POLITICAL CATHOLICISM IN

Political Catholicism was a crucial political force in interwar Europe and, in some ways, a precursor to post-war Christian democracy and the modern European People's Party. The ambivalent role of Catholic parties between democratic cooperation and the new Republican and democratic regimes after World War I, and the temptation to collaborate with authoritarian right wing dictatorships against the perceived dangers of social turmoil and Socialist revolution, are fundamental to understanding twentieth century European history and the politics of the European union.

For the first time, this book explains the role of Catholic parties in interwar Europe in a systematically pan-European comparative perspective. All country chapters address the same questions about the parties' membership and social organisation; their economic and social policies of corporatism; and their European and international policies at a time of increasing national and ethnic conflict. This book includes chapters on Catholic parties in East-Central Europe.

The first all-European and comparative perspective is strengthened by the inclusion of an introductory survey chapters on the roots of political Catholicism in nineteenth century Europe and a comparative chapter which draws together the main results of the country chapters. Two chapters on the much neglected transnational cooperation of Catholic parties and politicians in interwar Europe and in exile complement the comparative perspective.

POLITICAL CATHOLICISM IN EUROPE 1918–45

Volume 1

Editors
WOLFRAM KAISER
AND
HELMUT WOHNOUT

LONDON AND NEW YORK

First published in 2004
by Routledge, an imprint of Taylor & Francis
11 New Fetter Lane, London EC4P 4EE

Simultaneously published in
the USA and Canada
by Routledge
29 West 35th Street, New York, NY 10001

© 2004 Wolfram Kaiser and Helmut Wohnout
for selection and editorial matter;
individual contributors
their contribution

British Library Cataloguing in Publication Data:

A catalogue record for this book is available
from the British Library

ISBN 0-7146-5650-X (cloth)
ISBN 0-7146-8537-2 (paper)

Library of Congress Cataloging-in-Publication Data

A catalog record for this book is available
from the Library of Congress

All rights reserved. No part of this publication may be reproduced, stored in or introduced into a retrieval system or transmitted in any form or by any means, electronic, mechanical, photocopying, recording or otherwise without the prior written permission of the publisher of this book.

Typeset by Servis Filmsetting Ltd, Manchester
Printed in Great Britain by MPG Books Ltd, Bodmin, Cornwall

Contents

Notes on Contributors   vii
Introduction   1

1   Catholics, Christians and the Challenges of Democracy: The Heritage of the Nineteenth Century   7
John W. Boyer

2   A Microcosm of Society or the Key to a Majority in the Reichstag? The Centre Party in Germany   46
Jürgen Elvert

3   Catholics between Emancipation and Integration: The Conservative People's Party in Switzerland   65
Lukas Rölli-Alkemper

4   A Historical Detour: The Roman Catholic State Party in the Netherlands   80
Jan Roes

5   Religion, Class and Language: The Catholic Party in Belgium   94
Emmanuel Gerard

6   Christian Democracy and Centrism: The Popular Democratic Party in France   116
Jean-Claude Delbreil

7   Between the Crisis of the Liberal State, Fascism and a Democratic Perspective: The Popular Party in Italy   136
Tiziana di Maio

8   A Powerful Catholic Church, Unstable State and Authoritarian Political Regime: The Christian Democratic Party in Poland   150
Leszek Kuk

9	Middle-class Governmental Party and Secular Arm of the Catholic Church: The Christian Socials in Austria *Helmut Wohnout*	172
10	Collaborating with Horthy: Political Catholicism and Christian Political Organizations in Hungary *Csaba Fazekas*	195
11	Catholic People's Parties in East Central Europe: The Bohemian Lands and Slovakia *Arnold Suppan*	217
12	Catholic Politics or Christian Democracy? The Evolution of Inter-war Political Catholicism *Martin Conway*	235
13	Anticipated Exile of Catholic Democrats: The Secrétariat International des Partis Démocratiques d'Inspiration Chrétienne *Guido Müller*	252
14	Transnational Networks of Catholic Politicians in Exile *Wolfram Kaiser*	265
Index		286

Notes on Contributors

John Boyer is Professor of Modern History at the University of Chicago.

Martin Conway is Fellow of Balliol College, University of Oxford.

Jean-Claude Delbreil is Professor of Modern History at the University of Metz.

Tiziana di Maio is Senior Research Fellow at the University La Sapienza in Rome.

Jürgen Elvert is Professor of the History of European Integration at the University of Cologne.

Csaba Fazekas is Assistant Professor of Modern History at the University of Miskolc.

Emmanuel Gerard is Professor of Politics at the University of Leuven.

Wolfram Kaiser is Professor of European Studies at the University of Portsmouth and Visiting Professor at the College of Europe in Bruges.

Leszek Kuk is Professor of Modern History at the University of Toruń.

Guido Müller is Senior Research Fellow at the Institute of Contemporary History in Munich and lectures in history at the University of Stuttgart.

Lukas Rölli-Alkemper is Director of the Forum Hochschule und Kirche in Bonn.

Jan Roes (†) was Professor of History at the University of Nijmegen.

Arnold Suppan is Professor of History of Eastern Europe at the University of Vienna.

Helmut Wohnout is Director of the Karl von Vogelsang Institute in Vienna.

Introduction

As the liberal sociologist Ralf Dahrendorf concluded in 1979, the 'Social Democratic century has come to an end'.[1] Social democratic interventionist welfare state policies and deficit spending in times of economic expansion had contributed to the structural economic crisis in Western Europe that became evident after the oil crisis of 1973. The new policy agenda of global integration of markets, deregulation and privatization was not compatible with established social democratic ideology and values. At that time, moreover, many social democratic parties already seemed to have passed the peak of their electoral support. The beginning of the socio-economic transformation of Western Europe from an industrial society to a society based more and more on the service sector, without the same tradition of trade union organization or voting patterns, would inevitably lead to a further marked erosion in the social democratic predominantly working-class milieu and, thus, electoral decline, an analysis that seemed to be corroborated by the loss of power, for example, of the British Labour Party in 1979 and the West German Social Democrats in 1982.

But was the twentieth century really a social democratic century, or, in a narrower sense, a century of social democratic parties? In many ways, it was of course the fascist, National Socialist and communist dictatorships that exercised the greatest influence on the course of twentieth-century Europe, especially East Central Europe. Within the democratic spectrum, however, was not the twentieth century, if anything, a Christian democratic one? Were not the Christian democratic parties after 1945, in a Western Europe shaken by fascist and National Socialist rule, occupation and collaboration, of crucial importance for the stable evolution of democratic governance? Did not these parties, with their socio-economic policies anchored in Catholic social teaching, make an important contribution to relegitimizing the market economy through the extension of social security provisions, the introduction of neo-corporatist forms of consensual socio-economic policy making and the Europeanization of the welfare state in the context of the European Coal and Steel Community founded in 1951–52, and the European Economic Community founded in 1957–58? Were not the Christian Democratic parties, with their Catholic roots and orientation towards a 'supranational' Church, destined to put an end to national frictions and rivalries after 1945 and to construct the partly supranational European Union of the early twenty-first century?

Such a teleological interpretation of continuity in European Christian democracy from the late nineteenth century through to the post-war period sometimes shows in the historical literature on Catholic and Christian democratic parties. This is especially true as continental European research in the field has for a long time been dominated by the political parties themselves, their foundations and research centres and historians associated with them, who have sometimes fought the nineteenth-century culture wars by other, academic means.[2] In his analysis of Christian democratic ideas, for example, Jean-Dominique Durand tells a story of long-term democratic continuity by concentrating exclusively on democratic Catholic thinkers like the Italian Luigi Sturzo, the founder of the short-lived Italian Popular Party (Partito Popolare Italiano) in 1918.[3] Yet these thinkers and activists were mostly a small minority within their own parties in inter-war Europe. What is more, many Catholic 'democrats' in this period were not fully committed to the pluralist parliamentary system with a strong role for political parties. Some of them were even anti-Semitic.

Teleological interpretations of Christian democracy in modern Europe run the danger of overemphasizing both the continuity and the homogeneity of these movements and parties. In fact, inter-war political Catholicism as a precursor to post-war Christian democracy was characterized by a great plurality of political ideas and aims. Many conservative Catholics were still fundamentally opposed to important aspects of the modern world, as it had developed in the nineteenth century: rapid industrialization and many of its socio-economic and political consequences, the secular state, parliamentary government, republicanism and democracy. Catholic 'democrats' were often critical and in some cases opposed outright to the parliamentary system, which they saw as elitist and corrupt. They preferred a corporatist order, which was also advocated in the papal encyclical *Quadragesimo anno* of 1931. Many were initially enthusiastic about the creation of Catholic-influenced authoritarian regimes like the Portuguese *Estado Novo* of 1933 and the Austrian *Ständestaat* of 1933–34. In many cases they were anyway more interested in the 'social question' and Catholic social action in line with papal policy since *Rerum novarum* of 1891. In this encyclical, the Pope had called upon Catholics to work towards alternative solutions to the 'social question' to counteract the influence of socialism and communism on the working class, which he perceived as a major threat to the established social and moral order.

Catholic parties in inter-war Europe can best be described as coalitions of different social groups under the umbrella of the joint defence of Catholic religious, social and political interests. As such, they had developed in the course of the nineteenth-century European culture wars against the secularizing ideologies of liberalism and socialism.[4] The Catholic parties were people's parties, but only in the sense that to a much greater extent than any other parties in inter-war Europe, they comprised members and voters from all social classes (although much less so in the party elite) who were primarily united by their Catholicism. Their success in organizing practising Catholics and in influencing domestic politics varied a great deal. The German Centre Party (Zentrum), which had served as a role model for organized political Catholicism in nineteenth-century Europe, still managed to unite a majority of practising Catholics after 1918 and formed the core of all governments in the Weimar Republic. The Belgian Catholic Party, although internally very heterogenous, was the dominant political force and continued to control government formation. Some other parties were much less successful, however. In Poland and Hungary, for example, the Catholic parties were semi-integrated and not very influential in the authoritarian political regimes of those countries. Throughout the inter-war period, the Popular Democratic Party (Parti Démocrate Populaire) in France, where the originally anti-republican right was historically split, received only some 3 per cent of the popular vote in national elections.

On many of the core challenges of inter-war Europe, the Catholic parties were deeply split. As John Boyer demonstrates in his introductory chapter, by comparing the evolution of political Catholicism in Germany, Austria and France before 1918, the underlying fault-lines mostly originated in the nineteenth century. They concerned, first of all, the parties' attitudes towards democratic governance. By 1918, all European states had only limited experience with parliamentary government. Most of them introduced a democratic constitution with universal suffrage only after the First World War, and the introduction of the vote for women was even delayed in countries such as France and Belgium until after the Second World War. Almost immediately after the war the new democracies were threatened by domestic strife and, in some cases, civil war. They were undermined by ethnic or nationalist claims and conflicts, as well as economic problems, especially after the world economic crisis began in 1929. In this heated political climate many Catholics, too, sought non-democratic solutions in the form of a 'strong state' or a new corporatist order that was inspired and supported by the Vatican. Even when they agreed with Sturzo that such an order would have to be organized from below, not above, as in the case of Italian fascism, it was never quite clear how such corporatist professional bodies would relate to the institutions of representative democracy, or whether they would in fact replace them entirely.

The fault-lines in political Catholicism also concerned conflicting attitudes to the market economy. Some sections of the Catholic parties largely supported the capitalist system as it was, such as, for example, the Walloon-based industrialists within the Belgian Catholic Party. Others, especially in the Catholic trade union movement, favoured a much more interventionist state and redistributionary measures towards, mainly, small farmers and workers, especially after 1929. They were marginalized in most parties, however, as Catholic parties, when in government, generally opted for strict austerity programmes to stabilize state budgets and to counteract the effects of the world economic crisis, as happened, for example, in Germany and Austria in the early 1930s. Yet others in Catholic parties in Europe strove for economic corporatism and what they regarded as the potential harmonization of different social interests through the co-ordination of economic policy by organized professional bodies of, for example, farmers, civil servants, etc. As in the case of political corporatism, however, the relationship between these bodies and the existing institutions of representative government was never quite clear.

A third fault-line in political Catholicism related to diverging attitudes to ethnic and national conflicts and to inter-governmental co-operation within some kind of new European order after the experience of the European 'civil war' of 1914–18. Catholic parties, especially in the more multiethnic East Central Europe, frequently followed increasingly nationalistic policies towards ethnic minorities and, in particular, Jews. Following the post-war settlement, Catholics sometimes also supported revisionist foreign policy claims, such as in Hungary, for example. Other sections of Catholic parties were more open towards new forms of inter-state relations in Europe, especially following the Locarno Treaty of 1925, which the German Centre Party supported politically. After all, political Catholicism had developed in many countries in the nineteenth century in opposition to aggressive liberal and conservative policies of national integration and foreign economic and political expansion, emphasizing their common 'supranational' allegiance to the international Catholic Church. This had not, however, kept them from supporting the war effort in 1914, and these parties were still concerned in inter-war Europe to avoid being stigmatized as not nationally reliable political forces. As a result, the parties' transnational contacts were mostly organized by their left wings, which often had close contacts with the Catholic trade union movement and the international peace movement. While individual thinkers and politicians conceived of some kind of 'United States of Europe' in the inter-war period, the Catholics, as parties, did not.

Although there were other significant issues and fault-lines for political Catholicism in inter-war Europe, the country chapters in this book concentrate on the parties' membership and voters and their relationship with the Church; their attitudes to democracy; their socio-economic discourse, programmes and policies; and their foreign and European policies. All chapters include references to occupation, collaboration, resistance and exile, addressing the important question of continuity in political Catholicism from inter-war to post-war Europe. Research on political Catholicism in the period 1918–45 has so far not really developed a systematic European comparative perspective of this kind. When it has been attempted, as in the sole case of a book edited by Tom Buchanan and Martin Conway,[5] the scope has been limited to Western Europe, including countries where political Catholicism (as in Ireland) was a unifying, not a divisive factor within the national political culture and party system, and others (like Portugal and Spain) where significant Catholic parties existed for only a short time in the 1920s and early 1930s before the establishment of dictatorships. This book has a markedly different geographical scope. It takes a Europe-wide perspective, including political Catholicism in East Central Europe, which is much less well understood and about which very little has been published in English. In addition to Germany, the Netherlands, Belgium, France and Italy, this book includes chapters on Catholic parties in Switzerland, Austria, Hungary, Czechoslovakia and Poland. Martin Conway draws the experiences of these different countries together in his comparative chapter on political Catholicism in inter-war Europe. Lastly, the chapters by Guido Müller and Wolfram Kaiser analyse for the first time the rudimentary transnational networks of Catholic parties and politicians in the context of the Secrétariat International des Partis Démocratiques d'Inspiration Chrétienne, which existed in Paris from 1925–39, and in exile in the United Kingdom and the United States from 1936 through to the end of the Second World War.

This comprehensive approach demonstrates, most of all, that there was no straightforward continuity from the inter-war Catholic parties to post-war Christian democracy – with respect to the prevailing attitudes to parliamentary democracy or the mixed economy – let alone a new policy of European reconciliation and integration. To understand the transformation from inter-war to post-war (Western) Europe, which is analysed in a second volume on post-war Christian democracy,[6] it is necessary to analyse the effects of, for example, the experience of the totalitarian dictatorships in the 1930s, the Second World War and collaboration – which to a large degree discredited the nationalist right wing in European politics; the growing Cold War tensions and the renewed legitimacy of anti-bolshevism, which strengthened the agenda of Western integration; as well as post-war economic reconstruction and the resulting need for greater co-operation between states. Many ideas and concepts that were quite marginal in inter-war political Catholicism, such as, for example, consensual corporatist governance subordinated to parliamentary democracy, not replacing it, and closer European co-operation, could only be realized under these very different circumstances after the Second World War. Nevertheless, it would be impossible to understand the history of Christian democracy since 1945, or, indeed, the history of what is now the European Union, without systematic reference to the social structures, ideas and experiences of political Catholicism during 1918–45.

NOTES

1 Ralf Dahrendorf, *Life Chances: Approaches to Social and Political Theory* (London 1980).
2 See also the review article by Wolfram Kaiser, 'Christian Democracy in Twentieth-Century Europe', *Journal of Contemporary History*, 39/1 (2004), pp. 127–35.
3 Jean-Dominique Durand, *L'Europe de la Démocratie chrétienne* (Paris 1995).
4 In an all-European and comparative perspective, Christopher Clark and Wolfram Kaiser (eds), *Culture Wars: Secular-Catholic Conflict in Nineteenth-Century Europe* (Cambridge 2003). On the origins of Catholic parties in nineteenth-century Europe, see also Stathis N. Kalyvas, *The Rise of Christian Democracy in Europe* (Ithaca and London 1996); Ellen L. Evans, *The Cross and the Ballot. Catholic Political Parties in Germany, Switzerland, Austria, Belgium and the Netherlands, 1785–1985* (Boston 1999).
5 Tom Buchanan and Martin Conway (eds), *Political Catholicism in Europe 1918–1965* (Oxford 1996).
6 Michael Gehler and Wolfram Kaiser (eds), *Christian Democracy in Europe since 1945* (London 2004).

1

Catholics, Christians and the Challenges of Democracy: The Heritage of the Nineteenth Century

John W. Boyer

The country chapters in this book address the ways in which Catholic religious and political movements, mobilized from below and competing in the arena of electoral and associational politics, developed in interwar Europe, later contributing to the formation of generally stable political societies in Western Europe after 1945. This chapter involves an equally challenging, although slightly different question, which is how we can connect the nineteenth and the twentieth centuries. There is broad agreement that the traditions of political and social Catholicism that emerged with force and authority in the late nineteenth century, especially those associated with the idea of Christian democracy in its many forms, had important implications for the successful reinvention of European politics after 1945. Scholarly literature is certainly replete with variations of this argument. To take examples from American scholarship on Europe published in the last few years, Noel Cary, in a recent book on German political Catholicism, argues that the Centre Party (Zentrum) was a 'model among Catholics for what was fully achieved only after 1945 . . . a broad party that could integrate conservatives into a liberal democratic system'. Cary believes that 'the Center Party, the civic agent of the German Catholic *Sonderweg*, was, for better or worse, the closest example in the German past of a political culture that offered an ideal of tolerance'.[1] In a brilliant essay on Germany in the late twentieth century Michael Geyer has argued, in turn, that the history of Germany after 1945 is the history of two 'pariah nations' – Catholicism and socialism – both of which before 1914 were 'the foremost antistate, and, indeed, antisystem movements [that] had managed to check their respective particularist proclivities in order to generate programmatic national movements and cultural agendas with their own universal appeal', and which finally 'came to govern Germany for the "better", second half of the century'.[2] Finally, Raymond Grew has offered a similar assessment in a recent essay on liberty and Catholicism:

'Europe's Catholics can be said to have laid the groundwork before World War I for the parties of Christian democracy that would blossom after World War II and for the Catholic contribution to a European community.'[3]

One could duplicate these observations with parallel statements from many German, French, Austrian and other European historians. Yet the claims that scholars routinely make about links between the nineteenth and twentieth centuries are more often posited than demonstrated. Both Martin Conway and Stathis N. Kalyvas have recently cautioned against constructing cheerful, progressive narratives involving the history of Christian democracy that fail to explain the simultaneous existence of Catholic movements opposed to liberal values.[4] Kalyvas has rightly observed that '[l]ooking today at the benign Christian Democratic parties, one can easily forget the aliberal and often intolerant nature of the Catholic movement from which they emerged',[5] Michael Geyer himself has put the issue in a different light by warning against retrospective infatuations with 'the certainties of a nineteenth-century imagination' at the end of the twentieth century, infatuations that might lead historians to 'loop back to (and possibly renew) the hopes and expectations of the nineteenth century' and thus reaffirm the 'good intentions of the nineteenth century and their prospective fulfillment in the twenty-first'.[6]

Granted, the political and moral formations of 'Christian democracy', which were anchored in a corresponding Catholic civilizational milieu powerfully shaped by the nineteenth century and which blossomed so successfully in the late 1940s and early 1950s, were in many respects endangered, if not outmoded, by the later 1970s and early 1980s. Still, there is considerable irony if one stands at the vantage point of the logical end of the nineteenth century, namely 1914, and imagines the Catholics (or socialists) of that world having an opportunity to play the role of a post-1945 catch-all political movement responsible for broad-based regime stability. After all, in France, Catholics found themselves both embattled politically and still reeling from the consequences of the Separation Law of 1905. In Germany, three decades after the repudiation of the *Kulturkampf*, Catholics found themselves again dogged by militant Protestants seeking to engineer a second reformation, and in their own milieu were profoundly uncertain about how much of modernity they could or should assimilate. In neighbouring Austria, Catholics were trying to recover from the massive losses suffered in the 1911 national elections by the Christian Social Party. Nor were the German and Austrian cases all that dissimilar, for Catholics in both nations were having obvious trouble maintaining the political loyalties of working-class citizens living in large cities: Christian Social losses in Vienna in June 1911 were followed by the Centre Party's losses in Cologne, Düsseldorf,

Würzburg and elsewhere in January 1912.[7] The German Catholic Labour leader, August Pieper, would warn his colleagues in 1912 that 'we will have to organize ourselves and explain our cause completely differently among those who work in industry and commerce than we have previously been accustomed to do in a Germany that was primarily peasant-based'.[8]

We therefore confront a puzzle: the traditions of nineteenth-century political Catholicism, and, where they overlap, of social Catholicism, have been seen by many scholars to have great moment for the third and even the fourth quarters of the twentieth century; but standing at the beginning of the twentieth century, one might not have predicted these optimistic and fortuitous outcomes. Indeed, there are parts of the nineteenth-century narrative that are eminently unattractive, and difficult to fit into some imaginary Catholic or even Christian vision of the Whig theory of history. Christoph Weber has argued that many late-nineteenth-century Catholics greatly feared modernity and suffered from what he calls 'a feeling of loss and of catastrophe'.[9] True, Julius Bachem may have invited German Catholics to exit from 'the Tower' into a broader regime of interconfessional modernity, but this had costs as well as gains. As Marshall Berman once observed: 'To be modern is to find ourselves in an environment that promises us adventure, power, joy, growth, transformation of ourselves and the world – and, at the same time, that threatens to destroy everything we have, everything we know, everything we are.'[10]

It will be helpful in exploring this puzzle if we first consider the different and often conflicting histories of several of the major national sites of political Catholic action in Europe, and if we then examine some general cultural and intellectual processes that linked these sites together into a single Catholicism, all the while highlighting their differences. I conclude with some thoughts on what Catholics had learned from the nineteenth century, and on the unfinished business that they had before them in 1914. My narrative is not limited to parliamentary political history or to traditional issues of Church and state, moving as it does to encompass also mass political organizations, social theory and considerations of what might be characterized as the history of mentalities. Indeed, much of the most fascinating research in the last 20 years by European and American scholars on modern European Catholicism has resulted from the willingness of historians to move beyond the locus of a strict 'Church–State' lens to observe the many and varied ways that religion profoundly influenced the civic culture of modern European societies.[11] Rather, the story that I tell is that of a third way between the totalities of liberalism and collectivism, a way that I shall characterize as the politics of corporate modernity, a modernity that had a powerful effect on later twentieth-century European history.

CATHOLIC POLITICAL TRADITIONS, 1870–1914: THE CASE OF GERMANY

Three of the most prominent national sites for social and political Catholicism were Germany, France and Austria. The experience of Catholics in these states depended on the characteristics of their broader civic cultures, and especially their eighteenth-century antecedents. The seven decades between 1848 and 1914 saw tremendous institutional and political developments across Europe, and nowhere was this more evident than in Germany. Abandoning regimes of royal-bureaucratic absolutism, and overcoming centuries-long regional particularism, Germany not only became a nationally integrated state, but melded political absolutism into a constitutionally grounded regime of liberal law and representational procedure based on equality, certainty and uniformity before the law.[12] The zenith of this process of liberal and national institution-building came between 1870 and 1900.

By the beginning of the twentieth century German Catholics possessed what the distinguished French Catholic historian, Jean-Marie Mayeur, has characterized as a 'model' Catholic political party.[13] How did this come about? The *Kulturkampf* lies at the heart of German Catholic political experience, and it has had wide ramifications. That confessional identity became, and has remained, a major variable in modern German electoral politics is a testimony to the power of the impulses set off by Bismarck's attack on the Catholic Church from 1871 to 1878, and the resulting mass mobilization of German Catholics that endured long after his fall from power. The *Kulturkampf* defined Catholicism's future relationship not only to the German state, but to the majority Protestant community as well, since many of the most forceful proponents of anti-Catholic legislation were liberals intent on creating a community of values that were 'largely synonymous with those of enlightened Protestantism'.[14]

The founding of the Centre Party predated the onset of the *Kulturkampf* by several years, reflecting an already emergent political consciousness among Catholic voters during national institution-building of the later 1860s. Indeed, many historians believe that it was the Centre Party, rather than the Catholic Church as a confessional culture, that was the real object of Bismarck's scorn.[15] But the hard years of the mid-1870s forged a sturdy matrix of political relationships between the lower clergy and the Centre Party's lay cadres that endured long after 1890. Programmatically, the early 1870s saw the creation of a dense network of Catholic political and social organizations superior in scope to those enjoyed by liberals. This capacity for effective associational organization was revived after 1890 with a wave of new associations, of which the Volksverein für das katholische Deutschland was perhaps the most impressive.[16] In this movement, German Catholics did not lack determined, and even courageous, leadership from their bishops.[17]

These formative years resulted in what Margaret Anderson has called 'a massive political realignment of Catholics'.[18] The Centre Party that emerged under Ludwig Windthorst's resolute leadership was both confessional and interdenominational; rural and urban; aristocratic, clerical, and bourgeois; and, as Bismarck once put it, 'encompassing seven intellectual directions reflecting all the colours of the political rainbow, from the extreme Right to the most radical Left'.[19] The Centre Party did a superb job of coalescing Catholic support from many divergent social and cultural milieux into an impressive record of electoral support.[20] Between 1874 and 1912 the Centre's share of the total pool of eligible Catholic voters remained generally stable: 49 per cent between 1871 and 1878, rising to 52 per cent between 1881 and 1887, sinking to 46 per cent between 1890 and 1898, and returning again to 49 per cent between 1903 and 1912. Paradoxically, after 1900 the Centre began to lose more Catholic voters to the Social Democrats and National Liberals, but these losses balanced themselves out as it recruited more new voters and former non-voters.[21]

Recent research on the Centre Party and the confessional culture that it represents suggests, however, that Catholics faced a series of challenges after 1890 that were directly tied to new trends in the broader political milieu. The years after 1890 saw difficult, but powerful, transformations in the organization of parties and the associational structures that undergirded them, including the rise of a vast array of new special interest groups. Jonathan Sperber has recently argued that the Centre made the transition to an even more aggressive voter recruitment and mobilization quite effectively: 'The party accomplishing this [transformation] on the most massive scale and with the greatest effect was the Center.'[22] At the same time Wilfried Loth has made a robust argument that the Centre Party faced a process of upheaval after 1890 in which three very different electoral and cultural constituencies found voice and vote: a growing Catholic proletariat insistent on its rights, an agrarian and urban *Mittelstand* more and more defensive and fearful of change, and an emerging Catholic *Bürgertum* eager to profit from the high capitalism and new industrial culture that was enriching German society. In their diversity, these groups left the Centre Party without a coherent and durable political programme. What sturdiness the Centre did enjoy derived from Catholic confessional defensiveness, from a residual moral commitment by Catholics to the idea of social compromise, from the self-sustaining power of Catholic associationalism, and from the Centre's use of compensatory nationalism as a 'bonding agent'. Nevertheless, Loth views the Catholic political milieu as quite fragile by 1914, with ultramontane values incapable of holding it together in the long run. An 'erosion' of the Centre Party was thus irreversible, finally resulting in its collapse in 1933.[23] Still other scholars have challenged the strictly 'political' and somewhat reductionist lens of Loth's arguments, suggesting that Catholics lived in vibrant cultural and cognitive milieux that, taken together, were more than the sum of the Centre Party's constituent electoral parts.[24] As Josef Mooser puts it, 'the Catholic milieu was, despite all of its parochial-territorial gravitational force, *also* a translocal community of sentiment, analogous to the other great ideological-political forces in the second half of the nineteenth century'.[25]

Strategically, by the mid-1890s the Centre had ceased to be an oppositional party, and under the leadership of Ernst Lieber, and especially Peter Spahn, became a key element of the parliamentary majority upon which every German cabinet from Hohenlohe to Bethmann Hollweg (the Bülow Bloc of 1907–09 being the exception) had to depend.[26] Yet if Catholics felt at home in the early-twentieth-century administrative state, could they ever feel themselves to be full and equal members of the German nation? The 1890s and 1900s not only were a time of political accommodation on the part of the Centre Party, but also saw a vociferous campaign on the part of its more progressive, *bürgerlich* leaders seeking 'parity' with German Protestants.[27] Those Catholics most insistent on parity were also those most inclined to believe that they could reconcile confessionalism with German nationalism.[28] Yet, given the iconic and moral linkage posited in 1871 between Protestantism and the new German nation – parallel to the linkage between anticlericalism and the new republic in France – were not German Catholics fated to labour under an apologetic and deeply defensive aura in their search for cultural accommodation? Helmut Walser Smith has observed, of the period immediately before 1914, that 'nationalism, as the antagonism between Protestants and Catholics suggests, not only smoothed over conflicts but also sharpened them; it gave groups long existing in tension a new vocabulary with which to exploit their differences; and it lent to those differences a new, more modern urgency'.[29] Perhaps it is not accidental that the kind of *bürgerlich* interconfessional collaboration that occurred after 1945 – Germany's special brand of Christian democracy – took root only upon the collapse of the 'Protestant nation' invented in 1871.

THE CASE OF FRANCE

A systematic comparison of French and German experiences with political and social Catholicism in the nineteenth century would be both fascinating and illuminating, but it is surprising how little comparative work has been done. Certainly, their different paths were not unnoticed by contemporaries, both in Rome and elsewhere, and often this played to the disadvantage of the French. For example, in December 1906 the papal secretary of state Cardinal Merry del Val would argue to two visiting French Assumptionists that:

> [i]t would seem in effect that French Catholics are not interested in religious liberty, and that they wearily take up a defensive posture only when Rome demands it. It is, on the contrary, the duty of French Catholics to push intransigence to its ultimate limits, to reject utterly the laws that the government formulates against them, to go much further than Rome in resisting them, to be so militant that we need to restrain them . . . If our role was limited to being a moderating influence, you would have the situation that existed in Germany. There, resistance was vigorous, with no quarter given; the Catholics were admirably intransigent; Rome had to moderate them, and it was by no means easy to hold them back . . . But what a splendid position for the papacy, which thereby became the arbiter of the situation. In France, unfortunately it's just the other way round . . . Is it because *le sens catholique* no longer exists there?[30]

Nor did the different trajectories of the two Catholicisms fail to gain notice during the propaganda barrage conducted in the early months of the First World War, during which Hermann Platz, a clever German Catholic writer, asserted that:

> [t]he German *Kulturkampf* found the Catholics massed as one man on the battlefield of passive resistance, so that after a short time the ineffectual legislation springing out of the *Kulturkampf* had to be rescinded; the French *Kulturkampf* found the Catholics indifferent and before as well as after kindly disposed toward their anti-clerical deputies, so that the laws of the [French] *Kulturkampf*, once put into effect, have to the present day been able to inflict ever new wounds on the Church.[31]

Aside from the egregious partisanship of both statements, these two quotes allude to a fundamental difference between German and French Catholicism before 1914, namely, the French failure to develop a powerful, coherent political Catholic party. Given that they too faced a regime that was profoundly unsympathetic to their confession and their religion, why did French Catholics take such a different trajectory?

The history of French Catholicism in the later nineteenth century was circumscribed by the novelty, ingenuity and persistence of republican laic legislation. From the first laic education laws and decrees of 1879–81, to those providing for lay burials, the abolition of compulsory Sunday rest, and legalized divorce in 1880–84, to the Associations Law of 1901, the body of regulatory and punitive legislation applied against the Church grew in haphazard intensity until taking a more radical turn in 1905–06. Earlier laic legislation was Janus-faced, since it combined, in John McManners' paraphrase of Léon Gambetta's famous quip, 'the luxury of violent words with the security of moderate policies'.³² The legislation for separation initiated in July 1904 and finally approved in December 1905 may have been the logical telos of republican desire, but it constituted a break with past republican practice that sought to use the prerogatives of the concordat to protect the nation against the Church. By unilaterally abrogating the concordat, militant republicans now confidently ordered the Church to go away, to exist by itself, and to cease to be a nuisance in modern civic life.

Attempts by Catholic political leaders such as Albert de Mun and Jacques Piou to exploit Pope Leo XIII's call for a *Ralliement* in 1890 and create a conservative, Tory-like political party met with mixed and often contradictory reactions from Catholics throughout the mid-1890s. As Jean-Marie Mayeur has shrewdly observed, 'the moment that the Republic identified itself with laicization the Ralliement could only be a failure'.³³ Unfortunately, in the aftermath of the elections of May 1898, the ever-muscular capacity of anticlericalism *qua* republican 'concentration' again became evident, as the Catholics were isolated and then, in the context of the general political effluent of the Dreyfus affair, humiliated and punished. After 1900 the most plausible strategy for Catholic centrists like de Mun and Piou lay in brokering an alignment of the surviving Catholic parliamentary forces with right and right-centre republicans in a flexible conservative coalition, based on the premise that a left–right 'two grouping' structure would re-emerge to govern French politics.³⁴ The agent of this was to be the Action Libérale Populaire (ALP), founded in May 1902. Yet the ALP was held in suspicion by both the right and left, too moderate in the eyes of Catholic intransigents and too clerical for the tastes of many conservative republicans. Efforts to placate residual Catholic monarchist opinion cost it the support of many conservatives, however, and the ALP's miserable showing in the May 1906 parliamentary elections was a foretaste of its eventual disintegration. By 1912–13 de Mun, beset by Roman and French Integrists, had become (in Benjamin Martin's word) a 'semioutcast'.³⁵

The traditions of social Catholic action in France were equally sincere, but also disparate and in conflict. On the legitimist and conservative bourgeois side, de Mun's odyssey was representative, if not altogether typical. A sponsor of the corporatist Oeuvre des Cercles in the 1870s and of a network of Catholic youth groups called the Association Catholique de la Jeunesse Française founded in 1886, de Mun's once stodgy, employer-friendly approach gradually evolved to a respect for labour unions and an abandonment of paternalism.³⁶ Support from his own right-centre bourgeois and aristocratic allies was always unsteady, however. Several regional initiatives for Christian democracy led by renegade lower clerics were also put forward before 1900, but they succeeded only sporadically and were sometimes heavily invested with anti-Semitic and other 'new right' posturing.³⁷ Marc Sangnier and his Sillonists were perhaps the most distinguished representatives of a Christian democratic strain in French Catholicism after the turn of the century until their condemnation by Rome in 1910. Their most hopeful time lay ahead of them, in the more flexible conditions of the later 1920s and early 1930s.³⁸ The pre-war period ended with a fascinating symbol of the divisions within French Catholicism, when in the course of the 1914 election campaign the Christian democratic priest, Abbé Jules Lemire, who was first elected to the chamber of deputies in 1893, was openly opposed by the Church in his quest for re-election.³⁹

What accounts for the differences from Germany? Several factors seem reasonably clear. First, French Catholics not only confronted a broad ideological enemy seeking to eliminate their public influence, and confident that their cultic presence might slowly wither away; they also faced a constitutional regime that many Catholics viewed with scorn, if not open contempt. The struggle of clericalism against de-Christianization in France was thus inextricably caught up in the parallel war of monarchism against republicanism. True, German Catholics had to contend with a hostile, intimidating Protestantism, but as Margaret Anderson has correctly pointed out, this was a confessional competitor that kept Catholics focused on practical, goal-oriented initiatives: 'The constant, if unacknowledged, intellectual presence of the Protestant "competition" made Germany from the outset unfavourable soil for any kind of anti-intellectual fideism.' French Catholics, in contrast, faced a body of opinion and belief seeking in its most extreme form to eliminate religion from every corner of public life, and embracing de-Christianization as a starting and ending point for the nineteenth century.⁴⁰ Republicanism also fabricated an endless array of demeaning, if petty, challenges to the personal and professional authority of the clergy, a clergy that in many rural towns and villages of France was already held in low esteem.⁴¹

The self-congratulatory power of republican political culture embraced not only new constitutional arrangements and (eventually) a new system of Church–State relations, but also new notions about civic identity, personhood and citizenship that seemed fundamentally inconsistent with the core interests of Catholicism. French republicans of the 1880s, with their 'missionary zeal',⁴² come off sounding almost like Austro-Marxists before their time. Claude Langlois has remarked that the conflict over the republican cultural agenda 'engulfed the whole society', even to the point where mundane budget expenditures became fraught with high symbolic value: 'Minutes of parliamentary debates, for 1883 especially, show how republicans saw every decrease in the budget for religious functions as a direct contribution to the progress of public education.'⁴³

Because they were so much at odds among themselves over how to respond to the 'regime' question of monarchism versus republicanism, and because in France 'clericalism' signified hostility to the core iconic values of the revolutionary tradition itself, Catholics were bound to find themselves frustrated in developing coherent, internally consistent strategies for resistance. The extent, impact and endurance of state aggression and, perhaps even more important, its timing by decade were also of critical importance. It was certainly the case that Bismarck's *Kulturkampf* legislation was 'singularly less effective than that of Jules Ferry'.[44] But even more significant was that the decades after 1880 afforded Catholics no significant respite, for the Church was not only buffeted in the late 1870s and early 1880s, but, in the aftermath of the fall of Jules Méline's cabinet in June 1898, had to face a second and much more powerful assault between 1901 and 1905. The German *Kulturkampf* was a temporary disaster, with the Church not only surviving but growing stronger after 1890. As new possibilities emerged after 1900 for German and Austrian Catholics to exploit the institutions of the liberal administrative state and assert themselves politically (true, not all favourably and not all successfully), French Catholics found themselves worrying about how to pay their local priest's salary and who would own the local parish house and the local church. Because they felt relentlessly on the defensive, fears for the intergenerational cultural survival of Catholic values must have grown rather than diminished over time. Hence the extreme preoccupation of French Catholics with republicanism in all of its sundry cultural, as well as political forms, a reaction that was not static and may have even intensified over time.

Nor did Rome's ongoing proclivity to interfere in the affairs of the French Church help in the long run. During the critical assembly of French bishops in late May 1906 to discuss the implementation of the Separation Law, the Archbishop of Rouen, Édmond Fuzet, pointed out that Rome had accepted Church associations established in Prussia in June 1875 that were even less advantageous than those provided for by the 1905 legislation. Yet Pius X's encyclical, *Gravissimo officii*, two and a half months later led the French Church into a calamitous situation.[45] One is also impressed by Rome's genuinely harsh treatment of Marc Sangnier and the Sillon, as opposed to the rather fudging tactics applied to the Catholic labour leaders in Germany during the *Gewerkschaftsstreit*.[46]

Finally, some scholars have questioned the capacity of French Catholics to generate strong, viable, lay and episcopal leadership. Mayeur, Dansette and others have observed the absence of a Windthorst or a Ketteler in French political Catholicism.[47] French bishops were very divided on the 'regime' question, with a majority opposed to the secular republic while others were willing to go along with it sullenly or not so sullenly.[48] Perhaps, as Margaret Anderson has suggested, the unusually large number of episcopal sees had a retardative or at least fragmenting effect on broad co-operation – the 38 million Catholics in France were organized in 87 dioceses, whereas the 24 million German Catholics had only 26.[49] The republican authorities of the Third Republic were also extremely suspicious of French bishops trying to organize themselves or their clergy, or the clergy organizing their own political constituents.[50] Not only were plenary conferences of the French bishops forbidden, but the propensity of the republican regime to disallow proclerical election results must also have been humiliating and frustrating, especially since their Catholic counterparts in Germany did not suffer from similar discriminatory practices.[51] This orbit of negative regulations included numerous other kinds of petty and not so petty discriminatory practices, many of which were authorized by the concordatory regime itself. A development like the German (or later the Austrian) Catholic Congress movement would have been difficult to sustain in France, not only because of internal fragmentation among Catholics, but also because of likely government harassment. There seems to have been little interest in the social question among the majority of the episcopate, and many lower clerics followed their bishops' lead.[52]

Ironically, for all of this knotty, discordant history, the pre-war period in Catholic France concluded on two guardedly optimistic notes. First, despite the 'rejoicing at the Chaussée d'Antin' over Pius X's condemnation of the Sillon, the terrorism of the early Action Française could not suppress other tendencies in French Catholicism, that would come to play an important exemplary role in modern French politics.[53] The revival of Christian democratic and social Catholic impulses in inter-war France comes out of the tradition of the Sillon, just as the formation of the Parti Démocrate Populaire after 1924 depended upon leaders drawn from the pre-war ALP.[54] Second, although French Catholics found themselves embattled and humiliated in 1905, the new freedoms authorized by the Separation Law made possible strategies for associationalist defence within the context of the existing legal and administrative structures of the republic. As a fully defeated power, rather like Germany after 1945, French Catholicism could now proceed to reconstitute itself in the non-étatist terrain of civil society, and the period 1905 to 1914 sees the emergence, or further strengthening, of new lay groups including women's associations, youth organizations and others.[55]

THE CASE OF AUSTRIA

Germany and France present almost bipolar cases: a resolute political Catholicism playing a critical, if deeply resented, role in state affairs, as opposed to a political Catholicism that is, as Jean-Marie Mayeur put it, 'absent'. The situation in the Habsburg empire presents a third, hybrid-like model, for like France, Austria was an overwhelmingly Catholic country where Catholic confessionalism and public authority had long been closely associated historically, but, like Germany, it too developed a vigorous tradition of political Catholicism. The Austrian case also presents a new problem, for the ethnic and nationalist tensions plaguing the empire (and Catholics within it) created a unique political calculus that was absent from the immediate personal experience of Catholics in most parts of Germany and of France.

The history of Church and State in the late empire is bounded by the fact there was no 'regime question' as such, at least as it affected the role of religion or the status of one confession *vis-à-vis* other confessions.[56] Given the legitimacy of the Habsburg dynasty – which enjoyed broad popular support, enduring well into the war – and given the personal role of the emperor as a symbol of official co-operation between state authority and transnational Catholicism, this could hardly be otherwise. Instead, liberal law and sacral dynasticism combined by 1900 to favour both the Catholic Church and the administrative state in Austria.[57] True, in the late 1860s and early 1870s the new liberal parliament in Austria passed legislation that abridged the rights of the Church in education and in other areas of public law. Yet by the early 1890s at the latest it was clear that this legislation would be implemented in ways that were generally consonant with the interests of the Church. Thus, not only did the Habsburg Church not endure a Prussian-style *Kulturkampf*, but what passed for its local variant soon evolved a co-operative, mutually dependent relationship with the state, more rather than less pronounced as the twentieth century beckoned. Catholic critics of the 1874 legislation who accused it of having Josephinist tendencies were correct. But this was a Josephinism more substantial than its eighteenth-century predecessor, since it explicitly sought to reconcile the new authority of the anticlerical liberal administrative state with the traditional authority of the Catholic Counter-Reformation dynast who continued to serve as the first leader of that State. Robert Musil would shrewdly characterize 'the final outcome of the fateful struggle of Catholicism against the State' in 1912 as 'a struggle that began with the Church allowing itself to be misled into wanting to rule the State in the State's way, and ended with the Church being dominated by the State in the Church's way, that of invisible spiritual penetration'.[58]

In contrast to Germany, the Church–State narrative in the Habsburg empire is only indirectly related to the rise of a successful political Catholicism. Rather than hostile state intervention provoking or engendering the rise of mass political Catholicism, it would take a rather different convergence of social and class issues to spark a movement that eventually resulted in a para-Catholic 'Christian' framework. True, early forms of clerically led protests against liberal legislation had arisen in Tyrol and in some other Alpine lands in the 1860s and 1870s, resulting in the formation of conservative regionalist political groups with strong clerical participation. But these groups were restricted to rural electoral districts and could play at best a secondary, defensive role in collaboration with Polish and Czech nationalist parties throughout the 1870s and 1880s. They hardly added up to a political Catholic movement of the size and political effectiveness of the German Centre.

That Austria eventually came to have a mass-based, Centre-like party – the Christian Social Movement – reflected leadership emanating from the empire's metropolitan centre, the imperial capital of Vienna. Energized by strong anti-Semitic and economic protest rhetoric, and supported by sympathetic lower clerics with a keen sense for the benefits of social as well as confessional protests, a coalition of ill-tempered *bürgerlich* social groups came together in Vienna in the early 1890s and, under the enigmatic title of the 'Christian Social' Party, won control of the city government of Vienna in 1895–96.[59] Christian socialism thus began as an uneasy amalgam of religious protest and socio-economic unrest. Ironically, several of its key leaders, most notably Karl Lueger, came from the political world of Viennese municipal liberalism. The Christian Social Party in Vienna was more like a majority liberal Protestant party in Germany, since it depended more on what Dietmar von Reeken has characterized (for Oldenburg) as a *bürgerliches Milieu*, rather than a deeply confessionally anchored one.[60] The Christian Socials also profited from the fact that, unlike either Germany or France, Austria had no general suffrage of any kind until 1897, when a modest 'fifth' curia was introduced, and no system of universal male suffrage until 1907. Modern political parties took longer to emerge, and when they did emerge, *mittelständisch* protest groups like the Christian Socials had a unique chance to gain ideological coherence and organizational stability by employing a melange of anti-state and pro-state rhetoric, without having to depend upon or worry about the working classes.

Following their stunning victory in Vienna in 1895, the Christian Socials spent the next ten years securing control of Vienna and the surrounding Crownland of Lower Austria. In 1905–07 they merged with Catholic peasant forces based in the western Crownlands – especially in Tyrol, Salzburg, Styria and Upper Austria – to create a Christian Social *Reichspartei*. The net result was a transregional party with heavy *mittelständisch* and agrarian roots that in May 1907 became the largest political party in the imperial parliament, having the authority to nominate two of its key leaders to cabinet positions. Having defeated liberalism and co-opted many liberal voters in Vienna, the Christian Socials' only credible opponent was now the Austrian Social Democratic Party. In 1903 the socialist leadership concluded that: 'Social Democracy has shown itself to be the only opponent left against the Christian Socials which for the present can in any way be taken seriously in political terms. The struggle against clericalism essentially rests on the shoulders of our party.'[61]

The Christian Socials' subsequent ambition was to play the role of a German-based broker that would be able to forge religion and class into weapons with which to attack Austrian Social Democracy, while also neutralizing national and ethnic tensions in the empire at large. Between 1907 and 1914 a more 'Catholic' habitus settled upon the party, in part because of the effect of the merger of 1907, in part because Lueger's death in 1910 empowered a new generation of Catholic lay and clerical leaders to make their voices heard within the Viennese branch of the party, and in part because, with the onset of universal suffrage in 1907, the Christian Socials' main enemy now lay on the radical left.

CATHOLICISM IN A EUROPEAN PERSPECTIVE: THE PAPACY AND THE ULTRAMONTANE REVOLUTION

The different trajectories of the national political Catholicisms might call into question whether there were in fact common links, common traditions and indeed a common cause, such that one can agree with Sudhir Hazareesingh's recent observation that French Catholicism was part of a 'transnational community whose widely acknowledged source of authority was based in Rome'.[62] In his 1996 'Wiles Lectures', Adrian Hastings argued that Catholicism was associated with particular nations, but that it was also committed to a 'communion transcending such particularities'.[63] This communion was in fact far more than a liturgical or even confessional bloc. Rather, we might understand it as a civilization in the sense defined by the American anthropologists Robert Redfield and Milton Singer – namely, as a whole way of life involving many different folk communities, each having its own physical identity but bound together by a higher order (or, to use Redfield's language, a Great Tradition) of shared legal and moral norms, sacred cultural rites and performances, overlapping historical memories, common forms of reflective and systematic thought and collective aesthetic forms.[64] The bounded totality of the Great Tradition of Catholic cultural experience in Europe in the nineteenth century had important implications for the civic options available to European policy makers between 1945 and 1960. Catholics had many opportunities to experience their shared and collective way of life, among them the revolution in popular piety, the invention of a new system of papal and episcopal governance during the course of the nineteenth century, and the common discourse and ideological concerns posed by a new Catholic social theory.

PIETY AND MILIEU

The first development has to do with the powerful transformation of popular piety and devotion that swept across European Catholicism in the nineteenth century, which has been a subject of scrutiny by European social historians over the past two decades. David Blackbourn's brilliant work on Marpingen and Ruth Harris's equally noteworthy book on Lourdes are but two examples of this fascinating literature.[65] New forms of mass popular piety – pilgrimages, missions, relics, indulgences, the devotions to Mary (the Immaculate Conception) and the Sacred Heart of Jesus, shrines, visions, apparitions and miracle cures – together with frequent and early communion, intensified training for confirmation and expanded use of the rosary mark the cultural landscape of nineteenth-century Catholicism all over Europe. These new sacramental, ritualistic and performative transactions, many of them under the direct leadership, or at least influence, of the clergy, not only renewed Catholic pietistic consciousness, but also created new, common, transclass boundaries for Catholics against rival cultural ideologies. In many respects, no epoch was more ardently pious than this age of rampant secularism.

Along with the pietistic revolution, aided by defensive political action in states where political repression enhanced Catholic associational self-consciousness, came new solidarities of civic sociability and political-cultural interaction, which helped to bolster the particularistic, milieu-like quality of Catholic life. Both the pietistic revival itself, and parallel processes of political and social mobilization, enabled Catholics to exploit the literacy revolution of the nineteenth century and the many new avenues of mass communications, but on behalf of cultural worlds semi-isolated from the rest of European society.[66]

Judgements about the impact of the pietistic and organizational revolutions associated with ultramontane Catholicism and the many micro- and macro-cultural milieux nourished by them have been divergent. Christoph Weber has provided a critique of its most overt characteristics, arguing that it was nothing less than a massive exercise in fundamentalism.[67] Olaf Blaschke's recent characterization of German Catholicism as belonging to 'the especially backward formations of society' parallels Ralph Gibson's observation for France, that ultramontanism could involve 'a rampant anti-intellectualism which discredited the Church in many bourgeois eyes'.[68] The modernist and integralist crises that rocked the Church after 1900, which left it in disarray, have often been cited as evidence of a confessional culture defined by timidity and organizing itself in yet more powerful ghettos that, in turn, imposed heavy cultural opportunity costs on Catholics even in the twentieth century.[69]

But other scholars, particularly Thomas Nipperdey and Margaret Anderson, have emphasized the democratic, emancipatory implications of such mass popular mobilization, particularly in the leadership roles played by the lower clergy. Against the view that ultramontane ideas and culture are a form of hegemonic conservatism, Nipperdey has argued, 'Ultramontanism and democracy – populist and plebiscitary – they are clearly connected.'[70] Similarly, Margaret Anderson has made a powerful argument about the long-run connection between ultramontanism and democracy, suggesting that new forms of popular participation 'set in motion a revolution in social attitudes that shook the deference that had governed German social relations for centuries', and that 'religion, like rules, provided voters with civic courage, the gumption – of which Germans are traditionally said to be in such short supply – to stand up for one's rights, human and civil, against authority'.[71] Elections empowered powerless voters, and the political mobilization that began in the 1870s was a way of expressing one's rights. Thus, Anderson sees pro-ultramontane clergy as agents of civic democracy and, ironically, as less interested in strident nationalism. She points out that the most sympathy for Protestant-inspired nationalism in Germany came from Catholic liberals and modernists.[72]

This ultramontane revolution in piety was not uncontested, even within the Church. Nor were all Catholics caught up in it. Rituals congenial to the subcultural sensibilities of rural and small-town Catholics – certainly the majority in all European states before 1914 – might play very differently among their bourgeois confessional brethren in larger cities. Yet both the pietistic revival itself, and the regeneration of a variety of Catholic social milieux, occurred in the much broader context of civic community-building in nineteenth-century Europe, at a time when European society was seeing the invention of other subcollective ways of knowing and being, several of which claimed also to provide a 'whole way of life'. Those who criticize the alleged (antimodernistic) ghettoism of Catholics should remember that the late nineteenth century also saw a radicalized and particularistic civic consciousness among Protestants, replete with what Helmut Walser Smith has called 'different traditions, separate memories, another history'; a cult of republicanism in France that Philip Nord has characterized as 'an awakening republican opinion' that 'dramatized its arguments through ritual and symbol'; the creation of new 'faith' communities among European socialists with their own special rites and symbols; and new patterns of civic sociability focused on integral nationalist belief.[73] How exclusive could any of these communities and subcollective identities remain over time? More important, how much cultural autonomy could any one of these milieu-like ensembles claim via the ordering effects of liberal public law, without inflicting their cherished values and their world-views on the claims of other, rival groups or individuals?

A NEW CHURCH ORDER

The new developments of popular piety and associational mobilization evident in Catholic communities across Europe took place within a new organizational context, namely, the Church itself, as a transnational matrix of power based on formal rationality and hierarchical leadership.

This subject too has received increased attention, although it would justify a comparative analysis of its impact across European history. The drive to guarantee – indeed, to re-create – a common habitus of Catholic belief was tightly co-ordinated with the increasing levels of formal-organizational rationality and hierarchical bureaucratization that characterized the nineteenth-century Church. The result of what Michael Ebertz has termed a new 'bureaucratic-hierarchical system' of clerical authorities was an international Church that was not merely more 'papal', and thus more 'ultramontane', but also more priestly, more formally organized and more inclined to regulate and to systematize new and old cultic practices. Indeed, many scholars have linked the explosion of the new forms of popular piety with changes in the cultic disposition of the Catholic clergy, as modulated and authorized from Rome.[74]

The face of the new papacy was manifested in the style and substance of international diplomacy.[75] Leo XIII's precocious diplomatic interventions combined patent self-interest with a surprising unpredictability about the sensibilities of local Catholic political interests. His sense of the ambiguities of power led him to steer the Church in directions of compromise, but always with the broader goal of reanchoring Roman Catholicism as the pre-eminent transnational religion of continental Europe. His successor, Pius X, was no less concerned with internationalizing the Church's presence, although the latter's vision of a Church beset internally by renegade modernists and pillaged externally by heinous anticlericals led him to attack inevitably turning windmills.[76] But both Leo XIII and Pius X directed powerful efforts to build out the legal-moral-institutional impress of the papal Church across Europe, with professionalizing and systematizing interventions that achieved what Michael Ebertz has characterized as 'the organization of mass religiosity'.[77] As a latter-day version of enlightened absolutism, undertaken after rather than before the Industrial Revolution, this enormously complicated process of social and administrative disciplining left its traces in legions of ways.[78] For example, Rome's interest in the moral and professional discipline and material welfare of the lower clergy had powerful conformity-engendering effects that paid great dividends over time.[79] Ralph Gibson has argued that nineteenth-century seminaries created a 'docile, regimented, and uniform clergy, to a degree that even their eighteenth-century predecessors . . . had failed to do', whereas in Germany David Blackbourn has noted that 'more independent and ultramontane seminaries' led to an 'intensely Mariolatrous clergy'.[80]

SOCIAL THEORY AND SOCIAL PRACTICE

The experience of ideological order that accompanied the standardizing and homogenizing organizational strategies of Catholic leaders between

1860 and 1914 afforded new opportunities for an internationalization of intellectual perspectives.[81] One of the most fruitful sites for the construction of contemporary international perspectives came with debates about new Catholic social theories as they related to the working class. Such theory development inevitably forced educated Catholics to make tough decisions about the kind of civic values they most cherished, about the kinds of governmental structures they most esteemed, and about the capacity of those structures to use either coercive or redistributive power to effect social changes in their own societies. But such theory work was not exclusively national, since of necessity it depended upon comparative and international perspectives. Indeed, debates about social theory and social practice linked the new internationalism of the Church with the contingencies of the new national defence situations faced by each group of Catholics.

From Wilhelm von Ketteler, Franz Brandts and Georg von Hertling in Germany to Albert de Mun, René La Tour du Pin and Léon Harmel in France, the landscape of the last third of the nineteenth century is full of theoretical as well as organizational initiatives by Catholic laymen, lower clerics and bishops, by Catholic politicians, charitable associations and professional groups seeking to confront the social question.[82] The most notable, if not lauded, effort in social theory work came from Rome itself. Pope Leo XIII's great encyclical *Rerum novarum*, issued in May 1891, came at the crucial dividing line in the nineteenth century, at a point when liberalism had essentially created the civic constitutional world to which it aspired and mass socialism had not yet risen to full electoral power, when the constitutional frameworks of most large European states were more or less fixed, and when the generation of 'cultural struggles' so characteristic of the 1870s and early 1880s was over (as it happened, only temporarily in France) and the rise of radical nationalism not yet fully under way.

Although focused on the labour or 'social question', the document reflected wider concerns about how to position both the Church as an institution and Catholics as members of civic communities in their confrontation with an already successful political liberalism, while preparing the ground for the battle with socialism that lay ahead. Its power derived from several mediational interventions. First, the encyclical was an urgent effort to imagine a whole and thus harmonious way of life beyond the sustained reach of the strong administrative state, or (presumably) the large, anticlerical political parties of the late nineteenth century. Second, with its simultaneous defence of necessary, but also ethically responsible, differences in wealth based on the natural right of private property *and* of the natural legitimacy and efficacy of intermediate social organizations and collectivities (families, associations, churches, confraternities), *Rerum novarum* imagined a civil society that was both internally coherent and largely sustained by society's own subsidiary forces (although the state must involve itself in moments of crisis).[83] Third, it offered a plausible as well as sincere statement about the actual human dignities, if not always the real social rights, of the new industrial poor in European society.

Rerum novarum was thus a 'historic' document, because it inspired so many different contemporary understandings and divergent memories, each mirroring the political time and social place of the individual reader. Like the great polemical works of the French Enlightenment, it had a fascinating reception history, so much so that several generations of European and even American Catholics have felt compelled to produce Festschriften to celebrate its relevance to their worlds. A comparative analysis of these memorials would itself be illuminating about the history of twentieth-century Catholicism.[84]

Despite its paternalistic defence of workers' rights, *Rerum novarum*'s relentless condemnation of Marxian socialism should have been reassuring to Catholic businessmen. Indeed, what began as an attack on the inhumane practices of nineteenth-century capitalism ended up intimately connecting capitalism with socialism, to the ultimate disadvantage of the latter. As Michael Novak has shrewdly observed, the analytic line of the document is fundamentally asymmetrical: Leo may have criticized the excesses of liberal capitalism, but he fundamentally condemned socialism.[85] And as John Molony points out, unease in Rome about the negative consequences of connecting the Pope personally with further explanations of the idea of a just wage led to equivocations and demurs that were less than edifying but politically necessary.[86]

Still, by providing an unimpeachable endorsement of labour associations and sidestepping conservative demands for mixed (labour–management) corporations, *Rerum novarum* provided an intellectual platform that valorized serious Catholic labour movements across Europe over the next quarter century. It would be an overstatement to argue that the encyclical actually caused such movements, but because Leo XIII spoke commonly for all Catholics, he fostered a common discourse that gave European Catholics a shared starting point in dealing with industrial modernity. *Rerum novarum*'s imprecise, yet rhetorically powerful, defence of a living wage also legitimated the self-help strategies pursued by Catholic union activists, even if the Vatican subsequently felt uneasy with the direct democratic nature of some of those strategies. Finally, by counterposing associational organization to direct state intervention, Leo had unintentionally created a political as well as a policy space that Catholic labour activists could fill within their own Catholic electoral constituencies.

For all of its fascinating power, the international cause empowered by the encyclical – Catholic leadership on behalf of social justice for the working classes – had a deeply contradictory history all over Europe in the next twenty-five years. The fate of two of the encyclical's most notable contributions, associationalism and its critique of capitalism, help to illuminate the causes of this outcome. First, the instrumental agency of associationalism endorsed by the encyclical failed to anticipate that by the end of the nineteenth century, debates on social justice were pre-eminently political issues that would involve organized political parties much more than the Church and the administrative state. Catholic associationalism was not a thing unto itself, for it had to exist within a power matrix of larger political relationships, many of which had core missions that only partially overlapped with the visions of the various Christian labour activists. To defend the legitimacy of Christian labour unions or other democratic self-help organizations against possible incursions by the state said nothing about defending them against other, equally potent challenges, not the least of which would (within a decade) ironically originate from Rome itself. Pius X's condemnation of Marc Sangnier's Sillon movement in 1910 and his near condemnation of the interdenominational Christian unions in Germany in 1912 – the latter producing 'gloom and outrage' among Catholic union leaders – pointed to serious confusion among senior Catholic ecclesiastical leaders over who was authorized to accomplish what on the front of social justice.[87]

Second, the social and economic world inhabited by many European Catholics changed significantly after 1890, in ways that the core assumptions of Leonine social theory could not anticipate. Josef Mooser's research on the changing conceptions of the professions and their relations to modern capitalist business practices is valuable in this regard. Mooser argues that until well into the nineteenth century, Catholic attitudes about work were marked by a strong 'sociomoral traditionalism'.[88] Occupation and work were seen as necessary parts of an objective system of meaning: man as sinful, work as possibly unpleasant, but necessary to sustain virtue. Work did not lead to self-development (*Selbstbildung*), nor could it be expected to offer fulfilment. It was expected that most people would remain in the same class or occupation as their parents, that women would remain subject to men and that few people might enjoy a free choice of occupation.

After 1900, such static conceptions of employment and occupation were bound to become slowly anachronistic amid the powerful changes in the structure of the European urban labour markets in the late Industrial Revolution, and as Catholics began to move from a 'corporatist' to an individual-oriented occupational ethic. One also begins to see open and undisguised approval of capitalism among many Catholic political and intellectual leaders. The fascinating debates in the Christian Social Party leadership in 1910 on the legitimacy (and necessity) of an alliance between themselves and big capitalism took place only twenty years after Karl von Vogelsang's death, but they still constituted an intellectual revolution in

Austrian political Catholicism.[89] These cognitive changes in Catholic social milieux came as the range of social-interest representation in political Catholic movements became more complex, more regionally differentiated, with more subcomponents tending towards 'side-bar' interest-group affiliations. The 1890s were a time of 'accelerating organizing activity', in which new forces of social-interest politics emerged in many European countries.[90] However loyal German Catholic agrarian and small shopkeeper populists remained to the Centre, their policy concerns were often not readily reconcilable with those of their urban working-class colleagues. Similar centrifugal strains were increasingly prevalent in Austrian political Catholicism and French Catholicism after 1907.

WHAT HAD CATHOLICS LEARNED BY 1914 AND WHAT CHALLENGES LAY AHEAD?

On a positive note, many Catholics across Europe came to recognize the legitimacy (or at least the inevitability) of the modern liberal constitutional state as a normal way of doing public business. The 'noise' of right-wing nationalist groups, like the Action Française in France, should not be given more weight than it deserves. The 'liberalism' issue that perplexed Catholics in the 1880s was by 1914 increasingly anachronistic, as political liberalism won resoundingly (in France), or lost resoundingly (in Austria), or became fragmented and divided (in Germany). At the same time, the stark social upheaval that many feared was facing Europe in 1890 never came about. Whatever the fate of political liberalism in these states, liberal constitutional and legal institutions took root and Catholics learned to cope and even profit from them. Raymond Grew has thus correctly argued that Catholics came to terms with the liberal state and by their vigilant associationalism were able to exploit and mobilize a new level of freedom, although the procedures by which this happened differed widely and those differences had a profound import for the twentieth century.[91] The Church also accepted the fact that individual national Catholicisms had to make individual arrangements with secular states.[92]

The basic challenge faced by Catholics in the early twentieth century was how effective they and other non-liberal parties would be in sustaining the constitutional systems constructed in the liberal tradition, but in electoral circumstances where liberal notables no longer ran these systems. This in turn would hinge on two other flashpoints of European political culture – the social consequences of full democratic participation on the one hand and the fragmentation of national and ethnic identities on the other – which would have perplexed Catholics in the twentieth century even had Europeans not started a suicidal war in 1914. Paradoxically, because Catholics were so successful in mobilizing themselves and in engaging the state, they now found themselves embroiled in new problems involving equality and democracy, as well as those of ethnicity and national identity. On both fronts, to paraphrase Wilfried Loth, Catholics acted both for and against modernity.[93]

THE PROBLEM OF DEMOCRATIC PARTICIPATION: EQUALITY AND DEMOCRACY

Equality and democracy were the two most dangerous passions of nineteenth-century European modernity. Catholics played at democracy, while soundly rejecting equality. In most European nations by 1900 the pre-eminent advocates of democratic electoral procedures open to all adult men and women without restriction of wealth, education or residency requirements were the social democratic parties. Moreover, the ends to which the social democrats sought to put these democratic means involved not only utopian redistributive theories to cashier the bourgeois epoch, but also a host of concrete reform proposals and a coherent programme of union activity for the defence of the practical, day-to-day interests of the industrial labour force. By 1900 'socialism' was thus not only a salvific myth infused with anticlerical values, but also an evolutionary programme of radical liberalism on behalf of equalitarian values.[94]

It is a commonplace to argue that Catholicism and socialism bore many cultic similarities, so much so that they naturally and fundamentally detested each other. Ignaz Seipel captured this point when he observed to Heinrich Mataja, in 1928, that Austro-Marxism was not simply or not even a 'political party' in the traditional sense of the word. Rather, for Seipel it was a 'community with an all-encompassing world view' (*Weltanschauungsgemeinschaft*), whose only realistic rival was the Catholic Church.[95] Yet the opposition between socialism and Catholicism was not merely aesthetic or sacral, since it also encompassed profound differences in their views of human nature and of the possibility, if not the desirability, of social and economic equality.

As for democracy, many scholars have emphasized the mediation of political Catholicism in helping vast numbers of common people to learn the ropes of the competitive electoral political process by empowering them to challenge worlds of traditional deference and hierarchy. Margaret Anderson's arguments about the slow learning curve towards democracy involving a German Catholic laity being 'led' by a political party and an activist clergy should not be underestimated, and they are certainly applicable in other European regions beyond Germany.[96] Raymond Grew argues: 'The Church helped, in short, to bring the masses into political life and proved more effective at doing so than traditional liberals.'[97] What democracy in this usage did not comprehend, however, was support for full political rights for all, and for redistributive social policies that took full cognizance of the valence of *class*-based economic issues. This becomes clearer if one looks more closely at the isolated situation of Catholic worker groups within the various national Catholic parties after 1900, as many of those parties made clear their primary allegiance to what Philip Nord has characterized as 'middle-class defence'.[98]

The German case is perhaps the most famous, but also the most instructive. The *Gewerkschaftsstreit* (union struggle) between 1900 and 1912, which culminated in the encyclical *Singulari quadam*, under which the interconfessional unions were merely to be tolerated, a judgment that Catholic labour leaders like August Pieper, Heinrich Brauns and Adam Stegerwald found insulting and dispiriting, raised a host of dilemmas. *Bürgerlich* Centre leaders, especially progressive western leaders like Carl Trimborn and Julius Bachem, did try to protect their labourite colleagues, but were themselves under pressure from conservative forces.[99] They did so in the spirit of the Centre as a bourgeois, antisocialist, and (theoretically) interdenominational party, if also a party that was still deeply confessionally bounded in the Germany of 1908.[100]

Yet, as Wilfried Loth and Eric Brose have demonstrated, the end result of Rome's imputations about the confessional virtue of the labourites was to weaken their work, and not that of their *bürgerlich* or agrarian colleagues. This weakening came on the heels of a slow right-left polarization in German politics that left Catholic workers *qua* voters increasingly inclined to cross the cultural divide in the name of common class interests and to vote for the Social Democratic Party. At the same time, in spite of the labourites' frustration, the mother Centre Party remained resolute in opposing serious changes to the oligarchical Prussian three-class franchise, the epitome of antidemocratic electoral politics.[101] The frustration of the labourites in 1909 on the inheritance tax issue, and their misguided efforts to secure an antisocialist *Sammlung* of bourgeois parties in the 1912 elections, in the hope that Christian labour forces would also prosper, backfired. Instead, the Social Democratic Party gained a massive victory, whereas the Centre suffered what Noel Cary has rightly called 'an unprecedented and staggering defeat'.[102] On the eve of the war the Centre seemed headed in the direction of becoming 'more and more a bourgeois-dominated party of integration [*Integrationspartei*], with a strong *mittelständisch* accent'.[103] August Pieper would resign his position of director of the Volksverein in 1918 out of frustration with the reactionary stance taken by the Catholic clergy and major segments of the Centre Party on several issues, including their opposition to democratic voting reform in Prussia.[104]

Clearly, for many Catholic workers after 1900, social-class identities and cultural-confessional identities were increasing divisible.[105] This was a menacing development, for it confronted Catholic leaders with a pluralistic world in which vested socio-moral interests could no longer automatically hold their movement together. Certainly, Austrian Catholics found themselves in similar predicaments in Vienna and in the German-speaking Crownlands after 1907, and, in a different electoral context, French Catholics did so as well. To the extent that the Action Libéral Populaire led by de Mun and Piou was the most plausible representative of a moderate-conservative, post-*Ralliement* Catholic politics in France, the party's collusion with conservative republican forces on behalf of what Philip Nord has called 'middle-class defence' issues between 1901 and 1914 put it squarely in line with parallel developments in German and Austrian political Catholicism.[106] Indeed, Nord's research on the politics of retailers in Paris charts the gradual convergence of small shopkeeper militancy and conservative Catholic antisocialism under the aegis of the ALP. Like their counterparts in Vienna after 1900, anti-Semitic Parisian shopkeepers and artisans, at first candidates for a 'new' plebeian and even violent radical right, ended up being submerged in a more conservative, antisocialist, and Catholic *Sammlung*.[107] Interestingly, Pius's condemnation of Sangnier and the Sillon seems to have had a more dramatic effect on right-centrist French Catholics than the papal intervention against the Christian trade unions had in Germany. As Benjamin Martin has observed of the ALP after 1910:

> social Catholicism also quietly disappeared from the pages of the [ALP's] *Bulletin* since it might recall the fate of the Sillon . . . de Mun continued to shape legislation in the Labor Committee, to campaign for it in the press, and even to join in projects with a chastened and chary Sangnier, but about two-thirds of the party took this opportunity to cast off ideas with which they had never been quite comfortable. The deputies felt more secure embracing nationalism, and the ALP had always brandished the flag and the army.[108]

THE PROBLEM OF CULTURAL DIFFERENCE: NATIONALISM AND ANTI-SEMITISM

If the dual challenges of equality and democracy tested the capacity of Catholics to respond to the material and political potency of class, the challenges of ethnicity tested their capacities for civic pluralism and cultural diversity. I focus here on nationalism and anti-Semitism not only because of their subsequent import for European politics, but also because, paradoxically, they were the cultural and political tools that allowed Catholics not so much to resist, as to shape and control the democratization of civil society in the context of their own cultural traditions.

Nineteenth-century liberalism secured for the broad masses of society the right to monitor and control both the coercive and the redistributive powers of the state. Yet the century expired with important, if still fledgling streams of integral nationalism and political anti-Semitism, as it also ended with crescendos of militant anticlericalism and, in Germany at least, militant anti-Catholicism from groups like the Evangelical League.

The nationalisms of the late nineteenth century operated as patterns of collective memory and collected histories, arrayed on behalf of imaginary public associations based on the imputation of a common history, the availability of common language and the invocation of common civic sentiments.[109] As feelings of attachment to these newly imagined public associations became a powerful component of civic identity formation in most European societies after 1848, and especially after 1870, Catholics could hardly be expected to be unaffected. The ways in which individual Catholics understood such imagined public associations obviously differed from society to society and depended on broad existing demographic, class and regional variables. The embattled minority status of Catholics in Germany – arrayed as they were against a majority Protestant community whose leaders avidly identified Protestantism with the invented post-1871 German nation – put them in a different context from that of French Catholics, who could position themselves as legitimate advocates of what James McMillan has recently characterized as 'national Catholicism', linking French national greatness to the purity of its historic faith.[110]

Before 1914 most competitive invocations of national identity were deployed as much to buttress (or to undermine) regime stability within individual domestic European political systems as to create a divisive ethology of interstate hatred. Alon Confino is thus correct in cautioning us not to translate the nationalisms of the epoch before 1914 into the fate of Europe after 1933.[111] Indeed, Adrian Hastings has argued that ultramontane Catholicism historically served as an obstacle to militant nationalism: 'the Catholic Church was of its nature a restraining rather than inflaming influence upon nationalism', even if, as Hastings also argues, religion had a powerful effect on the ways by which national cultures came to be constituted over the centuries. Of the three major traditions I have explored in this essay, the Austrian Catholics bore the brunt of the challenge of responding to different ethnically constituted nations within their own political system, and the experience of the Habsburg Church and Austrian political Catholicism before 1914 does align with Hastings's suggestion.[112] The basic design of the Christian Social Party signified an attempt to substitute class and ideological politics for national tensions and thus preserve the multinational dynastic state, even though the execution of their plan was clumsy, partisan and, in the end, ineffective. In France, Catholics in and out of the ALP opted to pursue a more rigorous nationalist orientation, but their self-enhancing, self-defining nationalism was directed as much against the radical republican tradition as it was against their German neighbours to the east. In Germany, by contrast, Catholics found themselves playing at nationalism, not so much to attack the imperial-Protestant state as to gain eager recognition from it.

As a form of political and civic differentiation, anti-Semitism had none of the lustre of nationalism. Recent work on German Catholicism confirms that the top leaders of the Centre Party generally abstained from deploying anti-Semitic rhetoric, in part because of their sense of being a minority party and in part because it was ineffective as a means to unify Catholics of different social and class backgrounds.[113] Still, anti-Semitic images and rhetoric were widespread in Catholic popular culture, often used as a way of recovering or defending pre-modern conceptions of a historically rooted culture.[114] In Austria and France the situation was different. Political Catholic groups of various colours in those majority Catholic countries pursued a widespread engagement with anti-Semitism, most notably on the level of local and regional politics, and in the context of electioneering on behalf of petit bourgeois and agrarian economic causes, which Philip Nord has characterized in France in its more potent forms as 'smallowner utopianism laced with a powerful admixture of anti-Semitic venom'.[115] Just as Thomas Nipperdey argued that ultramontanism and democracy went well together, Olaf Blaschke has argued that ultramontanism and anti-Semitism could also go well together.[116]

In using political anti-Semitism in the open grid of competitive mass politics, Catholics, like other Europeans, had given dreadful hostages to the future. How dreadful depended, of course, on the shape and inevitability of that future. Much depends on how decisive one judges the effects of the First World War in making possible the conditions for European fascism of the 1920s and the 1930s, for ultimately, political anti-Semitism became most dangerous when it became a central, constituent part of modern fascism. Just as Confino has argued that pre- and post-1914 nationalisms should not be conflated, it is also important, as Robert Wohl has argued, not to obscure 'the vital role the Great War played in the development of fascist movements and regimes'.[117] Yet for some scholars the rise of a mass-based, political anti-Semitism in the late nineteenth century represents a marker of protofascism, a term that itself signifies a direct teleological connection between pre-war radicalism and post-war violence. This is and will remain a hugely controversial issue, but to the extent that Catholic parties made use of anti-Semitism, while also insisting on their dedication to representative government and a state of law, the historian confronts truly paradoxical situations that only dramatize the fragile and all-too-open-ended possibilities that lay at the end of the nineteenth century.

CONCLUSION: THE SITUATION AT THE END OF THE LONG CENTURY

Catholics were leaders of the effort to provide unrepresented or underrepresented classes in many European societies with significant representation in the state. To the extent that they succeeded in enlarging the realm of electoral representation and in expanding the range of social-interest responsibilities that the state accepted as its own, they must be considered forerunners of a democratic modernity. The profound tensions between Church and state that marked many European societies in the second half of the nineteenth century may have seemed superficially dangerous, but on a deeper level they were also productive of stable and controllable political-cultural change, for the disciplining force of the modern liberal state's universalizing law, when combined with the dialectical appropriation of and resistance to that law by the powerful private communities of the Church, created sturdy outposts of cultural resilience that allowed Catholic communities to defend, as well as to replicate, themselves generationally into the twentieth century.

Hence, although political Catholics were declared enemies of liberalism, they often served as its unwanted offspring, or at least as custodians of that originally suspect, but eventually tolerable system of power relations. It may seem ironic to posit a connection between these parties and liberalism, especially as one observes the crude anti-Semitic electioneering of Christian Social agitators or the staunch defence of Catholic confessional privileges by the German Centre. Yet this paradox simply suggests that it was possible to pick and choose among the discordant elements of nineteenth-century liberalism, all the while seeking its political demise.

Moreover, Catholic parties challenged the modern bureaucratic state in ways that the traditional liberalism of notables had failed to do.[118] In much of Europe Catholics developed a new style of class-based, competitive politics, one in which corporate, associational organization was at a premium. Their competitive social politics were infused with ideological and cultural preferences that postulated different visions of what the nineteenth century had been, in order to insist upon different scenarios of what the twentieth century should become.

In 1914 Catholicism was also both a local and a universal phenomenon. Most parishes had a cohesive local, often even ethnically uniform, community. At the same time most parishes were linked by piety, governance and self-conception to the Great Tradition of their universal Church. The result was that Catholics occupied a unique historical position. On the one hand, their identification with their civilization helped to compromise all other universalisms (nationalist, capitalist, or even totalitarian). To be a Catholic in a Catholic community gave solidity on the level of everyday life, and on the level of ideology and faith, with which to resist or at least modify and transform rival secular universalisms. On the other hand, their local cohesion helped to insulate them from the kind of isolation and anomie that a mere neighbourhood might suffer in the atomizing world of liberal, industrial modernity. When the tides of political turmoil – whether right-wing or left-wing collectivism or the atomization of capitalist democracy – washed over them, they were not easily swamped. They remained relatively secure in their sense of belonging to the stable order of a local community, within a universal structure that was meaningful but not totalizing.

The late German historian Thomas Nipperdey once distinguished between two kinds of modernist hope that he believed infused late-nineteenth-century German civil society. One was a liberal-individualist myth, deriving from the Enlightenment and undergirded by processes of economic progress, national unity and rationalism; the other was a cult of illiberal pessimism and radical nationalism privileging conflict and struggle as essential orders of nature and of life. Detlev Peukert has further glossed the first variant, arguing that the Weimar Republic was a prime site of a classical, but also not altogether positive modernity, since modernity as a 'dream of reason' not only brought with it advanced forms of capitalist production, economic rationalization and scientific rationality, but also engendered bureaucratization, dangerous social-policy utopias and mass conformity.[119]

Political Catholicism represented, however, a third variant of modernity, which I shall call corporate modernity. This form of modernity coupled mass party mobilization with the institutions of the liberal *Rechtsstaat* (constitutional state), and accorded to that state powerful interventionist responsibilities in maintaining and enforcing preconceived ethical-historical harmonies. But the maintenance and enforcement of these harmonies had to occur under the tutelage of the new political parties and the Church as collaborating agents on behalf of a whole way of cultural life, and not on behalf of some other imaginary universal such as the secular nation or the secular administrative state.[120] Individual liberty and rationality were not so much unappreciated as sublimated into larger cultural, moral and historicist wholes under the corporate umbrella sponsorship of a mass political movement. In this sense, parties such as the German Centre and the Austrian Christian Socials tried to reconcile the tensions inherent in Nipperdey's and Peukert's models, because they permitted some residue of 'liberal' individualist hope to prevail while also controlling mass society under the cultural disciplinary tutelage of the mass political parties and the parallel institutions of their cultural-civilizational-religious milieux. Even if these particular political formations were disrupted, indeed temporarily suppressed in the 1930s and 1940s, the combination of a resilient and identity-shaping Catholic pietistic tradition and a coherent approach to Christian ideological politics on a mass political basis – both legacies of the later nineteenth century – were still available to provide crucial anchors for the reconstruction of bourgeois European politics in many continental societies immediately after 1945.

Arnaldo Momigliano once observed of the relationship between religion and politics in the writing of modern history that, 'paradoxically, Christian ideas penetrated into modern historical books in the eighteenth and nineteenth centuries, when faith in Christianity was at its lowest'.[121] Something similar might be said for the penetration of 'Christian' politics as well. European Catholics made good use of the final third of the nineteenth century to come to terms with the political institutions and legal values of the various liberal and liberal-authoritarian constitutional regimes, to gain skilful experience in mass politics and mass organization, to defend their newly reconstructed and reimagined cultural communities, and to protect their unusually resilient faith. They, like their socialist competitors, made a stunning breakthrough to the twentieth century, inventing and reinventing themselves collectively as they crossed the divide of 1900 and again of 1918.

What they had not yet accomplished was to move beyond the formalities of the empowerment of the masses to a genuine political culture of democratization that would protect individual liberty and sanction the inevitability, if not desirability, of cultural diversity. This was a condition that was possible only in the desolation after 1945, but, in another paradox, such a recuperation and modernization was possible in the world of the 1950s *only* because enough of the Catholic civilizational heritage of the reconstructed nineteenth century had survived into (or perhaps stumbled through) the inter-war period and the Second World War and into the Europe of the *Stunde Null*. As one of Michael Geyer's two 'pariah nations', Catholics would eventually become the *de facto* heroes of the mid-twentieth century, but in 1914 they were immobilized by the transitional preferments they had so successfully garnered for themselves in the quarter century since 1890, and by larger determinants in each of their domestic political systems that limited their influence to minority-based brokering and subcultural exclusivity and defensiveness. It would take the experience of the next forty years of political upheaval and moral disorder, most of it not of their own making, to transform and to refit them for the more pluralistic and democratic roles we associate today with post-war 'Christian democracy', while also making it possible for their core ethical values – now wrapped in what Noel Cary has called an 'inclusive rhetoric of policy tenets' – to flow forward into the late twentieth century.[122]

NOTES

1 Noel D. Cary, *The Path to Christian Democracy. German Catholics and the Party System from Windthorst to Adenauer* (Cambridge, MA 1996), pp. 4,

9–10. For helpful comments and advice that I received in the course of writing this chapter, I am grateful to Margaret L. Anderson, Michael Geyer, Michael R. Jones and Anthony J. Steinhoff.
2 Michael Geyer, 'Germany, or, The Twentieth Century as History', *South Atlantic Quarterly*, vol. 96 (1997), pp. 663–702, here pp. 675–6.
3 Raymond Grew, 'Liberty and the Catholic Church in Nineteenth-Century Europe', in Richard Helmstadter (ed.), *Freedom and Religion in the Nineteenth Century* (Stanford, CA 1997), pp. 196–232, here p. 226.
4 Martin Conway, 'Introduction', in Tom Buchanan and Martin Conway (eds), *Political Catholicism in Europe, 1918–1965* (Oxford 1996), pp. 1–33, here pp. 10–11.
5 Stathis N. Kalyvas, *The Rise of Christian Democracy in Europe* (Ithaca, NY 1996), p. 258.
6 Geyer, 'Germany', pp. 672–3.
7 Wilfried Loth, 'Zwischen autoritärer und demokratischer Ordnung: Das Zentrum in der Krise des Wilhelminischen Reiches', in Winfried Becker (ed.), *Die Minderheit als Mitte. Die Deutsche Zentrumspartei in der Innenpolitik des Reiches 1871–1933* (Paderborn 1986), pp. 47–69, here p. 55; Jonathan Sperber, *The Kaiser's Voters. Electors and Elections in Imperial Germany* (Cambridge 1997), p. 262; John W. Boyer, *Culture and Political Crisis in Vienna. Christian Socialism in Power, 1897–1918* (Chicago, IL 1995), pp. 268–84; Raymond C. Sun, '"Before the Enemy is Within our Walls". A Social, Cultural, and Political History of Catholic Workers in Cologne, 1885–1912', Ph.D. (Johns Hopkins University 1991), pp. 692–730.
8 Quoted in Horstwalter Heitzer, *Der Volksverein für das katholische Deutschland im Kaiserreich 1890–1918* (Mainz 1979), p. 163.
9 Christoph Weber, 'Ultramontanismus als katholischer Fundamentalismus', in Wilfried Loth (ed.), *Deutscher Katholizismus im Umbruch zur Moderne* (Stuttgart 1991), pp. 20–45, here p. 34. For a parallel argument with a less polemical tinge, see Ronald J. Ross, 'Catholic Plight in the Kaiserreich: A Reappraisal', in Jack R. Dukes and Joachim Remak (eds), *Another Germany. A Reconsideration of the Imperial Era* (Boulder, CO 1988), pp. 73–94, especially pp. 88–9.
10 Marshall Berman, *All That is Solid Melts into Air. The Experience of Modernity* (New York 1982), p. 15.
11 The literature on Church and state as well as on religion and politics in the nineteenth and early twentieth centuries is enormous, on both regional and national levels. For the Habsburg empire the most important recent survey is Peter Leisching, 'Die römisch-katholische Kirche in Cisleithanien', in Adam Wandruszka and Peter Urbanitsch (eds), *Die Habsburgermonarchie 1848–1918. Band IV: Die Konfessionen* (Vienna 1985), pp. 1–247. For Germany, see the useful overviews of Kurt Nowak, *Geschichte des Christentums in Deutschland. Religion, Politik und Gesellschaft vom Ende der Aufklärung bis zur Mitte des 20. Jahrhunderts* (Munich 1995) and Karl-Egon Lönne, *Politischer Katholizismus im 19. und 20. Jahrhundert* (Frankfurt/Main 1986), the latter also offering comparative discussions of France and Italy. For France the older work by Adrien Dansette, *Religious History of Modern France*, 2 vols (Freiburg, Breisgau 1961), is still useful. But see also Philippe Joutard (ed.), *Histoire de la France religieuse, vol. 3: Du roi Très Chrétien à la laïcité républicaine (XVIIIe–XIXe siècle)* (Paris 1991) and René Rémond (ed.), *Histoire de la France religieuse, vol. 4: Société sécularisée et renouveaux religieux (XXe siècle)* (Paris 1992); Jacques Lafon, *Les prêtres, les fidèles et l'état:*

le ménage à trois du XIXe siècle (Paris 1987); and Geoffrey Cubitt, *The Jesuit Myth. Conspiracy Theory and Politics in Nineteenth-Century France* (New York 1993). For three recent insightful general surveys, see Martin Conway, *Catholic Politics in Europe, 1918–1945* (London 1997); Hugh McLeod, *Secularisation in Western Europe 1848–1914* (New York 2000); René Rémond, *Religion and Society in Modern Europe* (Oxford 1999).

12 See Michael John, *Politics and the Law in Late Nineteenth-Century Germany. The Origins of the Civil Code* (Oxford 1989), pp. 4–5, 95, 102–3.
13 Jean-Marie Mayeur, *Des partis catholiques à la démocratie chrétienne XIXe–XXe siècles* (Paris 1980), pp. 58–86.
14 See Helmut Walser Smith, *German Nationalism and Religious Conflict. Culture, Ideology, Politics, 1870–1914* (Princeton, NJ 1995), p. 20.
15 Margaret L. Anderson, *Windthorst. A Political Biography* (Oxford 1981), pp. 133–45; Ronald J. Ross, *The Failure of Bismarck's Kulturkampf. Catholicism and State Power in Imperial Germany, 1871–1887* (Washington, DC 1998), pp. 4–7.
16 Thomas Nipperdey, *Die Organisation der deutschen Parteien vor 1918* (Düsseldorf 1961), pp. 265–92.
17 For Catholic resistance in general, see Ross, *The Failure of Bismarck's Kulturkampf*; Jonathan Sperber, *Popular Catholicism in Nineteenth-Century Germany* (Princeton, NJ 1984), pp. 207–76.
18 Margaret L. Anderson, 'The Kulturkampf and the Course of German History', *Central European History*, vol. 19 (1986), pp. 82–115, here p. 82.
19 Heinrich von Poschinger (ed.), *Fürst Bismarck und die Parlamentarier*, vol. 3 (Breslau 1896), p. 231.
20 See Jürgen Schmädeke, *Wählerbewegung im Wilhelminischen Deutschland*, vol. 1 (Berlin 1995), pp. 192–268; Sperber, *The Kaiser's Voters*, pp. 75–107.
21 Ibid., pp. 82–5, 92, 105–6. The data cited are for constituencies where the Centre Party ran candidates.
22 Ibid., p. 97, also p. 271.
23 Wilfried Loth, *Katholiken im Kaiserreich. Der politische Katholizismus in der Krise des wilhelminischen Deutschlands* (Düsseldorf 1984); idem, 'Integration und Erosion. Wandlungen des katholischen Milieus in Deutschland', in Loth, *Deutscher Katholizismus*, pp. 266–81; idem, 'Soziale Bewegungen im Katholizismus des Kaiserreichs', *Geschichte und Gesellschaft*, vol. 17 (1991), pp. 279–310.
24 See Norbert Busch, 'Frömmigkeit als Faktor des katholischen Milieus. Der Kult zum Herzen Jesu', in Olaf Blaschke and Frank-Michael Kuhlemann (eds), *Religion im Kaiserreich. Milieus – Mentalitäten – Krisen* (Gütersloh 1996), pp. 136–65, here pp. 136–7. Several of the essays in this important volume offer critiques of Loth's thesis. None fundamentally overturns it, however. See also Margaret L. Anderson, 'Piety and Politics: Recent Work on German Catholicism', *Journal of Modern History*, vol. 63 (1991), pp. 708–14.
25 Josef Mooser, 'Volk, Arbeiter und Bürger in der katholischen Öffentlichkeit des Kaiserreichs. Zur Sozial- und Funktionsgeschichte der deutschen Katholikentage 1871–1913', in Hans-Jürgen Puhle (ed.), *Bürger in der Gesellschaft der Neuzeit. Wirtschaft – Politik – Kultur* (Göttingen 1991), pp. 259–73, here p. 270.
26 Cary, *The Path to Christian Democracy*, p. 23: 'From 1890 to 1932 – except for one two-year interval – the party held the pivotal parliamentary position.' See also John, *Politics and the Law*, pp. 200, 219, 238, 240.
27 Martin Baumeister, *Parität und katholische Inferiorität. Untersuchungen zur*

Stellung des Katholizismus im Deutschen Kaiserreich (Paderborn 1987), pp. 13–38; John, *Politics and the Law*, p. 219.

28 See the insightful observations about which Catholics were most likely to follow the allure of German nationalism, in Karl Rohe, *Wahlen und Wählertraditionen in Deutschland. Kulturelle Grundlagen deutscher Parteien und Parteiensysteme im 19. und 20. Jahrhundert* (Frankfurt/Main 1992), p. 157.

29 Smith, *German Nationalism*, p. 238.

30 Quoted in Maurice Larkin, *Religion, Politics, and Preferment in France since 1890: La Belle Époque and its Legacy* (Cambridge 1995), pp. 66–7.

31 Georg Pfeilschifter (ed.), *German Culture, Catholicism, and the World War. A Defense against the Book La Guerre Allemande et le Catholicisme* (St Paul, MN 1916), p. 259.

32 John McManners, *Church and State in France, 1870–1914* (London 1972), p. 140.

33 Jean-Marie Mayeur and Madeleine Rebérioux, *The Third Republic from its Origins to the Great War, 1871–1914* (Cambridge 1984), p. 169.

34 Maurice Larkin, *Church and State after the Dreyfus Affair. The Separation Issue in France* (London 1974), pp. 64, 70–1, 94–5; Benjamin F. Martin, 'The Creation of the Action Libérale Populaire. An Example of Party Formation in Third Republic France', *French Historical Studies*, vol. 9 (1975–6), pp. 660–89, especially pp. 663–4, 669; Eugen Weber, *The Nationalist Revival in France, 1905–1914* (Berkeley, CA 1959), pp. 10–11, 82, 111–12.

35 Benjamin F. Martin, *Count Albert de Mun. Paladin of the Third Republic* (Chapel Hill, NC 1978), pp. 276, 288; idem, 'The Creation of the Action Libérale Populaire', pp. 683, 686. See also Mayeur, *Des partis catholiques*, p. 89.

36 Martin, *Count Albert de Mun*, p. 99; McManners, *Church and State*, pp. 90–2, 98, 170.

37 See Jean-Marie Mayeur, 'Catholicisme intransigeant, catholicisme social, démocratie chrétienne', *Annales*, vol. 27 (1972), pp. 483–99; Stephen Wilson, 'Catholic Populism in France at the Time of the Dreyfus Affair. The Union Nationale', *Journal of Contemporary History*, vol. 10 (1975), pp. 667–705; Philip G. Nord, 'Three Views of Christian Democracy in *fin de siècle* France', *Journal of Contemporary History*, vol. 19 (1984), pp. 713–27 and Martin, *Count Albert de Mun*, pp. 124–5, 166.

38 The standard work is still Jeanne Caron, *Le Sillon et la démocratie chrétienne, 1894–1910* (Paris 1967). See also the excellent summary of the inter-war period in James F. McMillan, 'France', in Buchanan and Conway, *Political Catholicism in Europe*, pp. 40–54.

39 McManners, *Church and State*, pp. 172–4; Jean-Marie Mayeur, *Un prêtre démocrate: L'abbé Lemire, 1853–1928* (Paris 1968), pp. 494–522.

40 Margaret L. Anderson, 'The Limits of Secularization. On the Problem of the Catholic Revival in Nineteenth-Century Germany', *Historical Journal*, vol. 38 (1995), pp. 647–70, here p. 657, also pp. 649, 669; see also Thomas Nipperdey, *Religion im Umbruch. Deutschland 1870–1918* (Munich 1988), pp. 30–1.

41 See the insightful comments in Eugen Weber, *Peasants into Frenchmen. The Modernization of Rural France 1870–1914* (Stanford, CA 1976), pp. 357–74.

42 Philip G. Nord, *The Republican Moment. Struggles for Democracy in Nineteenth-Century France* (Cambridge, MA 1995), p. 246.

43 Claude Langlois, 'Catholics and Seculars', in Pierre Nora (ed.), *Realms of*

44 Ralph Gibson, *A Social History of French Catholicism 1789–1914* (London 1989), p. 237.
45 Dansette, *Religious History*, vol. 2, p. 241; Larkin, *Church and State*, pp. 198–200.
46 See Roger Aubert, 'The Modernist Crisis', in Hubert Jedin and John Dolan (eds), *History of the Church, vol. 9: The Church in the Industrial Age* (New York 1981), pp. 420–80, especially p. 477; and Anderson, 'The Kulturkampf', p. 113.
47 Mayeur, *Des partis catholiques*, p. 89; Dansette, *Religious History*, pp. 126, 250; Larkin, *Church and State*, p. 65.
48 See McManners, *Church and State*, pp. 24–6, 65–8, 75; Larkin, *Church and State*, pp. 50–1, 56–7; and Jacques-Olivier Boudon, *L'épiscopat français à l'époque concordataire (1802–1905). Origines, formation, nomination* (Paris 1996).
49 Anderson, 'The Limits of Secularization', p. 655, argues that the larger number of dioceses in France permitted tighter episcopal supervision over the lower clergy.
50 No general assembly of the French bishops had been held since the early nineteenth century. Interestingly, in the aftermath of the 1905 Separation, the French bishops were able to hold three assemblies between 1906 and 1908, after which the Vatican banned the practice.
51 I am grateful to Margaret Anderson for this insight. Margaret Anderson, *Practicing Democracy: Elections and Political Culture in Imperial Germany* (Princeton, NJ 2000) contains very insightful comparisons of German and French electoral practices in the later nineteenth century.
52 Dansette, *Religious History*, pp. 126, 288. Nothing close to the level of civic associationalism symbolized by the German Volksverein evolved in France.
53 Eugen Weber, *Action Française. Royalism and Reaction in Twentieth-Century France* (Stanford, CA 1962), p. 67.
54 See Jean-Claude Delbreil, *Centrisme et démocratie-chrétienne en France: Le Parti Démocrate Populaire des origines au M.R.P. (1919–1944)* (Paris 1990), pp. 13–22; Robert O. Paxton, 'France. The Church, the Republic, and the Fascist Temptation, 1922–1945', in Richard J. Wolff and Jörg K. Hoensch (eds), *Catholics, the State, and the European Right 1919–1945* (Boulder, CO 1987), pp. 69–72; William Bosworth, *Catholicism and Crisis in Modern France. French Catholic Groups at the Threshold of the Fifth Republic* (Princeton, NJ 1962), pp. 23–7, 36; Harry W. Paul, *The Second Ralliement: The Rapprochement Between Church and State in France in the Twentieth Century* (Washington, DC 1967), p. 183; McMillan, 'France', pp. 43–51.
55 Gérard Cholvy and Yves-Marie Hilaire, *Histoire religieuse de la France contemporaine*, vol. 2 (Toulouse 1986), pp. 150–69. For the history of Catholic women's associations before 1914, see James McMillan, 'Women, Religion, and Politics: The Case of the Ligue Patriotique des Françaises', *Proceedings of the Annual Meeting of the Western Society for French History*, vol. 15 (1988), pp. 355–64; and Odile Sarti, *The Ligue Patriotique des Françaises, 1902–1933. Feminine Response to the Secularization of French Society* (New York 1992), pp. 59–183.
56 Obviously, there was a very different kind of regime question in the issue of the constitutional and political relations of the various nationalities with each other.

57 This section draws upon John W. Boyer, 'Religion and Political Development in Central Europe around 1900. A View from Vienna', *Austrian History Yearbook*, vol. 25 (1994), pp. 13–57, especially pp. 31–2, 57.
58 Robert Musil, *Precision and Soul. Essays and Addresses*, edited and translated by Burton Pike and David S. Luft (Chicago, IL 1990), p. 21.
59 John W. Boyer, *Political Radicalism in Late Imperial Vienna. Origins of the Christian Social Movement, 1848–1897* (Chicago, IL 1981); idem, *Culture and Political Crisis in Vienna*; Peter G. J. Pulzer, *The Rise of Political Anti-Semitism in Germany and Austria*, revised edition (Cambridge, MA 1988).
60 See Dietmar von Reeken, 'Protestantisches Milieu und "liberale" Landeskirche? Milieubildungsprozesse in Oldenburg 1849–1914', in Blaschke and Kuhlemann, *Religion im Kaiserreich*, pp. 290–314, here p. 312.
61 *Protokoll über die Verhandlungen des Gesamtparteitages der Sozialdemokratischen Arbeiterpartei in Österreich. Abgehalten zu Wien vom 9. bis zum 13. November 1903* (Vienna 1903), p. 14.
62 Sudhir Hazareesingh, *Political Traditions in Modern France* (Oxford 1994), p. 103.
63 Adrian Hastings, *The Construction of Nationhood. Ethnicity, Religion and Nationalism* (Cambridge 1997), p. 203.
64 A good summary of this approach is in Robert Redfield and Milton Singer, 'The Cultural Role of Cities', in Margaret Park Redfield (ed.), *The Papers of Robert Redfield, vol. 1: Human Nature and The Study of Society* (Chicago 1962), pp. 326–50.
65 David Blackbourn, *Marpingen. Apparitions of the Virgin Mary in Nineteenth-Century Germany* (New York 1994); Ruth Harris, *Lourdes. Body and Spirit in the Secular Age* (New York 1999).
66 Gibson argues, for example, that France was flooded with a 'staggering quantity of pious literature' and that Catholics participated in and profited from the literacy revolution of the nineteenth century by means of this literature. See Gibson, *Social History*, pp. 234–5, and also Smith, *German Nationalism*, pp. 61–78.
67 Christoph Weber, 'Ultramontanismus als katholischer Fundamentalismus', pp. 21–3.
68 Olaf Blaschke, 'Wider die "Herrschaft des modern-jüdischen Geistes". Der Katholizismus zwischen traditionellem Antijudaismus und modernem Antisemitismus', in Loth, *Deutscher Katholizismus*, pp. 236–65, here p. 240; Gibson, *Social History*, p. 240.
69 For example, Hazareesingh explicitly associates the rhetorical motifs of clericalism, despair and ultramontane piety. See Hazareesingh, *Political Traditions*, p. 103.
70 Nipperdey, *Religion im Umbruch*, p. 45.
71 Margaret L. Anderson, 'Voter, Junker, *Landrat*, Priest. The Old Authorities and the New Franchise in Imperial Germany', *American Historical Review*, vol. 98 (1993), pp. 1448–74, here p. 1466.
72 Anderson, 'The Limits of Secularization', pp. 662–3, 666.
73 Smith, *German Nationalism*, p. 238; Nord, *The Republican Moment*, p. 13. The 'religious' aura of the European socialist movement has recently received important attention. Among a very large literature, see Thomas Kselman, 'The Varieties of Religious Experience in Urban France', in Hugh McLeod (ed.), *European Religion in the Age of the Great Cities, 1830–1930* (London 1995), pp. 165–90, especially pp. 179–83; Willfried Spohn, 'Religion and Working-Class Formation in Imperial Germany, 1871–1914', in Geoff Eley (ed.),

Society, Culture, and the State in Germany, 1870–1930 (Ann Arbor, MI 1996), pp. 163–87; Lucian Hölscher, *Weltgericht oder Revolution. Protestantische und sozialistische Zukunftsvorstellungen im deutschen Kaiserreich* (Stuttgart 1989), as well as the older essay by Vernon Lidtke, 'Social Class and Secularisation in Imperial Germany. The Working Classes', *Yearbook of the Leo Baeck Institute*, vol. 25 (1980), pp. 21–40.

74 Michael N. Ebertz, 'Herrschaft in der Kirche. Hierarchie, Tradition und Charisma im 19. Jahrhundert', in Karl Gabriel and Franz-Xaver Kaufmann (eds), *Zur Soziologie des Katholizismus* (Mainz 1980), pp. 89–111, here p. 105; Olaf Blaschke, 'Die Kolonialisierung der Laienwelt. Priester als Milieumanager und die Kanäle klerikaler Kuratel', in Blaschke and Kuhlemann, *Religion im Kaiserreich*, pp. 93–135, especially pp. 100–3; Gibson, *Social History*, p. 265; Blackbourn, *Marpingen*, pp. 29–30, 368, 373; Caroline Ford, 'Female Martyrdom and the Politics of Sainthood in Nineteenth-Century France: The Cult of Sainte Philomène', in Frank Tallett and Nicholas Atkin (eds), *Catholicism in Britain and France since 1789* (London 1996), pp. 115–34, especially p. 122.

75 See Owen Chadwick, *A History of the Popes, 1830–1914* (Oxford 1998), pp. 273–405; Peter C. Kent and John F. Pollard, 'A Diplomacy Unlike Any Other. Papal Diplomacy in the Nineteenth and Twentieth Centuries', in Peter C. Kent and John F. Pollard (eds), *Papal Diplomacy in the Modern Age* (Westport, CT 1994), pp. 11–21, especially pp. 15–16.

76 This led to the extraordinary protests of the Prussian and Bavarian governments in 1910 against official publication of *Editae saepe* in Germany. In 1910–12 German officials expressed concern over a possible negative judgement by Rome against progressive Catholics in the Christian labour unions dispute, for fear this would drive Protestant workers into the arms of the socialist unions. Horstwalter Heitzer, *Georg Kardinal Kopp und der Gewerkschaftsstreit 1900–1914* (Cologne 1983), pp. 158, 208, 220.

77 Michael N. Ebertz, '"Ein Haus voll Glorie, schauet . . .". Modernisierungsprozesse der römisch-katholischen Kirche im 19. Jahrhundert', in Wolfgang Schieder (ed.), *Religion und Gesellschaft im 19. Jahrhundert* (Stuttgart 1993), pp. 62–85, here p. 82; and idem, 'Herrschaft in der Kirche', p. 103.

78 Gerhard Oestreich, *Geist und Gestalt des frühmodernen Staates. Ausgewählte Aufsätze* (Berlin 1969), pp. 179–97.

79 See Roger Aubert, 'Light and Shadows of Catholic Vitality', in Hubert Jedin and John Dolan (eds), *History of the Church, vol. 8: The Church in the Age of Liberalism* (New York 1981), pp. 208–47, especially pp. 213–14.

80 Gibson, *Social History*, p. 89; Blackbourn, *Marpingen*, p. 368.

81 Anderson has recently argued that one feature of ultramontanism was that it inclined the clergy to look around themselves, obtaining what she calls an 'international perspective'. Anderson, 'The Limits of Secularization', p. 663.

82 Paul Misner, *Social Catholicism in Europe. From the Onset of Industrialization to the First World War* (New York 1991) provides an excellent overview of these many and varied efforts.

83 The imagination that governed *Rerum novarum* was *not* in favour of consistent and sustained state intervention. It argued rather for limited intervention where necessary and only where necessary. The encyclical explicitly says that 'the limits [of state intervention] are determined by the reason which moves the State to intervene, which means that the law must not go beyond what is required to repair the evil or to remove the danger'. John Molony, *The Worker Question. A New Historical Perspective on Rerum Novarum* (Dublin 1991),

p. 187. The general tenor of the encyclical is to defend corporatist intermediation, not state socialism. David J. O'Brien comes closest when he argues that 'this was a document of the ultramontane church ... the entire text reads as an analysis of and a prescription for society from the point of view of the institutional church. Winning workers to the Church is as important as defending their rights.' See David J. O'Brien, 'A Century of Catholic Social Teaching. Contexts and Comments', in John A. Coleman (ed.), *One Hundred Years of Catholic Social Thought. Celebration and Challenge* (Maryknoll 1991), pp. 13–24, here p. 17.

84 Of special interest is *Die soziale Frage und der Katholizismus. Festschrift zum 40jährigen Jubiläum der Enzyklika 'Rerum Novarum'* (Paderborn 1931).

85 Michael Novak, 'Transforming the Democratic/Capitalist Revolution', in Francis P. McHugh and Samuel M. Natale (eds), *Things Old and New. Catholic Social Teaching Revisited* (Lanham 1993), pp. 40–103, especially pp. 41–2, 59.

86 Molony, *The Worker Question*, pp. 122–3: 'The whole episode served to illustrate how difficult it was for the Church to deal with the increasing world of Catholic capitalism ...'

87 Cary, *The Path to Christian Democracy*, p. 30. Maurice Larkin notes that Merry del Val tended to lump together those who were willing to go along with the creation of the *associations cultuelles* in France in 1906 with the 'young priests and Catholics who have been won over to the freedom of the critical school, the advanced democratic school and all those who dream of reforms and novelties where the human and lay elements attempt to hold in check the divine and supernatural, and where the time-honoured structure of the Church would be turned upside down, in favour of the new Church of their dreams, adapted to the ideas of modern lay society'. Cited in Larkin, *Church and State*, p. 197. In this sense Pius X's *Vehementer nos* and *Gravissimo officii* (1906) were the logical prelude to his letter of 25 August 1910 attacking the Sillon.

88 Josef Mooser, '"Christlicher Beruf" und "bürgerliche Gesellschaft". Zur Auseinandersetzung über Berufsethik und wirtschaftliche "Inferiorität" im Katholizismus um 1900', in Loth, *Deutscher Katholizismus*, pp. 124–42, here pp. 128.

89 See Boyer, *Culture and Political Crisis*, pp. 251–4.

90 See Geoff Eley, *From Unification to Nazism. Reinterpreting the German Past* (Boston, MA 1986), p. 246. On the new political terrain of the 1890s, see idem., *Reshaping the German Right. Radical Nationalism and Political Change after Bismarck* (New Haven, CT 1980); David Blackbourn, *Populists and Patricians. Essays in Modern German History* (London 1987), especially pp. 217–45; and Boyer, *Political Radicalism in Late Imperial Vienna*.

91 Grew, *Liberty*, pp. 213–15.

92 Loth, *Deutscher Katholizismus*, pp. 12–13. David Blackbourn points out, however, that the situation in France and Spain was very different from that in Germany. See David Blackbourn, 'The Catholic Church in Europe since the French Revolution. A Review Article', *Comparative Studies in Society and History*, vol. 33 (1991), pp. 778–90, here p. 787.

93 'Eine moderne Bewegung gegen die Moderne', Loth, *Deutscher Katholizismus*, p. 11. See also Blaschke, 'Wider die "Herrschaft des modern-jüdischen Geistes"', p. 240.

94 See the insightful comments in John, *Politics and the Law*, pp. 232, 235.

95 Seipel to Mataja, 10 April 1928. Nachlass Seipel, Erzbischöfliches Diözesanarchiv, Vienna.

96 Anderson, 'The Limits of Secularization', pp. 669–70; idem, 'Clerical Election Influence and Communal Solidarity: Catholic Political Culture in the German Empire, 1871-1914', in Eduardo Posada-Carbó (ed.), *Elections before Democracy. The History of Elections in Europe and Latin America* (New York 1996), pp. 139–62, especially 142–3, 153–5.
 97 Grew, *Liberty*, p. 230.
 98 Philip G. Nord, *Paris Shopkeepers and the Politics of Resentment* (Princeton, NJ 1986), p. 472.
 99 See Eric D. Brose, *Christian Labor and the Politics of Frustration in Imperial Germany* (Washington, DC 1985), pp. 206–7, 257–9, 266–7, 272, 277, 340; and Rudolf Brack, *Deutscher Episkopat und Gewerkschaftsstreit: 1900–1914* (Cologne 1976), pp. 248, 331.
100 For the motives of the bourgeois leaders who did support Christian labour, see Thomas Mergel, *Zwischen Klasse und Konfession. Katholisches Bürgertum im Rheinland 1794–1914* (Göttingen 1994), p. 311. But see also Josef Mooser's comments about the hostility of some bourgeois Catholics over attempts to mix religion and labour reform, in idem, 'Das katholische Milieu in der bürgerlichen Gesellschaft. Zum Vereinswesen des Katholizismus im späten Deutschen Kaiserreich', in Blaschke and Kuhlemann (eds), *Religion im Kaiserreich*, pp. 59–92, especially p. 88.
101 Loth, *Katholiken*, pp. 187, 221–2, 229; Heitzer, *Volksverein*, pp. 130–4; Thomas Kühne, *Dreiklassenwahlrecht und Wahlkultur in Preussen 1867–1914. Landtagswahlen zwischen korporativer Tradition und politischem Massenmarkt* (Düsseldorf 1994), pp. 441–7, 463–5, 491–2, 547, 569–73.
102 Noel D. Cary, *Political Catholicism and the Reform of the German Party System, 1900–1957*, Ph.D. (Berkeley, CA 1988), p. 176, footnote 161. For the 1912 elections in general, see Sperber, *The Kaiser's Voters*, pp. 254–64; Schmädeke, *Wählerbewegung*, pp. 220–3, 232–8, 265; Jürgen Bertram, *Die Wahlen zum deutschen Reichstag vom Jahre 1912. Parteien und Verbände in der Innenpolitik des wilhelminischen Reiches* (Düsseldorf 1964), pp. 22–7, 212–13, 217–18. Karl Rohe, *Wahlen*, p. 132, points out that gender may have played a powerful structuring role. In the 1920 national elections Centre Party results in Cologne might have been different had not substantial support by newly enfranchised women voters been available to the Catholics. Such data might suggest that, even allowing for the effects of the war, the attractiveness of the Social Democratic Party for male Catholic voters should not be underestimated.
103 Loth, *Katholiken*, pp. 225, 229; see also Brose, *Christian Labor*, pp. 321–5.
104 Horstwalter Heitzer, 'Krisen des Volksvereins im Kaiserreich. Gründe und Hintergründe zum Rücktritt von August Pieper als Generaldirektor im Dezember 1918', *Historisches Jahrbuch*, vol. 99 (1979), pp. 213–54, especially pp. 215, 244–6, 253; idem, 'Der Parlementarier August Pieper. Auseinandersetzungen des Volksvereins für das katholische Deutschland mit dem Zentrum über die Fortführung der Sozialpolitik und die Wahlrechtsreform in Preussen im Ersten Weltkrieg', in Lothar Koch and Josef Stanzel (eds), *Christliches Engagement in Gesellschaft und Politik. Beiträge der Kirchen zur Theorie und Praxis ihres Sozialauftrages im 19. und 20. Jahrhundert in Deutschland* (Frankfurt/Main 1979), pp. 199–214; Reinhard Patemann, 'Der deutsche Episkopat und das preussische Wahlrechtsproblem 1917/18', *Vierteljahrshefte für Zeitgeschichte*, vol. 13 (1965), pp. 345–71.
105 Sperber, *The Kaiser's Voters*, p. 104; Brose, *Christian Labor*, pp. 324–8; Rohe, *Wahlen*, pp. 99, 109, 209, footnote 3.

106 When Jacques Piou proclaimed in 1901 that 'France is divided in two camps, on the one side the savage Jacobins, the sectarians, and collectivists, on the other, the patriots, liberals and conservatives', he was articulating right-centre Catholic hopes for a bipolar, two-bloc structure to refreeze French politics along an anti-socialist, pro-business axis, much as had almost happened between 1896 and 1898, only this time with the added option of a renewed nationalism. See Martin, 'The Creation of the Action Libérale Populaire', p. 665.
107 Nord, *Paris Shopkeepers*, pp. 468–71; idem, 'Le mouvement des petits commerçants et la politique en France de 1888 à 1914', *Le Mouvement Social*, vol. 114 (1981), pp. 35–55. Similiar trends occurred in Austria after 1907, where Albert Gessmann and Hermann Bielohlawek urged artisans and other small businessmen to adapt to the capitalist market, rather than trying to use protectionist legislation to avoid market forces; Boyer, *Culture and Political Crisis*, pp. 83–4.
108 Martin, *Count Albert de Mun*, pp. 256–7.
109 Alon Confino, *The Nation as a Local Metaphor. Württemberg, Imperial Germany, and National Memory, 1871–1918* (Chapel Hill, NC 1997), pp. 3–15.
110 James F. McMillan, 'French Catholics: *Rumeurs infâmes* and the *Union Sacrée*, 1914–1918', in Frans Coetzee and Marilyn Shevin-Coetzee (eds), *Authority, Identity, and the Social History of the Great War* (Providence, RI 1995), pp. 113–32, here p. 116; idem, 'Reclaiming a Martyr: French Catholics and the Cult of Joan of Arc, 1890–1920', in Diana Wood (ed.), *Martyrs and Martyrologies* (Oxford 1993), pp. 359–70.
111 Confino, *The Nation as a Local Metaphor*, pp. 211–15.
112 Hastings, *The Construction of Nationhood*, p. 203. The supranational 'ultramontane' variable here was as much Habsburg and imperial as it was Roman and papal.
113 Helmut Walser Smith, 'The Learned and the Popular Discourse of Anti-Semitism in the Catholic Milieu of the Kaiserreich', *Central European History*, vol. 27 (1994), pp. 315–28, especially pp. 327–8. Smith also suggests German Catholics tended to view Jews more often as a religious group than a race (p. 320), and that Protestants were generally more given to a strict political anti-Semitism.
114 See Olaf Blaschke, *Katholizismus und Antisemitismus im Deutschen Kaiserreich* (Göttingen 1997), especially pp. 235–60, and a convenient summary in idem, 'Wider die "Herrschaft des modern-jüdischen Geistes"', pp. 257–8. Blaschke argues that in the case of Ernst Lieber, 'die Taktik, an der Gleichberechtigung festzuhalten, beruhte weniger auf "Nächstenliebe", "Judenfreundschaft" oder einem modernen Pluralitäts- und Rechtsverständnis, als vielmehr auf politischem Räsonnement und der Sorge um den katholischen Selbstschutz'. Blaschke, *Katholizismus und Antisemitismus*, p. 245.
115 Nord, *Shopkeepers*, p. 380.
116 Blaschke, *Katholizismus und Antisemitismus*, pp. 152–3 ('die verheerende Liaison zwischen Ultramontanismus und Antisemitismus') as well as pp. 190–203.
117 Robert Wohl, 'French Fascism, Both Right and Left: Reflections on the Sternhell Controversy', *Journal of Modern History*, vol. 63 (1991), pp. 91–8, here p. 93.
118 Grew, *Liberty*, p. 209.
119 Thomas Nipperdey, 'Religion und Gesellschaft: Deutschland um 1900',

Historische Zeitschrift, vol. 246 (1988), pp. 591–615, especially pp. 599–600, 605; Detlev Peukert, *The Weimar Republic. The Crisis of Classical Modernity* (New York 1992), pp. xiii–xiv, 84, 164, 275–6; Frank Bajohr, Werner Johe and Uwe Lohalm (eds), *Zivilisation und Barbarei. Die widersprüchlichen Potentiale der Moderne. Detlev Peukert zum Gedenken* (Hamburg 1991).

120 Hence the resilience of corporate, party-political motivations and priorities in the face of seeming 'universal' processes of administrative rationalization and modernization. Not surprisingly, David Crew's recent critique of Detlev Peukert's theory of classical modernity is in part based on the residual presence of Catholic, Protestant and socialist interventions against the looming administrative welfare state. See David Crew, 'The Ambiguities of Modernity: Welfare and the German State from Wilhelm to Hitler', in Eley, *Society, Culture, and the State in Germany*, pp. 319–44, especially pp. 325–9; idem, *Germans on Welfare: From Weimar to Hitler* (New York 1998), pp. 16–17.

121 Arnaldo Momigliano, *The Classical Foundations of Modern Historiography* (Berkeley, CA 1990), p. 156.

122 Cary, *The Path to Christian Democracy*, p. 276.

2

A Microcosm of Society or the Key to a Majority in the Reichstag? The Centre Party in Germany

Jürgen Elvert

The Zentrum or Centre Party was founded in the late autumn of 1870 in the field of tension between, on the one side, the founding of the Kleindeutsches Reich along Prussian-Protestant lines, and on the other, the first Vatican Council's protective wall against *Zeitgeist* and modernity built in 1869–70.[1] With this context in mind, Golo Mann once characterized the party as a 'remarkable product both of German history and the European political climate around 1870'. The party appeared to him to be a product of German history, since Catholics had not represented such a strong minority in any European country other than the German *Kaiserreich*. In his opinion the Zentrum was determined by Europe, as the Protestant Prussians were able to triumph within a few years over the Catholic powers Austria and France and because it simultaneously came to revolutionary upheaval in Catholic Spain.[2] It was understandable to him that the Catholic Church felt threatened by such a development, as well as that the liberal state was scared of the reaction of a militant Church that appeared to be renewing its demands from its 'distant grey past'.[3]

THE HISTORICAL BACKGROUND

In choosing the name, the founders of the Zentrum in the late autumn of 1870 were thinking of the seating plan of the short-lived Paulskirche Parliament of 1848–49, which had in its time already constituted a Catholic club, later to become the nucleus of a conservative-liberal Catholic parliamentary group in the Prussian Landtag, which between the constitutional conflict and the Prussian–Austrian War of 1866 was to be worn down again. Thus there had already been several attempts before 1870 to give political Catholicism in Germany an organizational framework. It would therefore be a 'lop-sided polarization',[4] if one wanted to view the renewal and consolidation of the Zentrum in the 1870s exclusively as the direct reaction to the founding of the Reich and the *Kulturkampf*. Political Catholicism in Germany retained an organizational centre far longer with the Zentrum. As the German Reich was predominantly Protestant it needed this organizational centre in order to uphold its own political, economic and cultural interests. Looked at in this way, the founding of the party can be seen as one of the high points in the remarkable formative period of the Catholic milieu in Germany in the second half of the nineteenth century. This was, on the one hand, characterized by a conscious holding on to the traditional structures and essence of occidental Catholicism. On the other hand it set great reforming energy free, which not only promoted the opening up of Catholicism to influences of modernity, but also made a strong stand for inter-confessional co-operation, especially in the political and social fields.[5]

Tension between the two extremes was unavoidable. From a party-political viewpoint the most impressive clash came in the so-called *Zentrumsstreit*, which was triggered in 1906 by the demand of the Cologne Zentrum politician Julius Bachem for the transformation of the party into an inter-confessional Christian people's party.[6] In one sense, the Zentrum had already been a people's party, by self-definition as well as in reality. Those voting for it came from all social classes in the Reich. They were all, however, of the Catholic confession. Since the founding of the party, the Zentrum leadership had stressed time and again that the party was a political party, not a clerical one, and certainly not connected to and at the service of the Catholic hierarchy. This is why the party laid great emphasis on demonstrative independence from the Church, all the more so as the founding fathers had already hoped in 1870 for the formation of a Protestant wing in it, although fruitlessly. The possibility of the opening up of the party to other confessions was discussed again and again. In the 1920s, it even appeared to be a solution for raising the dwindling numbers of voters.

Yet the aim to become the organization for political Catholicism in the German Reich held the party and the Catholic Church together, despite occasional discussions about opening the party to Protestants. The party in fact depended on the Catholic Church reducing the endeavours for inter-confessionalism to a purely theoretical exercise. Efforts were made continually towards emancipation from the Church leadership, but these were without success between 1870 and 1933. It becomes clear that in an examination of the role of the Zentrum in the inter-war period certain basic issues and tendencies from the time prior to the First World War must be taken into consideration. After all, many of the problems that the Zentrum had to deal with in the 1920s were already there at the time of its building up. Knowledge of these problems is imperative for an adequate presentation of the party's development in the Weimar Republic.

THE ANCHORING IN SOCIETY AND THE RELATIONSHIP TO THE CATHOLIC CHURCH

The number of Zentrum members and voters represent a remarkable success story with respect to the political standing of the party in Germany. Between 1874 and 1907 estimated membership numbers rose from 1.45 million to 2.18 million, or by 85 per cent. This upward trend was disproportional to the growth in population (37 per cent) and in the number of potential voters (47 per cent) in the same period. The party could no longer fight for an increase in its proportion of the vote after the end of the *Kulturkampf*, but simply tried to retain what it already had, although it did not always succeed. The proportion of the vote that the Zentrum could hold on to thus sank from 27.9 per cent in 1874 to 16.4 per cent in 1912. This trend was to continue from the 1920s up until the disbanding of the party by the National Socialists: from 13.6 per cent in 1920 to 11.2 per cent in 1933.[7]

Thus, the Zentrum – despite occasional demands – never took up an exclusive position in the political representation of German Catholicism. During the time of the *Kulturkampf* the party could practically be sure of the German Catholic vote. In 1874, 83 per cent of these German Catholics voted for the Zentrum. By 1912 the number had sunk to 54.6 per cent and in the 1920s it fell to under 40 per cent outside of Bavaria.[8] The level could only manage to be retained at a little over 50 per cent throughout Germany by considering the Bayerische Volkspartei (BVP) as the representative of those Bavarian Catholics who had dropped away from the Zentrum in 1920. The other Catholic votes went mostly to the Social Democrats (SPD) – some 35 per cent. Then, in almost equal proportion with around 25 per cent, came the Communist Party (KPD) and the National Socialists (NSDAP). A much smaller percentage of voters, mainly the Rechtskatholiken, the right-wing Conservative Catholics, voted for the Deutschnationale Volkspartei (DNVP) – around 10 per cent.[9]

The Zentrum had been founded as an organizational platform for the championing of the interests of political Catholicism in the Prussian-Protestant-dominated German Reich. It comes as no surprise that such a position developed into basic opposition to Bismarck's politics during the course of the *Kulturkampf*. It arose from a centre-left position and developed through the collaboration with the left-liberal Freisinn and because of the anti-establishment stance reigning in the Catholic milieu. It lasted until the resignation of Bismarck in 1890.[10] That political Catholicism in these years held to the constitutionally laid-down basis of the Reich was primarily due to Ludwig Windthorst, one of the founding Zentrum thinkers. It was his strong sense of justice that was to become the guiding line for the party's programme between 1874 and 1891.[11]

Windthorst thus created the conditions for a turning point in the history of political Catholicism in the 1890s. Up until that time the leading positions in the Zentrum had been in the hands of priests, but now more and more middle-class professionals, especially lawyers, rose to prominence in the party. This was due, among other things, to the fact that the seats won by the Zentrum were predominantly 'safe seats'. In the last decade of the nineteenth century many older generation deputies were replaced by younger deputies. The Zentrum had established itself. The political pressure that had borne down on the German Catholics in the *Kulturkampf* had got weaker, and with it also the necessity of aligning the Church and political Catholicism. This transition of the Zentrum at the turn of the century into being a bourgeois party for the middle class was reflected in the example of its stance in the vote on Admiral Tirpitz's first Navy Law. By voting for this law the Zentrum deputies signalled their readiness to take on their share in the imperial and national power politics of the Reich. This strategy showed itself to be unusually successful. In the space of only a few years the Zentrum not only increased its political influence in the country, but was even declared by the liberal Friedrich Naumann to be the 'measure of all things', the creator of the majority in the Reichstag.[12]

The party picked up this thread again after the First World War. Although they (together with the BVP) usually won only around 15 per cent of the votes in the Reichstag elections, they were part of every government between 1919 and 1932. In nine out of twenty cabinets, the Chancellor of the Weimar Republic came from the party. This remarkable line of continuity showed that the Zentrum could master the transition from monarchy to republic without too many problems. It had been transformed overnight, so to speak, from being close to the monarchical constitutional order to become a republican party. This took effect apparently without having to give up any basic policy positions and in a coalition with moderate left parties. Parliamentary democracy was established in the German Reich with this coalition. Matthias Erzberger was a very important factor in the smooth transition. He had already been preparing the ground in Germany for the introduction of parliamentary democracy since 1917.[13] A man of the party's left wing, he collaborated with a series of Catholic workers' leaders. Furthermore, the November revolution of 1918 made agreement to an evolutionary transition from monarchy to republic easier for many Zentrum voters. The revolution was, in their opinion, clearly in opposition to a divinely ordained system. The upholding of the Church and the cultural-political concerns of the German Catholics in a new legal and constitutional order, on the other hand, appeared to them to be acceptable.[14] The coalition with the SPD, as had been in existence in the Reich and in Prussia since 1919, was, however, for many Catholics, far from being a matter of course. It even occasionally gave rise to hefty criticism.[15]

The Zentrum had never built up an actual party organization. Its proximity to the Church and the using of the clerics as a local network for electoral organization made a party organization seem unnecessary prior to the war. The Zentrum developed rather along the lines of a party composed of honorary dignitaries, a party in which the aristocratic elite in rural areas and parliamentary and bourgeois notables, who were experienced in life in the Catholic milieu, had the say in the towns.[16] Committees formed of such honorary dignities could hold out for years in the constituencies, despite occasional attempts to build up the organizational base of the party and to make reforms and extend them from the level of local associations.[17] The Zentrum thus largely remained up until its dissolution a party supported by voters on the day.[18]

Due to the lack of any effective party base organization there are still to this day no exact figures relating to the number of members. In the early summer of 1933, as the party leadership thought once again about the reorganization of the party just a few weeks before its dissolution, membership numbers could only be estimated. The estimate was at most 200,000 organized party members. The Windthorstbunde, as the Zentrum's youth organization, had 'more than 30,000 members' in its ranks. This organization was almost independent of the mother party. No exact figures are known about other party organizations or advisory boards, with one exception. The trade and industry advisory board had, in the middle of 1932, exactly 1,584 members. Still nothing is known about the social and age structure of the membership of the Zentrum, its distribution throughout the regions or the percentage of women voters. The latter could have been relatively high, however, as a disproportionally large number of women belonged to the Zentrum's electorate. The reason for this lay in the Zentrum's women voters having such strong roots in the Catholic milieu. These women voters could, in turn, send proportionally many representatives to the Zentrum's parliamentary parties on a regional and Reich level.[19] Hedwig Dransfeld, the leader of the Katholische Frauenbund, the Catholic women's organization, and simultaneously a member of the Zentrum's leadership, had declared the close interweaving of the Catholic milieu and the Zentrum to be the principal aim of the work of the Catholic women's organizations. She did this at the end of 1918, on the occasion of a convention of Catholic women's organizations in Cologne. In addition, she called for appropriate advisory work on a local level to guide German Catholic women towards supporting the Zentrum.[20]

The macro-structure of German Catholicism in the 1920s allows for further conclusions to be drawn about the social structure of the Zentrum members and voters. The middle-class component outweighed all others and according to the regions was either agrarian, petit bourgeois or proletarian tinted. To be more precise, the broad base of the Catholic social pyramid at the end of the *Kaiserreich* was formed by industrial workers and smallholders. Then came a relatively broad middle class, including non-academic Catholic civil servants, large landowners, craftsmen, wholesalers and small-business people. Built on to the middle level of this pyramid was a thin layer of academics working as civil servants or clerics, economically independent entrepreneurs and freelancers. At the top came the Catholic aristocracy.[21] That nothing had essentially changed in the make-up of this pyramid up until the end of the Weimar Republic, inclusive of the resulting problems for the party, was shown by a party self-assessment of October 1932. It was said at that time, rather tersely, that one did not belong to the wealthy part of German society.[22] Others observed that the Zentrum or its electorate did not represent any specific social group, but rather a political microcosm of Weimar (Catholic) society.[23]

This set it apart from other Weimar parties and, of course, represented an existential problem for the party, which it did not solve in a satisfactory way until 1933. It did not manage to integrate the political and social interests of all the German Catholic groups and classes in a unified Church, confessional and cultural-political programme. Furthermore, the Zentrum had never developed its own republican tradition, and after the revolution of 1918–19 – despite constant participation in the Reich government – it never understood itself to be a decidedly republican party.[24]

The rather feeble response to the call by Centre Party politician Joseph Wirth for the founding of a 'republican union' in July 1926 demonstrates how limited was the image of themselves as republican held by party members and the electorate.[25] The recognition of the republic as a legitimate political order ensured the Zentrum a share in power, albeit at a high price. It meant a distancing from parts of the former leadership class, mainly from the clerics, the episcopate, the academic middle class and the agrarians. What is more, the participation in the building up of the republic in 1920 led to the defection of the Bavarian wing. The signal sent at that time to the Zentrum's leadership with the founding of the BVP was clear: an unconditional profession of loyalty to the republic, as was asked time and again especially of the left wing, had put off a large part of the Zentrum's electorate. In doing so it probably led to a loss in the party's tactical room for manoeuvre.[26] The near violent conflict that occurred at the Deutschen Katholikentag, the National Congress of Catholics, between the convinced republican Konrad Adenauer and Cardinal Michael von Faulhaber, who was in close sympathy with the House of Wittelsbach, reflected this dilemma, which remained unsolved up until 1933.[27] The longer the party remained in government in changing coalitions, the more its inner unity was strained by political, economic and social special interests.

The rather weak level of organization prevented a cushioning of the impact of the accompanying disintegration process. The formation of professional advisory boards, actually meant to be a means of unifying diverse currents, served only to strengthen the diversity of the Zentrum and threatened to overtax the party's ability to integrate in the 1920s.[28] The intra-party orientation crisis was obvious within the parliamentary party ('parliament in parliament') and reached its climax in the years 1927–28, when representatives of the different wings even threatened to form their own parties. In January 1927, Wilhelm Marx, as party leader, formed a centre-right coalition government. The left wing of the Zentrum interpreted this as a shifting of the political weight within the party to the right. The anti-republican right wing of the party, however, feared that the conservative Deutschnationale were to be bound into the republican 'system'.[29] Marx, as an exemplary representative of the traditional leadership of local dignitaries, could not solve this conflict and resigned from party leadership. Such a resignation was unique in the history of the party. In addition, it showed clearly that the party at this time was no longer in a position to function as a generally recognized representative of the Catholic population at large. It soon became apparent, too, that the new leader, Ludwig Kaas, was unable to fulfil the hopes placed in him by a large part of the Zentrum's members to tackle the unhealthy state of the Catholic party by providing it with clear political leadership and guidance.[30]

Kaas was the first cleric to become the leader of the national party. His success in the vote did not, however, introduce a new clerical leadership for the party, even if up to the end of the 1920s one might have thought so because of the previously unseen increase in the number of clerics in leading positions in the party. Six clerics were part of the parliamentary party in the Reichstag between 1930 and 1933, and clerics also sat in various state parliaments. In addition, the BVP parliamentary parties in the Bavarian parliament and the Reichstag were both led by clerics.[31] The clerics did not, however, see themselves as being the recipients of orders from the Church hierarchy. They mostly tried consciously to keep a certain distance. Prelate Karl Ulitzka, one of the leaders of the Upper Silesian Zentrum, once gave the following explanation for his political occupation: 'As a priest I can justify political activity in that I stand for peace and order.'[32] This statement was made not least as a justification to the Vatican, which was, for pastoral reasons, rather sceptical about the dual commitment involved in looking after both spiritual welfare and party politics.

Seen in this way, the increase in clerics in leading positions in the Zentrum at the end of the 1920s showed the inner conflict within the party. Non-clerical politicians were increasingly less in a position to overcome the polarization of the party, as they were mostly affiliated to certain intra-party interest groups and thus lacked the integrative strength necessary to overcome intra-party differences. Priests, on the other hand, were thought to be independent of different interest groups. That Ludwig Kaas also did not succeed in tackling the challenges of the early 1930s, and could not help the party to overcome particularistic currents by a fundamental modernization, was partly due to his professional background. He was more of a vacillator than a dynamic leader, and saw himself primarily as the representative of political Catholicism and not as a power-conscious politician. He was not a politician who, in the first instance, would have tried to promote political co-operation in the Reich and in so doing find a way out of the crisis in the first German Republic, including warding off National Socialism.

THE SOCIAL QUESTION AND THE BAVARIAN SPECIAL PATH

In 1890 the Volksverein für das katholische Deutschland was established. Its founding fathers hereby fulfilled the wish that was widespread in the Catholic milieu for a general Catholic societal association. This was particularly pertinent in that in Erfurt in 1884 a Protestant association had been founded that avowedly strove for a strengthening of the Protestant consciousness in the German Reich. Furthermore, the final thwarting of the anti-socialist laws led to a shift of Catholicism's main opponent from liberalism to socialism. Against the backdrop of growing popularity for Social Democracy, it appeared neccessary to leading German Catholics to create an instrument for the immunization of the Catholic masses against the Social Democrats.[33] The changed perception of socialism was eased by the widespread supposition in German Catholicism at that time that socialism was just a child of liberalism, or to be more precise, a 'rebellious son' (Wilhelm Ketteler), as both shared the same ideological-cultural ground and had the same aims, growing out of the same conditions. Liberalism had, however, the middle class as its target group while socialism appealed more to the working class.[34] This interpretation of socialism got backing from the social encyclical *Rerum novarum*, of 1891, in which Pope Leo XIII held that economic liberalism was the cause of the increasingly bad plight of the working class. On the other hand, he also rejected the socialist path to solving social issues in a class struggle. As an alternative, a programmatic framework was outlined that promoted state-controlled social policies informed by the principles of solidarity and subsidy, and which was later to serve the Zentrum after the end of the First World War as an economic and social-political framework.[35]

The Volksverein offered social, social reformist and democratic left-wing Catholicism an institutional home on the eve of the First World War, even if its 800,000 members represented a much wider political spectrum.[36] Its existence promoted the coming into being of Christian Catholic unions, and thus bound social Catholicism as well as a large part of the Catholic working class into the spectrum of the Zentrum. The Volksverein could develop into a kind of 'substitute mass organization' for the Zentrum[37] that set Catholic social teaching, with its idea of a society based on solidarity and private ownership informed by natural law, against social democracy. The Jesuits Heinrich Pesch and Gustav Gundlach contributed a great deal here.[38] Pesch conceived an economic programme, outlined in his writings, which was occasionally described as being 'Christian socialist'. It was essentially corporatist, foreseeing the important role of organized professional groups.[39] Gundlach used this as a starting point and developed it with special emphasis on the principles of subsidiarity and personality.

Gundlach was a member of the Königswinter circle, the intellectual leadership group of the Catholic workers' movement of the 1920s. Another member of this circle was Oswald von Nell-Breuning, who had made a great contribution to the publication of the second papal social encyclical, *Quadragesimo anno*, in 1931 on the occasion of the fortieth anniversary of *Rerum novarum*.[40] This encyclical pressed for a new classless society, a demand that was translated in the German version into 'corporatist order'.[41] *Quadragesimo anno* had thus contributed to the debate about the ideal form for government and society, but not, however, in the sense of unreserved support for the republican system – even if Gundlach, as well as Nell-Breuning, emphasized that their idea of 'corporatist order' was compatible with the principles of parliamentary democracy.[42]

The encyclical could be interpreted in different ways and testified to an ambivalent relationship between the Catholic Church leadership, the republican state and parliamentary democracy. The Zentrum leadership noticed this ambivalence, but in democracy's years of crisis they remained sceptical regarding demands for a corporatist ordering of society. The party had, after all, taken on the role of a reliable backer-up of the republic in the time since the end of the First World War. On the other hand, some reservations that members and voters had about the emergency decrees by Reich Chancellor Heinrich Brüning were swept aside by pointing to *Quadragesimo anno*. Thus the Zentrum leadership tried to find a compromise in the early 1930s, as it was defining its own position in the debate. A purely corporatist order was expressly rejected.[43] On the other hand, it was also true that the ever louder demands coming from some circles of members for the curbing of 'party despotism' had to be taken into consideration.

The party leadership developed its concept of 'authoritarian democracy' against this backdrop in the course of 1930. This concept was to be reflected in the programmatic basis of the Zentrum. It was, in the autumn of 1932, still opposed to the attempts of the new Reich Chancellor, Franz von Papen, to destroy 'the rule of parties'.[44] In addition, during the death throes of the republic, it led to a long unseen solidarity in the party once again, as the Christian unions as well as the Catholic workers' movement in western Germany expressively supported 'authoritarian democracy'.[45] The Zentrum differed quite considerably in this interpretation of *Quadragesimo anno* from other interpretations of the papal encyclical. Thus Engelbert Dollfuss in Austria likewise looked to the encyclical when forming the programmatic basis of his 'authoritarian corporatist state' after the dissolution of parliament.[46]

The end phase of the Weimar Republic is, from the viewpoint of the Zentrum, marked by a new rapprochement of the left and right wings of the party. While a basic intra-party consensus about the retention of the Reich constitution[47] existed until March 1933, the concept of 'authoritarian democracy' offered enough room for differences of interpretation. The different ideas about the state constitution held by Zentrum members could all be taken into consideration. This new relative solidarity of the Zentrum's membership could certainly not be taken for granted in the years after the First World War, but was rather an exception. More typical of the party was the programmatic dispute between 'Christian' and 'political' democracy, including very divergent ideas about the meaning of the terms 'Christian democratic' and 'political democratic', which could only just gloss over the fact that there was a lack of a clear political concept.[48]

While this conflict was the everyday business of the party, the Zentrum had, meanwhile, already survived its first big test of endurance in the mid-1920s – the separation from the Bavarian wing. This separation was the result of an open quarrel between the party left on the level of the Reich, and the Bavarian Zentrum, which primarily had its roots in the Christian Social peasant associations in rural areas. The dispute was about the collaboration of the party with left-wing Liberals and Social Democrats. It was not only Heinrich Held, the leader of the Zentrum parliamentary party in the Bavarian parliament, who saw this collaboration to be 'a betrayal of our programme in the direction of parliamentarism'.[49] Erzberger's demands for the democratizing of the Reich's political structure as well as the peace resolution of 1917 that he had initiated had caught the Bavarian Zentrum quite clearly unprepared. In the ranks of the predominantly monarchical party supporters, the resolution grew to follow a special path in Bavaria, party-politically speaking, which was to take into consideration the federalism that was especially strong in Bavaria.[50] This approach was seen to be threatened by the strategy of the party leadership at the Reich level to opt for parliamentary government, since Matthias Erzberger had made the declaration at a meeting of the Reich party committee that 'Left is life, Right is death'.[51] The Bavarian Zentrum withdrew its co-operation with the Reich party after hearing this comment, and constituted itself as the Bayerische Volkspartei (BVP), the Bavarian People's Party.[52]

The separation led to a temporary withdrawal of the BVP from Reich politics to a Bavarian 'ordered compartment' south of the river Main. There it was, however, as a result of its collaboration with the Deutschnationale and the semi-military defence organizations drawn into a conflict between Bavarian federalism and anti-democratic nationalism, which reached its climax in 1923 with the Hitler coup.[53] One way out of the isolation the BVP had brought on itself was opened up in the summer of 1924, by the election of the BVP leader Heinrich Held to Bavarian Minister President. He led the BVP back into Reich politics. This return was completed in January 1925 with the entry of Karl Stingl into Luther's Reich government as Post Minister. Whilst the Zentrum out of 'a feeling of responsibility for the whole [i.e., the Reich]' and basic readiness to compromise, co-operated in different Reich governments, the BVP was motivated to act to defend Bavaria against centralizing unitarian forces.[54] The party had the support of around a million voters who primarily came from Catholic agrarian regions. They were thus saved from any great loss of voters, but on the other hand had already in 1920 used up a great part of their reservoir and did not have any further possibilities for development in the party spectrum of the Weimar Republic.[55]

The accusation of partial responsibility for the splitting up of the Bavarian Catholics bore down on the centre-left from 1920 on, and was to weaken its position within the party until its demise. What is more, the lasting rivalry between the particularistic interest groups within the party meant that the Zentrum was unable to win any programmatic independence, in the sense of creating a decidedly Christian economic and social-political model. It rather allowed the assembling of certain elements of political Catholicism that could facilitate a consensus. From an economic point of view the right of private ownership took a central position. Furthermore, there was a declaration of loyalty to the idea of the use, as well as the increase of capital as the deciding motivating force in modern industrial economics, in addition to the holding on to the principle of open competition and the central position of enterprise in the production process.[56] The social reform programme was defined by the self-portrayal of the party, which pointed to the necessity of solidarity within the *Volksgemeinschaft*.[57] Heinrich Pesch had specially coined the term 'solidarity' for this as a mark of the most important lesson that had been learned. At the centre of this lay, on one side, the rejection of economic liberalism and socialism, and on the other that the Christian working class, unionists and politicians were under obligation to push for the establishment of social peace and the integration of the working class.[58] Nevertheless, it was his fellow clerics Gundlach and Nell-Breuning who, after Pesch's death, picked up from where he left off in his thinking and developed his ideas further from a corporatist point of view.[59] The central question then in their considerations was whether the 'solidarity of the members of professions' could be transformed into a system incorporating the entire spectrum of society. Nell-Breuning presented the basic characteristics of the imagined system in 1931 in his commentary to *Quadragesimo anno*.[60]

The effect of the concept of solidarity on the social-ethical ideas of leading Zentrum politicians is hard to measure. It appears, however, to have been rather limited. Very few statements from that time from leading Zentrum politicians are as clearly recognizable as being under the influence of solidarity as the study, *Lebenshaltung aus Fürsorge und Erwerbsstätigkeit*, written by the Reichstag deputy Helene Wessel. She expressly laid great emphasis on individuality and responsibility of man for himself and his life, under the safeguarding of the Christian principle of loving thy neighbour.[61]

THE EUROPEAN DIMENSION

The Zentrum leadership, on the occasion of the Reichstag elections in 1930, produced a handbook of key programmatic points. It was published by the Münster church historian Georg Schreiber, who was one of the 'house prelates' of the parliamentary party in the Reichstag.[62] There is no entry under 'Europe' in the index. This in itself indicates that the Zentrum of the Weimar years lacked a European concept in the sense of some kind of integration. The eight pages about the party's foreign policy programme confirm the absence of a European policy. In this section, the great task of foreign policy is seen to be the return of the German Reich on an equal basis into the group of European nations and the world. Furthermore, one can read that the great idea of the nation state leading to 'great fulfilment', meant, among other things, the *Anschluss* of Austria. Further foreign policy aims were the securing of world peace and good relations between recognized nations, with complete sovereignty and in the framework of international co-operation, primarily in the League of Nations. International disarmament was to be pushed further, as the Reich had already largely been demilitarized by the Treaty of Versailles. The demand for a revision of the peace treaties followed, in which the removal of legal inequalities, the revision of the borders in the east and the reintegration of the Saar region before 1935 were aims that were especially emphasized. This was not, however, to be bought at too high a price for Germany, such as the completion of a customs union with France.[63] The party's official foreign policy followed the line that had been traced out by the Liberal foreign minister, Gustav Stresemann, in his years in office. The foreign policy, which in the handbook was expressly described as a continuation of the policies introduced by the former Zentrum Chancellors Wirth and Marx,[64] had no concept for Europe in the sense of the post-war integration model. Instead, what the Zentrum (and many other German parties too) strove towards, was the establishing of German supremacy in Central Europe. On closer inspection, this is what was really being demanded, hidden behind the demands for an international position for the German Reich, which the German nation, because of its history, cultural development and economic efficiency, was thought to be owed.[65]

Alongside this official setting of targets in foreign policy, a spectrum of European political concepts was in existence, which had been drawn up by various interest groups within the party at different times. On the one side were ideas about the restoration of a German *imperium sacrum* in Central Europe, whose territory would be like that of the Holy Roman Empire of the early thirteenth century.[66] This idea was mainly to be found in right-wing Catholic circles. On the other side were integrationist ideas that sought to bridge the divide between Western and Central Europe. Konrad Adenauer's thinking along the lines of a German–French equilibrium, by means of an interweaving of their industrial potential in the Rhein-Ruhr area, the Saarland and Alsace Lorraine, can be seen as the direct precursor to the European integration efforts of the early 1950s. Adenauer's concept for Europe was in the 1920s still seen as that of an outsider. Consideration of the possibility of striving towards the restitution of the German leading role in a newly ordered Central Europe met with greater general approval, including approval from within the Zentrum.

Of course, by supporting this option, numerous attention-grabbing anti-democratic European concepts that surfaced in the 1920s were also implicitly supported.[67] None of them wanted to accept the new European order of the Paris Peace Conference. They strove rather for a newly ordered German Reich as a great power in an appropriately newly ordered Central Europe.[68] This was in step with Arthur Moeller van den Bruck's call for a 'Third Reich'. The adoption of arguments from the right-wing anti-democratic forces by the parties of the first German Republic led to its opponents gaining a reputation that, at the end of the day, allowed the National Socialists to appear to be a legitimate alternative for a large part of the German electorate. The accusation remains that the Zentrum did not take a firmer stance on the basic values of the republic of which it was a supporting part. Rather the opposite is true. It added fuel to the fire at the time of the crisis in its compliance with the demands of the proposed authoritarian solutions.

AN END AND A NEW BEGINNING

Only a few weeks after the National Socialist accession to power, it was evident that this path would lead to a dead end. A large part of the

Zentrum membership rejected the new system, but most of them remained in the country and tried to accommodate themselves to the new state of affairs. After the so-called self-dissolving of the BVP in July 1933, which was forced by violent acts against the party branch offices as well as by the arrest of around two thousand functionaries and members,[69] there was no longer doubt that the National Socialists considered all democrats to be enemies. Those who remained in the country had to find ways of surviving under the NSDAP regime. The Catholic Church helped, where possible, with the provision of employment, for example in Church welfare institutions such as Caritas-Notwerk or other communal and regional welfare organizations. Other former Zentrum politicians were forced to earn their living outside the Church and state.[70] At least this was still possible under the prevailing conditions in the Third Reich. In contrast to many Social Democrats and Communists, most former Zentrum politicians were not directly threatened by the National Socialist regime, even if they were kept under surveillance. Only after the assassination attempt of 20 July 1944, in the context of the so-called *Aktion Gewitter*, did former members of the Zentrum count among those whom the National Socialists arrested.[71]

Prior to this, only a few leading party functionaries had fled abroad. They made up 5 per cent of those in exile who were politically active.[72] The contribution the Zentrum exiles were able to make in the European resistance's work against National Socialism in its formative phase up until 1935–36 was correspondingly small. The difficulties experienced in the building up of a Christian democratic exile resistance front against National Socialism can be attributed to the Zentrum's lack of systematic co-operation with Christian democratic parties in the neighbouring countries in Europe before 1933. While the German Social Democrats were part of a European network, which after the Nazi usurpation of power made the development of organized political activity in exile considerably easier, the Church in countries outside Germany, and other Zentrum exile relief organizations, offered at first only limited comparable help. Only with the consolidation of National Socialist power in the course of the 1930s was a network of Christian democratic exile organizations formed that were now also inter-confessional. These exile organizations had their own papers, such as *Abendland* and *Europa*.[73] Thus, at the climax of National Socialist power on the eve of the Second World War, a forum for discussion of alternatives to its ideas about the state and Europe came into existence, which after the collapse of the Third Reich was later to influence the European integration programme of the German Christian democrats.

When the National Socialist regime collapsed, the ideas about the European political aims of future Christian democratic politics still reflected the various standpoints that Zentrum members had taken up on this issue during the time of the Weimar Republic. How far the aims continued to diverge becomes clear when comparing Jakob Kaiser and Konrad Adenauer. While Kaiser strove to rebuild a new improved republic based on the example of Weimar, which was to overcome the ever deepening chasm between East and West Germany, Adenauer strove, right from the start, for as close a collaboration with the Western powers as possible. Kaiser's political master plan was a synthetic one. It was supposed to unite Germany internally and to establish it as a bridge between Eastern and Western European ideas, in order to allow for the coming into being of a socially peaceful European community as the harbinger of a new and lasting understanding in Europe.[74]

The plans of Kaiser, who was elected leader of the East German Christian Democrats, clearly bore the imprint of Ernst Troeltsch's views about a cultural synthesis between Central and Western European thought as a prerequisite for a European understanding aiming at overcoming the tensions that had arisen after the end of the First World War.[75] It becomes clear that Kaiser continued to stand in the tradition of a German special self-consciousness, that phenomenon in the history of thought which among other things had as a starting point the 'special' German mission in Central Europe. This time it was, of course, its function as a bridge between East and West, stabilizing Europe as a whole. Kaiser's idea was supported by many Protestant conservatives.[76] However, it overlooked the real political constellations and possibilities in Europe after the obvious failure of Roosevelt's 'one world' approach. The increasing systemic conflict did not allow Germany to return to the 'see-saw policy' of the interwar period. The Western powers did not want an 'honest broker' with state sovereignty, neutrality and its own armed forces resulting in renewed latent unpredictability. They wanted rather a reliable partner who could contribute to the security of the Western system of alliances.

This aim, which, should the occasion arise, could be bought for the price of the dividing up of Germany, corresponded with the political ideas of a group of former Rhenish Zentrum politicians under the leadership of Adenauer. This group had already in the 1920s pronounced itself to be for an interweaving of the industrial potential in the Rhineland, the Benelux states and in northern France. A continuation of Germany's special position in Central Europe after 1945 was out of the question for Adenauer. He mistrusted the Soviet Union too much. Furthermore, he was extremely sceptical of the political maturity of his countrymen. A policy of neutrality between East and West would have required an enormous degree of political maturity. Instead of this, Adenauer saw the only chance of survival for Germany in peace and freedom to be an uncompromising orientation towards Western Europe. Directly after the German surrender he was only able to formulate such thoughts, as no German politician could actually implement them. But because of the great compatibility between their own aims with respect to 'Europe' and Adenauer's thinking, the former mayor of Cologne quickly became the leading contact and negotiating partner of the Western military governments, simultaneously enhancing his role in West German politics. Jakob Kaiser's fate was completely different. Although he was re-elected as leader of the East German Christian Democrats in September 1947 with an overwhelming majority, he soon had to realize that after the enforced integration of communists and socialists in the Socialist Unity Party in 1946, there was no more room for him in the politics of the Soviet zone of occupation. In January 1948, the East German authorities, on the instigation of the Soviet military administration, forbade him freedom of speech and of movement in East Germany.

Adenauer and Kaiser are here representative of all those former Zentrum and BVP politicians who made great efforts to rebuild a democratic Germany after 1945. As in the 1920s, a wide spectrum of political wishes and aims was represented, and these were, occasionally, impossible to bring together. The survivors of the Nazi dictatorship had, however, learnt their lesson from the past. Referring to Ludwig Windthorst, Julius Bachem, Adam Stegerwald, Konrad Adenauer and Heinrich Brüning, this time they avoided a renewed fragmentation of party politics along confessional lines. They used the chance to build up an inter-confessional, Christian democratic or Christian Social people's party.

NOTES

1 For the anti-modernist character of the First Vatican Council, see Michael Klöcker, 'Erneuerungsbewegungen im römischen Katholizismus', in D. Krebs and Jürgen Reulecke (eds), *Handbuch der deutschen Reformbewegungen 1880–1933* (Wuppertal 1998), pp. 565–80, especially pp. 565–6.
2 Golo Mann, *Deutsche Geschichte im 19. und 20. Jahrhundert* (Frankfurt/Main 1958), pp. 422–3.
3 Ibid., p. 422.
4 Thomas Nipperdey, *Deutsche Geschichte 1866–1918*, vol. 2, *Machtstaat vor der Demokratie* (Munich 1998), p. 338.
5 See Klöcker, 'Erneuerungsbewegungen', pp. 566–7.
6 Such efforts were not new. Ludwig Windthorst had already wanted an inter-confessional party instead of a confessional one in 1870.
7 See Rudolf Morsey, *Der Untergang des politischen Katholizismus. Die Zentrumspartei zwischen christlichem Selbstverständnis und 'nationaler Erhebung' 1932/33* (Stuttgart and Zurich 1977), p. 14.
8 Ibid.
9 Josef Becker, 'Die Deutsche Zentrumspartei 1918–1933', in Oswald Hauser (ed.), *Politische Parteien in Deutschland und in Frankreich 1918–1939* (Wiesbaden 1969), pp. 59–74, here p. 60; see also Winfried Becker (ed.), *Die Minderheit als Mitte. Die deutsche Zentrumspartei in der Innenpolitik des Reiches 1871–1933* (Paderborn 1986).

10 Nipperdey, *Deutsche Geschichte 1866–1918*, p. 544.
11 Rudolf Morsey, 'Der politische Katholizismus 1890–1933', in Anton Rauscher (ed.), *Der soziale und politische Katholizismus. Entwicklungslinien in Deutschland 1803–1963*, vol. 1 (Munich and Vienna 1981), pp. 110–64, especially pp. 114–15.
12 Nipperdey, *Deutsche Geschichte 1866–1918*, pp. 547–8.
13 Klöcker, 'Erneuerungsbewegungen', p. 568.
14 Alfred Milatz, *Wähler und Wahlen in der Weimarer Republik* (Bonn 1965), p. 94.
15 Elisabeth Friese, *Helene Wessel (1898–1969). Von der Zentrumspartei zur Sozialdemokratie* (Essen 1993), p. 21.
16 Nipperdey, *Deutsche Geschichte 1866–1918*, pp. 345–7.
17 Ibid., p. 542.
18 Morsey, *Der Untergang des politischen Katholizismus*, p. 34.
19 For membership figures, see Karsten Ruppert, *Im Dienst am Staat von Weimar. Das Zentrum als regierende Partei in der Weimarer Demokratie 1923–1930* (Düsseldorf 1992), p. 413.
20 Monika Pankoke-Schenk, 'Katholizismus und Frauenfrage', in Rauscher, *Der soziale und politische Katholizismus*, vol. 2, pp. 278–311, especially p. 296.
21 Becker, 'Die deutsche Zentrumspartei 1918–1933', pp. 63–4.
22 Morsey, *Der Untergang des politischen Katholizismus*, p. 34.
23 Becker, 'Die deutsche Zentrumspartei 1918–1933', p. 64.
24 Ruppert, *Im Dienst am Staat von Weimar*, pp. 409–10.
25 Heinrich Küppers, *Joseph Wirth. Parlamentarier, Minister und Kanzler der Weimarer Republik* (Stuttgart 1997), pp. 228ff.
26 Ruppert, *Im Dienst am Staat von Weimar*, p. 410.
27 Peter Koch, *Konrad Adenauer. Eine politische Biographie* (Reinbek 1985), pp. 76ff.
28 Becker, 'Die deutsche Zentrumspartei 1918–1933', p. 65.
29 Ruppert, *Im Dienst am Staat von Weimar*, p. 417.
30 Becker, 'Die deutsche Zentrumspartei 1918–1933', pp. 63, 65–6.
31 Morsey, *Der Untergang des politischen Katholizismus*, pp. 27–8.
32 Ibid., pp. 27ff.
33 See Heinz Hürten, 'Katholische Verbände', in Rauscher, *Der soziale und politische Katholizismus*, vol. 2, pp. 215–77, 248–9.
34 Anton Rauscher, 'Sozialismus', in idem, *Der soziale und politische Katholizismus*, vol. 1, pp. 294–339, especially p. 303.
35 For *Rerum novarum*, see for example Lothar Roos, 'Kapitalismus, Sozialreform, Sozialpolitik,' in Rauscher, *Der soziale und politische Katholizismus*, vol. 2, pp. 52–148, especially pp. 109–10.
36 Ibid., p. 260.
37 Nipperdey, *Deutsche Geschichte 1866–1918*, p. 543.
38 For Pesch and Gundlach, see for example Rauscher, 'Sozialismus', especially pp. 307–11 and 319–22; also Klöcker, 'Erneuerungsbewegungen', pp. 571–2.
39 Concerning Pesch's influence on the Belgian Catholic Party, see Emmanuel Gerard's chapter in this book.
40 See Klöcker, 'Erneuerungsbewegungen', p. 572.
41 Ibid.
42 Rauscher, 'Sozialismus', pp. 322ff.
43 See Georg Schreiber (ed.), *Zentrum und Reichspolitik. Ein politisches Handbuch in Frage und Antwort* (Cologne 1930), p. 215.
44 Morsey, *Der Untergang des politischen Katholizismus*, p. 70.

45 Ibid.
46 Concerning the relevance of *Quadragesimo anno* for the Austrian Christian Socials' concept of a corporatist state and with this, implicitly, the importance of Engelbert Dollfuss, see Helmut Wohnout's chapter in this book.
47 See the appropriate statements made at the meetings of the Zentrum parliamentary party and parliamentary party leadership between 13 October 1930 and 2 February 1933: *Die Protokolle der Reichstagsfraktionen und des Fraktionsvorstandes der Deutschen Zentrumspartei 1926–1933* (Mainz 1969), pp. 479–618.
48 See Herbert Hömig, *Das Preussische Zentrum in der Weimarer Republik* (Mainz 1979), p. 290.
49 Klaus Schönhoven, *Die Bayerische Volkspartei 1924–1932* (Düsseldorf 1972), p. 18.
50 Georg Heim was one of the leading figures in the Bavarian 'special path'. Sebastian Schlittenbauer was another of the founders of the Bavarian Christian farmers' society and national deputy of the Zentrum from 1897–1912, as well as director of the Regensburg Central Association of the Bavarian farmers' society. Both men had single-mindedly prepared the split since 1917. See Morsey, *Der politische Katholizismus*, p. 143.
51 Schönhoven, *Die Bayerische Volkspartei*, p. 19.
52 Ibid.
53 Ibid., pp. 279–80.
54 Ibid., p. 280.
55 Concerning the BVP in the context of the elections in the 1920s see Milatz, *Wähler und Wahlen in der Weimarer Republik*, pp. 127, 134.
56 Ruppert, *Im Dienst am Staat von Weimar*, p. 414.
57 See for example the relevant section in Schreiber, *Zentrum und Reichspolitik*, pp. 139–58.
58 Anton Rauscher, 'Solidarismus', in idem, *Der soziale und politische Katholizismus*, vol. 1, pp. 340–68.
59 Ibid., p. 362.
60 Rauscher, 'Solidarismus', p. 363.
61 Friese, *Helene Wessel (1898–1969)*, p. 37.
62 Schreiber, *Zentrum und Reichspolitik*, pp. 37–8.
63 Ibid.
64 Ibid., p. 39.
65 Ibid., p. 37.
66 Representative of many others and reminiscent of the ideas of the Cologne historian Martin Spahn. See also Gabriele Clemens, *Martin Spahn und der Rechtskatholizismus in der Weimarer Republik* (Mainz 1983). Spahn had left the Zentrum, joined the DNVP and later became a member of the Reichstag. He was the son of Peter Spahn, the long-standing leader of the parliamentary party of the Zentrum in the Reichstag.
67 See Jürgen Elvert, *Mitteleuropa! Deutsche Pläne zur europäischen Neuordnung (1918–1945)* (Stuttgart 1999), for the right-wing, anti-democratic ideas of a European system.
68 Ibid.
69 Günter Buchstab, Brigitte Kaff and Hans-Otto Kleinmann, *Verfolgung und Widerstand 1933–1945. Christliche Demokraten gegen Hitler* (Düsseldorf 1986), p. 15.
70 See for example the fate of Heinrich Krone, the former national leader of the Windthorst Group. He was at first a member of the board of the Caritas-Notwerk,

before having to become a travelling salesman. See Heinrich Krone, *Tagebücher. Erster Band: 1945–1961* (Düsseldorf 1995), pp. x–xi.
71 Friese, *Helene Wessel (1898–1969)*, pp. 45–6; also Krone, *Tagebücher*, p. xi.
72 Buchstab et al., *Verfolgung und Widerstand*, p. 77.
73 Ibid.
74 Christian Hacke, *Weltmacht wider Willen. Die Aussenpolitik der Bundesrepublik Deutschland* (Stuttgart 1988), pp. 20–1.
75 Ernst Troeltsch, *Der Historismus und seine Probleme* (Tübingen 1922).
76 Hacke, *Weltmacht wider Willen*, pp. 17–18.

3

Catholics between Emancipation and Integration: The Conservative People's Party in Switzerland

Lukas Rölli-Alkemper

Self-portrayals of political parties – especially those presented during electoral campaigns – usually show more of the condition a party would like to be in than the condition in which it really is. It is therefore advisable not only for voters, but even more so for historians and political scientists, to observe with a certain suspicion the way a party portrays itself towards the public and towards its electorate. These self-portrayals can, however, reveal structures and themes that are crucial for the state of the party portrayed.

A wood-engraving dating from 1933 is in fact such an exquisite illustration of the way Swiss Conservative Party Catholics saw themselves in the inter-war period. It was first used on a brochure during the cantonal elections in St Gallen in 1933 and published again during the national electoral campaign of 1935 in *Vaterland*, the leading conservative paper of Catholic Switzerland. The comment on the 1933 brochure said: 'Firmly rooted in its *weltanschauung* the Conservative People's Party forms the unsurmountable barrier against the revolutionary powers on the left and the un-Christian totalitarian movements on the right.'[1] The picture shows the Catholic Conservatives united around the Cross as the symbol of the Church, forming a well-organized battle formation made up of numerous social organizations all holding up their banners against the stormy winds, standing on the solid foundation of Christian values, facing the tempestuous waves of the class struggle. The main elements of this powerful image form useful guidelines for the analysis of the Swiss Conservative People's Party, the Schweizerische Konservative Volkspartei (SKVP): as a People's Party it united different social groups with different interests; as the party of the Catholics it had a close relationship to the Catholic Church, and as a *Weltanschauungspartei* it built its policy on a clearly defined ideology. The party saw itself as part of a larger Catholic world, and at the same time wanted to integrate itself into a Swiss nation dominated by the Liberal Party.

The SKVP of the inter-war period has to be seen as part of the social phenomenon of Swiss Catholicism. In the second half of the nineteenth century conservative Catholics had formed a Catholic subculture or milieu essentially characterized by the following three features:[2] a uniform *weltanschauung* with a system of corresponding values and social codes; a network of social institutions to transmit these values and to defend them against society; and the state and cultural codes that translated the meanings of the *weltanschauung* into the language of everyday life and helped to maintain its values. The SKVP played a crucial part within this milieu. The history of the party was therefore closely linked to the history of Swiss Catholicism. Up to the 1950s conservative Catholicism defined itself as the counterweight to modernity.[3] Anti-modernism, anti-liberalism and anti-socialism formed its ideological foundations in the first half of the twentieth century. However, social changes in the cause of industrialization and the continuing integration into the system of the federal state challenged the party's attitude towards modernity. Its history reflects the tensions between integration into the modern federal state of Switzerland and emancipation as an independant conservative force within this state.

THE SKVP'S SOCIAL BASIS: TENSIONS BENEATH THE SURFACE

The SKVP had emerged in the last third of the nineteenth century as the parliamentary representation of the losers of the civil war of 1847.[4] The Liberal winners of this civil war had formed the modern federal state of Switzerland. They were firmly rooted in the mainly Protestant midland cantons, where industrialization had already made great progress. The Liberals governed the country on their own for more than forty years. The Conservative Party represented, first of all, the seven conservative Catholic cantons that had opposed the transformation of the loosely knit Swiss confederation into a modern federal state: Lucerne, Uri, Schwyz, Unterwalden, Zug, Fribourg and Valais. After the Conservatives had successfully regained power in these cantons during the 1850s and 1860s they became the so-called *Stammlande*, or heartland, of Catholic conservatism in Switzerland. The party's leaders followed a strict course of opposition against the federal government, which finally forced the ruling Liberals to take a member of the Catholic Conservatives into government.[5] In 1891 the parliament elected Josef Zemp from Lucerne as the first Catholic conservative member of the Bundesrat, the federal council. The Catholic Conservative faction in parliament was clearly dominated by the representatives of the *Stammlande*, as was the SKVP, which only became a nationally united party in 1912.

The conservative heartland in the alpine regions of central Switzerland was characterized by a socio-economic backwardness that was to last up to the middle of the twentieth century. Until the 1950s more than 90 per cent of the population of these cantons was Catholic.[6] From the 1870s up to the late 1920s Catholics formed the almost invincible fortress of the conservative electorate in Switzerland, and were therefore regarded as the core of the party: small farmers, craftsmen and businessmen firmly rooted in the close-knit rural world under the umbrella of a strong Catholic faith. The Catholic subculture they formed experienced its golden age during the time between the two world wars. Politically, these representatives of the lower-middle and middle class favoured an extremely particularistic course, and they were strongly opposed to any policy decided on by the federal government in Berne.

Yet the alpine mountains could not bar modernity for ever. Industrialization drew numerous young farmers to the factories of the mainly Protestant midland cantons. The Catholic population outside the *Stammlande* region grew rapidly during the last third of the nineteenth century. The town of Zurich, for example, counted only 8,800 Catholics in 1870, or 13.3 per cent of its population.[7] In 1900 the figure was up to 42,200 Catholics or 25 per cent, more than in any of the larger towns in the Catholic cantons. Only about a third of the Catholic population in the so-called diaspora was firmly attached to the Church and its numerous social organizations. One-third at least voted for liberal or socialist parties. Although the social migration slowed down in the first half of the twentieth century, its wide-ranging impact became perceptible only after the First World War. By then, Catholic voters from Protestant and from mixed cantons had become very important for the SKVP as a whole. Their share of the party's votes rose from 57 per cent in 1931 to 60 per cent in 1947.

The well-organized Catholic Workers' Movement had its bases mainly in the cantons of the midlands dominated by Protestants. In 1919 traditional Catholic workers' associations, Christian trade unions, cooperatives and Christian Social Party groups united in the Christian Social Workers' Union, or Christlichsozialer Arbeiterbund (CAB). Under the leadership of Josef Scherrer, the union gained great influence on Catholic politics.[8] In many cantons outside the *Stammlande* the conservative parties had strong left wings that sometimes formed separate parties and even competed with the SKVP.[9] In the 1930s Christian social politicians from the diaspora gained more influence on the leadership of the SKVP. They were less opposed to the building of a modern federal state than the party members from the *Stammlande*. They were less eager to defend the cantons' particular cultural or political authorities against the federal state, and they argued for a federal social security system.

The Young Conservatives were the third group within the SKVP. After a painful defeat in the national election of 1925 the party's secretary, Paul Kubick, and the young journalist and editor of the fundamentalist paper

Die Schildwache, Otto Walter, had launched the idea of a youth organization within the party to mobilize Catholic voters in future elections.[10] The Young Conservatives movement soon came under the influence of right-wing conservative leaders such as Otto Walter, Josef Beck – a professor of theology at the university of Fribourg who was active in social politics up to the 1920s – and Jean-Marie Musy from Fribourg, a Conservative federal councillor from 1919 to 1934. This group of politicians was called the *Schildwache* movement[11] after its leading paper. They defended fundamentalist Catholic positions and fiercely fought against both socialism and liberalism. They criticized the 'egalitarian' democratic system of the federal state, and admired authoritarian regimes such as those of Mussolini, or later those of Franco in Spain or Salazar in Portugal. Among the members of the *Schildwache* movement were the most fervent anti-Semites within Swiss Catholicism.[12]

At the beginning of the 1930s the Young Conservatives took part in the movement of national restoration that was led by the fascist 'fronts'. During this time their influence on the SKVP grew rapidly. Together with the fascist 'fronts' they launched a petition for the complete revision of the federal constitution.[13] The vague aim of this petition was the transformation of Swiss liberal democracy into an authoritarian corporatist state. After a heated debate, the party congress of 27 January 1935 decided to support the petition of the Young Conservatives. In the subsequent poll, however, 511,578 voters were against the revision of the constitution and only 196,135 supported the petition. The clear defeat of the referendum weakened the position of the Young Conservatives within the party, and thereafter it refrained from fundamentalist positions.

The party's elite, which mainly consisted of its members in parliament, did not fully reflect the social structures described above. It was long dominated by professional politicians from Catholic cantons, lawyers and civil servants. Up to the late 1920s party leadership lay in the hands of three prominent politicians from central Switzerland: Joseph Räber from Schwyz, the party's president; Heinrich Walther from Lucerne, who led the faction as party whip from 1919 to 1940; and Hans von Matt from Nidwalden, president of the Swiss Catholic People's Association, Schweizerischer Katholischer Volksverein (SKVV). In the 1930s the party bodies became more independent of the parliamentary faction in parliament. The growing influence of politicians from diaspora cantons can be traced in the rising number of functionaries and journalists who came mainly from the industrialized cantons of the midlands.

The party leaders followed a pragmatic line, carefully avoiding anything that could have endangered the party's position as junior partner in the Liberal-dominated government. After the Catholic Conservatives had proved most loyal citizens during the general strike of 1918, the party gained a second seat in the government of seven federal ministers in 1919.

During the whole inter-war period the party's representatives in parliament never really wanted to give up this share of power. The different wings of the party nevertheless had great freedom of manoeuvring. Because the Swiss governmental system did not have provision for a vote of no confidence against the government, the position of the SKVP could vary quite distinctly from the course of the liberal–conservative coalition government.

The tensions between farmers and workers, ultra-federalists, fundamentalists and pragmatists remained a characteristic feature of the Conservative People's Party up to the 1940s. In referenda on questions that touched upon the cantonal authority or on social policies, the deep differences of opinion could paralyse the party as a whole. Ultra-federalists in the *Stammlande* cantons quite regularly overruled the pragmatic recommendations of party leaders in national votes. Such was the case in the vote on the National Security Act in 1922, on the Working-time Act in 1924, on the constitutional amendment preparing a Social Security Act in 1925 and in the vote on the Social Security Act itself in 1931, in the vote on the Corn-dealing Act in 1926, on the petition for a complete revision of the federal constitution in 1935, on the Penal Law Act in 1938 and on the Act for early military training in schools in 1940.[14]

There were four predominant strategies to keep the different wings of the party together and to mobilize the Catholic voters in referenda and in elections. First of all, Catholic faith and Christian values were the best means to keep farmers, craftsmen and workers from splitting from their party. Their economic interests were often opposed, yet they shared the same faith. The social network of Catholicism played an important role in creating common ground in all the different social groups. The strength of this common band was clearly shown during the economic crisis of the 1930s, when protest movements such as the Independents, or Landesring der Unabhängigen, or the Young Farmers' Party, the Jungbauernpartei, gained many votes in Protestant cantons. In the rural Catholic regions, however, they received little support.[15]

The other ideological weapons were strong anti-liberalism and fierce anti-socialism. After the general strike in 1918, Catholic Conservatives, who themselves had been treated as second-class citizens in the nineteenth century, had singled out the socialists as a group that they could stigmatize as unreliable members of the state. Anti-socialism worked as a most effective means of mobilization in the national election of 1928,[16] and it formed the most reliable troops in the campaigns against socialist referenda. Anti-liberalism was most characteristic of the Young Conservatives. In their view, both the cultural crisis after the First World War and the economic crisis of the 1930s were consequences of the politics of liberalism. Anti-Semitic stereotypes that were widespread among Young Conservatives were closely combined with their anti-liberal and anti-socialist attitudes.

A third means to integrate the divergent economic interests of the party wings was structural reform within its organization.[17] The different regions of the country were proportionally represented in all party bodies, as were the groups of the Christian Workers' Movement. In 1923 farmers, craftsmen and workers were given five seats each in the party's central committee. In addition, the party leaders tried to set up special committees to discuss agricultural and middle-class topics. In 1930 an agricultural committee, the Bäuerliche Arbeitsgemeinschaft, and a committee of trade and commerce, the Mittelständische Arbeitsgemeinschaft, were formed within the party.

The fourth means to prevent political tensions from destabilizing the party was to give the cantonal parties great liberty in making recommendations for votes on controversial matters. Before referenda, the national party congress usually made recommendations to the Catholic electorate on how to vote. If the matter of a referendum was controversial within the party, cantonal party congresses often made differing recommendations. The national party bodies usually did not interfere in such cases. In order to avoid serious tensions between the different wings of the party they accepted that the Catholic conservative electorate did not vote unanimously.

THE RELATIONSHIP BETWEEN PARTY AND CHURCH

Until the 1940s the Conservative People's Party saw itself as the 'sword and protection of Swiss Catholicism in the political field'.[18] This definition reflected the Catholic position in the *Kulturkampf* of the 1870s, which cast its shadow over Swiss politics right up to the 1940s. As a result of the *Kulturkampf*, 'special regulations' concerning religious affairs had been implemented in the revised constitution of 1874: Jesuits were banned from Switzerland, the founding of new monasteries was forbidden and priests were not allowed to take parliamentary mandates.[19] These 'special regulations' of the constitution were maintained up to 1973, and remained a bone of contention for the Conservative Catholics in Switzerland. Another fact that they criticized was the poor representation of Catholics in the federal administration. Up to the middle of the century the institutions of the federal state were dominated by liberal Protestants. The number of Catholics among the upper ranks of the civil service was far below their proportion of the Swiss population. In 1938 only 16 per cent of the civil servants in upper ranks were Catholic, well below their 36 per cent of the Swiss population.[20] More than two-thirds of the posts in higher administration were occupied by members of the Liberal Party, the Freisinnig-demokratische Partei.

In the 1920s, national Catholic Congress, the *Katholikentage*, staged vociferous protests against the discriminatory regulations and demanded equal representation of Catholics in the civil service and in cultural life.[21] The Conservative leaders supported these goals, but they were very careful not to raise the suspicion of radical liberals by uttering political claims too loudly. They never seriously put the 'special regulations' on the political agenda. The only time they made a slight effort was during the campaign for the referendum on the petition for the complete revision of the constitution in 1935.[22] In the draft of a revised constitution published by the leading Young Conservative, Otto Walter, government support for confessional schools was favoured openly. These plans caused the Liberals, who opposed the complete revision of the constitution, to call a new *Kulturkampf* in order to prevent the so-called 'confessionalization' of public life. The clear defeat of the petition warned the Conservative leaders not to touch the delicate matter of the 'special regulations' again. They were supported by the Church leaders, who themselves were taking care not to disturb the religious 'peace'.

The relationship between the party leaders and the bishops was close. It was mainly based on the personal relationship of the leading politicians with their local bishop. However, not too many of the bishops were politically interested.[23] Bishop Aloisius Scheiwiler of St Gallen was exceptional in his political activities.[24] He had taken part in the Catholic Workers' Movement and was the founder of the Catholic Farmers' Organization, the Schweizerische Katholische Bauernvereinigung. Josef Scherrer, the leader of the Christian Workers' Movement, was his intimate friend. Through him he had a strong influence on the policy of the Catholic workers. Scherrer, on the other hand, found in his bishop an adviser whom he consulted on all political matters.

Apart from personal advice to party leaders, the bishops generally refrained from interfering in the political decision-making process. This was to avoid the impression that the Church was influencing the party's policies. So when the party leaders presented their new economic programme to the bishops in 1929, the Church leaders approved it, but they would not allow their approval to be printed in the booklet by which the programme was to be made public. In 1937, when the delicate question of a ban on Freemasonry was to be voted on, the bishops officially declared they would not utter an opinion on the question.[25] The party was split on this question. Its fundamentalist wing saw in Freemasonry a threat to religion and Church, whereas its pragmatic members feared the totalitarian aspects of a ban. Catholic voters were therefore in a dilemma. Many of them did not go to the poll. Yet the results in the Catholic cantons clearly showed that the aversion to Freemasonry was stronger among Catholics than among the rest of the population.[26]

In the 1930s, the withdrawal from politics was clearly to be felt among the Church leaders. It was a consequence of the papal *Actio catholica*, which made the bishops concentrate more on pastoral questions. In 1931, there were still five prominent priests in the central committee of the party; in 1939 only three remained, and they were not very influential. During national or cantonal elections the Church fully supported the party of the Catholics. In 1928, for example, Victor Bieler, Bishop of Sion, wrote to his clergy:

> Maybe during your sermon you can point out that a Catholic man has to confess his belief in the elections, too, because it is a duty to his conscience to vote only for men who confess our Catholic religion in word and in deed, and that it is also a duty of their religion not to vote for men who are deriding and trampling all over our religion.[27]

Not only in 1928, when the fear of a socialist success in the elections was at its peak, did the bishops ask their priests to advise the churchgoers to vote for truly Catholic candidates alone. Bishop Scheiwiler forbade his flock to join protest movements such as the Young Farmers' Movement, the Jungbauernbewegung, in the 1930s. The party's leaders, of course, welcomed such strong support from the Church. Yet even more important than the support by clergymen was the help of Catholic lay organizations. The party did not have any organizational structures on the local level. That is why it fully depended on the lay organizations in villages and small towns. The organizations recruited the conservative electorate and instructed the Catholics how to vote. The Catholic press played a very important role. Numerous editors of Catholic papers were priests, and they clearly supported the SKVP. The lay organizations were united in the SKVV.[28] Its leaders were closely linked to the party. A third of the members of its directing board were also members of the SKVP's central committee. In the 1930s, however, the People's Association lost much of its former influence on the policy of the party.[29] It was the bodies of the political party that took over the lead within the Catholic society on a national level. In the 1940s Martin Rosenberg, the party's general secretary, established an excellent collaboration with Josef Meier, the secretary of the People's Association. The party decided on political matters, whereas the association served as an instrument of propaganda.

THE ECONOMIC AND SOCIAL PROGRAMME

When the SKVP was founded in 1912 it lacked a clearly defined economic and social programme. This was surprising in a sense, for the party looked back on a great tradition of social ideas in the 1880s and 1890s. Josef Beck, Caspar Decurtins and Ernst Feigenwinter, three of its leading figures, were closely linked to the Union de Fribourg, an international club of theologians and politicians who developed many of the ideas of the encyclical *Rerum novarum*.[30] This papal letter developed its influence on the Conservative political programme only in the 1920s.[31] It was the Christian Social Movement of the French-speaking part of Switzerland that, under the leadership of Abbé André Savoy and Ernest Perrier, took up the corporatist ideas of the Union de Fribourg.[32] The founding of co-operatives played an important part in their concepts. During the 1920s corporatist ideas spread in the organizations of the Christian Social Workers' Union.

The Conservative Party's ideas on social reform were not as clearly defined as the concepts of the corporatists. They were vaguely based on the social philosophy of solidarism that Heinrich Pesch had developed in Germany. The situation of the middle class played an important role for the Swiss conservatives. Craftsmen and small businessmen constituted a crucial part of the conservative electorate. Therefore, Oskar Leimgruber, one of their leading representatives within the party, developed a specific social philosophy called *mesonism* which put the sustaining of an independent middle class at its centre.[33] The social ideas of the conservative Catholics were much too vague to form clear guidelines for their social policy. The Christian Social Workers' Movement demanded social reforms, yet the deeply rooted suspicion of all federal policies made fundamentalist Conservatives block such reforms in the 1920s and 1930s. The party leaders realized that a common economic and social programme was needed to hold the different wings of the party together.[34] The first congress of Christian Social politicians in 1927 was the starting point for programmatic debates that resulted in the party's economic and social programme of 1929. The programme was strongly influenced by *Rerum novarum* and favoured corporatist solutions to social problems. Scherrer, leader of the Christian Workers' Movement and author of the programme, had been in touch with the international Circle of Mechelen of Cardinal Désiré Mercier during the programme's preparation.

The hopes Conservative leaders had invested in a common economic and social programme were soon dashed. The defeat of the old-age pension scheme in the vote of 1931 clearly showed how little cohesion there was on social policy within the party.[35] The only common ground for a Conservative social policy was the analysis of the social problems of the time. In the eyes of all Conservative Catholics, social problems were a consequence of the abandoning of the Christian faith in society. Their solution lay in establishing a 'Christian democracy'.[36] However, the form this democracy was to take remained quite indistinct. It was supposed to be an organic mixture of traditional, authoritarian, federal and corporatist elements. The forcefully established corporatist *Ständestaat* system of Austria was not seen as a model for Switzerland, however.

Corporatism was one of the key solutions the Young Conservatives proposed during the campaign for a complete revision of the constitution.[37] Therefore, their clear defeat in the vote of 1935 had to be regarded as a serious setback for corporatist ideas in general. Furthermore, the authoritarian forms of corporatism in Austria and Italy discredited this concept. The party did not give up its principles, however. When the federal government declared comprehensive pay agreements compulsory for all members of the respective industrial branches in 1941, the Conservatives regarded this measure as the first step towards a corporatist system.[38] At the beginning of the 1940s favouring families was at the centre of the Conservatives' social policy. Their concept of family allowances was clearly based on corporatist ideas.[39] Although the Conservative family programme could not be fully realized, industrial boards played an important part not only in the social security schemes established after the Second World War but also in the economic system of post-war Switzerland as a whole. Corporatism, among other ideas, was one of the social concepts behind this system.

EUROPEAN CONCEPTIONS OF SWISS CATHOLIC CONSERVATIVES

Switzerland's relationship to Europe had to be redefined after the First World War. Strict official neutrality during the war had been the only means to prevent a split between the entente-favouring French and the Germanophile German-speaking parts of Switzerland. This 'split of languages' went right through the Catholic population, too. It was still virulent in 1920, when the Swiss electorate was asked to decide whether Switzerland should join the League of Nations.[40] German-speaking right-wing Conservatives regarded the League as an anti-papal conspiracy of capitalists and Freemasons. The SKVP's pragmatic leaders had to exert all their authority to convince Catholic voters that accepting the treaty with the League of Nations was vital for the Catholics' position in domestic politics. Although a majority of the Conservative electorate accepted the treaty, international politics never played an important part within the SKVP. It remained the domain of a few conservative intellectuals.

The international isolation of Germany and Austria at the beginning of the 1920s was apparently the main reason for the fact that contacts with international intellectual elites were mainly established in the French-speaking part of Switzerland. Fribourg, with its Catholic university and the tradition of the Union de Fribourg, played an important part. Georges de Montenach and Gonzague de Reynold, two of its best-known conservative intellectuals, were leading figures in the Union catholique d'études internationales in Paris.[41] This circle of intellectuals was founded in order to secure Catholic influence on the policy of the League of Nations.

Similarly, leading Catholic conservative students in Fribourg took the initiative in developing the concept of Pax Romana – an international union of Catholic students.[42]

The French-speaking intellectuals were also among the first to take part in the Catholic restoration palpable all over Europe in the 1920s. In Switzerland this restoration was mainly inspired by the Fribourgeois aristocrat, Gonzague de Reynold, who was strongly influenced by the Action Française.[43] He was of the opinion that the liberal era of the nineteenth century and its system of parliamentary democracy had come to an end after the First World War. According to Reynold, the future belonged to a new form of state that combined aristocratic and democratic elements. He admired authoritarian fascist regimes, such as those of Mussolini, Franco or Salazar. Although Reynold was never a member of the Conservative People's Party, he had a great influence on conservative intellectuals in the party such as Jean-Marie Musy, Joseph Piller, Ferdinand Buomberger, Karl Hackhofer, Karl Wick and especially Philipp Etter, one of the leading members of the federal council in the late 1930s. A deeply rooted anti-liberalism and a high esteem of authority, together with a strong belief in Christian values, characterized the conservative analyses of society. Fascism was seen as a reaction to the crisis of liberal democracy and of the capitalist economy. The concept of a 'Christian democracy' has to be seen as a reaction to these social and political changes.

Yet, Swiss German intellectuals, warned by the developments in Nazi Germany, clearly mistrusted totalitarian centralization. They developed a specific concept of Swiss identity that defined the state as a nation of will, held together by its common history, its Christian values and its federal system of government.[44] In the late 1930s their concepts, which can be interpreted both as part of a reactionary *Zeitgeist* or of an ideology of national integration, were officially sanctioned by the national programme of the *Geistige Landesverteidigung*, a kind of spiritual defence that the Swiss government launched against the propaganda both from its northern and southern neighbours. Foreshadowing the troubles that totalitarian dictatorship might bring to Europe, Swiss intellectuals created the myth of Switzerland as a model for a peaceful European community. However, it was not until after the Second World War that such ideas were to become a realistic alternative in European politics.

CONCLUSION

As a people's party the SKVP was characterized by strong tensions between the different social groups that it united. Catholic faith, and a fierce anti-socialism as well as a strong anti-liberalism, were the bands that held these groups together. The Catholic Church, with its moral and social teaching and its social network, was the firm foundation of the party. However, Church leaders withdrew from day-to-day politics in the 1930s, and the party became more independent in its decisions. The economic and social programme, which the party developed on the basis of Catholic social teaching, served more as a means to integrate different economic interest groups than as a clear guideline for concepts of a conservative social policy. If the Swiss political and economic system took up corporatist elements in the 1940s, it can therefore hardly be seen as a result of SKVP policies. The concepts of 'Christian democracy' that conservative Catholic intellectuals developed in the 1920s and 1930s were a reaction to the social crisis after the First World War and after the world economic crisis. Although these concepts seemed illusory in the 1930s, they formed the common ground on which Swiss Conservative politicians were able to meet their European colleagues after the war.

NOTES

1 Broschüre zur Grossratswahl 1933. Staatsarchiv des Kantons St Gallen, Archiv CVP. Quoted in Walther Baumgartner, *Die Christlichsoziale Partei des Kantons St. Gallen 1911–1939. St. Gallen Arbeiterschaft und Angestellte zwischen Katholizismus und Sozialismus* (St Gallen 1998), p. 537.
2 Urs Altermatt, *Katholizismus und Moderne. Zur Sozial- und Mentalitätsgeschichte der Schweizer Katholiken im 19. und 20. Jahrhundert* (Zurich 1989), pp. 49–62, 103–18. Altermatt is one of the first scholars in German-language historiography to have approached the history of the Catholics' party under this premise. In the series *Religion – Politik – Gesellschaft in der Schweiz*, directed by Altermatt, a number of volumes have been published on the history of the SKVP: Joseph Jung, *Katholische Jugendbewegung in der deutschen Schweiz. Der Jungmannschaftsverband zwischen Tradition und Wandel von der Mitte des 19. Jahrhunderts bis zum Zweiten Weltkrieg* (Freiburg, Switzerland 1988); Quirin Weber, *Korporatismus statt Sozialismus. Die Idee der berufsständischen Ordnung im schweizerischen Katholizismus während der Zwischenkriegszeit* (Freiburg, Switzerland 1989); Lukas Rölli-Alkemper, *Die Schweizerische Konservative Volkspartei 1935–1943. Politischer Katholizismus zwischen Emanzipation und Integration* (Freiburg, Switzerland 1993); Dieter Holenstein, *Die Christlichsozialen der Schweiz im Ersten Weltkrieg. Entwicklung der christlichsozialen Organisationen und ihre Stellung in der Schweizerischen Arbeiterbewegung und der katholischen Sondergesellschaft 1914–1920* (Freiburg, Switzerland 1993); Urs Altermatt (ed.), *Schweizer Katholizismus zwischen den Weltkriegen 1920–1940* (Freiburg, Switzerland 1994); Markus Hodel, *Die Schweizerische Konservative Volkspartei 1918–1929. Die goldenen Jahre des politischen Katholizismus* (Freiburg, Switzerland 1994); Urs Altermatt, *Der Weg der Schweizer Katholiken ins Ghetto. Die Entstehung der nationalen Volksorganisationen im Schweizer Katholizismus 1848–1919*, 3rd edition (Freiburg, Switzerland 1995); Bernhard Wigger, *Die Schweizerische Konservative Volkspartei 1903–1918. Politik zwischen Kulturkampf und Klassenkampf* (Freiburg, Switzerland 1997).

3 Urs Altermatt, 'Conservatism in Switzerland: A Study in Antimodernism', *Journal of Contemporary History*, vol. 14 (1979), pp. 581–610.
4 Altermatt, *Ghetto*; Altermatt, *Katholizismus und Moderne*, pp. 133–80; Wigger, *Die Schweizerische Konservative Volkspartei*.
5 The Swiss federal government consists of seven ministers who are elected by parliament. Each minister is both head of an administrative department and a member of the governing Federal Council, or Bundesrat, which makes its decisions as a body. Parliament has no means to dismiss the Federal Council or one of its members. Urs Altermatt, 'Bundesrat und Bundesräte. Ein historischer Aufriss', in idem (ed.), *Die Schweizer Bundesräte. Ein biographisches Lexikon*, (Zurich and Munich 1991), pp. 17–43.
6 Rölli-Alkemper, *Die Schweizerische Konservative Volkspartei*, pp. 17–19.
7 Altermatt, *Katholizismus und Moderne*, pp. 181–202, here p. 181.
8 Holenstein, *Die Christlichsozialen der Schweiz*; Baumgartner, *Die Christlichsoziale Partei*; Otmar Gehrig, *Das Christlichsoziale in der Politik unter besonderer Berücksichtigung des Christlichsozialen Arbeiterbundes der Schweiz 1919–1939* (Winterthur 1969); Roland Ruffieux, *Le Mouvement Chrétien-Social en Suisse Romande 1891–1949* (Freiburg, Switzerland 1969).
9 Rölli-Alkemper, *Die Schweizerische Konservative Volkspartei*, pp. 169–76; Baumgartner, *Die Christlichsoziale Partei*, pp. 394–492.
10 Hodel, *Die Schweizerische Konservative Volkspartei*, pp. 133–45.
11 Urs Altermatt and Franziska Metzger, 'Der radikale Antisemitismus der rechtskatholisch-integralistischen Zeitung "Schildwache" 1912–1945', *Zeitschrift für Schweizerische Kirchengeschichte*, vol. 92 (1998), pp. 43–72; Hodel, *Die Schweizerische Konservative Volkspartei*, pp. 402–9; Jung, *Katholische Jugendbewegung*, pp. 161–5.
12 Urs Altermatt, *Antisemitismus in der katholischen Schweiz 1914–1945* (Frauenfeld 1999); Altermatt and Metzger, 'Der radikale Antisemitismus'.
13 Rölli-Alkemper, *Die Schweizerische Konservative Volkspartei*, pp. 30–7; Josef Widmer, 'Von der konservativen Parteinachwuchsorganisation zur katholischen Erneuerungsbewegung. Die Schweizer Jungkonservativen in den dreissiger Jahren', unpublished thesis (Freiburg, Switzerland 1983), pp. 117–47; Peter Stadler, 'Die Diskussion um eine Totalrevision der Schweizerischen Bundesverfassung 1933–1935', *Schweizerische Zeitschrift für Geschichte*, vol. 19 (1969), pp. 75–169.
14 Hodel, *Die Schweizerische Konservative Volkspartei*, pp. 258–307; Rölli-Alkemper, *Die Schweizerische Konservative Volkspartei*, pp. 233–43.
15 Rölli-Alkemper, *Die Schweizerische Konservative Volkspartei*, pp. 66–75.
16 Hodel, *Die Schweizerische Konservative Volkspartei*, pp. 182–98.
17 Ibid. pp. 352–71; Rölli-Alkemper, *Die Schweizerische Konservative Volkspartei*, pp. 124–34.
18 Martin Rosenberg, *Die Schweizerische Konservative Volkspartei. Geschichte, Aufgabe, Programm* (Berne 1943), p. 26.
19 See also Peter Stadler, *Der Kulturkampf in der Schweiz* (Frauenfeld 1984).
20 Ulrich Klöti, *Die Chefbeamten der schweizerischen Bundesverwaltung. Soziologische Querschnitte in den Jahren 1938, 1955 und 1969* (Berne 1972), pp. 96–8; Rölli-Alkemper, *Die Schweizerische Konservative Volkspartei*, pp. 93–8.
21 Markus Hodel, 'Die konfessionellen Ausnahmegesetze in der innenpolitischen Diskussion nach dem Ersten Weltkrieg', in Altermatt, *Schweizer Katholizismus*, pp. 279–95; Armin Imstepf, *Die schweizerischen Katholikentage 1903–1954. Geschichte, Organisation, Programmatik und Sozialstruktur* (Freiburg, Switzerland 1987), pp. 74–83.

22 Rölli-Alkemper, *Die Schweizerische Konservative Volkspartei*, p. 35.
23 Patrick Bernold, *Der Schweizerische Episkopat und die Bedrohung der Demokratie 1919–1939. Die Stellungnahme der Bischöfe zum modernen Bundesstaat und ihre Auseinandersetzung mit Kommunismus, Sozialismus, Faschismus und Nationalsozialismus* (Berne 1995).
24 Walther Baumgartner, 'Alois Scheiwiler (1930–1938): Der "(christlich) soziale Bischof"', in Joachim Müller (ed.), *Die Bischöfe des Bistums St. Gallen – Lebensbilder aus 150 Jahren* (Freiburg, Switzerland and Konstanz 1996), pp. 136–58; Baumgartner, *Die Christlichsoziale Partei*, pp. 255–68.
25 Rölli-Alkemper, *Die Schweizerische Konservative Volkspartei*, pp. 153–4, 210–12; Josef Widmer, 'Die Jungkonservativen und die Fonjallaz-Initiative 1934', in Altermatt, *Schweizer Katholizismus*, pp. 297–316.
26 The ban on Freemasonry was defeated by 513,553 against 323,466 votes. See Boris Schneider, 'Die Fonjallaz-Initiative. Freimaurer und Fronten in der Schweiz', *Schweizerische Zeitschrift für Geschichte*, vol. 24 (1974), pp. 666–710.
27 Letter of Bishop Victor Bieler to his clergy, 16 October 1928. Quoted in Hodel, *Die Schweizerische Konservative Volkspartei*, p. 191.
28 Hilmar Gernet, 'Der Schweizerische Katholische Volksverein im Spannungsfeld von katholischer und politischer Aktion (1930–1960)', Ph.D. (Freiburg, Switzerland 1988).
29 Rölli-Alkemper, *Die Schweizerische Konservative Volkspartei*, pp. 149–51.
30 Altermatt, *Der Weg der Schweizer Katholiken ins Ghetto*, pp. 123–6.
31 See Aram Mattioli and Gerhard Wanner (eds), *Katholizismus und 'soziale Frage'. Ursprünge und Auswirkungen der Enzyklika 'Rerum novarum' in Deutschland, Liechtenstein, Vorarlberg und St. Gallen* (Zurich 1995).
32 Ruffieux, *Le Mouvement Chrétien-Social*; Weber, *Korporatismus statt Sozialismus*; Philippe Maspoli, *Le corporatisme et la droite en Suisse romande* (Lausanne 1993).
33 Hodel, *Die Schweizerische Konservative Volkspartei*, pp. 468–71.
34 Ibid., pp. 471–8, 483–6.
35 Ibid., pp. 278–88.
36 Ibid., pp. 490–4; Rölli-Alkemper, *Die Schweizerische Konservative Volkspartei*, pp. 205–7.
37 Weber, *Korporatismus statt Sozialismus*, pp. 184–95; Rölli-Alkemper, *Die Schweizerische Konservative Volkspartei*, pp. 30–7.
38 Rölli-Alkemper, *Die Schweizerische Konservative Volkspartei*, pp. 249–56.
39 Ibid., pp. 256–74.
40 Hodel, *Die Schweizerische Konservative Volkspartei*, pp. 225–37.
41 Aram Mattioli, 'Gonzague de Reynold und die Entzauberung der Welt', in Altermatt, *Schweizer Katholizismus*, pp. 81–101; Philippe Trinchan, 'Adaptation ou résistance des catholiques au nouvel ordre international: le cas de l'Union catholique d'études internationales 1920–1939, in Altermatt, *Schweizer Katholizismus*, pp. 103–16.
42 Michela Trisconi, 'Une Internationale pour les universitaires catholiques. "Pax Romana" et ses tentatives de propagation en Amérique latine durant l'entre-deux-guerres', *Traverse*, vol. 5, no. 2 (1998), pp. 112–22.
43 See Aram Mattioli, *Zwischen Demokratie und totalitärer Diktatur. Gonzague de Reynold und die Tradition der autoritären Rechten in der Schweiz* (Zurich 1994).
44 Josef Mooser, 'Die "Geistige Landesverteidigung" in den 1930er Jahren. Profile und Kontexte eines vielschichtigen Phänomens der schweizerischen politischen

Kultur in der Zwischenkriegszeit', *Schweizerische Zeitschrift für Geschichte*, vol. 47 (1997), pp. 685–708; Rölli-Alkemper, *Die Schweizerische Konservative Volkspartei*, pp. 200–5; Francis Python, *Les aspirations à une rénovation nationale dans les milieux conservateurs romands 1919–1941. Les débuts d'idées dans les revues de deux Sociétés d'étudiants* (Freiburg, Switzerland 1995).

4

A Historical Detour: The Roman Catholic State Party in the Netherlands

Jan Roes

The history of the Christian and Catholic parties in the Netherlands offers a characteristic example of the historical detour that was made in the twentieth century by the Christian democratic parties, before reaching the crossroads they faced at the beginning of the twenty-first century. The situation changed significantly after the first half of the last century. At that time Protestants and Catholics had lived in the same country for centuries, albeit next to, rather than with one another. A gradual change was brought about by party political developments that began at the end of the nineteenth century. The main thesis of this chapter is, therefore, that the path of the Rooms Katholieke Staats Partij or Roman Catholic State Party (RKSP) to Christian democracy was decisively determined by the religious relationships and conflicts in the history of the Netherlands – not primarily in the inter-war period, but rather in its confessional prehistory, not only in the long nineteenth century, but essentially since the time of the Reformation.[1] Against this background, some key themes in the history of the formation of the Catholic Party in the Netherlands need to be analysed: the dynamic dialectic of emancipation and coalition, the 'being spoilt for choice' between the Scylla of a Church party and the Charybdis of Catholic unity, and connected to this the even more agonizing search for a middle course in view of the social contrasts in its own ranks; and lastly, the efforts of the RKSP to develop into a socially and nationally united party despite these contrasts and tensions. The RKSP wanted to make its contribution to the building up of a 'Christian state of the future'.[2]

THE LONG NINETEENTH CENTURY

Since its founding at the time of the Reformation, the Dutch state had a multi-confessional and multicultural character. It was only in the

Netherlands that the principle of *cuius regio, eius religio*, i.e. the right of monarchs to determine the religion of their subjects, was not upheld, and in this it is unique among all the other European nations. There was, it is true, a public (Calvinist) Church, but no state Church as in neighbouring states. In the 'confessional co-existence' of different beliefs, Catholics had to develop a readiness to compromise as a survival strategy within the Dutch Polder model of tolerance. The Netherlands' identity as a 'religious testing-ground' has to this day prevailed as a creative force.[3] This characteristic of Dutch society and the Dutch state should not, however, be presented as more than it actually was in historical reality, since Catholics were, for centuries, pushed to the edge of society. Despite this political and social marginalization, the Catholics made up, until the middle of the twentieth century, about a third of the population. In the course of the nineteenth century the social and political situation gradually changed, so that the Catholics were able to establish themselves as a new factor in the political scene by 1900. The nineteenth century was for the Dutch, more than for most other European states, a very 'long century' and this is true especially for Catholicism in this country. It took from the end of the eighteenth century to the First World War for freedom and equality of religion, which had been constitutionally introduced under the influence of the French Revolution, to be realized as a social, political and cultural reality.

After the intermezzo of a united kingdom with Belgium which existed until 1830, Protestants and Catholics in the Netherlands resigned themselves to being condemned to working together to build a modern democratic state. Both confessions made increasingly greater efforts to put their stamp on the national identity. The Protestants made great efforts in the nineteenth century to give prominence to their own identity, while the Catholic citizens on their side tended more and more to the ultramontane identity orientated towards Rome. Not least, the Catholics, with the help of the prevailing liberal conception of the state, managed to achieve a legally guaranteed standing for their Church, which was strengthened by the formation of a proper Church province in 1853. The hefty anti-papal reactions in the Netherlands demonstrated the continuing differences and rivalry between Catholics and Protestants.

Characteristic of the long nineteenth century in the Netherlands was the late modernization. As the German writer Heinrich Heine once put it: in the Netherlands everything happens fifty years late. Only at the end of the century did the country begin to catch up. In the decade before and the decade after the turn of the century fundamental modernization transformed the Dutch political and social landscape. Three vital questions were crucial in achieving this: the school issue, the social question and the demand for universal male suffrage. It was remarkable that the Dutch Catholics played a leading role in these debates. There were three reasons: first, the late modernization, second, the larger backlog, which meant that the Catholics did not have much to lose but a lot to gain, and third, the impulse from two rival social movements, the socialists and the Protestants.

The formation of political parties was a part of this process of modernization. Up to this point there had been quite a loose system of, on the one side, liberal and on the other side conservative currents. In 1879 the first modern party was founded by the Protestants – the Anti-Revolutionary Party. The Socialists then organized themselves in the 1880s. The forming of a party by the Catholics also began at this time, albeit very casually and hesitantly. The Liberals saw themselves forced to join in this party development. At the beginning of the twentieth century, this four-party political landscape developed its main characteristics, which can be seen as the political basis for Dutch pillarization, i.e. the segregation of Dutch society and politics along confessional and political lines. Pillarization took on its final form in the inter-war period and was, for decades, the hallmark of Dutch politics.

BETWEEN EMANCIPATION AND COALITION

The Catholic Party came into being only gradually. There were several reasons for this. The Catholics had first of all to overcome their closeness to the Liberals, who had contributed decisively to the emancipation of their Church. In the 1860s the Catholic deputies became closer to the politics of the Conservatives. The Liberals became alienated ideologically from their Catholic colleagues by their radical, left-liberal transformation. The Catholics, on their part, went off at the same time in an ultramontane direction. The liberal battle for public, as opposed to private schools was a decisive factor leading to the split.

The formation of the Protestant Anti-Revolutionary Party was a landmark for the political development of Catholicism. The priest Herman Schaepman, who was at this time elected to the second chamber, brought the Catholics in their own right as a party on to the political stage. In 1883 he published a draft of a Catholic Party programme, which can be seen as the trigger for the formation of the RKSP. It would still take half a century, however, before the official formation in 1926. A further ten years went by before a proper party programme was adopted. The name RKSP was, at this point, already part of the Dutch political vocabulary. Schaepman, who had actually wanted an inter-confessional party of the political centre along the lines of the German example of the Centre Party (where inter-confessionalism, however, was not realized either), formed a historical coalition with the founder of the Anti-Revolutionary Party, the pastor Abraham Kuyper. Protestants and Catholics formed an alliance for the first time since the Reformation. The school issue, a milder Dutch version of the German *Kulturkampf*, brought the traditional enemies together. To interpret this as an early sign of Christian democratic development would, however, be unhistorical.

The RKSP had, first of all, more pressing internal problems to solve. In Church issues, and these included the school question, it was united and worked for the emancipation of the Catholic population.[4] In other matters, however, especially in social and political questions – such as the workers' question, and universal suffrage – there was strife within the party. This is why it had taken so long for the party to be founded in the first place. What made it even more difficult was that there had been a right to vote since the constitution of 1848, but this right was, at the start, limited to higher income groups. The census voting system and division into districts greatly favoured the conservative wing of the party, above all because the Dutch Catholics mostly belonged to the lower social classes as a result of their historical discrimination. This promoted internal tension in the RKSP from the outset.

The political situation only changed as universal male suffrage was introduced in 1918 and the vote for women in 1922. Afterwards and for decades, 80 to 90 per cent of Dutch Catholics voted for the Catholic Party. Two further fundamental decisions changed the political landscape fundamentally after the First World War: the school question was settled, with financial and legal equality for public and private schools, and the foundation for social legislation was laid. Likewise, in 1918 Charles Ruys de Beerenbrouck was called upon, as the first Catholic, to form a government. A proper Catholic Party did not yet formally exist, but despite this the struggle for political emancipation was considered successful, at least regarding its first basic target.

The political scientist, Arend Lijphart, was right when he drew attention to the fact that the inter-war era was a pacifistic phase in Dutch politics and one that was to ensure remarkable stability for half a century.[5] A new era dawned for the RKSP, in which it achieved a key position in the political balance of power. It was only able to use this favourable position in a limited way, however. W. H. Nolens, a priest and long-standing leader of the Dutch Catholics, who had an awe-inspiring reputation as the sphinx at the centre of power in The Hague,[6] defended the political interests of his party, but did not achieve an appreciable breakthrough. Internally, the RKSP was lamed by intra-party dissidents and curbed from without by the alliance with the Protestant parties, because the main purpose of the coalition – the school question – had in the meantime been solved.

There was no question of any inter-confessional Christian democratic bonding between the RKSP and the Protestant parties, neither in domestic politics nor in foreign policy. Because of its neutrality policy the Netherlands had hardly any interest in trans-national party co-operation.

The RKSP took part in the meetings of the Secrétariat International des Partis Démocratiques d'Inspiration Chrétienne (SIPDIC) which took place from 1925 onwards,[7] but there was no trace of a supranational policy, despite the universalist demands in the day-to-day politics of the party; its direction was at that time still very introverted.[8] There was, however, one important exception, namely Nolens, who participated actively as an authority on employment issues and social law-making during his political career, especially in the International Labour Organization in Geneva and in the Peace Movement.

THE PRIMACY OF UNITY

Although the RKSP was closely allied to the Catholic Church because of its emancipatory aims, historians agree that it was not a Church party.[9] It was, however, led by two priests for almost half a century, but it was just these men who put particular emphasis on the party's independence from the Catholic Church. A Church party would have been rather counterproductive for achieving emancipation against the background of the Dutch tradition of a separation of State and Church. The efforts made not to give a pretext for anti-papal feelings had also become an important leading line. It was not a Church party, but to a great degree a Catholic one, as its most important task was to uphold Catholic interests, and that is why ensuring Catholic unity always had the highest priority for the Church as well as for the Catholic political elites.

Schaepman may have represented the growing Catholic self-confidence in the Dutch public. Within the RKSP itself, however, he remained a loner for almost all his political life, as more conservative colleagues in the second chamber left him standing solitarily on the left because of his progressive stance. He has even been described as 'a political leader without a party'.[10] Nolens acted a great deal more skilfully than his predecessor and role model Schaepman. He ran a tight ship after the First World War, leading the RKSP parliamentary party in the second chamber. But even he could not control the ever returning dissident tendencies within the party. Despite this continual worrying about Catholic unity, the RKSP voters remained remarkably faithful in the inter-war period. About 85 per cent of the Catholics voted for them, winning them a third of the seats in parliament and making them the strongest party.[11]

The bishops took a somewhat ambivalent stance during these years. On the one hand, they made great efforts for the upholding of the political unity of the Catholics, because they feared a split. On the other, they usually did not intervene directly on concrete political issues.[12] With pastoral matter of factness they made their voices heard on political issues that had a Church and moral dimension. They also took positions on philosophical and ideological matters and did not hesitate to warn, not only against communism and National Socialism, but also social democracy. The last was, however, a political border area that could not be entered without special attention, as the bishops were also advised from among their own Catholic ranks. In the first years after the First World War they directly interfered twice in political issues, which led to an immediate reaction. In 1919 the Archbishop of Utrecht turned to the new Catholic Minister for Employment, P. J. M. Aalberse, in the name of the entire episcopate, because of the composition of the newly formed high council for employment, especially concerning the Catholic representatives. Two years later, the bishops wrote a letter to the party leadership in which they forbade any collaboration with the Socialists. In both cases, the Catholic politicians made it more or less clear that an interference of this kind was unwanted and, with respect to safeguarding Catholic interests, actually counter-productive.

The bishops accepted the warning and in the remaining inter-war years limited themselves to upholding the unity of the Dutch Catholics. With their pastoral letters, often issued just before the elections, they gave the RKSP influential support and tried to at least minimize the dissident movements in their own ranks. The 'bishops' fire-brigade' was, when necessary, brought into action to put out political fires ignited among the Catholics that blazed up more and more as a result of conflicting views on the social question. Hardly any other issue occupied the episcopate as much in these years as the formation of the Catholic pillar – a label that first started to be used in the 1950s in the parcelled social and political landscape in the Netherlands. It occupied them even more than the upholding of unity. Aware of the social frictions within Catholicism, the bishops made repeated efforts to separate political and social activities. In most cases they could leave the guarding of Catholic unity to the clergy, as on the local and regional level the priests and chaplains were often the best promoters of the Catholic movement, including the RKSP. These lower clerics could, as 'clerical advisers', best promote the social and cultural organizations and control Catholic voters in the interests of the Catholic Party.

THE DIFFICULT CENTRE

Catholic unity was constantly being put to the test because of internal social contradictions. The social differences in the Catholic milieu were considerable. At the beginning of the twentieth century around two-thirds of the Catholic population were working-class. Their social and political interests were, however, represented by the other social groups in the party. In the last decade of the nineteenth century the workers began to organize themselves, which led to an interweaving of Catholic and social emancipation. The continuation of collaboration with the Protestant parties seemed to be the logical path towards Catholic emancipation, although the coalition showed signs of wear and tear after winning the school question, and old confessional contradictions were stirred up again. An alliance with the Socialists appeared to make more sense for the upholding of the social interests of the Catholics. However, despite the emancipatory affinity on the social question, the ideological gap between Catholicism and socialism during the entire inter-war period was too wide to be bridged.

Much more difficult than occupying, in a very general sense, the political centre between socialism and liberalism was to set a political course within the RKSP itself; internal harmony turned out to be far more difficult to realize than the external pacification in the context of pillarization. The danger of a split between the left and the right wings loomed. Priests, as 'clerical advisers', had a special task in keeping the Catholic Workers' Movement away from their Socialist anticlerical rivals. Moreover, the way the Workers' Movement was organized became exemplary for the other Catholic organizations in the social sphere, especially for the farmers and the middle class: no inter-confessional groupings, a double structure of corporatist organizations and unions, and alongside national also regional organizations at the diocesan level, and this all under the hierarchical protection of the 'clerical advisers'.

The Catholic social movement was extremely important for the political mobilization of Dutch Catholicism because of its thorough organization. At the same time, its unity always appeared vulnerable, representing the RKSP's Achilles' heel. This was because the orthodoxy – or rather, orthopraxy – of the Dutch Catholics as regards Church matters was uncontested, but with regard to politics they could be tempted to base their decisions on their interests as workers or as members of other social groups. For a people's party with a broad base, such as the RKSP wanted to be, the Workers' Movement was, without doubt, essential as a social basis. It was indeed an indispensable cornerstone. It could also be used as an ideological foundation for the ever recurring claim for the necessity of Catholic unity. The Catholic Workers' Movement had already, before the First World War, occasionally demonstrated its growing political weight. Because of the census voting system it did not have at this point the necessary strength, but with the introduction of universal suffrage the situation changed significantly. From this time on the workers formed two-thirds of the Catholic electorate. They were called upon to vote for 'their' party, that is to say the Catholic Party. These democratic influences changed the balance of power in the party. The influence of the Workers' Movement within the party was at first far less than the proportion of their votes, which led to considerable tension. The growing conflicts between the conservative and the democratic wings of the party were a ticking time-bomb for Catholic unity. The leadership dealt with this problem, which was so difficult to overcome, by a functional differentiation almost amounting to a political instrumentalization of social contrasts.

The official founding of the RKSP in 1926 as well as the drawing up of its political programme in the following years facilitated this functional differentiation. From the end of the 1920s a maximum of two-thirds of the RKSP parliamentary seats were 'reserved' to 'satisfy' certain social and regional needs or 'qualities', the so-called 'quality seats'.[13] Four seats were earmarked for the Workers' Movement. With the help of such a divide-and-rule-like compromise the party managed to not only marginalize the dissidents, but also to largely realize the desired unity as far as possible. This could be seen at the elections, as well as with the members: around a third of all Catholic voters were also members of the party. The RKSP was thus the strongest and largest Dutch party in the inter-war years – an uncomfortable party, but one of social integration, which practised, at least within the Catholic sphere, successful politics of the centre.

SOCIAL AND NATIONAL: THE IDEOLOGICAL ADVANCE TO CHRISTIAN DEMOCRACY

The encyclical *Rerum novarum* of 1891 was an unpleasant surprise for the conservatives in the RKSP, because in their eyes it vindicated the social demands of the Workers' Movement, which had just begun to rise. The encyclical came at the right time, however, for the Workers' Movement. The first steps in the direction of a Catholic Workers' Movement in the Netherlands were made in the 1880s, albeit rather tentatively. Directly after its publication the encyclical was deemed to be the guiding Magna Carta of the Catholic Movement in the Netherlands, first of all in the social field and then gradually also in the political field. The solidarity between the social classes advocated by the Pope came at just the right moment for the convinced ultramontanes that the Dutch Catholics were proving ever more to be. Workers' leaders called on their comrades to take part in the social movement with the slogan, 'Catholic workers of the world unite: *Rerum novarum!*' The first task of the bishops and priests was to put the teachings of the encyclical into practice. Young priests such as the 'workers' chaplain', Alphons Ariëns, knew that from this time on they were on a secure ideological path; the encyclical meant a sort of social Damascus experience for the leading politician, Schaepman.[14] *Rerum novarum* was for his successor Nolens the social basis of his politics, in the second chamber as well as in other public activities.[15] The modern awakening that had begun at the turn of the century was pushed on considerably by *Rerum novarum*, as the papal blessing provided for a specific chemistry: a combination of Catholic and social emancipation that contributed to a lasting transformation of Dutch society. Thanks to *Rerum novarum*, Catholic social teaching became the motivating force in the RKSP. Although Pope Leo XIII tried with his encyclical *Graves de communi re* in 1901 to keep Christian democracy away from politics, social reformist ideology for forming a 'Christian state of the future' became a characteristic feature of twentieth-century Christian democratic politics in the Netherlands as elsewhere. Because of the special historical conditions in the Netherlands, it took until after the Second World War for their ideas actually to be politically implemented. Yet to a certain extent, these ideas were already a kind of state philosophy from the turn of the century onwards.

It was of great importance for the new socio-political orientation that partly before the First World War, but above all in the inter-war period, a new generation of politicians took up office. Along with the priest and parliamentary party leader, Nolens, the young lawyer Aalberse accomplished a great deal for the Catholic social movement in the decade before the outbreak of war. He founded Catholic Social Action in 1904, which had its own weekly newspaper and was modelled on the Mönchengladbacher Volksverein, in the German Rhineland.[16] Together with another layman, Ruys de Beerenbrouk, a friend from his university days, he also started up the so-called 'Social Weeks'. Ruys was the first Catholic Prime Minister in 1918, and Aalberse Minister for Employment. They and other laymen were ideologically supported and encouraged by a number of social priests, among them J. D. J. Aengenent, Ariëns and H. A. Poels.[17] The priest Nolens guaranteed the clerical influence on Catholic politics.

Shortly after the First World War the political scene in the Netherlands changed fundamentally. The fever of a socialist revolution rose briefly, but was soon fought off energetically with the help of Catholic forces, which used this unforeseen opportunity to demonstrate their national reliability. It was above all two structural changes that over a longer period transformed the social and political landscape. The first of these was the end of the battle over the school issue, which served as a model for the building of a pluralistic society. The second was the introduction of the new electoral system, which changed the political balance of power.[18] In the 1920s, the traditional Catholic elite had to come to terms with the fact that 'their' RKSP had changed into a people's party, which should represent the interests of a greater part of the population and which also aimed at a Christian transformation of society. This social-political reorientation caused considerable tension: the transformation went too far and too fast for the conservative Catholics, whereas for the 'Catholic democrats' it was too slow and did not go far enough. This cleavage invited recurring dissident tendencies, however minimal and fleeting they perhaps appeared to be.[19] J. A. Veraart, a radical Catholic, was one such democratic tick in the conservative Catholic fur. He made passionate efforts during the whole inter-war period to transform the RKSP into a Christian Social party.[20]

The RKSP was forced to choose a more social course because of the pressure from the Catholic Workers' Movement, which every now and again threatened to form its own party. In so far as the party succeeded in binding the Workers' Movement move tightly to itself by developing into a people's party, it was necessary and possible to make Catholic social teaching into one of the basic tenets of the party. The ideal was a Christian state of the future, on the basis of an organically organized society. A corporatist societal order would be based on the principles of solidarity and subsidiarity. Dutch Catholicism tried just after the First World War to put this teaching into practice with the introduction of R. K. Bedrijfsradenstelsel, a works council.[21] This first attempt at a public organization of works councils in modern society turned out to be a failure. Yet it did force the RKSP to discuss the underlying social theory of its policies more thoroughly. The party tried, in the following period, to develop its Christian democratic identity in this direction.[22]

The RKSP also developed its national identity in the inter-war period. Socio-economic questions had become, since the First World War, ever more the main concern of politics.[23] This led to the RKSP – as well as the other parties, especially the Social Democratic Labour Party (SDAP) – becoming ever more aware of their task of seeing to public welfare and, as a result of this, their national responsibility as well, not just for 'their' pillar. In the measure of their wanting to be a proper people's party, the Catholics progressively moved away from their antagonism towards the SDAP of the pre-war period and from their coalition with the Protestants. At the same time, they adopted to some extent Christian democratic thinking inclusive of a national mission.[24] The new ideological orientation was connected to one of the biggest political issues of the inter-war years: would the two parties, the Socialists and the Catholics, have anything to do with each other or not? When and how could the alignments in Dutch politics change? As a reaction to the bishops' forbidding of a collaboration with the Socialists, Nolens, as the Catholics' political leader, created some room for manoeuvre by formulating the policy that the RKSP would only strive for such a collaboration in the case of 'extreme necessity'. This policy could be used, depending on the circumstances, either as a threat or as a bait.

A possible collaboration with the Socialists remained hotly contested in the Catholic camp: first, because the bishops forbade it and in the 1930s even brought out a pastoral letter that was read out from the pulpit every year, in which socialism and communism were judged to be principally anti-Church and anti-religious and a more serious threat than National

Socialism at its most extreme;[25] second, because socialism was all the more threatening for the Catholic leadership elite, not only the bishops, but also the social and political elites, as Social Democracy distanced itself from revolutionary views and turned out to be a normal party that was acceptable to Catholic citizens. Under pressure from the economic and political crisis of the 1930s, the question was whether the time of 'extreme necessity' had come. The Catholics, prompted by the encyclical *Quadragesimo Anno* of 1931, were especially aware of the task of creating a 'new society'. This was even more the case as the SDAP, with its 'plan of action' and other socio-political proposals, proved to be a challenging alternative to the long-lived Catholic coalition with the Protestants. A government was finally formed in 1939 in which both Socialists and Catholics took part. The social and national conditions for such a political change of course were for the RKSP at last fulfilled, or in other words, the Catholics ended their historical detour towards Christian democracy. But before they could put their newly acquired Christian democratic identity to the test, National Socialist Germany invaded the Netherlands in 1940.

AN END AND A BEGINNING

The Second World War was simultaneously an end and a new beginning. The German occupation destroyed the political and social structures in the Netherlands within a year. The RKSP was liquidated on 4 July 1941 by a command coming from the head of the German occupation, Reichskommissar Arthur Seyss-Inquart. The party secretary at that time, H. A. M. T. Kolfschoten, brought important archive material into safety just in time before the German occupiers closed the party office.[26] From then on the Dutch Catholics were in a political diaspora. Numerous attempts to keep up contacts within the party and between the remaining democratic parties were not particularly successful.

At the beginning, efforts were still being made to find a *modus vivendi* in the new political order. Some Catholic politicians wanted to save, through compromise, what there was to salvage of confessional and national values.[27] There was no question of an organized resistance to the German occupational powers in the ranks of the former RKSP. The former political elites were not in agreement about their position as regards the resistance movement; some wanted to keep their distance from it, others out of conviction or by chance joined the resistance. Some top functionaries of the RKSP were taken hostage by the German occupiers and deported to concentration camps. Two former party leaders – C. M. J. F. Goseling and T. J. Verschuur – died in concentration camps, one in Buchenwald and the other in Sachsenhausen.

In this terrible time of terror and political homelessness the bishops took over the political leadership of the Dutch Catholics. Jan de Jong, the Archbishop of Utrecht, especially showed the faithful the way on fundamental questions of human rights and national independence. His moral and political influence went far beyond his own Catholic Church; he became a symbol of Catholic resistance and contributed greatly to Catholics being at last recognized as fully equal Dutch citizens. Immediately after the war De Jong was made cardinal by Pope Pius XII for his achievements. He was the first Dutch cardinal since the time of the Reformation.

What the Dutch parties did not succeed in doing before the war was forced upon them by the German occupiers, and this quite literally. They imprisoned, for a time, the entire Dutch political, social and cultural leadership elite in the same internment camp.[28] Thus, the leaders of the different pillars came together in a way that might not otherwise have happened, giving a decisive impulse to mutual acceptance, a nudge even in the direction of a breakthrough, which was supposed to go beyond the merely necessary. This coming together allowed the different parties to prepare for a new political and societal beginning after liberation.[29] When this came, it turned out, however, that a complete break with the pre-war period was impossible. The fact that the Dutch were liberated from the German occupiers in two phases, first the southern provinces, and then the northern provinces, only at the end of the war, significantly reduced the chances of a new party-political beginning. This was especially true of the Catholics, as the southern, predominantly Catholic provinces were liberated first and their process of restoration could be started several months earlier.

J. A. Bornewasser has aptly characterized the transformation of the RKSP into the Catholic People's Party (KVP) as 'a new-old party'. Considering the continuing strength of the old Catholic elites, which did not want a break with the political and social structures of the pre-war period, the Catholic renewers, who were relatively poorly organized,[30] did not succeed in their aim of forming an inter-confessional party. Those thinking along the same old lines could, with the support of the bishops, build the KVP on the foundations of the RKSP in the first years after the war. This 'new-old' party learned from history. There was no break with the pre-war period, structurally speaking, but a new era did dawn in terms of its policies. Collaboration with the Socialists proved to be necessary. On the international level new perspectives gradually opened up in the direction of a closer transnational Christian Democratic alliance. The time for neutrality was over, and from the Christian democratic standpoint a new European beginning was imminent. The Catholics ended their historical detour, from collaboration with the Social Democracy Party in the case of 'extreme necessity' to a Christian democratic orientation. It was only after the Second World War that the 'Roman–red' or 'black–red' collaboration contributed greatly to social reforms and the formation of an elaborate welfare state. Two general characteristics of all Christian democratic parties came then finally to the forefront: a social profile as well as the potential for greater national and European integration.

NOTES

1 For the history of the Catholic People's Party in the post-war period and its prehistory as the RKSP, see J. A. Bornewasser, *Katholieke Volkspartij, 1945–1980*, vol. 1, *Herkomst en groei (tot 1963)* (Nijmegen 1995). With respect to leading RKSP politicians, see among others Gerald Brom, *Schaepman* (Haarlem 1936); Jules Persyn, *Dr. Schaepman*, 3 vols ('s-Gravenhage and Antwerp 1912–27); J. C. van Wely, *Schaepman. Levensverhaal* (Bussum 1954); J. H. J. M. Witlox, *Schaepman als Staatsman*, 3 vols (Amsterdam 1960) J. P. Gribling, *P. J. M. Aalberse, 1871–1948* (Utrecht 1961); idem, *Willem Hubert Nolens, 1860–1931 Uit het leven van een priester-staatsman* (Assen 1978); Jac Bosmans, *Romme. Biografie 1896–1946* (Utrecht 1991). Of special relevance, because it deals with the attitude of the Catholic Workers' Movement to the formation of a Catholic party in the Netherlands, is Jos van Meeuwen, *Lijden aan eenheid. Katholieke arbeiders op zoek naar hun politiek recht (1897–1929)* (Hilversum 1998). For confessional politics in the Netherlands in the twentieth century and also for the problems of inter-confessionalism in the inter-war period, see Paul Luykx and Hans Righart (eds), *Van de pastorie naar het torentje. Een eeuw confessionele politiek* ('s-Gravenhage 1991).
2 There are some key confessional terms that are indispensable for understanding the complex confessional relationships in the Netherlands. If one can talk about Christian democracy at all in the period before the Second World War, if not even up until the 1960s, then it was only in a Catholic context. The term 'Christian' is in the Dutch language historically claimed by the Protestants, and this is why it was so difficult to speak about Christian democracy.
3 Jacques Janssen, *Nederland als religieuze proeftuin* (Nijmegen 1998).
4 In order to avoid misunderstanding, it is necessary to draw attention to the fact that the term 'Catholic emancipation' has its own special importance in Dutch historiography. It describes a Catholic movement that made great efforts to get rid of the historical discrimination against the Catholic population on a social, cultural and political level. The RKSP was the political instrument of this movement.
5 Arend Lijphart, *The Politics of Accommodation. Pluralism and Democracy in the Netherlands* (Berkeley and Los Angeles, CA 1968).
6 J. P. Gribling, 'Uit de geschiedenis van de RKSP', special issue of *Politiek perspectief. Tweemaandelijks tijdschrift van het Centrum voor Staatkundige Vorming* vol. 5, no. 6 (1976), pp. 3–55.
7 See Guido Müller's chapter in this book.
8 Bornewasser, *Katholieke Volkspartij*, p. 93.
9 Ibid., p. 73; Gribling, *Staatspartij*, p. 32.
10 Gribling, *Staatspartij*, pp. 10–17.
11 Bornewasser, *Katholieke Volkspartij*, pp. 40–2, 96–7.
12 Van Meeuwen, *Lijden aan eenheid*, pp. 152, 523.
13 Bornewasser, *Katholieke Volkspartij*, pp. 62–3.

14 Document, 'The Social Question 17.12.1891', in Jan Roes, *Bronnen van de katholicke arbeidersbewegung in Nederland. Toespraken, brieven en artikelen van Alphons Ariëns, 1887–1901* (Baarn 1982), pp. 96–126; H. J. A. M. Schaepman, *Rerum Novarum. Rede over de jongste encyclick van Z. H. Paus Leo XIII, gehouden op 15 juli 1891 te Vlissingen* (Utrecht 1891).
15 See Gribling, *Nolens*.
16 See Gribling, *Aalberse*.
17 For comprehensive biographies of two influential priests, see Gerard Brom, *Alphons Ariëns*, 2 vols (Amsterdam 1941); J. P. Colsen, *Poels* (Roermond and Maaseik 1955).
18 D. Th. Kuiper, 'Een eeuw "confessionele politiek" in ontwikkelingsperspectief', in Luykx and Righart, *Van de pastorie*, pp. 161–74, here pp. 166–8.
19 Bornewasser, *Katholieke Volkspartij*, pp. 44–6; Gribling, *Staatspartij*, p. 36.
20 Sjef Schmiermann, 'Prof. dr. J. A. Veraart (1886–1955). Een recalcitrant katholiek democraat', *Jaarboek van het Katholiek Documentatie Centrum*, vol. 20 (1990), pp. 122–42. See also Renier Rutjens, 'Tussen groepsbelang en solidarisme. De "ideologie" van de rooms-katholieke vakbeweging en haar verhouding, tot de katholieke sociale leer, 1900–1920', *Jaarboek van het Katholiek Documentatie Centrum*, vol. 23 (1993), pp. 22–54. Veraart later led the alliance of Catholic politicians in exile in London, the International Union of Christian Democrats. See also Wolfram Kaiser's chapter in this book.
21 W. G. J. M. Tomassen, *Het R.-K. Bedrijfsradenstelsel (1919–1922). De eerste poging tot publiekrechtelijke bedrijfsorganisatie op organisch-solidaristische grondslag binnen de moderne industriele samenleving in Nederland*, Ph.D. (University of Leiden 1974).
22 Bornewasser, *Katholieke Volkspartij*, pp. 39–40, 91–4.
23 Rudolf Anton Koole and Hans Martien ten Napel, 'De riante positie in het vermaledijde "midden". Confessionele machtsvorming op nationaal niveau', in Luykx and Righart, *Van de pastorie*, pp. 72–92, here pp. 78, 86.
24 Bornewasser, *Katholieke Volkspartij*, pp. 68–72.
25 Ibid., p. 97; Bornewasser calls it an 'episcopal faux pas'. See Paul Luykx, 'Van de dorpspastorie naar het torentje. Kerken en de macht der confessionele partijen', in Luykx and Righart, *Van de pastorie*, pp. 35–71, here pp. 45–6.
26 Bornewasser, *Katholieke Volkspartij*, p. 155.
27 Ibid., p. 117.
28 Madelon de Keizer, *De gijzelaars van Sint Michielsgestel. Een eliteberaad in oorlogstijd* (Alphen aan den Rijn 1979).
29 Jan Bank, *Opkomst en ondergang van de Nederlandse Volks Beweging (NVB)* (Deventer 1978).
30 A. F. Manning, 'Geen doorbraak van de oude structuren', in idem, *Mensen en situaties. Scènes uit het katholiek leven in de negentiende en twintigste eeuw* (Baarn 1990), pp. 302–28.

5

Religion, Class and Language: The Catholic Party in Belgium

Emmanuel Gerard

The history of the Catholic Party in inter-war Belgium is marked by an important shift. It evolved from a party of Catholics, encompassing different, if not contradictory, political forces in one confessional federation, into a people's party that anticipated the post-war reforms. In the 1920s the Catholic Party was characterized by a lack of organization, of programmes and of leadership. In the 1930s a new party concept developed, one that stressed structural as well as programmatic unity and the integration of formerly separate forces. This evolution was the result of an interaction with the dynamics of the political regime, especially the need for strong governmental parties, as well as with the emergence of a new generation, moulded in the spirit of Catholic Action. The relationship with the Church and the programme of social and economic reform have to be considered with respect to these two forms of the Catholic Party in the inter-war period.

PARTY FORMATION IN THE NINETEENTH CENTURY

Significantly, Belgium had a stable political regime from its foundation in 1830. The most important characteristics were the monarchy, parliamentary government and a broad set of rights and freedoms. Although parliamentary government became firmly established after 1848 and the role of parliamentary groups increased, the King continued to play an important role even after the First World War, especially in the process of cabinet formation. The King used his prerogatives to nominate fairly moderate politicians, especially when the Catholic Party was in power. Political participation was limited to a census elite during the nineteenth century. In 1893, a system of universal male suffrage combined with plural votes was introduced. Proportional representation was implemented for the first time in 1899 and was strengthened in 1919, when the principle of 'one man, one vote' was also accepted, although the vote was not given to women. The transition to mass politics after the First World War did not threaten the foundations of liberal democracy, although the formation of the first post-war cabinet in November 1918 was considered a *coup d'état* by many conservatives.

Moreover, it is important to note that Belgium did not experience a rupture between State and Church in the nineteenth century. The national revolution of 1830 was the result of the combined forces of liberals and Catholics, and consequently the liberal constitution of 1831 met the grievances of the Church. After the separation from the predominantly Protestant Netherlands, Catholicism as the religion of most Belgians was able to develop and expand, due to constitutional provisions such as freedom of education and freedom of association. However, the national role of the Catholics did not prevent a growing polarization between an emerging Liberal Party, grouped around the masonic lodges, and a Conservative Party, which was closely connected with the Church. The Liberal Party, representing the interests of the new urban middle class, fought the monarchical tendencies of the new regime as well as the prominent role of the Church in public life. It came to power in 1847 and maintained this until 1884. The Conservative Party, which started to organize itself in the 1850s, was hindered by a tension between clerics and lay politicians. The latter stressed their autonomy and the national character of their party, refusing a 'Catholic' label. The core of the Conservative Party was constituted by the parliamentary right, the electoral committees united in the Fédération des Associations Conservatrices et des Cercles Catholiques (1868) and the press. As a result of the so-called school war of 1879, the Conservative Party assumed a more confessional character and the influence of the bishops increased.

The Catholic Party came to power in 1884 and managed to stay in government until the First World War. This longstanding dominance was due to the popular basis of the Catholic Church and the growth of a dense network of popular associations, built up more intensively from the end of the nineteenth century. Party competition increased, however, when the Socialist Parti Ouvrier Belge was founded in 1885. As an alternative to socialism, Catholic priests and laymen tried to organize industrial workers, craftsmen and farmers, especially in the Flemish provinces. In 1890, the Belgian Farmers' League, the Belgische Boerenbond, was launched, followed in 1891 by the Belgian People's League, the Belgische Volksbond/ Ligue démocratique belge. These organizations had a firmly established Catholic foundation and were supported by a number of younger clerics, encouraged by the appeal of the Pope in the encyclical *Rerum novarum*. They constituted the core of a nascent Christian democracy and gained more and more influence in the Catholic Party at the expense of the older Fédération des Cercles, dominated by the conservative urban middle class, which nevertheless retained its dominant position until 1914. Backed by a powerful Catholic Party, the Catholic Church created an impressive network of schools, charitable institutions and social organizations in the framework of a liberal democracy. This explains to a large extent the attachment of the Church to the parliamentary strategy of the Catholic Party, and the absence of intransigent positions *vis-à-vis* a fundamentally liberal regime.[1]

Belgium was initially a unitary state with limited autonomy for the nine provinces and some 2,500 municipalities. The unity of the state, however, was threatened by pronounced regional differentiation in the sphere of economics and culture. From the start of the nineteenth century the Walloon provinces of Hainaut and Liège, in the south, experienced rapid industrialization. In contrast, the Flemish provinces in the north (with the exception of Ghent and Antwerp), lagged behind in the economic development and retained a largely agrarian character. This economic antagonism was emphasized by a difference in language and cultural development. From 1830 onwards, French became introduced as the language of government, justice and education all over the country, even in the northern provinces, where the vernacular language was and still is Flemish. The inferior position of the north, in economic as well as cultural respects, constituted the basis of the Flemish movement and a growing Flemish identity within the Belgian state in the second half of the nineteenth century. The duality was deepened by the German occupation during the First World War. The German *Flamenpolitik* nurtured an anti-Belgian Flemish nationalism. In the inter-war period, important language reforms were carried out to meet the grievances of the Flemish movement. The importance of this issue for our subject lies, first, in the strong position of the Church and the Catholic Party in the north and in the close connection between Catholics and the Flemish movement, and, second, in the different orientation of the Flemish and the francophone Catholics, the former being more oriented towards the Netherlands and Germany, the latter towards France and the Latin world.

A FRAGMENTED PARTY IN THE 1920S

In August 1921, the Catholic Party was reformed and the Katholiek Verbond van België/Union Catholique Belge founded. This Catholic Union was a confederation of four organizations, namely, the Fédération des Cercles, which was the old federation of electoral committees recruiting among the bourgeois middle class; the Belgische Boerenbond; the Algemeen Christelijk Werkersverbond/Ligue Nationale des Travailleurs Chrétiens, the National League of the Christian Workers, created in 1921; and the Christelijke Landsbond van de Middenstand, or National League of the Christian Middle Class, an organization for lower-middle-class shopkeepers and businessmen, founded in 1919.[2] According to its founders, the Catholic Union was built on the idea of social harmony – a concept cherished by social Catholicism. The Catholic Union had a misleading name, however. It created the illusion that political unity was realized. This was not the case. On the contrary, strong centrifugal forces came to the fore in the post-war years.

The war put an end to the Catholic hegemony of thirty years. In June 1912, the Catholic government still stood firm and was successful in an electoral confrontation with the left, the *Cartel des gauches*, on the school question. The outbreak of the war in August 1914 then led to a *union sacrée* between all the parties. Gradually, the Catholics had to yield terrain to the left. In January 1916, the Catholic government in exile at Le Havre in France reluctantly accepted some leaders of the former Liberal and Socialist opposition as cabinet members. Finally, in November 1918 the Catholic Party had to give up its dominant position. King Albert, alarmed by the revolutions in Europe and preoccupied that the monarchy could be held responsible for the longstanding conservative and Catholic government, used the days of confusion after the armistice to sack the war cabinet and replace it with a real cabinet of national unity, the so-called Loppem cabinet.[3] The Catholic Party, although still possessing an absolute majority in the two houses of parliament, received only half of the ministerial portfolios, the other half being given to Liberals and Socialists. Moreover, it had to accept the introduction of the single vote.[4] The general elections of 16 November 1919 then resulted in a fundamental redrawing of the political map. The Catholic Party lost its absolute majority, although it remained the largest formation. It was nearly matched by the Socialist Party, which was the real winner of the election. The Liberal Party was reduced to a minor third party. However, the constituencies of these three parties differed considerably. The Catholic Party held an overall majority in Flanders, while the Socialist Party dominated Wallonia and the Liberal Party Brussels. These electoral figures were reproduced during the entire inter-war period, except for the 1936 elections.[5]

The democratic spirit of the post-war period also caused a shift of power within the Catholic Party. The Fédération des Cercles lost its leading position and had to give way, especially in Flanders, to *flamingants* and Christian Democrats. In September 1919, a Catholic Flemish League, the Katholieke Vlaamse Landsbond, was founded, demanding language reforms and especially the use of the Flemish language in government, justice and education. It was strongly supported by the Flemish Catholics. Catholic deputies supporting this programme formed a separate parliamentary group, the so-called Catholic Flemish Group, or Katholieke Vlaamse Kamergroep, led by Frans Van Cauwelaert. At the same time the Christian Labour Movement became radicalized. Unions and workers' associations rejected the paternalism of well-intentioned middle-class politicians and clerics. They called for autonomy and founded in July 1921 the National League of Christian Workers, the Algemeen Christelijk Werkersverbond/Ligue Nationale des Travailleurs Chrétiens ACW/LNTC, imitating the Socialist Parti Ouvrier. The ACW was an umbrella organization in which unions, co-operatives, mutualities, women and youth organizations were bound together. The ambitions of the ACW were clearly political: it wanted participation of the Catholic workers in political life through their own representatives and the realization of a programme of social reform. The deputies linked to the ACW also formed a separate parliamentary group, the so-called Christian Democratic Group.[6] The term 'Christian democracy' – a rather suspect expression before 1914 – was now used without any hesitation by the Christian Labour Movement.[7]

This shift in power was accompanied by huge tensions, which in the first half of the 1920s led to overtly expressed antagonism and even to a rupture. At the elections of 1919, 1921 and 1925 Catholics fought in dispersed order, especially in Flanders, and in several districts two Catholic lists competed for votes. The Catholic parliamentary group, the so-called Droite (Right), continued to exist nominally, but it consisted of several subgroups. The cabinet formation from 1921 on – after the fall of the last cabinet of national unity – increased the tension. Would the Catholic Party form a coalition with the Liberals or with the Socialists? Christian Democrats and Flemish Catholics fought, almost overtly, the Conservative Theunis cabinet (1921–25), supported enthusiastically by Liberals and conservative Catholics. In 1925 the Catholic Party split when Christian Democrats and Flemish Catholics supported a coalition with the Socialists, the so-called *gouvernement démocratique* Poullet-Vandervelde (1925–26), which was attacked and brought down after only eleven months by conservative Catholics and Liberals.

Why then did the Catholic Party, facing a diminution of its influence in government, disintegrate? The explanation for the increased fragmentation of the Catholic Party is to be found in the climate of confessional pacification during and following the war.[8] It was a period of *union sacrée* between Catholics, Liberals and Socialists. Although the old antagonism between the Liberal and Socialist left and the Catholic Right did not disappear during the war, there were signs of mutual respect. Cardinal Désiré Mercier, the Archbishop of Malines (1906–26), enjoyed general prestige as a symbol of the patriotic resistance against the German invader, and numerous Catholics collaborated with left politicians in the Comité National de Secours et d'Alimentation. In the Loppem cabinet, Liberals and Socialists accepted the school truce in a gesture of national reconciliation and thus the granting of state subsidies to Catholic schools, in return for universal male suffrage.[9] In still other fields the parties of the left met some of the demands of the Church. They no longer opposed a legal position for congregations and charitable institutions and accepted the legal recognition of union pluralism. The necessity to have a Catholic Party seemed to have disappeared. Instead of confessional issues, other political problems came to the fore: the international position of Belgium and the attitude towards Germany, monetary and fiscal problems, the social protection of the workers through reductions in their working time, the indexation of salaries and social insurance schemes, the recognition of the Flemish language in public life, etc. Not religion, but class and language became the main cleavages. They were what divided Catholics. At the same time, the left also experienced a rupture. The *Cartel des gauches* was no longer effective after the war. It made the Catholic Party a centre party that was necessary in the numerous inter-war coalitions. Post-war reconstruction thus created the opportunity for new alliances.

With hindsight, the Catholic Union seems to have been the answer to the setbacks of the post-war period, a means to overcome and transcend internal division and to fight the rise of the left. It was not.[10] The Catholic Union, based on the so-called representation of interests, is the formula by which workers and farmers tried to end the domination of the bourgeoisie. It confirmed the fragmentation of political forces by devolving autonomy to the farmers' and workers' organizations against the will of the Fédération des Cercles, which tried to defend its leadership role. At the same time it resulted in a shift from the francophone to the Flemish Catholics. The Fédération accepted the Catholic Union, because it could not refuse it, but it did not co-operate.

Based on a false symmetry, the Catholic Union was not able to bring about real unity. The four founding organizations had an equal representation on the executive committee, but they were very different in nature, importance and regional distribution. The Farmers' League and the Workers' League were mass organizations combining educational activities, social action and political representation; their constituency was mainly in Flanders. The Workers' League was in itself a complex and all-embracing network of unions, mutualities, co-operatives, women's and youth organizations. The core was formed by the Confederation of Christian Trade Unions, the Algemeen Christelijk Vakverbond-Confédération des Syndicats Chrétiens. The organization for the lower-middle class was a negligible force in political, as well as in social respects. The Fédération des Cercles was an exclusively political body, strongly established in Brussels and Wallonia, but very weak in Flanders. It did not accept the idea of a political representation of group interests. On the contrary, it considered the farmers' and workers' associations as exclusively social organizations, and tried to strengthen its claim to political leadership by itself creating associations for workers, employees and the lower-middle class.[11] In fact, the Catholic Union did not prevent the Catholic

Party from being characterized by a strong antagonism between a conservative and mainly francophone wing, and a Christian Democratic and mainly Flemish wing.

The Catholic Union did not create strong leadership and a well-organized party structure. It was only a committee – and for most Catholics an obscure committee – meeting irregularly. It was a national committee of representatives of the four founding organizations, without any link to the local party organization or to the parliamentary groups. At the local level, party organization could vary according to the division of power between the competing sections of the Fédération des Cercles, the Farmers' and the Workers' League. The parliamentary groups made decisions without any interference from outside, except for the Christian Democrats who established a close relationship with the national leadership of the ACW. The most important contribution of the Catholic Union was the drafting of an electoral platform, and the arbitration it offered on the occasion of the general elections.

In fact, what was called the Catholic Party continued to be an alliance of organizations, newspapers and deputies, organized more informally than formally. It was built upon a *modus vivendi* between Catholic organizations. The 'representation of interests' – also called the federal formula – was a convenient device to keep Catholics 'united', notwithstanding their political, social and regional differences. The term 'Catholic Party' did not refer to a clearly structured, strongly directed and programme-based political organization, but to the Catholic world in all its forms. The Catholic Union was only one element of this machinery, and a badly functioning one.

The pre-war *modus vivendi* between conservatives and Christian Democrats was disturbed by the democratization in the post-war years, and then re-established after 1927. Three reasons appear to be important for this. First of all, the failure of the 'democratic government' and the refusal of the Socialists to co-operate in government from 1927 to 1935. This alleviated much tension, because there was no alternative to the Catholic–Liberal coalition. Second, the conservative leader, Jules Renkin, campaigned to restore Catholic unity in order to contain socialism. He especially addressed his conservative followers and advocated concessions to Christian Democrats and Flemish Catholics as a lesser evil. Third, Cardinal Mercier intervened discreetly during the formation of the 'democratic government' in June 1925. He warned the Christian Democrats not to destroy Catholic unity.[12] His successor, Cardinal Van Roey, the new Archbishop of Malines (1926–61), also intervened discreetly during the formation of the Jaspar cabinet in November 1927, in order to prevent Christian Democrats from taking radical positions on the military question and jeopardizing the chances for reconciliation with the conservative wing through collaboration in the new cabinet.

These interventions highlight the important role of the Catholic hierarchy.[13] The bishops had intervened in Belgian politics since 1830, but since the school war of 1879 their intervention was more systematic and their influence on the Catholic Party more direct. They imposed their arbitration to solve internal conflicts, and exhorted the faithful from the pulpit during electoral campaigns. However, in the aftermath of the First World War they were troubled by the new setting of Belgian politics. It should be noticed that the bishops did not intervene collectively and publicly during the electoral campaigns of 1919, 1921 and 1925 although the division among Catholics had never been so deep. They were in fact themselves divided on several issues, especially on the Flemish question.[14] Finally, in September 1925, they condemned Flemish nationalism. And in October 1932, when the parties of the left threatened to abolish state subsidies to Catholic schools, the bishops issued a pastoral letter to support the Catholic Party, dubbed as 'the only bulwark of our religious freedoms'.[15] These public interventions by the bishops did much to strengthen the image of the Catholic Party as a confessional party.

Its confessional character was also enhanced by the involvement of the clergy at the parochial level and by the influence of the workers', farmers' and middle-class organizations. These organizations, with many priests as leading figures, were considered by the bishops as subordinate to the Church, and were assigned as their main objective the re-Christianization of society. Yet the Christian democratic lay leadership opposed this view and claimed autonomy for themselves. They were eager to play a political role. At the local level, the involvement of the parochial clergy was direct, and to all intents and purposes the parochial community of practising Catholics was the local Catholic Party.

On the other hand, the term 'confessional party' is not entirely appropriate. It did not mean either that the Catholic Party was a branch of the Church, or that it would address only Catholics. Actually, the Fédération des Cercles continued to reject the confessional label. Its leaders continued to declare publicly that the Catholic Party was an autonomous and national party, open to everyone. The closer one got to the local level, the stronger the impact of the clergy on the organization and the stronger the confessional character, but the closer to parliament and government, the more autonomous and less exclusively confessional was the *modus operandi* of the Catholics. At the top level, there was an ongoing co-optation of moderate politicians through the King's action during cabinet formation. Technocrats such as Léon Delacroix, Henri Jaspar and Georges Theunis were appointed Prime Minister by the King, and as such were imposed as leaders on to the Catholic Party.

Between 1918 and 1927, some conservative Catholics in particular considered religious defence as too small a foundation for a political party. They proclaimed the end of a Catholic Party, advocating a lasting conservative alliance with the Liberals. But most conservatives did not want a break-up of the Catholic Party. Maurice Houtart, representative of the Fédération des Cercles in the executive committee of the Catholic Union, declared in May 1926, referring to conservative threats to leave the Catholic Union, that it was essential to maintain the formula as it could become necessary again at any time to defend religious interests together.[16]

The public declarations of the bishops were not so much destined for Christian Democrats and Conservatives within the Catholic Party, but for the Flemish nationalists. The new demands of the Flemish movement after the war resulted in a strongly profiled position of the Flemish Catholics in the Catholic Party. However, the 'moderate programme' of these Flemish Catholics was rejected by an emerging Nationalist Party that claimed self-government. The condemnation of Flemish nationalism by the bishops in September 1925 marked the start of a hard struggle between Catholic Flemish nationalists and the bishops. The former disputed the right of the Catholic hierarchy to intervene in political matters. They criticized, for the first time, what they called 'political Catholicism', especially after their electoral success in 1929. The growth of an almost exclusively Catholic Flemish nationalism destroyed the unity of the Catholic world and of the Catholic Party, since from then on two parties recruited among Catholics.[17]

If one tries to assess the Catholic political ideas, especially those with respect to social and economic reform in the 1920s, one should, of course, take into account the division of Catholics. Catholics are bound together not by a political programme, but by the defence of Church and religion. They are strongly divided on some important aspects of public life. In addition, it is necessary to distinguish between the political body of the Catholic Party *stricto sensu* and some Catholic periodicals, groups or intellectual circles interested in political affairs. Of course there was some interaction, but Catholic deputies were not responsible for the sometimes fantastic – and mostly anti-democratic – blueprints that circulated in some circles. In the 1920s for instance, the influence of Charles Maurras and the Action française on francophone Catholic middle-class youth was strong, but its direct influence in the Fédération des Cercles was rather limited.[18]

The Catholic Union offered a political platform of generalities. It was written in a pragmatic spirit and was rather moderate, since the Catholic Party was a government party. The Fédération des Cercles and the workers' and farmers' organizations had more elaborate programmes, sometimes containing conflicting ideas. In general, the programme of the conservative wing was rather inspired by a middle-class preoccupation with good management: budget orthodoxy, as little state intervention as possible, minimal taxation. This had nothing to do with a Catholic political doctrine. In contrast, the farmers' and the workers' organizations also offered a set of concrete reforms, but mostly as part of a broader view of society based on *Rerum novarum*. The liberal economy should be substituted by an organized economy, in which ethical considerations were to be more important than profit and competition. An essential part of this Christian Democratic programme was the collaboration between capital and labour that was to be realized through some form of corporatism. In the 1920s this corporatism did not threaten the foundations of liberal democracy, since it focused on consultations in social and economic affairs, legal recognition of joint committees and their conventions. From 1921 onwards the idea of a so-called *bedrijfsorganisatie* formed part of the programme of the Christian trade unions. In that year a first Christian Democratic proposal was introduced in parliament.[19] In fact, the first joint committees resulted from an initiative of the Socialist Minister of Labour in 1919. There was less interest in this programme in the second half of the 1920s, as a result of economic prosperity, however.

One topic existed in the social sphere that rallied all Catholics, and that was the family issue. Closely linked to a programme of religious defence, the defence of the family was one of the basic features of the Catholic Party programme. 'Religion, property, family' was one of the old slogans to rally all Catholics. In government and in parliament, Catholics supported all measures to guarantee the rights of the family and to improve its material conditions. An important law on allocations to families was passed in 1930, partly inspired by the idea that women should be banned from the workplace.

THE EMERGENCE OF A PEOPLE'S PARTY IN THE 1930S

Fifteen years after the foundation of the Catholic Union, which had confirmed the existing fragmentation rather than creating unity, a fundamental party reform was undertaken in 1936. In that year the Catholic Union was replaced with the Blok der Katholieken van België/Bloc Catholique Belge, which in many respects can be seen as prefiguring the Christelijke Volkspartij created in 1945. This reform affected not only the structure of the party, but also its relation to the Church and its social and economic programme. Two factors appear to be important in explaining the shift that occurred. On the one hand are the requirements of a political system that lacked stability and needed stronger parties. On the other, the influence of a new generation, socialized within Catholic Action or inspired by the so-called revolution from the right. They advocated a single-party organization to carry out political, economic and social reform.

In the inter-war period, from November 1918 until May 1940, Belgium was characterized by remarkable governmental instability. No fewer than 22 cabinets and still more cabinet crises succeeded. One of the reasons for this instability was the new phenomenon of coalition cabinets. Coalition government not only required compromises among parties, but also strong party leadership to implement them. In this respect the Catholic Party was an additional element of instability. Catholics participated in every cabinet, and with only two exceptions named the Prime Minister. But they were divided. In every cabinet at least two Catholic strands can be distinguished: Conservatives and Christian Democrats. They each had their own congresses which decided on government policy.

One example of the lack of direction in the Catholic Party was the Van Zeeland cabinet. In March 1935, Belgium suffered from a severe banking crisis. The deflationary policy appeared to have exhausted the economy. An important shift in economic policy was carried out by the technocrat Paul Van Zeeland and his cabinet of national unity, which the Socialists joined after eight years of opposition. Although a Catholic believer, Van Zeeland explicitly distanced himself from the Catholic Party. He announced a devaluation and a new economic policy that contained some *dirigiste* measures, such as banking regulations. The parliamentary Right, which as a group was ignored by the new Prime Minister during the negotiations, reacted in a divided way: 31 Catholic deputies supported the government, with 31 opposed.[20] Of course, this weakened the Catholic position. This and other incidents convinced some Catholic politicians that it was necessary to establish an effective leadership, within as well as outside parliament. Hubert Pierlot, who in May 1935 was elected chairman of the Catholic Union, was one of these leaders. His main objective was to strengthen the authority of the Catholic Union, which was until that time mostly a construction on paper. Pierlot started a reform that was to go further than he himself had expected.[21]

A second factor of change was Catholic Action. Official Catholic Action in Belgium started with the Association Catholique de la Jeunesse Belge (ACJB) formed in 1921. The ACJB leadership – in particular Abbé Picard – took Catholic Action in Italy as its example, implying no involvement in politics. In Italy, where the Partito Popolare Italiano (PPI) was discredited and fascism on the rise, such an orientation could perhaps seem justified. But in Belgium, where Catholics were still a major force in government, it was a peculiar orientation, especially as Catholic youth had traditionally been at the service of the Catholic Party. The new orientation was not inspired by a choice for political pluralism among Catholics, nor by a simple division of labour, but – just as in Italy – by a distrust and even a rejection of liberal democracy. For the ACJB, democracy and secularization were two sides of the same coin.

Symptomatic of this orientation of Belgian Catholic Action was the conflict between the ACJB leadership and the Christian Democrats. Abbé Picard reopened the old controversy about the encyclical *Graves de comuni re* of 1901, and accused the Christian Democrats of contravening papal instructions. Their first mission should be a spiritual and not a political one: to re-Christianize the workers through social action. In that respect they should be considered part of Catholic Action, with all of the ensuing consequences. The conflict focused on the Jeunesse ouvrière chrétienne (JOC) – originally the Jeunesse Syndicaliste – created as part of the Christian Workers' Movement by Abbé Joseph Cardijn. The ACJB leadership did not accept the division of the youth movement based on the class principle, and the absorption of the workers' youth by the Christian Democrats. In the eyes of the ACJB, the Christian Democrats were simply imitating the Socialists. This conflict used up a lot of energy – sometimes it seemed a sterile scholastic dispute among clerics – but eventually brought about a compromise, supported strongly by the new archbishop, Van Roey. Official Catholic Action was to be based on the class principle[22] – this was obviously a concession to the JOC – but all youth organizations had to accept the bishops as their leading authorities (and not lay organizations such as the ACW) and could not become involved in politics. The implementation of this compromise caused many difficulties, especially in the relationship between the JOC and the ACW.[23] However, the most important effect of this compromise was the rallying of all youth organizations under one single banner, that of Catholic Action, with its offensive rhetoric of a social reign of the Christ the King and its diffuse criticism of liberal democracy, which was incompatible with the opportunist practice of a Catholic Party involved in parliamentary politics.

Catholic youth was not indifferent towards politics, but it could not identify with the politics of the day. When this youth became the young adults of the 1930s, they wanted to engage in politics, but not in the 'old' politics. This scepticism resulted in the creation of several political movements that were rather critical towards the Catholic Party. The best known of these was the Rexist movement led by Léon Degrelle, Rex being derived from *Christus Rex*. These movements demanded that the Catholic Party carry out a real 'Catholic policy'. In that way, they were more intransigent Catholics than the politicians involved in the Catholic Party. At the same time, they asked for more than a confessional party, since the Catholic policy they advocated was not simply a confessional one, based on the rights of Church and religion, but a policy of social reform derived from the papal encyclicals.[24]

The years 1933–36 constituted a decisive period in the design of a new Catholic Party. Five important events can be seen as catalysts. First of all, there was the Nazi seizure of power in Germany in January 1933. Although National Socialism drew much criticism, this event and the following National Socialist 'revolution' increased the interest of many Belgian Catholics in some kind of 'reform of the State'. From 1933 onwards, more and more was published on this issue and congresses organized. The leitmotiv was a strengthening of authority. Some Catholics were sympathetic towards the authoritarian regimes in Portugal and Austria. Corporatism – in all its vagueness – was always an important aspect of the social blueprints, but few Catholics wanted to replace liberal democracy with a corporatist and authoritarian regime.[25] The most radical voices could be heard in the younger generation, where many called for a 'new order'. Social democracy was considered more important than political democracy, a social insurance scheme better than universal male suffrage. In 1936, Rex advocated signing a concordat between the Belgian state and the Church, in order to make the Catholic Party redundant.

A second important event was the financial crash of the Boerenbond in December 1934. The Farmers' League was one of the main pillars of the Catholic Party in Flanders. Not only did it have a monopoly representing the interests of farmers in the Flemish countryside, but its commercial and financial affairs had expanded in a spectacular way. The bank of the Boerenbond formed the core of nascent Flemish capitalism. The economic boom of the late 1920s had, however, encouraged imprudent investment and, like many other banks, the Boerenbond suffered badly from the depression. In December 1934, the bank was put under state control and a moratorium was introduced.[26] The bank's failure had three major consequences. First of all, farmers lost their savings and their confidence was shaken. This had electoral effects in the Flemish countryside in May 1936. Second, the crash reopened the controversy on the position of the Catholic 'social' organizations. The bishops decided to redefine the relationship between Catholic Action and social and political activities. They wanted the involvement of clerics in financial affairs to be limited, and the educational activities to be accentuated at the expense of politics. These guidelines also affected the Christian Democratic workers' organizations. Finally, the financial débâcle of the Boerenbond shed light on some dubious financial practices, which were to be exploited under the suggestive phrase of 'political-financial collusions' by the Rexist movement. In short, the 'old regime' was badly hurt by the Boerenbond crash.

The rupture with Rex in November 1935 was a third major event. At the beginning of 1935, Léon Degrelle left Catholic Action and turned Rex into a political movement. On 1 May 1935 he held his first big meeting in Italian fascist style. His declared aim was not to fight the Catholic Party, but to achieve its renewal from within. The Boerenbond affair affected Degrelle's attitude, however. As the scandal deepened under the investigation of a parliamentary committee, Degrelle became more radical and called for a 'purification' of the Catholic Party, bringing him into conflict with the Fédération des Cercles in November 1935 and provoking sharp criticism from the ACW, the Catholic Union and the bishops. The rupture was complete when, in February 1936, Degrelle nominated Rexist candidates for the next elections. From a dissident Catholic movement, Rex was to evolve into a heterogeneous coalition of malcontent people. Three major groups can be distinguished: the movement created by Degrelle himself, appealing especially to younger people coming out of the ranks of Catholic Action and inspired by the need for a 'spiritual revolution'; the lower-middle class, which had many economic grievances, especially in relation to big business, big labour and concerning high taxation;[27] and the veterans of the Great War, patriots who were alarmed by the weak reaction of the Belgian government to German rearmament.[28]

A fourth and decisive event was the electoral defeat of the Catholic Party on 24 May 1936. Although the Van Zeeland cabinet was successful in redressing the economic situation, the three government parties were severely battered in the general elections. The damage to the Catholic Party was great. It lost 10 per cent of the vote and barely kept 29 per cent (63 seats) against 11 per cent for Rex (21 seats) and 7 per cent for the Flemish Nationalists (16 seats). There were also gains for the Communist Party with 6 per cent (9 seats). The Catholic Party, much weakened in Wallonia, lost more than 400,000 voters, mainly Catholics, who turned to Rex and the Flemish Nationalists. The threat to the Catholic Party and to the regime increased when, in September 1936, Rex and the Flemish Nationalists signed an agreement.

The fifth and last event leading to a fundamental transformation of the Catholic Party was the Spanish Civil War. While the Catholic constituency was disintegrating and some observers denounced the Catholic Party as redundant, the success of the Popular Front in Spain and in France created a somewhat opposite reaction, especially after the outbreak of civil war in Spain. Communism was portrayed as a threat to Belgium and to Christian civilization in general, seemingly strengthening the need for a common Catholic reaction. But anti-communism offered more than a confessional foundation so typical of the past. Not only the Church or religion seemed to be at stake, but Western civilization, deeply influenced by Christendom.

The Catholic Party responded to the challenges of 1936 with a reform that met the desires of the younger Catholic generation as well as of the Flemish Catholics. The reformers strove to integrate the diverse Catholic groups into a single party structure, based on real unity with a corresponding political programme. At the same time, they gave more autonomy to Flemish and Walloon Catholics to allow separate action. In fact two opposite movements can be traced: national disintegration, and regional integration of structure and programme.[29]

On 11 October 1936, the Belgian Catholic Bloc was formed as an umbrella organization containing two fairly autonomous wings: the Catholic Flemish People's Party, the Katholieke Vlaamse Volkspartij, for the Flemish north of the country, and the Catholic Social Party, the Parti Catholique Social, for the francophone south. The party adopted a modern structure, with local sections based on individual membership and with regional and national councils. The national leadership also gained control over the parliamentary groups, which now had a firm place in the party structure. The position of the organizations that had previously constituted the Catholic Union was also redefined. These 'social organizations' – a new term – continued, according to the party statutes, to participate in the selection of candidates and the drafting of the programme, but they accepted the creation of a streamlined party structure and a political leadership that could decide party policy. While the Workers' League and the Farmers' League easily adjusted to this new situation, the position of the Fédération des Cercles (having only a political mission) was severely weakened. In the Katholieke Vlaamse Volkspartij it was no longer recognized. In the Parti Catholique Social it retained an ambiguous position. The weakening of the conservative Fédération removed an important obstacle to structural integration and programmatic innovation.

In terms of its organization and functioning as a political party, the Catholic Bloc marked a step forward. In terms of the transformation of a confessional party into a political one, the Bloc was again a step forward. As a result of the attacks by Rex and the Flemish Nationalists on 'political Catholicism', it paid more attention to the political legitimation of its existence. The Catholic Bloc presented itself as a people's party, no longer referring to the rights of Church and religion, but to a political doctrine based on personalism and to a political programme. It also offered an elaborate set of social and economic reforms based on the guiding principles of personal dignity, the family and the profession. In this respect it anticipated the Christelijke Volkspartij created in 1945.

It is not quite clear who introduced personalism. The term was not part of the political vocabulary of the Christian Democrats, but did feature in the pamphlets of the young middle-class intellectuals attracted by a growing criticism of liberal democracy. They referred to the French philosopher, Jacques Maritain, and were in contact with Emmanuel Mounier.[30] In 1932 – and before the appearance of the French review *Esprit* edited by Mounier – the Belgian group Esprit nouveau was the first to publish a declaration that contained personalism as its core.[31] The introduction of personalism into the new party programme seems, however, to stem from the neo-Thomist philosopher Edgar De Bruyne, one of the leading members of the Flemish party leadership. Personalism was also a key concept in the party programmes of Rexism, the Flemish Nationalists and in the vocabulary of the Socialist leader, Hendrik De Man. It was a platform for all kinds of anti-liberal forces and an alternative to fascist and communist totalitarianism. The same is true of the concept of a people's party that meets the desire of national and social unity. Such essentially anti-pluralist thinking is typical of the 1930s and also appears in the discourse of De Man.[32]

In its policies of the late 1930s, the Catholic Bloc opposed collectivist tendencies in education, social insurance schemes and health services. Instead, it advocated state recognition of and support for private initiatives, such as Catholic schools or union unemployment funds. The Bloc opposed economic planification and focused on a reform introducing the 'organized professions'. The term corporatism was dropped because of its new fascist connotations. The idea of *bedrijfsorganisatie* cherished by the Christian Democrats in the 1920s had thus conquered the whole Catholic Party by the end of the 1930s.

Relations with the Church also changed to some extent in the late 1930s. In a significant pastoral letter of February 1935, Cardinal Van Roey made a clear distinction between the Catholic Party and the Church. He praised the Catholic Party, but continued, 'one may not identify the Catholic Party with the Church. It is not even an emanation of it. It does not depend on it for its political action. It drafts its economic, financial and military programme in all freedom.'[33] The Catholic Union, in turn, declared in a manifesto of February 1936 that it had 'never been a confessional party. Its mission is not of a religious, but of a political character ... The Church is one reality, but the State another. They are two separate and independent institutions in their respective spheres.'[34] The Katholieke Vlaamse Volkspartij and the Parti Catholique Social proclaimed even more vehemently than before not to be confessional parties: they insisted that they were not limited to Catholics, but open to anyone who accepted their political programme. One member of the reform committee of the Catholic Union in fact proposed to replace the label 'Catholic' with 'Christian', although this was not accepted at the time.

The new party tried to reconcile two contradictory elements: rallying all Catholic forces against communism, and rallying them on a political programme opposed to Rex and the Flemish Nationalists. The name of the new formation, Catholic Bloc, indicated clearly that it was still the aim to rally all Catholics within one party. This was also the explicit demand of the Belgian bishops, formulated at the Catholic Congress of Malines, in September 1936, and in an important pastoral letter of Christmas 1936. In this letter the bishops rejected communism as well as a dictatorship of the right. They praised the confessional social organizations as efficient instruments in the struggle against communism, and they stressed the necessity of a party defending the rights of the Church.[35] Before the electoral contest between Prime Minister Van Zeeland and the Rexist leader Degrelle on 11 April 1937, Cardinal Van Roey condemned Rex publicly as a 'danger for the country and for the Church'.[36] For the bishops, inclusion of all Catholics in one party still seemed necessary. Political pluralism among Catholics was not tolerated. These interventions by the bishops naturally compromised the supposedly non-confessional position and the political autonomy of the Catholic Bloc.

The non-confessional character was also undermined by two other factors. The fact that the Catholic social organizations – with close connections to the Catholic hierarchy – continued to play a major role in the Catholic Bloc strengthened its confessional character. Finally, the repeated reference to the social teaching of the Church as justification for the programme of the Catholic Bloc also compromised its political character. Although the contours of an autonomous party with a political programme inspired by Christian values, but independent of the Church, did become clearer in the late 1930s, the sociological reality of 'political Catholicism' in its old form continued to exist.

THE EUROPEAN DIMENSION

Was the Catholic Party in Belgium affected by influences from abroad and did it see itself as part of a broader political phenomenon? There was always, especially in and around the university of Louvain – the Belgian centre of Catholic intellectual life – a great interest in developments outside the country. Such interest extended noticeably to the Christian Labour Movement and Catholic Action. In their periodicals, such as the *Gids op Maatschappelijk Gebied* or *La Cité Chrétienne*, intellectual and political currents in other countries were closely studied. Generally speaking, the Flemish Catholics were more oriented towards the Netherlands and Germany, while the francophone Catholics were rather oriented towards the Latin world. Moreover, transnational communication in Europe became more intense as a result of the war. The Pope played a central role in the Catholic world. His prestige and influence increased considerably. The autonomy of national hierarchies was constantly eroded. The 1931 encyclical *Quadragesimo anno* was a key reference point for all Catholic political thinking in the 1930s, including in Belgium.[37]

It is clear that Catholic Action in Belgium was part of a larger ecclesiastical movement with directives originating in Rome, although local differences clearly existed. Concerning the origins of Catholic Action in Belgium, it is quite remarkable how the Pope's rejection of the Partito Popolare was translated into a rejection by the ACJB leadership of Belgian Christian democracy as a political movement. It is also important to note, however, that class-based Catholic Action 'made in Belgium' was exported to other countries. At the political level, however, only Christian Democrats had international contacts. The ACW showed great interest in the PPI experiment, and on 10 October 1920 it discussed a proposal to establish international collaboration with the Dutch and Italian Christian Democrats.[38] The ACW, and not the Catholic Union, participated in the Secrétariat International des Partis Démocratiques d'Inspiration

Chrétienne (SIPDIC) from its creation in 1925, and some of its leaders – Father Rutten, Hendrik Heyman, P. W. Segers – participated in its annual meetings.[39] Their participation, however, does not seem to have influenced their position at home. The Christian Labour Movement had numerous international contacts, which undoubtedly indirectly affected its political position and vision. The International Confederation of Christian Trade Unions was an important meeting point from 1919 on,[40] but so was the Catholic Workers' International founded in 1928. The core countries of this International were Belgium, Germany and the Netherlands. It was mainly preoccupied with the defence of the Catholic social organizations against the pretensions of an expanding official Catholic Action.[41] There was no mention of international collaboration between states or parties in Catholic Party programmes, however. European civilization only became a major theme in the political discourse as a result of the successes of National Socialism and communism in the 1930s. With the sole exception of the Belgian Catholic youth, which established contacts with Maritain and Mounier and his movement, the horizon of Belgian political Catholicism remained very much national.

WAR AND OCCUPATION

The war and occupation interrupted the Catholic political reform movement. After the German invasion on 10 May 1940 and the Belgian capitulation on 28 May, Belgium was put under military administration. At the beginning, however, members of the Belgian establishment believed that a rapid normalization of public life was possible, since they – like many Belgians – considered the Germans as victorious and the war to be over. Inspired by the French Vichy regime, King Leopold III, who surrendered against the will of his ministers and stayed in the country, aimed at a restoration of Belgian sovereignty. He was supported by some Catholic leaders as well as by some liberals and socialists. They designed a new and strong regime based on corporatist principles.[42] Catholic union leaders were prepared to dismantle the existing Catholic unions, and in November 1940 they joined the single union imposed by the Germans.[43] Yet Hitler remained undecided concerning Belgium's future position, and at the end of 1940 it became clear that the country was to remain occupied territory. From the start, the German military administration tried to introduce a 'new order' in political, economic and social life and subjected all public activities to prior authorization. It tried to eliminate as many representatives of the 'old regime' from public life as possible, favouring Flemish Nationalists and Rexists, who were willing to collaborate closely with the Nazi regime. Finally, in August 1941, Catholic union leaders were expelled from the single union.

Because the traditional political parties were disbanded, the Bloc Catholique Belge was not active during the occupation. Neither did it organize clandestine activity, although Catholic leaders of course met privately and did make plans for the future. The foundations of the Catholic Party remained intact, however, since with the exception of the unions, the Catholic social organizations were tolerated and maintained regular activities. So did Catholic Action. Some Catholics engaged in civil and armed resistance, but as individuals. The only exceptions to the general rule were some initiatives emanating from the Christian Labour Movement. Although no consensus existed regarding Belgian politics after the war, most Catholic leaders preferred to maintain a Catholic Party.[44] Cardinal Van Roey, for example, was convinced of the necessity of such a Catholic Party after the war.[45] In designing the post-war party, Catholic leaders wished to avoid the fragmentation of the 1930s, so they aimed at a solid party structure within a strong political system. This preference for 'strong' party organization and government was to recede after liberation, however. Inspired by a renewed Belgian patriotism, most party leaders also wanted a national party. Collaboration between labour and capital was a crucial aspect of all the draft programmes. The Christian Labour Movement hesitated to accept a unitary party structure built on individual membership, but felt growing pressure from a younger Catholic Action generation, which did not want Catholic social action to be compromised by political activity. At the same time, fear of communism was an important motive for the leadership of the labour movement to accept the creation of a Christian People's Party.

With the exception of the national structure, the party reform debated under the occupation strengthened the tendencies of the 1930s. Dissident voices could be heard among the refugees in London, where the Belgian government in exile had its seat. Some Catholics and socialists cherished the idea of a joint Labour Party. After liberation these ideas eventually led to the birth of the Union démocratique belge, which, however, turned out to be stillborn.[46]

NOTES

1 The studies by Simon and Van Isacker dating from the 1950s for a long time framed the historical interpretation of the origins of the Catholic Party. Simon stressed the transition from a conservative to a confessional party in 1884: Aloïs Simon, *Le parti catholique belge 1830–1945* (Brussels 1958). Van Isacker paid much attention to the cleavage between the 'liberal-Catholic' strand of the parliamentary Right and intransigent Catholic opinion: Karel Van Isacker, *Werkelijk en wettelijk land. De katholieke opinie tegenover de Rechterzijde 1863–1884* (Antwerp 1955). These interpretations have been criticized by Lode Wils, 'De katholieke partij in de 19e eeuw: organisatie, programma en aanhang', in Emiel Lamberts and Jacques Lory (eds), *1884: un tournant politique en*

Belgique (Brussels 1986), pp. 69–97. Wils views the Catholic Party as a slowly growing formation that until 1914 maintained a very loose structure, and for which the year 1884 did not mark a major change. A recent study is Jean-Luc Soete, *Structures et organisations de base du parti catholique en Belgique 1863–1884* (Louvain-la-Neuve 1996). For the growth of the Catholic pillar, see Emiel Lamberts, 'Van Kerk naar zuil: de ontwikkeling van het katholiek organisatiewezen in België in de 19e eeuw', in Jaak Billiet (ed.), *Tussen bescherming en verovering. Sociologen en historici over zuilvorming* (Leuven 1988), pp. 83–133. For the impact of the intransigent (ultramontane) current, see Emiel Lamberts (ed.), *Kruistocht tegen het liberalism. Facetten van het ultramontanisme in België in de 19e eeuw* (Leuven 1984).

2 Documents on the foundation of the Catholic Union have been collected and edited by Emmanuel Gerard, *Documenten over de katholieke partijorganisatie in België (1920–1922, 1931–1933)* (Leuven 1981). See also Emmanuel Gerard, *De katholieke partij in crisis. Partijpolitiek leven in België 1918–1940* (Leuven 1985), pp. 141–70.

3 Named after the village near Bruges where the King's headquarters were established at the time of the armistice.

4 Henri Haag, *Le comte Charles de Broqueville, Ministre d'Etat, et les luttes pour le pouvoir (1910–1940)* (Louvain-la-Neuve 1990); Jan de Maeyer and Leen Van Molle (eds), *Joris Helleputte* (Leuven 1998).

5 Electoral figures in Roger E. de Smet, René Evalenko and William Fraeys, *Atlas des élections belges 1919–1954* (Brussels 1958).

6 Emmanuel Gerard and Paul Wynants (eds), *Histoire du mouvement ouvrier chrétien en Belgique*, vol. 1 (Leuven 1994), pp. 146–73. In the Belgian context, Christian effectively means Catholic.

7 The original name of the ACW was Christian Democratic League.

8 Emmanuel Gerard, 'Grondlijnen van de katholieke verzuiling tussen 1914 en 1945', in Billiet, *Tussen bescherming en verovering*, pp. 135–69.

9 Jeffrey Tyssens, *Strijdmunt of pasmunt? Levensbeschouwelijk links en de schoolkwestie 1918–1940* (Brussels 1993).

10 In 1986 Hans Righart argued that the Catholic Union was the end of a process of integration: Hans Righart, *De katholieke zuil in Europa. Het ontstaan van verzuiling onder katholieken in Oostenrijk, Zwitserland, België en Nederland* (Meppel 1986), p. 169, also pp. 28 and 174–5. There is no evidence for his thesis, however, according to Gerard, *De katholieke partij in crisis*.

11 Such initiatives can be found in Brussels and in Charleroi. They caused a permanent conflict with the Christian Democrats. See Emmanuel Gerard, 'Tussen apostolaat en emancipatie: de christelijke arbeidersbeweging en de strijd om de sociale werken (1925–1933)', in Emmanuel Gerard and Jozef Mampuys (eds), *Voor Kerk en werk. Opstellen over de christelijke arbeidersbeweging* (Leuven 1986), pp. 203–60.

12 Mercier to bishops, 14 June 1925. Mercier Papers 78, Archbishopal Archives Malines.

13 Until the 1960s, Belgium formed an eccleciastical province with six dioceses.

14 For the antagonism between the Bishop of Liège and the Archbishop of Malines, see Roger Aubert, 'Le cardinal Mercier et Mgr Rutten', *Bulletin de la societé d'art et d'histoire du diocèse de Liège*, vol. 57 (1990), pp. 161–200.

15 Pastoral letters on political affairs have been collected and edited by Karel Van Isacker, *Herderlijke brieven over politiek 1830/1966* (Antwerp 1969).

16 Protocol of the executive committee of the Catholic Union, 4 May 1926. Delvaux Papers, Katholiek Documentatie en Onderzoekscentrum Leuven.

17 Bruno De Wever, *Greep naar de macht. Vlaams-nationalisme en Nieuwe Orde. Het VNV 1933–1945* (Tielt 1994).
18 Eric Defoort, *Charles Maurras en de Action Française in België* (Bruges 1978). Degrelle made the distinction between *pays légal* and *pays réel*.
19 Godfried Kwanten, 'De bedrijfsorganisatie in de christelijke arbeidersbeweging', *De Gids op maatschappelijk Gebied*, vol. 75 (1984), pp. 337–47.
20 Bregt Henkens, 'De vorming van de eerste regering van Zeeland (maart 1935). Een studie van het proces van kabinetsformatie', *Revue Belge d'Histoire Contemporaine*, vol. 26 (1996), pp. 209–61.
21 For the Pierlot reform, see Gerard, *De katholieke partij in crisis*, pp. 419–56; Godfried Kwanten, *August-Edmond De Schryver (1898–1991). Politieke biografie van een gentleman-staatsman* (Leuven 2001).
22 In the official terminology this was called *spécialisation par milieu*.
23 On the conflict between Catholic Action and Christian Democracy, see Marc A. Walckiers, *Sources inédites relatives aux débuts de la JOC 1919–1925* (Leuven 1970); Emmanuel Gerard, 'Cardijn, arbeidersbeweging en Katholieke Actie (1918–1945)', in *Cardijn. Un homme, un mouvement* (Leuven 1983), pp. 119–47; Emmanuel Gerard, *Église et mouvement ouvrier chrétien en Belgique. Sources inédites relatives à la direction générale des oeuvres sociales (1916–1936)* (Leuven 1990).
24 Pierre Sauvage, *La Cité Chrétienne (1926–1940). Une revue autour de Jacques Leclercq* (Brussels 1987); Martin Conway, 'Building the Christian City: Catholics and Politics in Interwar Francophone Belgium', *Past and Present*, vol. 128 (1990), pp. 117–51.
25 Griet Van Haver, *Onmacht der verdeelden. Katolieken in Vlaanderen tussen demokratie en fascisme 1929–1940* (Berchem 1984); Dirk Luyten, *Ideologisch debat en politieke strijd over het corporatisme tijdens het interbellum in België* (Brussels 1996).
26 Leen Van Molle, *Ieder voor allen. De Belgische Boerenbond 1890–1990* (Leuven 1990).
27 Peter Heyrman, *Middenstandsbeweging en beleid in België 1918–1940: tussen vrijheid en regulering* (Leuven 1998), analyses lower-middle class support for Rexism.
28 For Rexism before 1940, see Jean-Michel Etienne, *Le mouvement rexiste jusqu'en 1940* (Paris 1968); Emmanuel Gerard, 'La responsabilité du monde catholique dans la naissance et lessor du rexisme', *La Revue Nouvelle*, vol. 35 (1987), pp. 67–77. For Rexism during the war, see Martin Conway, *Collaboration in Belgium. Léon Degrelle and the Rexist Movement 1940–1944* (New Haven, CT 1993). For the Flemish Nationalists, see De Wever, *Greep naar de macht*.
29 For the Catholic Bloc, see Gerard, *De katholieke partij in crisis*, pp. 485–506.
30 Pierre Sauvage, 'Jacques Maritain et la Belgique', in Bernard Hubert (ed.), *Jacques Maritain en Europe. La réception de sa pensée* (Paris 1996), pp. 133–79.
31 'Directions', *Esprit nouveau*, August 1932.
32 See Annemieke Kijn, *Arbeiders – of volkspartij? Een vergelijkende studie van het Belgisch en Nederlands socialisme 1933–1946* (Maastricht 1990).
33 Van Isacker, *Werkelijk*, p. 124.
34 Union Catholique Belge, *Exposé de la politique catholique. Progamme de réformes*, February 1936.
35 Van Isacker, *Werkelijk*, pp. 132–3.
36 Ibid., p. 136.
37 Martin Conway, 'Introduction', in Tom Buchanan and idem (eds), *Political Catholicism in Europe, 1918–1965* (Oxford 1996), pp. 1–33.

38 Emmanuel Gerard, 'Uit de voorgeschiedenis van het ACW: het einde van de Volksbond en de oprichting van het Democratisch Blok (1918–1921)', *De Gids op Maatschappelijk Gebied*, vol. 19 (1978), p. 514.
39 Roberto Papini, *Il coraggio della democrazia. Sturzo e l'Internazionale popolare tra le due guerre* (Rome 1995), pp. 131–2; see also the chapter by Guido Müller in this book.
40 See Patrick Pasture, *Histoire du syndicalisme chrétien international. La difficile recherche d'une troisième voie* (Paris 1999).
41 Luc Vandeweyer, 'De Katholieke Arbeiders-Internationale. Standsorganisatie in internationaal perspectief', in Emmanuel Gerard (ed.), *De kracht van een overtuiging. 60 jaar ACW* (Zele 1981), pp. 61–80.
42 Jan Velaers and Herman Van Goethem, *Leopold III. De Koning, het Land, de Oorlog* (Tielt 1994). King Leopold III, formally a prisoner of war, stayed at his Laeken palace under close German supervision. The Pierlot cabinet, having failed to convince the King to continue the war, fled to France on 24 May 1940. After the French armistice, four of its members eventually fled to London in October 1940 and joined the Allied war effort.
43 The decision to join the single union was supported by the Flemish leadership and created a split with a mainly Walloon minority. Forced into clandestine action, the Walloon minority favoured the foundation of a Labour Party and supported the UDB after liberation. See Jean Neuville, *La CSC en l'an 40* (Brussels 1988).
44 For the ideas debated among Catholics during the occupation, see Mark Van den Wijngaert, *Onstaan en stichting van de CVP-PSC. De lange weg naar het Kerstprogramma* (Brussels 1976).
45 At a private audience held on 11 July 1942 with ten Catholic leaders, he argued that the bishops believed a Catholic Party was necessary. Addressing the criticism that a Catholic Party might compromise the Church, he replied that one could change the name of the party. Quoted in Alain Dantoing, *La 'collaboration' du Cardinal. L'Église de Belgique dans la Guerre 40* (Brussels 1991), p. 451.
46 See Wilfried Beerten, *Le rêve travailliste en Belgique. Histoire de l'UDB 1944–1947* (Brussels 1990).

6

Christian Democracy and Centrism: The Popular Democratic Party in France

Jean-Claude Delbreil

The Parti Démocrate Populaire (PDP), founded in 1924, can be considered as the first instance of a political party of Christian-based democracy in France, without being directly so called and having no openly denominational reference. As in most other European countries, the party had its origin in a multiplicity of complex traditions, but it had an originality and subtle features of its own, stemming from a combination, to some extent, of Christian democracy in its strict sense, social Catholicism and liberal Catholicism.[1] France, however, unlike other countries, and for a range of historical reasons dating back to the Revolution, was alone in that no 'Catholic' party was founded there. Although the parties of that tendency, in France and elsewhere, could not be called Christian democrat until 1945, they were referred to, notably in the inter-war years, as 'Christian-inspired democratic parties', and all attempts to form 'Catholic' parties failed. Development in France was further complicated by the emergence, at the end of the nineteenth century and the beginning of the twentieth, of another movement that shaped the outlook of a whole generation: the Sillon, founded in 1894 by Marc Sangnier.[2]

After the condemnation of the Sillon in 1910 by the Pope, Sangnier launched another movement of a distinctly political nature: the Ligue de la jeune République. Some leading figures from the Sillon, from the Christian democratic movement and from a section of social Catholicism who had democratic leanings had begun to form the Fédérations de républicains-démocrates. Social Catholicism, which was not necessarily democratic and was of a more hierarchical nature than Christian democracy, had undergone change since the encyclical *Rerum novarum* of 1891.[3] It had developed in a profusion of organizations, around movements as powerful as the Association catholique de la jeunesse française (ACJF), the Semaines sociales, the Union d'étude des catholiques sociaux, etc. Following the conflict, many looked to Marc Sangnier to co-ordinate a mass meeting. He, however, refused, fearing it would be too right-wing in nature despite the launch in 1920 of the Ligue nationale de la démocratie between the Jeune République and the Fédérations de républicains-démocrates which finally collapsed in 1922.

As for the 'democratic republicans', they produced another formula, inclining towards the leaders of the large Catholic social organizations in the form of the Bureau d'action civique, which planned political action at the time of the 1924 elections, following which 13 deputies who shared these views constituted the 'democratic' group. A few months later the PDP was formed at the Bureau's conference in November 1924. Broadly speaking, the PDP, in order to make a political impact, was to be composed of a 'left wing' of social and liberal Catholicism and a 'right wing' of those of the Christian democratic movement who refused to follow Marc Sangnier.[4] In 1924 the party drew up a programme with a centrist Catholic political tone, positioning it on the right of centre in French politics. The new party was to be among the 'popular' or 'populist' parties of post-war Europe, on the pattern notably of the Italian Partito Popolare (PPI) launched by Luigi Sturzo in 1919. It was an example among others of those parties, alongside the justly named 'Catholic parties' such as those in Belgium and Holland, and Christian social or people's parties of Central and Eastern Europe.

THE PDP AND ITS SOCIOLOGICAL ROOTS

The PDP was a minor political force, never supported by more than 3 per cent of the electorate. It was, then, small compared with other, roughly similar, European parties and was one of the weakest parties inspired by Christian democracy, and this must be stressed when comparisons are made. In the *Conseil national* of 1924 it was the professions, along with the middle and upper-middle classes, who set the tone; the contribution of wage-earners, particularly manual workers and even the rural and farming community, was somewhat limited. In 1924, then, the PDP was in effect very much a party of the middle classes.[5] The situation was generally the same at the level of party officials. The farming community was represented in a complex fashion, as was a large section of the legal profession. Several eminent PDP representatives were from a traditional bourgeois background.

It is more difficult to make an exact sociological study of the membership of the PDP. An attempt can be made via such sources as the lists of paid-up members, which provide some indication of their occupations. It can be seen, for instance, that those who were farmers and growers constituted only 5 per cent. Seven per cent were skilled manual workers, and a particularly large proportion came from the various professions (17 per cent), compared with industrialists (6 per cent), general merchants (5 per cent) and shopkeepers (4.5 per cent). All these categories, along with farmers and skilled manual workers, formed 45 per cent of the total, and 33 per cent without them – i.e. one-third were in the socio-economic category of the upper and upper-middle classes. The number of priests on the lists is surprisingly high (8 per cent). There were also students (4 per cent), teachers and writers (4 per cent) and engineers (4 per cent). The group that can be classified as clerical workers came to a total of 25 per cent. There was, then, penetration into the realm of the white-collar worker, where the setting up of Christian trade unionism could have played a part. Manual workers, however, were in the minority (7.5 per cent). The middle classes accounted for a large number of the members, as did clerical workers, and together they formed the sociological core essential to the party. As for the popular democratic electorate, it may be wondered if it was really specific, even though the party had an inter-class ideology that aimed to integrate certain members of the lower-middle and working classes. Nevertheless, the PDP sought to include all social classes, and tried to draw up a specific programme for each one without managing to achieve the hoped-for balanced result. This was a relative failure, and the reflection of certain grey areas in its thinking on the social level.[6] This sociological diversification can, of course, be found in all major parties inspired by Christian democracy.

Regarding relations with the 'world of work' in general, those with Christian trade unionism and the Confédération française des travailleurs chrétiens (CFTC), founded in 1919, were the most important. They existed in particular when the party was launched in 1924 and involved the CFTC leaders around their secretary general, Gaston Tessier. However, these leaders always made a point of having no direct involvement in party disputes.[7] They also avoided being directly involved in the leadership of the PDP, even though that led to a number of problems locally and nationally. The map of Christian trade unionism, although not corresponding exactly with that of the PDP, showed parallels in a region such as the *Nord*. Christian trade unionism, however, did not adequately swell the ranks of the party. Furthermore, in line with its inter-class ideology, the PDP maintained links with the Catholic employers' unions within the Confédération française des professions (CFP), which, in 1929, instituted a *commission mixte* with the CFTC. The party was in contact with both of them as a kind of liaising agent.[8] In any case, with the CFTC, contacts involved leaders or prominent members rather than the rank and file.[9] There was, then, an imbalance between the membership of the PDP and that of the CFTC. However, the specific dimension of the relations with Christian trade unionism should not be overlooked; they probably played a part in engaging the party in a number of social campaigns.

Alongside these complex sociological elements in the world of work involving both employers and workers, the PDP was also involved, through its ideology and sociology, with the rural world, but once again with complications. What came about was something of a victory of traditional tendencies over more advanced tendencies with socialist leanings, which were apparent from the outset in the association of farmers and growers, l'Association des 'cultivateurs-cultivants', set up by the Abbot Mancel and supported by Abbot Trochu and the newspaper *L'Ouest Éclair*.[10] However, other influences closer to traditional agrarianist milieux with a nuance of social Catholicism also came into play.

The popular democrats remained linked to social Catholic organizations and inspired by the social doctrine of the Church. The PDP was founded in 1924 with the firm support of certain of these milieux. There were relations with those organizations that provided it with leaders, such as Semaines sociales or the ACJF. In theory these relations were purely personal, as the social Catholics did not commit their own associations. But one of the party's problems, as was the case with other parties of a Christian democrat nature in the inter-war years, proved to be that of its relations with such organizations and contacts between a Christian democrat-inspired party and the social Catholic milieu in the broad sense. Yet it was far from true that all social Catholics were sympathetic to the PDP. The real commitment in social Catholic circles was weak, and this was one of the main reasons for the failure of the party.[11] The fact was that the PDP, unlike other similar parties, had somewhat tenuous links with a range of organizations that could have given it greater support. Despite this, it was in contact with certain of them, which, at least as regards their leaders, gave it their initial support. Such was the case with l'Union d'étude des catholiques sociaux – the social welfare administrative offices. It was in fact especially the case with the Semaines sociales group, which had gradually come to be of pivotal importance in social Catholicism and Christian democracy, in which an attempt was made to establish a common doctrine overriding different political and social persuasions, in relation with the Lyon group of the journal *Chronique sociale*. *Semaines sociales* had nevertheless become a crossroads where different shades of social Catholicism and Christian democracy came together. This did not prevent clashes of opinion, however. This was also true of the ACJF, whose relations with the PDP and Christian democracy were always indisputable.[12] The AJCF was also one of the starting points and main contributors in terms of the leadership of the PDP – Charles Flory, for example, and subsequent leaders such as François de Menthon and Georges Bidault. After the departure of Flory in 1926, the ACJF reaffirmed that the ground on which it meant to operate was that of political neutrality, thus marking the end of a period in which it had been prepared to follow almost any party line if it seemed expedient to do so. The association of former members of the ACJF can be seen as a recruiting centre for the PDP.

RELATIONS WITH THE CHURCH, THE CATHOLIC WORLD AND RELIGIOUS QUESTIONS

The party, for all its partial successes, also ended in relative failure for a number of reasons, notably the extent of the right–left split which almost invariably steered it towards the moderate right, despite its avowed wish for 'concentration' between the centre-right and the centre-left and for what it called a 'downgrading of parties', particularly with regard to religious matters and the question of whether secularity should be the criterion for differentiating between right and left. On these points the party finally achieved only partial success. The problems arose with the choice of the party's name, a complicated matter influenced by the French Christian democratic tradition, the 'popular' current of thought then prevailing in Alsace and the 'popularism' of Sturzo. A point had been made of avoiding any denominational labels, and it was decided to create neither a Catholic party nor one that was officially Christian democrat. The PDP was opposed to any form of 'Catholic' party, and was unable and unwilling to call itself 'Christian democrat'. Agreement was reached on a formula such as 'State secularity as it was meant to be', which was soon set against 'secularism'. This aspect constituted one of the four 'cardinal points' of the party.[13] It is also against the background of what was called the *second ralliement* of Catholics to the Republic, spelt out after 1919, that the birth of the party must be reset.[14] A *de facto* rapprochement had taken place between the moderate lay republicans and the Catholic republicans.

Robert Cornilleau, in *Le ralliement a-t-il échoué?*, published in 1926, provided a positive assessment of this period,[15] rejecting what he called the 'ill-timed demands' against the hard line of probably a majority section of French Catholicism. Nevertheless, the 'religious question' was a key feature of the 1924 elections and the conflict between 'conciliators' and 'intransigents' intensified. It was at least established that religious harmony was vital if democratic institutions were to function properly, and that it was possible to have only 'perfectible' laws, not 'inviolable' ones.[16] This was one of the major features of the action of the party and probably one of its *raisons d'être*. Its 'centrist' stance was also apparent in relation to the so-called school question and to educational freedom, in not adopting the proposals of the Catholic Right for 'mixed ability schools'. But the PDP arrived on the scene at the time of the Cartel des gauches – an electoral coalition of the left – when there was a resurgence of lay and anticlerical politics. However, integration with the Radicals as the main moderate republican party was still its aim and its means for reaching a solution to the 'religious question' against the policy of the blocs, since the Catholics might one day become one of the major elements in a new *grand parti républicain*.

Despite everything, the PDP succeeded in mustering to its ranks only a fraction – probably a minority – of organized French political Catholicism, and that initial state of affairs was to remain unchanged. On the political front it never managed to attract the majority of those Catholics who remained faithful to other more conservative forces and to a party that later became that of the conservative right – the Fédération républicaine. All this reflects the multiparty system in France, and the preference on the part of conservative Catholics for a non-denominational party. The PDP was to clash with this party at every turn. From then on, it was a case of two indirectly (not explicitly) Catholic parties on the political map of France: the Fédération républicaine, more to the right, and the more centrist PDP.[17] The majority of Catholic voters opted for the traditional right, which, in the 1920s, was favoured by church leaders. It was the embodiment of a moderate clerical alliance, especially at the outset of the period of the lay offensive. The PDP in any case had to confront new forms of Catholic action and defence, and in particular the Fédération nationale catholique (FNC) led by General de Castelnau. This gave rise to complex problems, since a large number of democrat leaders took part in demonstrations and rallies organized by the FNC.[18] In the 1928 elections the FNC presented a list of demands, allowing its members a 'free vote', but the myth was again raised that the PDP was a 'Catholic party' that could prosper only on a programme that was confined to religious matters. More and more acute problems arose as time went by and in relation to the early stages of the new organization of the Action catholique.

Regarding the question of the Action française (AF), with which the PDP had been in conflict since before the Vatican condemned it in 1926, an effort was made to present the problem as being not so much political as intellectual; not wanting to mix politics and religion, and this was seen as a prudent step.[19] This wish was hampered by the fairly vicious attacks by the AF against the Christian democrats as a whole, who were accused of being responsible, along with Aristide Briand, for the Vatican's condemnation of French nationalism.[20] It was with considerable prudence that the PDP handled the matter, still opposing the 'untimely demands' from a religious point of view. But this ostensible prudence did not prevent it from taking more discreet steps aimed at eventually achieving a new statute from the Catholic Church of France. At first, the period of the Cartel des gauches was not favourable to this policy of appeasement. But, although once again opposing 'secularism', the PDP declared itself to be against any blatant demonstration against it. After the period 1926–28 a change in the political climate took place, as did a continuation of the interrupted *second ralliement*.

The question of relations with Vatican politics must also be raised, for it can be said that, whereas Pope Benedict XV had been in favour of Christian democracy, Pius XI adopted a more cautious attitude. He was above all the pope of Action catholique. Although certain key features of Vatican politics coincided with those of the PDP, both internal and external, fundamental questions remained, such as the possible concordat concerning the political position of the FNC. The condemnation of the AF by Pius XI should not distort the picture, and, although support was afforded to the policy of *ralliement* and international conciliation, it was not afforded to Christian democracy as a political force. The place of Christian democrats was accepted in so far as they respected Action catholique, currently being set up. Relations between the Vatican and a party almost unknown in Rome were somewhat complicated. Among the French bishops, however, the conciliatory *concordataires* were initially in a minority, and the situation improved only in the 1930s.[21] But the will of the PDP to adopt a free and political stance enabled it to be relatively independent. For the clergy as a whole, there were also some elements of ambiguity. Although some of them supported the PDP, it is hard to gauge how much impact this had. Regarding relations with the bishops, after 1932 a greater number of them were more sympathetic towards Christian democracy, but their sympathies, casual or whole-hearted, were always tempered by great caution. By and large they adopted an attitude of occasionally benevolent neutrality. Although the PDP benefited from approval, any direct expression of it might have been an embarrassment. In point of fact, the problem was that of the liberty of action of a party composed essentially of Catholics who were engaged in organizations more or less subject to a hierarchy.

The 'politico-religious' problems kept arising throughout the 1930s. At its 1930 conference, the party expressed its support for a general reform of the education system as part of a grand plan recognizing the place of educational freedom itself, as opposed to the partial acceptance of the unitary school system – a system having no segregation between the primary and secondary sectors.[22] In 1929 the possibility of an 'overall concordat' between France and the Vatican was mooted. The PDP was bound to support this general move towards 'appeasement', through an entente involving groups of the centre-right and the centre-left. Regarding education, the party tried to maintain a balance between its policy of co-operation with the public authorities and the defence of educational freedom. The PDP remained faithful to a means of rapprochement with republicans, including the Radicals. This attitude did not lead to very spectacular results, but a slow transformation of opinion came about. The Popular Front period did not prevent the *séparation cordiale*. With the government led by Édouard Daladier and the presence within it of Auguste Champetier de Ribes, the PDP was at the heart of a body of support approved by the hierarchy, which brought about the rapprochement with the centre-left and the Radicals.[23]

It was mainly during the 'phoney war' of 1939–40, when Champetier de Ribes was Under-Secretary of State for Foreign Affairs, that a plan called by some the 'Champetier Concordat' was drawn up. However, Daladier's government resigned without achieving these aims, which remained merely intentions. The Vatican attempted to obtain advantages in the form of a compromise that would virtually have signalled the end of the Popular Democrats' religious policy. From the point of view of the Church, however, the problem of relations between political and religious action remained poorly presented and poorly resolved, and the PDP, despite being non-denominational, could not ignore the Catholics' way of intervening in political and civic life. The party therefore moved towards defining its plans more precisely, while continuing to position itself on the shifting boundary between politics and religion. The PDP – and this was perhaps one of its weaknesses – always remained apart from the Action catholique and had no wish to reduce the distance, as many, especially in the new splinter group, Action catholique spécialisée, objected to Christian democracy. This was regrettable for a so-called Christian democrat-inspired party. On the other hand, although the PDP was a minority party compared with the moderate right, and although it did not succeed in making a name for itself in Catholic political circles, it was weakened, from the outset, by the absence of such groups as the Jeune République, which continued to form a left wing of Christian democracy. In the 1930s it appeared, to the new generation, to be irrelevant and outdated.

ECONOMIC AND SOCIAL POLICY: MIDWAY BETWEEN LIBERALISM AND SOCIALISM?

The connection between the PDP as the first party in France inspired by Christian democracy, social Catholicism and the social doctrine of the Church is somewhat complex, in relation, for example, to the encyclical *Rerum novarum* of 1891, which was largely updated by *Quadragesimo anno* of Pius XI in 1931. The social programme of the PDP drawn up in 1924 certainly succeeded in combining different doctrinal trends, and it was probably in the social sphere that this was best achieved, in the form of what was called *centrisme social*. The policy was governed by the second of the four 'cardinal points': 'We wish to establish democracy in the social and economic order through bold reform and development: not through the class struggle and pointless violence, but by the sincere co-operation of all the different groups involved in the production process.'[24] One can also see the inspiration for the social doctrine of the Church regarding professional organization and trade unionism, and the social legislation to be favoured under the supervision of the state. An important aspect is that trade union and professional action were to be developed by encouraging permanent joint committees and the setting up of employers' unions on the lines of the CFTC. Reference is also made to the participation of workers, who must 'play an increasing part in managing their work-related interests', to profit sharing, and to worker and trade union share ownership. Thus employer–employee co-operation and the introduction of worker participation were advocated. Such measures could transform the socio-economic system. All these ideas fitted in with a certain social Catholicism and with Christian democracy. Alongside this concern for the working class, however, considerable concern was also shown for the middle classes.

The PDP 'handbook' for 1928 acknowledged that the economic role of the state had inevitably become considerable. Between liberalism and socialism, both of which it refused to support, social Catholicism – of which it claimed to some extent to be an expression – seemed to be only like one of the varieties of 'interventionism', but with an economic purpose that was unfamiliar to and transcended it. Social Catholic teaching held that the state had a positive part to play in economic activity. Another privileged area was that of rural policy, which proved to be of great importance to the party.[25] Family policy was also stressed; everything had to be done to ensure family stability, and this was an 'inter-class' matter in which each social class lived out its own independent appointed destiny 'for the common good'. The role of the state was accepted to the extent that it had a positive part to play in the economic and social sphere. Unbridled liberalism and the socialism of the class struggle were equally condemned. An appeal was made to the social sense of the bourgeoisie, with the backing of the Catholic working class. This gave rise to a concept of democracy that was no longer the radical and individualist concept, but one that was 'organic and of the people'.

Such were the doctrinal problems that influenced the PDP. Alongside the social doctrine of the Church, there was an important ambience with, in particular, the 'popularism' built up into a doctrine by Sturzo and popularized to some extent by Marcel Prelot; it led to an 'organic concept of society and of the people' considered as an articulated whole of varied groups. The 'popularism' was disseminated notably by the review *Politique*, while several articles by Sturzo were published in French, particularly in the *Cahiers de la Nouvelle Journée*.[26] Marcel Prelot stressed the 'profound intellectual affinities' between the founder of the PPI and the PDP.[27] It was a case of the systematizing of the traditional doctrine of the Christian democrats and the social Catholics on the so-called 'intermediary bodies' representing professional groups, with a series of 'natural communities' that had to interlock, culminating in a necessary reform of the state. This reform was based on a regionalist conception of a more decentralized France.

The 1927 party conference attempted to spell out the principal features of this social programme.[28] There was another doctrinal influence – that of 'democratic personalism', associated with Paul Archambault and the *Cahiers de la Nouvelle Journée*. 'Democratic personalism' was set against the 'revolutionary personalism' of Emmanuel Mounier.[29] The 'theory of the institution' associated with Maurice Hauriou and echoing the theory of intermediary bodies again exercised an influence. Hauriou and Georges Renard later saw this theory as being the basis of a renewal of the social order.[30] An abundance of doctrinal wealth came to light in a sort of laboratory, in which the teachings of the Church provided the guidelines for the conceptual development of an economic and social organization opposed to both liberalism and socialism. But this overall aim did not prevent interest being taken in concrete social problems and in what was called the 'social movement', leading to constant support by the PDP for the new social legislation.

In particular, thought was given to the question of business relations, the position of wage-earners and working conditions – everything that could foster co-operation between workers' and employers' organizations. In 1929 François Reille-Soult, a democratic deputy, set out in the chamber the broad outlines of PDP social policy as a kind of 'third way' between liberalism and socialism.[31] No attempt was made to exclude social progress in a certain 'rationalization of labour', and a certain 'American' and 'modernist' influence was brought to bear in the 1920s on a part of social Catholicism, as were the topics of modernist and social 'neo-capitalism'. Initially at least, the PDP's 'practical social action' had concrete effects such as the support given to the new social legislation. The new law on social insurance was approved, and the PDP rebelled against all the moves to hamper the application of the law adopted in 1928 and recast in 1930.[32] The same was true of the support given to the new legislation of 1932 on family allowances.

The social welfare problems changed in tone with the onset of the crisis of the 1930s, which the PDP saw as a sign of economic imbalance and of the failure to respect the basic principles of a 'Christian welfare economy'. On no account was it to be an excuse for revising social benefits, but rather an opportunity to show a more determined spirit of social co-operation. A *plan démocrate populaire* was drawn up in 1934.[33] There was to be a restructuring of the economic and social system by the organization of business corporations, and certain reforms in the republican state. There was condemnation of the ambiguities of the 'planned economy' that could lead to a totalitarian state. State intervention was to take place in a clearly defined context, thus avoiding the excesses of both 'liberal anarchy' and the 'planned economy' of the Soviet or fascist kind. The PDP also expressed its opposition to the corporatist state of Mussolini's Italy, and its backing of an economy 'ordered' or 'organized' from above, by the state.

However, it was at that time that the question of 'corporatism' arose once more in social Catholic – and to some extent Christian democrat – circles.

The PDP sought to re-examine in some depth its social policy between individualistic capitalism and state socialism, just when social Catholicism was about to be gripped by the temptation of corporatism.[34] The corporative idea was still alive in those circles and some politicians, like Prelot, even spoke of 'corporative democracy' in the ideological summary of the journal *Politique*. In the 1930s a corporatist revival occurred. The Semaine sociale held in Angers in 1935 was devoted to 'corporatist organization'. It ended with the acceptance of a sort of 'toned down' corporatism, which to some – notably the Christian democrats – may have seemed excessive. In the doctrinal domain of the popular democrats there was a certain reticence with regard to the spread of these ideas. There, too, uncertainties arose, although there was still opposition to the nature of what PDP politicians called 'state corporatism' of the Italian type. For the popular democrats those ideas had some attractive aspects, such as the search for a third way, and other aspects that prompted mistrust, such as certain authoritarian aspects.

There was also uncertainty as to what position to adopt at the end of the period with regard to the social legislation of the Popular Front. In the main the reforms, many of which featured in their programme, were given wholehearted support, but there were some reservations as to their root causes and their economic consequences. The fairly rapid economic failure of the experiment, however, did not cause too much regret and the so-called liberal reorientation, from 1937–38 onwards, was sustained. The popular democrats were among those who supported France under Daladier: a time when the beginning of an experiment in 'co-operation between the classes' was thought possible. The inter-war years ended with a period during which the popular democrats believed more than ever that they could assert their social ideas, and also their family policy with their support for the new 'family code'. Similarly, constant support had been given to the CFTC and to its 'plan' of 1936. Right to the end, relations with the major organizations of the social Catholics remained fruitful. It was in that incomplete and imperfect symbiosis, based on an appeal to moral forces and respect for religious conscience as the third 'cardinal point', that the PDP found the basis for its social actions and policies.

PRO-EUROPEAN AND INTERNATIONAL INITIATIVE

The PDP also developed a major policy and initiative, both European and international. However, the stance it adopted in this domain was not immediate. Throughout the period prior to its official launch in 1924, divergences in the field of international and European politics had existed between the 'democratic republicans' and the supporters of the Jeune République of Marc Sangnier, who had begun to veer towards a more or less pacifist and internationalist position.[35] But this direction was not well received by the 'democratic republicans'. The constitution of the Ligue nationale de la démocratie (LND) in 1922 provided no solution to the problem, at a time when Sangnier, for his part, was launching the Internationale démocratique. Prior to the founding of the PDP, the attitudes of the 'democratic republicans' were much more nationalist than those of the Jeune République; the future Popular Democrats thus remained faithful to the 'France first' policy of the Bloc national.[36] There was also an initiative on the part of the PDP and Sturzo in favour of a 'black' or 'popular' International, aimed at bringing together tendencies grounded in Christian democracy throughout Europe with different objectives from those of the Internationale démocratique of Sangnier, who operated in a less political sphere and wanted to broaden out his activity into tendencies that were even non-Catholic or left-wing. Relations between the Internationale démocratique and the Internationale populaire soon became strained. Following the break-up of the LND and the launch of the PDP, Sturzo chose to ally himself with the PDP.

At the time of its launch in 1924, the PDP already revealed in its programme certain signs of the shift in its approach to international problems that constituted its fourth 'cardinal point'. It proposed 'a foreign policy that was resolutely French but at the same time definitely in favour of measures aimed at international reconciliation'. It expressed the wish for 'the advent of an international order able to ensure peace'.[37] The initial programme, however, was marked by complex influences, before developing towards a moderate internationalism. Over the period from 1924–28 the PDP inclined towards Briand's policy of European entente and Franco-German rapprochement, and engaged actively on the international scene. After the launch of the PDP and also his exile in London, where he kept in touch with Sangnier, Sturzo travelled to Paris in 1925 to suggest to the newly founded PDP that it should take the initiative in arranging a meeting of parties to examine the possibility of founding an international organization. The first meeting was held in Paris in December 1925. The decision was made to set up in Paris a Secrétariat International des Partis Démocratique d'Inspiration Chrétienne (SIPDIC).[38]

There was now a new setting for the action of the PDP; it was located in an embryonic International comprising parties with the same outlook and, moreover, the awareness of being in touch with Germany's Centre Party in the context of the policy of Briand. The PDP took part in the SIPDIC conferences in Brussels in 1926 and in Cologne in 1927. In 1928 the SIPDIC was further reinforced around a general secretariat in Paris, which was entrusted to the PDP in the person of Henri Simondet. The 1928 conference was held in the Dutch town of s'Hertogenbosch. The theme of the 1929 conference was particularly close to the democrats' heart: 'organization in the workplace in the modern state'. The year 1930 was the start of a period of difficulties. In the forefront of these was the return of the German problem with the electoral rise of National Socialism, and in 1931 the Germans took no part in the conference held in Luxembourg. Franco-German relations collapsed, although contact was made with the Italians in exile and dialogue was opened up between European parties. Despite this support, on the international front the PDP still had to defend a more or less 'centrist' policy between what it saw as the internationalist demagogy of the left, and the right that was bedevilled by the extreme views of Charles Maurras.[39]

It was also at this time that the effects of the condemnation of Action française tended to arouse yet more hostility towards expressions of nationalism, the popular democrats having distanced themselves on the matter from the Catholic Right. To an increasing extent after 1927, discussion about European affairs was taken up by the journal *Politique*, which had a somewhat 'Briandist' tone. The party spoke of a 'transnational policy' based on a primarily moral concept of the role of the nation. The time had come to settle the major problems brought about by the war. In 1929 an issue of the *Cahiers de la nouvelle journée* was devoted to the Franco-German problem and favoured rapprochement. Briand's plans for a European federation were welcomed and *Politique* echoed, with Sturzo, the appeal of Richard Coudenhove-Kalergi, the founder of the Pan-European Movement.[40] It was not until 1930 that new anxiety arose concerning the worsening political situation. The PDP remained attached to the trilogy of arbitration, security and disarmament, centred on an 'organized Europe'. A manifesto entitled *Notre programme de politique extérieure* was published in 1930, and *Politique* launched an 'Investigation into European Union'.[41] In 1931 the conference declared: 'European union was never more essential'. It was not until late 1932 that this policy came under attack. Thus, without concurring with the pacifism of the Jeune République, the PDP distanced itself from the traditional Catholic Right.

The political sympathies of Pope Pius XI were made clear by his support for Briand and for Franco-German rapprochement. Action française later held that this policy, with its allies in France, was responsible for the Pope's condemnation. It is difficult to tell whether perhaps the Pope's views, or his relations with Sturzo, were at the root of these attitudes. This was a point on which the Christian democrats and the left as a whole were in agreement – one of the convergences mentioned by Cornilleau in his *Pourquoi pas?* for an alliance with the Socialists, and one of the points that united the groups associated with journals such as *La Volonté, Le Rappel, Le Nouveau Siècle, Paris-Phare, Notre Temps, La Jeune République*, etc., who were known as the *jeunes équipes* and who advocated a 'United States of Europe'. The convergences between the Vatican's policy and that of Briand were undeniable, even though, from that time on, their interpretation provoked somewhat heated debate. A form of 'European idea' began to develop within the PDP, and certain of its intellectuals and political theorists went a considerable way towards a certain idea of a 'United States of Europe'. This period probably explains why there was a rapid resurgence of the same themes in the early years following the Second World War.

There were those who attempted to codify these movements, like Ernest Pezet, for example, on the problems of Central and Eastern Europe.[42] Here again contacts made through SIPDIC played a part, as did Catholic solidarity in a number of these countries such as Poland in particular, but also Austria with its Christian Social Party, even though, following 1931, Austria was seen to be 'at the crossroads' with regard to its domestic and foreign options. During 1931–32 Pezet collaborated on the so-called Tardieu Plan for economic co-operation between the countries bordering the Danube. His visits to those countries had led him to believe that it was necessary to establish an economic agreement among them under the supervision of the future European Union.

Ideas concerning European co-operation were not without specific problems, like relations with fascist Italy. Of all the moderate parties, the PDP, in the light of its contacts with the anti-fascist Partito Popolare emigrants such as Sturzo, Francesco Luigi Ferrari and Domenico Russo, was the first to express its hostility to fascist ideology and the fascist regime. It launched a fierce attack on the major features of Italy's fascist policies, both domestic and foreign. Announcing its hostility to all forms of totalitarianism, the PDP believed that both fascism and bolshevism were interconnected and inimical to 'Catholic supranationalism'. However, a dispute arose between Sturzo, who had replaced Ferrari on his death in 1933, and the popular democrats over the role of the Austrian Christian Social Party in the suppression of Social Democratic riots in Vienna in February 1934, against the imposition of a corporatist state. In Russo's view, an end had to be put to the fiction of an International of Christian democrat parties, given that truly democratic parties were now effectively in a minority.[43]

Furthermore, the PDP had begun to edge towards a certain distrust of Germany.[44] After January 1933 and the arrival on the scene of Adolf Hitler who, initially, received an unworried welcome, the PDP attitude towards Germany was somewhat ambivalent. At the end of 1934, despite the 'neophytes' who continued to favour the policy of Franco-German rapprochement, Pezet realized that this policy had failed.[45] This was the start of the party's change to a firm approach towards the Germany of Hitler. The PDP essentially shed its illusions regarding international co-operation. The problems of Central Europe still worried the party. All had to be done to ensure the survival of Austria, and there was a redoubled wish to oppose Hitler's expansion in that region. However, hostility to fascist foreign policy was the primary concern, although the PDP did not openly condemn Italy's invasion of Ethiopia and the atrocities committed by Italian troops while Franco-Italian relations remained close at the governmental level. On the other hand, with regard to the USSR, whereas the rejection of totalitarianism was maintained, a realistic approach to a possible Eastern alliance against Nazi Germany became apparent, even though the ratification of the Franco-Soviet Pact of 1935 caused some unrest. The PDP no longer really believed in 'collective security'. It was very concerned about the so-called *Anschluss*, or annexation of Austria by Nazi Germany in March 1938. Following the Czechoslovakian crisis in the late summer, early autumn of the same year, the PDP eventually approved the Munich agreement in parliament, including the cession of Czechoslovak territory mainly inhabited by German speakers, although most of its members held strongly 'anti-Munich' views.

As part of the Daladier government, the PDP reaffirmed its progressive shift towards firmness against Nazi Germany. Previously, regarding the Spanish Civil War, the PDP had already been less sympathetic than the bulk of Catholic opinion towards Franco, because of his links with fascist Italy and Nazi Germany. The question of forming possible alliances to safeguard peace was more and more frequently raised, disappointment being all the greater in view of the Soviet–German Pact signed in 1939. Throughout the 'phoney war' of 1939–40, the PDP continued to pursue its policy of firmness. In principle, they remained faithful to the concept of a united Europe that they had defended during 1925–32. They nourished the idea of a Europe inspired by the democratic spirit, grounded in Christianity and tracing its roots to a certain Catholic universalism, or indeed internationalism. Religious motives were at the heart of their vision, buttressed by the idea of Christian charity in international relations, along with justice and the need for reconciliation between wartime enemies. The themes that arose over a few years were those that were to be taken up again, after 1945, in the same Christian democrat context.[46]

LIFE AND DEATH OF A PARTY

In 1924 the PDP wanted to fashion itself as a party on a pattern closer to that of the French Socialists, for example, than to those of the moderate right and the radical left: a party of the 'masses', not of the 'class of functionaries'. It remained a small political force that juxtaposed in its structures a certain centralism and sustained federalism. However, it had a national conference, a national council and executive committee, a general secretariat, a research department and a range of committees and subcommittees. It was always short of funds and it remained at best a party of only average political influence, even though it tried to engage in propaganda on much the same scale as the large parties with more than 20,000 members.[47] It was one of the Christian democrat-inspired parties in Europe in the broad sense that had the least direct political impact, thus showing the difficulty – greater and more specific in France – of founding a party of that sort. This was due notably to a certain persistence of the 'religious question'. The founding of the PDP came about through the Fédérations de républicains-démocrates, but its expansion, which was rapid in the 1920s, tapered off during the 1930s. Its network was patchy, and varied from region to region. The party also had widespread publicity in the press, although it failed to acquire a national daily newspaper, which the major parties in France had.

The PDP drew up an official programme and endeavoured to devise an overall political philosophy. It was, then, a Catholic programme based socially and doctrinally on social Catholicism and Christian democracy, while adhering politically to liberal democracy. It was, furthermore, a particular concept of 'popular democracy' broadly inspired by the 'democratic popularism' of Sturzo and by an organized concept of society originating farther back in the past. The PDP, of course, also developed a plan of direct political action at the very outset of what could be considered its 'ascendant phase', from 1924 to 1932. It played a political part in the period 1924–28 when it straight away took up a centre-right position against the Cartel des gauches. It was confronted by the problem of its political classification and had to adopt a position in relation to the parties of the so-called moderate right, notably the Fédération républicaine. It distinguished itself from them in a number of fields by its more 'progressive' views on social policy and international relations, favouring, as it did, international understanding and support for the policy of Briand. At any rate, it was opposed to all the shades of the far right and to the setting up of leagues, just as it was opposed to the AF in the fields of politics and religion. The question of possible collaboration with left-wingers, in particular the Radicals, arose fairly soon: it was the question of the so-called republican concentration. With regard to the socialists, in 1927 Cornilleau, one of the party's political theorists, in his book *Pourquoi pas?*[48] launched the idea of a possible future political and parliamentary entente, which caused a sensation. Attempts were also made to establish contacts in what were called the various *jeunes équipes*, marking a wish to bypass the old traditional divisions.

These characteristics continued to be apparent in the period 1928–32, when overall support was given to the governments of the centre-right. There were constant clashes with the extreme right, who started calling the Popular Democrats and the other Christian Democrats 'Christian Reds'. The underlying crisis with the Fédération républicaine remained permanent and eventually came to a head in 1931–32. Whereas the 1928 elections had been a relative success, those of 1932 marked the beginning of the party's decline. The ensuing period 1932–39 was one of slow relative decline, but also of total transformation. Although the PDP fought the second cartel, it distanced itself somewhat from the popular unrest against it of February 1934, and yet it once again supported the governments of national union. The party again lost ground in the 1936 elections. Despite this, it remained in fairly calm opposition with regard to the Popular Front government of Radicals and Socialists (1936–38) tolerated by the Communists and, initially, to the government of the socialist Léon Blum. It later rallied to the Daladier government by becoming a 'government party' at the end of the inter-war period, along with the Radicals. The patient effort of contact accomplished over a period of some fifteen years with certain secular milieux finally yielded results. The activity of the PDP in the 1930s also had to be resituated within the framework of both a party crisis and an overall renewal of Christian democracy. Internal divisions were pointed up by the launch in 1932, by Francisque Gay, of the newspaper *L'Aube*, on which Popular Democrats and members of the Jeune République collaborated. Although an attempt at revitalizing the party was made by the Jeunesses démocrates populaires, it did not yield immediate results.

It could be said, then, that there were partial successes for the PDP, probably marking a necessary stage in the political growth of Christian-inspired democracy in France, but also relative failure if judged by initial aspirations. The PDP undeniably made its mark in the political heritage of France, which can be appreciated only when viewed as part of a continuous process of change. The party was an indispensable stage in the political gathering together of a tendency that hitherto had been mainly intellectual and social. It also played a role in the transnational organization of the SIPDIC, and in that international impulse it found part of its *raison d'être* as one of several parties of the same sort, or of somewhat similar inspiration, elsewhere in a Europe the complexity and diversity of which it demonstrated all on its own.[49]

In any case, the 'pre-Resistance' attitude developed by the majority of Popular Democrats during 1933–39 was to become a reality, first of all during the 'phoney war' of 1939–40. It ranged from support for a certain 'war propaganda' to a vote against the granting of 'full powers' to Marshal Pétain after the French military defeat, by three of their deputies (Champetier de Ribes, Paul Simon and Pierre Trémintin), which can be seen as a first act of resistance. Under the occupation and the Vichy regime a section of the PDP, seeing that the regime had adopted part of the social Catholic programme, succumbed to a certain 'pro-Vichy' temptation, and a small minority even drifted towards collaboration. However, other Popular Democrats adopted, at an early date, a certain 'sullenness' towards the regime, while yet others opted for the 'first resistance', which was often Christian-inspired to some extent.

The Resistance began in this setting in a casual, almost haphazard manner and centred on Alphonse Juge, Champetier de Ribes, etc. But the

Popular Democrats played a more precise role within movements such as Liberté (with François de Menthon, Pierre-Henri Teitgen and Alfred and Paul Coste-Floret), which was soon absorbed by Combat, led by Henri Frenay. Similarly, a number of other militant democrats joined Témoignage chrétien, in whose networks they met representatives of the other shades of opinion that constituted the Christian democrat sphere, thus paving the way to later expansion. Some popular democrats also gravitated towards parallel movements, such as Résistance, La voix du Nord, le Groupe de la rue de Lille, etc. On the other hand, however, a number of them played an important role in the official Resistance institutions such as the Press and Information Bureau directed by Georges Bidault, and the General Research Committee, of which Pierre-Henri Teitgen became the Secretary General and which published the *Cahiers* that showed the influence of Popular Democracy. On the founding of the Conseil national de la Résistance (CNR), the 'Christian Democrats' were represented by Georges Bidault, who, following the arrest of Jean Moulin, took over as head of that top-level body which organized internal resistance, thus giving the PDP a new boost. The Christian and Popular Democrat tendency, then, approached the run-up to the Liberation benefiting from a soundly based position in the Resistance; its standing was markedly higher on the political scene than it had been in 1940.

This situation was to be the basis for major changes made possible at the Liberation in 1944–45 and which led to the launch of a new party, the Mouvement Républicain de Libération (MRL) that later became the Mouvement Républicain Populaire (MRP), with which the majority of popular democrats agreed to merge even though they were outnumbered – particularly in the case of the ACJF – and to some extent sidelined. However, what occurred here was a sort of transformation of the PDP and a sudden increase in the influence of the tendency it represented, since the MRP became the foremost party in France in the early post-war years.

NOTES

1. See Gérard Cholvy and Yves-Marie Hilaire, *Histoire religieuse de la France contemporaine* (Toulouse, 3 vols, 1985–88); Jean-Dominique Durand, *L'Europe de la démocratie chrétienne* (Brussels 1995); Jean-Marie Mayeur, *Des partis catholiques à la démocratie chrétienne* (Paris 1980).
2. See Jeanne Caron, *Le Sillon et la démocratie chrétienne* (Paris 1966) and Madeleine Barthelemy-Madaule, *Marc Sangnier 1873–1950* (Paris 1973).
3. See Jean-Marie Mayeur, *Catholicisme social et démocratie chrétienne, principes romains, expériences françaises* (Paris 1985).
4. See Jean-Claude Delbreil, *Centrisme et démocratie chrétienne en France. Le parti démocrate populaire, des origines au MRP: 1919–1944* (Paris 1990). Jean-Claude Delbreil, 'Le parti démocrate populaire des origines au MRP 1919–1944'. Thesis (Nanterre 1984); Marcel Prelot, 'Les démocrates populaires

français. Chronique de vingt ans 1919–1939', in *Scritti di sociologia e politica in onore di Luigi Sturzo* (Bologna 1953), pp. 203–29; Jean Raymond-Laurent, *Le parti démocrate populaire 1924–1944* (Le Mans 1965).
5 Delbreil, *Le parti démocrate populaire*, p. 207.
6 Ibid., p. 275.
7 Ibid., p. 231.
8 Ibid., p. 780.
9 Michel Launay, *La CFTC. Origines et développement* (Paris 1988); idem, *Le syndicalisme chrétien en France de 1885 à nos jours* (Paris 1984).
10 Delbreil, *Le parti démocrate populaire*, p. 755; *Pour les ruraux, la politique agricole du PDP* (Paris 1930).
11 Delbreil, *Le parti démocrate populaire*, p. 783.
12 Ibid., p. 793. *Discours de Charles Flory. Librairie de la Jeunesse catholique* (Paris 1925).
13 *Petit Démocrate*, 24–30 November 1924. See also Paul Simon, *République et laïcité. La politique religieuse des démocrates populaires*, Speech in the Chamber of Deputies, 26–27 January 1925 (Paris 1925).
14 See also M. W. Paul, *The Second Ralliement: the Rapprochement between Church and State in the Twentieth Century* (Washington, DC 1967).
15 Robert Cornilleau, *Le ralliement a-t-il échoué?* (Paris 1926). See also idem, *De Waldeck-Rousseau à Poincaré. Chronique d'une génération 1896–1924* (Paris 1927).
16 Jean Raymond-Laurent, *Manuel politique et social. Le programme des démocrates* (Paris 1924).
17 Delbreil, *Le parti démocrate populaire*, p. 503.
18 Ibid., p. 543; Philippe Portier, *Église et politique en France au XXe siècle* (Paris 1955), Archives Raymond Laurent, Box 50.
19 Delbreil, *Le parti démocrate populaire*, p. 525.
20 Jean-Claude Delbreil, *Les catholiques français et les tentatives de rapprochement franco-allemand dans l'entre deux guerres* (Metz 1972).
21 Marc Minier, *L'épiscopat français de 1921 à 1932* (Paris 1977).
22 *Petit Démocrate*, 23 November 1936; Auguste Bastianelli, *La réforme générale de l'enseignement*, Editions du Petit Démocrate (Paris 1930).
23 Delbreil, *Le parti démocrate populaire*, p. 1067; Philippe Dazet-Brun, 'Auguste Champetier de Ribes', Thesis (Nanterre 1995), Archives Champetier de Ribes. See also Jean-Marie Mayeur, *La question laïque (XIXe–XXe siècles)* (Paris 1997); Laurent Laot, *Catholicisme, Politique et laïcté* (Paris 1990).
24 Delbreil, *Le parti démocrate populaire*, p. 360; *Le Parti démocrate populaire. Compte-rendu de l'assemblée générale constitutive des 15–16 novembre 1924* (Paris 1924).
25 Raymond Laurent et Marcel Prelot, *Manuel politique* (Paris 1928).
26 *Cahiers de la Nouvelle Journée*, vols 18 (1931) and 32 (1936).
27 Marcel Prelot, *Démocratie populaire et réforme de l'État* (Paris 1932); Durand, *L'Europe de la démocratie chrétienne*, p. 180.
28 *Petit Démocrate*, 27 November 1927.
29 Delbreil, *Le parti démocrate populaire*, p. 397.
30 Ibid., p. 408.
31 *Journal Officiel, Débats parlementaires. Chambre des Députés*, 22 January 1929 (Paris 1929).
32 *Petit Démocrate*, 18 June 1929.
33 Jean Raymond-Laurent, *Face à la crise. Les solutions du PDP* (Paris 1936).
34 Delbreil, *Le parti démocrate populaire*, p. 1120.

35 Barthélemy-Madaule, *Marc Sangnier.*
36 See Delbreil, *Les Catholiques français*; Roberto Papini, *L'internationale démocrate chrétienne 1925–1986* (Paris 1988); Roberto Papini, *Il corragio della democrazia. Sturzo e l'internazionale popolare tra le due guerre* (Rome 1995); Hugues Portelli and Thomas Jansen (eds), *La démocratie chrétienne, force internationale* (Nanterre 1986).
37 Delbreil, *Le parti démocrate populaire*, p. 367.
38 See in greater detail the chapter by Guido Müller in this book.
39 Delbreil, *Les catholiques français*, p. 143.
40 *Politique*, 15 September 1929.
41 *Politique*, 15 January 1931.
42 Ernest Pezet, *Chrétiens au service de la cité. De Léon XIII au M.R.P.* (Paris 1969).
43 Delbreil, *Le parti démocrate populaire*, p. 1165.
44 Ibid.
45 *Journal Officiel, Débats parlementaires, Chambre des Députés*, 1 December 1934 (Paris 1934).
46 See Philippe Chenaux, *Une Europe vaticane?* (Brussels 1990); Serge Berstein, Jean-Marie Mayeur and Pierre Milza (eds), *Le M.R.P. et la construction européenne* (Brussels 1993).
47 Delbreil, *Le parti démocrate populaire*, p. 265.
48 Robert Cornilleau, *Pourquoi pas? Une politique réaliste* (Paris and Valois 1929).
49 Delbreil, *Le parti démocrate populaire*, p. 1301. Also on Christian democracy, see Michael Fogarty, *Christian Democracy in Western Europe 1820–1953* (London 1957); Pierre Letamendia, *La démocratie chrétienne* (Paris 1977); B. E. M. Irving, *Christian Democracy in France* (London 1973); François-Georges Dreyfus, *Histoire de la démocratie chrétienne en France de Chateaubriand à Raymond Barre* (Paris 1988).

7

Between the Crisis of the Liberal State, Fascism and a Democratic Perspective: The Popular Party in Italy

Tiziana di Maio

The first political experience of organized Catholics in Italy was permeated by events that occurred in the period from the end of the First World War to the start of fascism. The history of the Partito Popolare Italiano (PPI) was consequently a very short one: founded in 1919, it was already banned by a fascist law in 1926. During the very few years of its existence it none the less made an important contribution to the democratic life of the country, and at the same time formed the basis for the long-lived Christian Democratic party in Italy after the Second World War. Leading PPI figures took part in its formation. In its brief life the PPI also promoted an important, but similarly short-lived initiative: Catholic politicians came together in the Secrétariat International des Partis Démocratiques d'Inspiration Chrétienne (SIPDIC), with important contributions from Italians, especially Luigi Sturzo.

Despite its officially non-confessional character and a certain independence from the Church authorities, the PPI was, of all the Christian parties in Europe, the one most under the influence of the Church. This was due to historical and geographical factors. In an analysis of the relationship between the PPI and the Church, its economic and social policies and its contribution to the SIPDIC, it is necessary to throw light on the historical events from 1919 to 1926. Only in so doing can it be understood why the PPI, despite the difficulties arising from the crisis of the liberal state and the rise of fascist power, could retain its strong programmatic and ideological coherence. This was despite the fact that a national-Catholic synthesis was never accomplished. The history of the PPI is likewise incomplete without taking Sturzo's role into consideration. He was not only founder of the party, but also its inspiration and ideas man.

THE POPULAR PARTY IN ITALY

ORIGINS AND GENERAL CHARACTER OF THE PPI

The founding of a Catholic-oriented party in Italy took place later than in other European countries. This was due to the opposition between the Vatican state and the newly formed Italian kingdom of 1859–61. The achievement of national unity threw up the so-called 'Roman Question': the objections of the Pope and the entire Catholic Church to the occupation and dissolution of the Vatican state in 1870. The relationship between the Vatican and the Italian state was very much put to the test in the first decades. Between 1861 and 1871 many Catholic groups refused to field candidates or to vote. Up until 1870 the Vatican took no official position on the question of abstention from voting. In 1874 the *Non expedit* actually banned Catholics from participating in parliamentary elections. They were, however, actively encouraged to take part in local elections. The first years of the Italian state were consequently characterized by the non-participation of Catholic citizens in political life. The solving of the 'Roman Question' remained the main aim of the government and of Catholic citizens. Only in 1905 did Pope Pius X modify the *Non expedit* with the encyclical *Il Fermo Proposito*. Italian Catholics were now motivated to prepare themselves for political life with 'care and seriousness', for the time when they would be called upon to do so.

After the publication of this encyclical, Sturzo realized that the moment had come for Italian Catholics to form a political party. In a speech in Caltagirone he laid down the basis for a democratic party, which, although inspired by Catholicism, should officially remain non-confessional.[1] Before taking the step of forming a Catholic party it was, in Sturzo's opinion, necessary to resolve the problems resulting from the coming into being of the Italian state. Most importantly, the relationship between the monarchy and the Church had to be clarified.[2] The future party, according to Sturzo, had to influence the government's decisions regarding the Church. It should stand for Catholic principles without becoming a clerical party, because this would not be of use either to the Pope or to the Italian nation. As regards the monarchy, Sturzo's position was shrewd and far-sighted. Italian Catholics had fought against the sovereignty of the House of Savoy on different levels, because it was seen as both socially conservative and frivolous. Sturzo's position was that the national Catholic Party had neither strong opinions about the monarchy nor the intention to change the existing structure of society, as 'we see the unity of the country and the portrayal of authority in the existing monarchical institution combined and one in the figure of the throne'.[3] Furthermore, the aim of the future party should not be the solving of the Roman Question, as this was not to be solved by parliament but by the Pope himself, who was a unique instance.[4] Sturzo was influenced by the autonomous teaching of the German Centre Party.

In his opinion, this model 'addresses the real conditions of the time in which we live'.[5] The political weight of the Catholics was underlined in 1913 on the occasion of the first general election with universal male suffrage. In the framework of the so-called *Patto Gentiloni*[6] the Vatican allowed Catholics to participate. It was on 17 November 1918 that Don Luigi Sturzo announced the official entry of the Catholics on to the Italian political scene. He stressed that this was as a result of the situation after the war, which was characterized by the decline of the old political elite.[7] After this speech the Vatican State Secretary, Cardinal Gasparri, gave his go-ahead for the formation of a 'Party of Catholics'. Sturzo, in turn, agreed not to speak in the name of the Vatican and not to name the party either 'Christian' or 'Catholic'. His aim was to clear away the suspicion that the party represented the Vatican, which wanted to remain politically neutral. After this declaration and also later, the non-confessional nature of the PPI came, however, to be questioned and doubted. The press wrote that the PPI had been formed 'under Vatican orders', so that its interests could be better represented in the state.[8]

CONNECTIONS TO THE CHURCH AND THE SOCIETAL BASIS OF THE PPI

The PPI was founded on 18 January 1919, when the party publicized a call to the nation and its first programme. It was something quite new in the history of Italian politics that a party presented itself with a written manifesto. It is very important to stress the new character that this party embodied. Through the integration of the Catholics into the state, they *de facto* confirmed, first of all, the definite solution to the Roman Question. Moreover, the PPI programme reflected ideological and policy reforms. The party presented itself as independent of the Church hierarchy.[9] Sturzo declared at the first PPI congress in Bologna that a distinction should be made between the universal, such as religion, and the concrete, which was practical politics. For this reason the party was not named 'Catholic'.[10] Sturzo chose the name *popolare*, a name that had already been used by the Catholics in the Austrian Trento region. He wanted originally to add the word 'Christian' to indicate the principles on which the party's programme were based. But he then abandoned this idea in order to facilitate the breakthrough of the basic principle of non-confessionalism. At the congress in Bologna, he explained the choice of the name Popular Party and stressed the necessity of uniting Christian ideas, social movements and organizations and working-class interests in a political synthesis. In his endeavours for autonomy, he consciously wanted to detach the PPI from previous attempts to organize Catholicism and from other parties – in the basic principles as well as in the action taken:

For a popular idea to work one would like to see a certain level of national unity and social common sense, collective freedom, the organization of political forces and moral values. This has been shown in the history of mankind from that time on when all people were named 'the chosen people ... and Christian people'.[11]

The second essential aspect of the PPI consisted in the assertion of non-confessionalism and a political programme not necessarily determined by common Catholicism. The PPI presented itself not as the party of the Catholics, but rather as the party of Catholics in general. This left open the opportunity for non-Catholics to join, without working against other political groups that also had their basis in Christian values. The PPI was a party with its own ideological, programmatic and organizational character.[12] It created a modern structure for itself comparable to that of the other larger parties, such as the Socialist Party, with a political office, national council, a network of local party groups, periodically held national congresses and its own press. The PPI members of parliament demanded well-defined alliances and programmatic agreements before they agreed to their own participation in government. The parliamentary party was not homogenous. The deputies came from different Catholic organizations. Among them were journalists, smallholders, industrialists and unionists. Above all, the PPI had its roots and broad base in rural Italy. Its special character allowed it to bring together different social classes. These included at the same time the interests of the big landowners who saw in *popolarismo* an effective means of combating socialism and of avoiding far-reaching social reforms, as well as the interests of the lower-middle class who wanted limited economic and social reforms from the Liberals. The common denominator of these different strands consisted of a shared Catholicism and democratic alignment.

THE ECONOMIC AND SOCIAL PROGRAMME

The PPI's programme aimed at securing Christian values and at addressing the long-perceived demand from Catholics to formulate a programme that would change life in Italy positively, above all for the poor and deprived. The objective was the upholding of freedom for Catholics and improving their opportunities within the state, and this was combined with Christian social and ethical values. In order that the value of the individual and human dignity could be upheld as a measure for the state administration, the PPI programme included the explicit aim to improve the lot of the individual in every area of civil life. In particular, the founders of the PPI demanded moderate agrarian reform and supported smallholders. The character of the party, with its appeal across all classes, was already a distinguishing feature at its first conference. While Agostino

Gemellis on the right wing of the party recommended a closer relationship with the Church authorities, and Guido Miglioli on the left wing suggested rather working together with other popular and proletarian forces, the programme tried to unite the interests of a wide spectrum of voters and to bring about Catholic unity.

The twelve points in the programme were advanced with vehemence during the short life of the party. The internal political principles are representative, therefore, of stages in numerous parliamentary struggles, showing that the PPI wanted to reform the state and political life. Proportional representation, freedom of teaching, decentralization of administration, tax reform, the right to work, improvement of the conditions of the industrial and agricultural worker, as well as freedom for the unions, were among the most important points. In its economic and social ideas the programme was related to that of the Austrian Catholics, and especially to the experience of the nineteenth-century social reformer Karl von Vogelsang, who was hailed as 'the proud adversary of the capitalistic economy'.[13] Sturzo declared at the Bologna congress:

> The programme is the truth, and as such is a living thing. It is in a constant state of development, it is specific, it creates a struggle to assert itself in theory and in practice and it describes in its development the path and the progress of the party. Our programme is developed by us and is strengthened by everyday concerns. Everything will contribute to bringing us ever nearer to the reality of life.[14]

In the year of its formation in 1919, the PPI took part in an election for the first time. It stood alone and declined all forms of electoral alliances, to find itself exposed to merciless attacks coming from the camp of those forces that had seen the Catholic movement as a reservoir of votes destined exclusively for them, as well as from the ranks of the maximalist socialists. Many of those fearing a rise of revolutionary socialism placed their hopes in the PPI. Simultaneously, sections of the rural population and conservative entrepreneurs accused the PPI of 'white bolshevism'. The PPI won 100 seats and became the largest parliamentary party at the heart of the Italian parliamentary system. As Francesco Malgeri has explained, electoral success was a mixed blessing:

> The election success of the PPI paradoxically changed its plans. The short history of the party was marked by a contradiction: on the one side it wanted to push through its programmatic ideas, and on the other side it was being worn down in government.[15]

The PPI was at its most committed as regards state reform, and the revival and freshening up of political life within the existing constitutional order. As a result, it was in a position to stop the advance of the Socialists. The PPI belonged to the governments towards the end of the liberal state. It also took part in Benito Mussolini's first government.[16] In the years in which the party participated in government it presented important plans for legal changes which were, for the most part, the result of party congress debates and analyses. On 3 April 1919 the PPI leadership sent out a circular in which the following directives of the party regarding agrarian reform were laid out: defence of small private ownership, representation for the agrarian working class and measures to benefit the day labourer. The agrarian question became one of the fundamental issues at the second PPI congress in Naples,[17] where deputies pressed for the expropriation of large landowners.[18] The PPI, resting on Sturzo's premise of 'bringing the people back to agriculture', subsequently presented a draft for a change in the law aiming at a large increase in small landownership, as well as comprehensive measures for the recultivation of land. The party rejected all forms of collectivism. It preferred small and middle-sized landownership, provoking sharp criticism from the Socialists. The resulting PPI draft law was described by Sturzo as late as 1942 as 'the best initiative in Italy since the Risorgimento'.[19]

The union disturbances of the 1920s, the taking over of the factories and the barricades, prompted Sturzo's party to analyse the position of the factories in the Italian capitalist economy. Party members suggested solutions that were later, in collaboration with the Catholic union, Confederazione Italiana Cavoratori (CIL), turned into a draft law. This draft was not, however, accepted by the government. The PPI promoted the introduction of profit-sharing schemes, as in its opinion this was one of the best methods for facilitating possibly a better and more economically profitable development of production – and without damaging employer or employee. These suggestions, however, only brought about the opposition of the government as well as of the Socialists.[20]

FOREIGN AND EUROPEAN POLICY

Questions of foreign policy were very important in the PPI's programme. According to Stefano Jacini, it was probably the only Italian party in the first years after the First World War that seriously concerned itself with the complex issues involved.[21] The PPI's conception of international politics was based on the conviction that fruitful and sustainable relations between states were those that corresponded to the interests of the peoples, guaranteeing them an influence over foreign policy making. Sturzo disagreed with the traditional Italian subordination of foreign policy to domestic political affairs.[22] He devised a foreign policy programme built around the principles of anti-imperialism, internationalism and a pro-European attitude.[23]

Among other points, the PPI promoted unilateral disarmament, supported the League of Nations, opposed the division of countries into victors and vanquished and pleaded for the right of entry to the League of Nations for those states that were defeated in the First World War. The PPI, in *Appello al paese* and in its programme, referred directly to the principles contained in Pope Benedict XV's declaration, 'Against the unnecessary blood bath',[24] and to US President Woodrow Wilson's 14 Points, which, however, remained largely of a declaratory character. The party's foreign policy aimed at economic and political equality across Europe, facilitating a Franco-German rapprochement. The PPI understood that the French policy of containing Germany economically as well as politically – in the sense of retribution – served only to foster feelings of revenge.[25]

In the opinion of the PPI, the Franco-German conflict had been transformed into a structural economic problem for Europe as a result of the Treaty of Versailles. The intention of the French appeared to be the distribution of foreign loans, with which Germany could rebuild its economy and pay for war damages.[26] The PPI suggested that the problem of reparation should be combined with inter-allied debts, to allow Germany an extended deadline and temporary discontinuation of payment of debts to Great Britain and the USA.[27] The PPI also expressed its uneasiness and discontent as regards the occupation of the Ruhr area. An economic balance had to be achieved in Europe, protectionist tendencies curbed, the value of currencies stabilized and the purchase of raw materials facilitated. In the suggestions for economic, emigration and colonial policy, it becomes apparent that the PPI's foreign policy goals reflected what it regarded as Italian national interests.

The eleventh point in the PPI's programme promoted 'colonial policy connected to the interests of the nation and a programme geared to progressive civilization'. The colonial question was not seen by the PPI as an imperialistic function or serving economic exploitation, but rather as an additional means for emigration in order to curb overpopulation in Italy. This was seen, above all, as an answer to the agrarian question, especially in relation to the problems in southern Italy. The PPI also hoped for greater markets for Italy's economy. In addition, the party laid great emphasis on national self-determination for European nations, and the resulting necessity of seeing this defended in an international context and respected as a peace-inducing instrument. This position was similarly reflected in the PPI's explicit expression of its disappointment about the prohibited unification of Austria and Germany. The PPI also supported the nationalist demands of the Irish, who gained independence in 1921.

THE PPI AND THE CRISIS OF THE LIBERAL STATE

It can be said with regard to the role of the party in a state in which the Liberal Party was dominant, that the PPI contributed, in a paradoxical way, to the crisis it experienced in that it hoped to overcome its structural shortcomings with constructive criticism. It gave political consciousness to those southern Italian farmers and workers who, up until this time, had not fully identified with socialist ideology. The efforts of *popolarismo* helped the farmers to combat the political dominance of the old liberal governing classes. This also had the side-effect that the basis of the Liberal Party system, that is, the tacit understanding between the protectionist bloc of northern industrialists and the great landowners of the south, was no longer safe. The PPI did not, however, achieve its aims, as the mass of the deprived, which had increased, saw its chance in the rise of fascism. In October 1922, after the fascist 'March on Rome', Mussolini was called to form a new government. He suggested the PPI take part. The party leadership consented to the participation of some deputies in a personal capacity.[28]

Stefano Jacini, a leading figure in the history of the PPI, and a deputy from 1919 to 1924, later recalled the leadership's decision in his book, *Storia del P.P.I.* After weighing up the possible courses of action, the leadership allowed 'the individual and conditional participation in the government of a number of deputies'.[29] They were instructed to guard the rights and values of the citizens, 'who had first survived the bolshevist and then the fascist storm', thus contributing to a return to constitutional government.[30] Mussolini had given the PPI guarantees, especially on the retention of proportional representation and the continued freedom of trade union organization.[31] The PPI representatives believed in the normalization of political life and in a constitutional anchoring of fascism. The hope that the fascists could be guided towards a democratic approach turned out to be an illusion, however, as they did not keep their promises, so that the PPI could only observe the destruction of parliamentary institutions.

Sturzo himself inaugurated the end of the policy of collaboration in a speech in Turin on 20 December 1922.[32] He disputed there, above all, the oft-quoted thesis that with the rise of fascism, *popolarismo* no longer had the right to exist, because the government itself had taken over the protection of religious interests. The Sicilian priest voiced his disapproval of fascism and called for unity in the party. He stressed the autonomy of the Catholics in political activities and underlined the programmatic relevance of the PPI in opposition to 'clerical fascism'. The end of the collaboration of PPI representatives in Mussolini's government was eventually decided at the fourth party congress, which took place in Turin on 12 April 1923. For some, like Stefano Cavazzoni and the PPI's right wing, collaboration with Mussolini had been ideologically motivated all along, which resulted in 1924 in the separation of the right wing and the formation of the Centro Nazionale Italiano. In Turin, Sturzo emphasized the deep-seated differences between fascism and *popolarismo* in internal and foreign policy.[33]

He firmly opposed the inclination of the party's right wing to hand over the representation of Catholic interests to the facists. The PPI's anti-fascist stance was now quite obvious. Mussolini was very irritated and called Sturzo a 'devious priest'. Some days after the end of the congress he suspended the PPI deputies from the government. After repeated pressure from the Vatican, Sturzo eventually left the party, was replaced by Alcide De Gasperi and went into exile, first in Paris, then London and New York.

It was now completely clear that fascism and the Vatican were seeking an agreement without the unwelcome intermediary role of the PPI. The PPI suffered a great defeat in the 1924 elections against the backdrop of fascist violence, leading to Sturzo's enforced stand down from the leadership and the splitting of the clerical-fascist right wing,[34] with a resulting loss of favour from the press and complete indifference on the part of the Vatican and Catholic Action towards the fate of the party. They lost, not least of all, because of a new election rule brought in by the fascists, the so-called Acerbo Law. This gave to a list of candidates who had gained 25 per cent of the vote, two-thirds of the seats in parliament. The hope of being voted in without being on the fascist list for the elections was therefore very slim, even at the outset. As a result, some of the PPI deputies argued in favour of boycotting the elections. But once again the idea that the democratic ideal and Christian principles could be united and defended only within the political system was permanent. The PPI stood again with its own list of candidates.[35] It won 9 per cent of the votes and, with its 39 seats, formed the largest opposition group in parliament.

After the assassination of the Socialist deputy, Giacomo Matteotti, who had had the courage to openly denounce the fascist violence and electoral manipulation, the Catholics, together with the Socialists and the Communists, walked out of parliament in protest in the so-called Aventine Secession. The PPI, in this phase, attempted to form a coalition with the Socialists for the second time. It based itself on the model of the co-operation of the Germany's Centre Party with the Social Democrats, which had greatly interested Sturzo and De Gasperi. If the failure of the first attempt at forming a coalition in 1922 could be attributed to the wavering position of the Socialists, then the failure of the second could be attributed to negative attitude of the Church. Several factors must be remembered that led the Church authorities to judge Mussolini's government positively and to place its hopes in it. Mussolini moderated the anti-clerical undertones that had at the start been a mark of his speeches. He tried at this point to portray himself as a champion of Catholic interests.

Furthermore, it should be stressed that the death of Pope Benedict XV left a great scar on party life. Pius XI valued Sturzo, but not the party. After the fascist March on Rome, the new Pope felt that the party would increasingly impede the solving of the Roman Question. The relationship between the party and the Vatican was as a result more distanced. In addition, a great part of the public was of the opinion that with the rise of fascism, *popolarismo* had no real reason for existing, as the government had taken on the role of safeguarding religious interests.

When the PPI opted for co-operation with the Socialists, De Gasperi stressed in 1924 that the PPI would not lose 'the purity of its ideas' and its identity in this coalition. The Jesuit journal *Civiltà Cattolica* declared in a leading article that the government, thanks to Mussolini, had done a great deal for religion. It went on to describe the possible oppositional alliance as 'neither fitting, nor appropriate nor permitted'.[36] A collaboration between the PPI and the Socialists was really the sole attempt systematically to oppose the rise of fascism. The temporary hope of normalization and achieving a constitutional orientation of fascism turned out to be illusory, because of the clearly totalitarian nature of fascism. In addition, the Aventine Secession was destined to end up as an ethical protest, and had no political basis. The party eventually received fascist orders to disband in 1926. It had, however, already given up its political power and its leading members had already been, for the most part, persecuted or arrested. The party disappeared, but not *popolarismo* itself.

THE DEMOCRATIC PERSPECTIVE

Many anti-fascist *popolari* went on to collaborate with other anti-fascist political forces. These forces tried to weaken their anti-clericalism, in order to find a common political solution that could be used to transform Mussolini's Italy into a state with a democratic basis. A collaboration of this kind represented an important attempt by the anti-fascist forces to come to an agreement in preparation for republican state reform in Italy. The anti-fascist forces agreed that the monarchy, which had shown no resistance to fascism, had lost its legitimacy. A revision of the constitution was seen to be unavoidable, even at this early stage. The main worry that the *popolari* had was that the Catholics could be excluded from the political life of a new Italian democracy. The banned anti-fascist *popolari* activities were extremely limited, as a result of their small number and their political isolation. Their activities were also hindered by the continued anticlericalism of many socialists and exiled liberals and democrats, as well as by the initial Vatican support for fascism. The Lateran Treaties of 1929 finally put an end to the hopes of the *popolari* for the formation of a democratic anti-fascist alliance that included themselves.

The position of those in exile as regards the Lateran Treaties was not unified. Sturzo justified on the one side the position of the Vatican, in order to defend it from heavy attacks. On the other side he criticized the Vatican, if not openly, for the support the Italian episcopate and clerics gave to the anti-democratic and imperialistic intentions of the fascist regime. Francesco L. Ferrari, however, had nothing good to say about the Vatican's politics, and he revealed to Sturzo his disappointment, disgust and fears for the future.[37] De Gasperi remained in Italy, was interned for one year during 1927–28 and worked in the Vatican library from 1929. He tried to overcome the confusion that followed the conclusion of the concordat attempting to justify what he saw as a politically false step.[38] His efforts arose from his desire to retain some degree of universal respect for the Catholic hierarchy.[39]

According to Gabriele De Rosa, the Lateran treaties forced the *popolari* into a 'second, further exile'.[40] The Italian anti-fascist outlaws, who were united in the Concentratione antifascista, complained that the Church was more responsible for the political situation than fascism itself. The Church was seen, as it had been in the Risorgimento, as the real enemy in Italy. The Socialists suffocated the last possibilities of collaboration with the *popolari*. The Church was again perceived to be the anti-modernistic institution of the *Syllabus errorum* of 1864,[41] and following this logic, had to be combated, together with fascism. The Catholic emigrants were thus excluded from the Concentratione antifascista and the Lega Italiana dei Diritti dell'Uomo (LIDU). They contributed substantially, however, to the thinking about the crisis of the liberal state and the rise of the fascist regime in Italy. In doing so, they also contributed to the basis of the future republic.

The Catholics in exile also tried to foster the international co-operation of Catholic parties. The idea of international collaboration between Christian democratic forces was already in existence with the founding of the PPI. The groups advocating such collaboration were convinced that a close connection existed between internal and foreign policy and international relations. The members of the PPI were also inspired by the pacifistic stance of Pope Benedict XV, and they aligned their party programme with his views. Suggestions for international collaboration between Catholic unions, farmers, co-operatives and national parliaments were presented from the first party congress onwards. The trips to Germany by Sturzo, De Gasperi and Rufo Ruffo della Scaletta in 1921 can be seen as the first concrete steps to an international understanding and co-operation between Catholic and popular parties. It was not by chance that they chose Germany. The Catholic Centre Party was one of the major forces with a Christian leaning at that time. Sturzo felt that Italy had a central role to play in the foundation of an international organization, thanks to what he saw as its intermediary position between victorious and conquered states. The keeping of the peace on the Continent was to be brought about by the constitution of the 'United States of Europe'. Sturzo conceived his idea for the PPI programme, an idea that had a far-reaching innovative character and anticipated the end of the Franco-German antagonism. In 1922 Sturzo presented his international project in Paris, too, as his trip to Germany had been interpreted by the French press as an understanding between the Italians and the Germans and damaging to French political interests. Sturzo presented another initiative of this kind in the same year at the Genoa conference.

These attempts at international co-operation were undermined by the rise of fascism. Sturzo's plans could only be taken up again during his years in exile. The three essential basic policies that he recommended to the SIPDIC in Paris were 'Church autonomy', 'non-confessionalism' and a 'democratic direction'. He added, however, that this basis would not mean the indifference of the parties with respect to religious interests. A democratic way of thinking had to be the basis for the coherence of the individual parties and their co-operation. It was Sturzo's intention, in this way, to warn those Catholics, especially the German, Austrian and Spanish fellow believers who had shown some readiness to collaborate with the radical right in their home countries, from the National Socialists to the nationalist militia in Austria and the Falange in Spain. Sturzo took an especially firm stance against a synthesis of nationalism and Catholicism, something that was being promoted by Engelbert Dollfuss in Austria, Gil Robles in Spain and Antonio Oliviera Salazar in Portugal, for example. Those attempts at interpreting fascism that were offered by Italians in exile were often quite different to those made by other European party representatives in the SIPDIC. Sturzo held fascism to be unacceptable to the Christian democratic conscience, as this ideology identified morality with power and no longer recognized the autonomy of ethical boundaries. Ferrari saw fascism as the negation of the natural rights of the individual. The Italians had already personally experienced fascism very early on and seen its rise. On the basis of this experience they tried, unsuccessfully however, to warn their Catholic party colleagues of the rise of totalitarianism.[42] The SIPDIC was unable to organize effective resistance against fascism and National Socialism in Europe.

NOTES

1 'I problemi della vita nazionale del cattolici italiani', Speech by Don Luigi Sturzo in Caltagirone, 24 December 1905, in Francesco Malgeri (ed.), *Gli Atti dei congressi del Partito popolare italiano* (Brescia 1969), pp. 3–33.
2 Ibid., pp. 17–24.
3 Ibid., pp. 23–4.
4 Ibid., pp. 21–2.

5 Luigi Sturzo, *Nazionalismo e internazionalismo* (Bologna 1971), p. 88.
6 The agreement consisted of a seven-point programme, which was to be signed by every candidate in order to be able to get the Catholic vote. The seven points comprised the upholding of the freedom of teaching; religious education; unity of the family (opposition to divorce); recognition by law of the economic and social Catholic organizations; and tax and law reforms. This was negotiated with the Conservatives, so as to stem Socialist political activity.
7 'I problemi del dopoguerra', Speech by Luigi Sturzo in Milan on 17 November 1918, in Luigi Sturzo, *Il partito popolare italiano*, vol. 1 (Bologna 1956), pp. 13–23.
8 *La Tribuna*, 25 January 1919, which threw open the question, 'Which side would the PPI have been on if a conflict between Italy and the Vatican had broken out?' *Epoca*, 21 January 1919; *Il giornale del Popolo*, 21 January 1919. The Socialists also thought (*Avanti!*, 27 May 1919) that the PPI was nothing more than the reorganized old *partito cattolico*; Antonio Gramsci recognized the strength of the People's Party and its ability to stand competitively against the Socialists. He thought, however, that they would disband when they had fulfilled their task. *Ordine Nuovo*, 1 November 1919.
9 The seventh article in the Italian People's Party programme was 'Freedom and Independence of the Church through the full expansion of its position as spiritual teacher. Freedom and respect of the Christian conscience as a structure for the Nation by which to live, freedom for the people and conquests for the civilized world.' See Sturzo, *Il Partito popolare italiano*, vol. 1, pp. 69–70.
10 'La costituzione, la finalità e il fondamento del Partito Popolare', Speech by Luigi Sturzo at the congress in Bologna on 14 June 1919, in Malgeri, *Gli Atti*, p. 48.
11 Ibid.
12 'Alone, specifically different to the Liberals and Socialists, free in conduct, sometimes right, sometimes left, with a concrete programme, based on the elements of democracy, this is the way we would agree to take part in political life. Neither the monarchy, nor conservatism, nor reform socialism can tempt us, we will, out of necessity, always be Democrats and Catholics.' 'I problemi della vita nazionale dei cattolici italiani', Speech by Luigi Sturzo in Caltagirone on 24 December 1905, in Malgeri, *Gli Atti*, p. 28.
13 Sturzo, *Nazionalismo e internazionalismo*, p. 88.
14 'La costituzione, 14 June 1919', in Malgeri, *Gli Atti*, p. 50.
15 Francesco Malgeri, 'Storia del Partito popolare italiano', in idem (ed.), *Storia del movimento Cattolico* (Milan 1980), p. 74.
16 The first concrete action of the parliamentary deputies was the laying down of an order of the day in which, among other points, measures against unemployment, the participation of the farmers in landownership, the breaking up of great landownership, and the partial ownership by the workers of the means of production through shares were proposed.
17 In connection with the PPI's agrarian policy, see an interview with Luigi Sturzo in the newspaper *La Tribuna*, cited in Sturzo, *Il partito popolare italiano*, vol. 3 (Bologna 1957), pp. 139–44.
18 The Socialists reacted negatively to the resolutions of the Naples congress regarding agriculture. They described the suggestion of an increase in small landownership as utopian and regarded it as an attempt to oppose their intended socialization of rural Italy.
19 *La voce del Popolo* (New York), 4 December 1942.
20 Angelo Tasca, *Nascita e avvento del Partito popolare* (Florence 1950), p. 91.
21 Stefano Jacini, *Storia del P.P.I.* (Milan 1951), p. 147.

22 Speech by Luigi Sturzo in Rome, 2 May 1921, in Sturzo, *Il Partito popolare italiano*, vol. 1, p. 177.
23 See the twelfth point in the programme.
24 *Civiltà Cattolica*, 1 September 1917, pp. 389–92.
25 The PPI politicians believed that the efforts being made towards weakening and isolating Germany would awaken an imperialist spirit, which could lead to new demands and conflicts.
26 On the basis of this intention, the resolution made by the national council of the PPI was published on 6 May 1922. Igino Giordani, *La politica estera del Partito popolare italiano* (Rome 1924), p. 114.
27 See Giordani, *La politica estera*, p. 129.
28 The PPI deputies in government were Stefano Cavazzoni, Employment Minister; Ernesto Vassallo, Deputy Foreign Minister; Fulvio Milani, Deputy Secretary for Justice; Giovanni Gronchi, Trade and Industry Secretary; Umberto Merlin, Deputy Secretary for the new regions. Sturzo was suddenly against the decision, but left it to the committee.
29 Jacini, *Storia del P.P.I.*, p. 147.
30 Ibid., p. 147.
31 See especially the PPI leadership's announcement of 1 November 1922, which reflects Mussolini's assurances to De Gasperi and Cavazzoni that all illegal and wrongful activities would be put to an end and proportional representation upheld. *Corriere d'Italia*, 1 November 1922, quoted in Giulio De Rossi, *I popolari nella XXVI legislatura* (Rome 1923), p. 417.
32 'Rivoluzione e ricostruzione', Speech by Luigi Sturzo in Turin, 20 December 1922, in Sturzo, *Il Partito popolare italiano*, vol. 1, pp. 264–308.
33 For the other events at the Turin congress, see Malgeri, *Gli Atti*, pp. 264–5.
34 Before the Acerbo Law was passed, a meeting of the PPI party took place in which it was decided to abstain from voting. Ten right-wing delegates voted for the law, however. They were immediately expelled from the party and stood in 1924 for the *lista nazionale*.
35 See the PPI's election proclamation, 6 April 1924, in Sturzo, *Il Partito popolare italiano*, vol. 2, pp. 273–5.
36 *Civiltà Cattolica*, 16 August 1924. In 1921 the third PPI congress in Venice defined the basis for a collaboration with the Socialists: 'The People first and then the Programme'. This slogan was to be repeated by Luigi Sturzo at the congress in Turin. See also Luigi Sturzo, *Italia e fascismo* (Bologna 1965), pp. 73–100.
37 See Francesco Malgeri, *Chiesa cattolica e Stato da Sturzo a De Gasperi* (Brescia 1990).
38 In 1926 De Gasperi was forced to give up his position as party leader and member of parliament. In 1927 he was charged with illegal crossing of a border and convicted to four years' imprisonment. He was pardoned after one year. In 1929 he took up a position in the Vatican library.
39 Alicide De Gasperi, *Lettere sul Concordato* (Brescia 1970).
40 Gabriele De Rosa, *Luigi Sturzo* (Milan 1977), pp. 304ff.
41 The document published on 8 November 1864, together with the encyclical *Quanta cura*, comprised 80 philosophical, moralistic, political and religious arguments against liberalism and modernity.
42 On the SIPDIC, see also Guido Müller's chapter in this book.

8

A Powerful Catholic Church, Unstable State and Authoritarian Political Regime: The Christian Democratic Party in Poland

Leszek Kuk

The first organizations of a Christian democrat nature began to appear on the political scene of the three regions of Poland belonging to Russia, Prussia and Austria shortly after 1890. Prior to the creation in November 1918 of the independent Polish state, however, the Christian democrat movement was relatively weak and scattered. This dispersion was primarily the result of marked social and political differences between the different parts of Poland. It was in the territories annexed by Russia that the Christian democrat movement was most strongly represented: territories where, in 1916 – when the region was under German occupation – a Christian democrat party, the so-called Workers' Democratic Party, was launched. Two other sizeable groups were operating in the territory annexed by Prussia: one in the region of Great Poland and in Pomerania, and the other, which was less active, in Upper Silesia. Wojciech Korfanty,[1] who was later to become the most prominent politician in the Christian Democratic Party in independent Poland, and the only one really known by Polish people at large, was associated with the party from the outset. In Galicia, the region annexed by Austria, several small groups operated but they were isolated from one aother and of minor political importance.

The Christian democrat movement and its first representatives surfaced in Polish political life shortly after the emergence of the major political strains of thinking that were to dominate until the communist era. These were represented notably by the nationalist movement, the most representative vehicle of which was the National Democratic Party, or National Democracy (popularly called *endecja*, after its initials, ND), the peasant movement represented by several large groups, and finally the socialist movement represented by the Polish Socialist Party and the Social Democratic Party. However, from the outset the Christian democrat movement was by far the weakest and the least active.

The creation of the independent Polish state raised the question of the merger of the groups comprising the Christian democrat movement. Prior to the summer of 1919 it played no important or autonomous role; in the territory formerly annexed by Russia it served as the weak and passive partner of the powerful right-wing party, *endecja*. Independently of ideological similarities, this co-operation contributed to the forming of an image of the Christian democrat movement: an image that closely associated it, until the end of the 1920s, with *endecja* and one that the Christian democrats had great difficulty in altering. Decisive changes came about in 1919. In September, at a conference held in Cracow, the Christian democrat groups of the territories once annexed by Russia and Austria formed Polskie Stronnictwo Chrześcijańskiej Demokracji, or the Polish Christian Democratic Party (PSChD). Six months later, in March 1920, a party was launched uniting the Christian democrat groups operating in the Great Poland region and in Pomerania. The party adopted the name Chrześcijańsko-Narodowe Stronnictwo Robotnicze, or National Christian Workers' Party (Ch-NSR). The two parties, PSChD and Ch-NSR, merged in May 1920 to become the Chrześcijańsko-Narodowe Stronnictwo Pracy (Ch-NSP). The union took place during a conference that was later regarded as being the first conference of the Christian Democratic Party. Two years later, in 1922, the Popular Christian Union of the region of Silesia united with the Ch-NSP. In this way, the definitive unification of the Polish Christian democrat movement came about. From the second conference of the party, which was held in May and June 1925, the party was generally known as the Chrześcijańska Demokracja, or Christian Democracy, or, more briefly and familiarly, *chadecja*.

In analysing the functioning of the Christian Democratic Party, the exceptional context of social and political life in inter-war Poland must be taken into account. It was a vast country with a sizeable population (35 million in the summer of 1939), but poor and backward. The political and cultural integration of the country, which for a hundred years was under the sway of foreign empires, was the greatest achievement of Poland in the period from 1918 to 1939. Its economic life, despite considerable effort and a number of successes, was characterized by widespread stagnation. In 1938 industrial output was virtually at the level it had been in 1913; the same was true of agriculture: farms of less than five hectares accounted for two-thirds of all agricultural land. It was estimated that there was an overpopulation of 4.5 million living in rural areas. Political life in Poland, however, although somewhat chaotic, was very active. As in other countries in Central Europe, the political changes that took place in Poland between 1918 and 1939 led to a certain authoritarianism. In 1922 the first president of the country was assassinated. Following a bloody *coup d'état* led by Marshal Józef Piłsudski in 1926, Poland became a state under dictatorial government. The second constitution, imposed on the country in 1935 after illegal machinations by the marshal's political coterie (called *sanacja*), abandoned the model of parliamentary democracy. The economic – and consequently military – potential of the country was totally at variance with the political aspirations of the elites, mainly from the post-feudal minor gentry, who wanted to exercise regional influence. In the 1930s, in contrast to its impressive neighbours – Germany and the USSR – with their totalitarian regimes, Poland became more and more outmoded.

In the inter-war years the Catholic Church played an extremely important role in Poland.[2] Its political and legal position was set out under the concordat of 1925, an arrangement that proved to be of great advantage to the Church,[3] which enjoyed numerous political and financial privileges: it was a wealthy Church in an impoverished land. The Catholic clergy was clearly sympathetic towards the nationalist right wing, and especially towards the *endecja*. On the other hand, the right, headed by the *endecja*, prided itself on its fervent attachment to Catholicism and on its readiness to defend the rights and interests of the Church.[4] There is no doubt that it tried to put the Church and Catholicism to the service of its 'national policy'.[5] This situation began to change towards the end of the 1920s, to the extent that the Catholic hierarchy began, with some success, to seek a compromise with the camp in power – the *sanacja* – towards which it harboured considerable misgivings concerning not only the socialist pedigrees of its many representatives, especially Piłsudski, but also the muted anticlericalism sometimes shown by that group before 1926.

The Catholic Church was considered by the majority of Polish people and their governing classes to be one of the main pillars of the state, of Polish national identity and of the established social order. That the actions of Church and state were closely interdependent was broadly seen as axiomatic. The right-wing parties were pressing for the creation of a Polish 'Catholic' nation state; following the death of Piłsudski in April 1935, the *sanacja* was well on the way to adopting such a programme. The response of the left was weak. However, Polish Catholics constituted only two-thirds of the population of the Second Republic. The programme of Catholic Poland was seen as being yet another provocation by the national minorities, the largest of which were the Jews, the Ukrainians and the Germans. The problem of the minorities was a burning political issue that had never been settled. The state pursued openly a policy of Polonization, and anti-Semitism was deeply ingrained in the population. In the inter-war years the position of the ethnic minorities grew progressively worse. The Catholic Church was very largely responsible for aggravating this tendency.

When the Christian Democratic Party was set up in the period 1919–20, nobody thought it would last long or that it would increase in importance. It was supposed that the party had come about merely because of clashes within the nationalist camp. However, it was precisely in the first half of the 1920s that the party was the most active. During that time it was relatively well represented and influential in parliament. The major split in public opinion, and consequently in parliament, meant that the Christian Democrats had more impact on public affairs than could have been expected, given the limited number of their members in parliament. Representatives of the party served in several governments between 1923 and 1926. One, Antoni Ponikowski, even served as Prime Minister, and two other politicians, Korfanty and Józef Chaciński, came close to doing so.

Following the *coup d'état* the PSChD went into a partial decline. The Christian Democrats in Silesia severed links with the party and operated independently for three years from 1927 to 1929. In the 1928 and 1930 elections the Christian Democrats gained few votes, and the 1930 result showed that the party had solid political support only in Silesia. This prompted a change of direction in the PSChD, which was once more led by Korfanty. The situation became even more difficult: in 1929 the Christian Democratic Party joined the alliance of parties of the centre and left (Centrolew) in opposition to the camp of Piłsudski. The alliance collapsed in 1930, following defeat in the election. Attempts at collaboration with the *endecja*, which was becoming ever more aggressive and expansive and closer to the totalitarian ideology that was alien to the Christian Democrats, proved to be impossible. Another approach, this time to the largest peasant party, Stronnictwo Ludowe, came to nothing because of that party's rapid political and social radicalization. The alliance with Narodowa Partia Robotnicza (NPR), rightly considered to be ideologically closest to the Christian Democratic Party was, for numerous reasons, impossible to achieve.[6]

During the 1930s an attempt was made to subdivide the Christian Democratic Party. In November 1931, the section active in the former Austrian territories separated off and joined forces with the *sanacja* camp. Other splits occurred in 1934 and 1935, and the groups involved co-operated with the government camp. The party experienced its period of greatest instability in 1933 and 1934, when serious attacks were made on Korfanty, who was accused of embezzlement – an accusation that later proved to be largely unfounded. In the 1930s the PSChD practically became a 'Silesian regional party'.[7] Its political decline was partially arrested by the progressive disintegration of the *sanacja* camp after the death of Piłsudski. At a time in Polish political life when more and more importance was attached to totalitarian – and in extreme cases, fascist – theories, the Christian Democratic Party suddenly became the most important party of the traditional right. Those referred to as the 'old guard' of the *endecja*, as well as the Union of Soldiers of General Haller, who distanced themselves from the *endecja* because of the changes mentioned above, began to side with the Christian Democratic Party. They included such eminent and highly respected figures as Stanisław Grabski and Haller. Korfanty and his party took part in the forming of a liberal, anti-government bloc of the centre-right led by General Władysław Sikorski. Although this bloc lasted for only a brief period, in 1937 this episode produced a definitive merger of the Christian Democratic Party and the National Workers' Party and, consequently, the launch in 1937 of the Stronnictwo Pracy, the Labour Party (SP).

ORGANIZATION, STRUCTURE AND SOCIAL COMPOSITION

The PSChD was never properly organized or efficiently administered, and its structures were not uniform throughout the whole country. In the 1930s it was even seen to be 'a weak and disorganized party'.[8] Prior to 1923 in particular, it had few members, all of whom had to be Christians, who had only to register and pay a small membership fee. A considerable majority of the members were artisans, manual workers and peasants. It is not known how many members there were in the 1920s, but probably some 30,000.[9] Everything seems to indicate that membership plummeted drastically in the 1930s. Local groups of from ten to 100 people made up the basic cells. There are thought to have been 270 of them in 1926, 170 of which were in the territories belonging, before 1918–20, to Germany. Their actual political activity was very limited, and occurred particularly in places where it met with the approval of the clergy – usually at the regional level.

The Christian Democrats decided upon their strategic programme during their conferences, held in 1920, 1925, 1931, 1932, 1934, 1935 and 1937. The party was headed by the supreme council (*Rada Naczelna*) which met once a year and consisted of a few dozen people, of whom 25 were elected during the conferences, and the rest were party deputies and senators. Executive power was in the hands of the Zarząd Główny, or directorate, comprising ten people. As a rule the deputies and senators played a decisive role. A chairman presided over the party: the deputies Ludomir Czerniewski (1919–20), Chaciński (1920–21), Tadeusz Błażejewicz (1923) and Father Stanisław Adamski (1924–29). None of them had a very striking personality, and the leadership of the party was, to some extent, of a collective nature – a state of affairs that did not change until the 1930s, when Korfanty was again in charge of the PSChD. In June 1931 he became its chairman.

The party was never homogeneous and was, therefore, very poorly centralized. It made little effort to insist that its members, even those in high office, be fully of one mind on policy matters. Divergent views and regional variations always featured prominently. For a long time the Silesian group kept its distinctive character. Although strictly speaking the PSChD did not have its own press organ until the 1920s, it had a fairly solid foothold in the media until the beginning of the 1930s. It spread its influence via ten to fifteen journals or newspapers,[10] several of which carried considerable weight: *Postęp* in Poznan, *Głos Narodu* in Cracow, *Dziennik Bydgoski* in Bydgoszcz, *Polonia* in Katowice and, from 1924, *Rzeczpospolita* in Warsaw. The last two belonged to Korfanty and his family. This sound state of affairs began to change in the 1930s. Either the Christian democrat press was closed down or, more frequently, the newspapers severed their links with the declining party. In 1936 the party no longer had more than three publications at its disposal.

The Christian Democratic Party had its greatest influence in the territories belonging, before 1918–20, to Germany, in particular in Silesia, where in 1922 it achieved a record 41 per cent of the vote. It was also influential in the major cities, more especially in Warsaw. It was least successful in former Austrian territory. The party played a more important role in the large cities than in the rural areas; in the towns it was supported by artisans, the intelligentsia,[11] clerical workers and teachers, and also by manual workers, especially those employed in small factories and workshops (except in Silesia). Traditionally, its sphere of influence was among domestic servants. In the 1930 elections 430,000 electors voted Christian Democrat, 33 per cent of whom lived in Silesia.

PARTY PROGRAMME

The draft programme was accepted at the first party conference, and the programme that remained in force until 1931 was approved during the second conference. In October 1931 the third conference took place, during which a new programme was formally adopted. It was, by and large, a continuation of the previous one and remained in force until the party ceased to exist, but it was updated several times by the addition of detailed clauses. Particular importance was attached to the clauses relating to the reconstruction of the socio-economic system approved during the fourth Christian Democrat conference in November 1932, and to the constitutional clauses approved by the supreme council of the PSChD in October 1933. The Christian Democratic Party based its programme on the teaching of the Church, and in particular on the recommendations included in the encyclical *Rerum novarum* and, after 1931, on those in the encyclical *Quadragesimo anno*.

Christianity was set against socialism and bolshevism, both of which were accused of arousing inter-class hatred and limiting individual freedom. There was also opposition to capitalist liberalism, which perpetuated 'selfish instincts'. The good points of national ideology were emphasized, but jingoism of the kind that aroused enmity between nations was reprehended. Social harmony and solidarity were stressed as being worthy of esteem. The principle of private property was accepted, but it was also agreed that the state had a duty to prevent such property being used in the pursuit of undesirable ends. Small and medium-scale landownership was openly welcomed; the prime objective of social policy was concerned with the emancipation of employees:

> Property in general and private property in particular is contrary to neither justice nor natural law: it is a direct and natural result of work. There is, therefore, no contradiction between work and property . . . Christian Democracy sees its social programme and the resolution of the labour question as serving to raise each member to the status of co-owner of a certain part of the means of production, and as a consequence, to increase, within the company, the application that accompanies socio-economic undertakings. The key word in this domain is emancipation. Christian Democracy, unlike Socialism, declares war not on property but on the exploitation of wage-earners.[12]

The setting up of all sorts of co-operatives was enthusiastically urged. The capitalist system was to undergo change and be transformed into a social Christian system. Social policy matters were to be regulated by legislation. The possibility of worker participation in the management of companies and in profit-sharing was guaranteed. In 1923 Korfanty, who was a miner's son, stated in a debate in parliament: 'The modern worker, who nowadays is fully aware that the labour he is selling is closely linked to himself, his health and the welfare of his family, wants – as is his right – to play a full part in the running of the production process.'[13]

The Christian Democrats opposed any attempt to reduce social legislation, since it protected workers' dignity. The party was opposed to any schemes that would benefit the economy at the expense of the workers. When it came to matters concerning employment, they did not shrink from using radical language. On the matter of Poland's much-needed agrarian reform, the PSChD acted with great caution. There was support for reform that would involve the compensation of landowners. There was also a call for the creation of a strong peasantry but, at the same time, it was feared that a drop in agricultural output might result from the dividing up of the big estates. In 1925 the PSChD proposed that the problem of land division should be put into private hands. The party was even more cautious concerning the dividing up of lands belonging to the Church, and insisted that the Vatican should be consulted on the subject.

The Christian Democrats demanded state control on social questions, but were against extending state involvement in economic matters. Only shortly before the party's eventual collapse was it to ask for increased state intervention on the economic front. The programme of the Labour Party in 1937 called for nationalization and state control of big businesses that were vital to society and to the state. In 1932, at the fourth conference of the PSChD, the old clauses concerning the socio-economic system were abandoned. Strictly speaking, the new programmatic demands were merely a supplement to the 1931 programme. They stipulated the introduction of planning measures in matters to do with the economy, and a restructuring, along corporatist lines, of the social system. However, they did include several new features that amounted to a radical criticism of capitalism. The criticism stemmed in part from the major economic and social crisis that reached a peak in 1931 and 1932, but it was prompted mainly by the encyclical *Quadragesimo anno*, which contained a severe criticism of capitalism. In the party's new programme, capitalism was depicted as being contrary to Christian morality. It was seen as having a pagan nature, which was displayed both in its extreme individualism and its liberalism. Capitalism, it was felt, led to the total elimination of property belonging to the working classes, to unemployment, the deterioration of agriculture, the collapse of the middle classes, the undermining of family values and, eventually, in the field of international relations, to the strengthening of imperialist tendencies and to war. Concomitants of capitalism, such as the abuse of property and money, unfettered competition, monopolies, the amassing of wealth, financial speculation and the 'artificial creation of unwholesome needs', were all held to be unacceptable. Hitherto, these matters had not featured in Christian Democrat thinking in Poland.

The 1931 programme also introduced certain corporatist elements. According to what was set out in *Quadragesimo anno*, the corporatist system was understood to be an alternative to the liberal capitalist system on the one hand, and to socialist collectivism on the other. Social solidarity was given greater emphasis. The setting up of compulsory workers' organizations was sought. The creation in the workplace of workers' councils was proposed. There was a call for the widening of work-related legislation, the general implementation of bilateral contracts between management and workers, the launch of special committees of employers and employees to oversee working conditions, the guarantee of freedom of assembly, and the adoption of measures to avert strikes and lockouts through compulsory arbitration. The overall objective of this policy was to increase the number of landlords, to extend property ownership to all and to reconcile opposing interests for the good of both society and the nation. The clauses of the programme adopted in November 1932, at the conference held in Łódź, set out a detailed model of the corporatist system that made provision for the setting up of a corporatist hierarchy: a new vertical power system at whose head would be a corporative national chamber. The constituent corporations were to be granted a certain autonomy. While some Christian Democrats were sceptical regarding the 'state corporatism' in fascist Italy under Mussolini, others saw it as the direct embodiment of the principles contained in *Rerum novarum* and *Quadragesimo anno*. The most prominent of those was Ludwik Caro.[14]

In the field of domestic policy, a strong link between the State and the Church was demanded. Numerous demands involved the creation of 'a Catholic State, that is to say a State integrating the Catholic religion but at the same time formally respecting freedom of worship'.[15] During a debate on the draft constitution that took place in 1920, one of the Christian Democrat deputies demanded that the Church and religion should occupy the same position in the state that had been guaranteed to them under the constitution of 3 May 1791, which forbade the abandonment of Catholicism. The 1925 programme stated that 'Christian Democracy looks upon religion not as something private and individual, but as a wholly social matter',[16] and, that being the case, the party declared it necessary to 'base the State and society on Christian teaching ... and to organize the Polish nation under the banner of Catholicism'.[17] It must be stressed, however, that the Christian Democrats did not think it appropriate that the clergy should play a direct part in the exercise of power. A party member summed up the question as follows:

> Christian Democracy is a genuinely Catholic party which respects the authority of the Pope and of the bishops regarding moral and religious matters, but it is not especially in favour of clericalism nor, consequently, of the direct participation of the clergy in the ordering of social and political life.[18]

The Christian Democrats called for close co-operation between Church and State in the sphere of morals, culture and education, and for church schools and family legislation based on the teaching of the Church. All the party's programmes demanded a guarantee of the influence of the Church in schools, and of religion in society at large. Indeed, the Church was seen as having a vital part to play in the inculcating of family values. Hence the concern to maintain national 'purity' in the schools. At the very first conference of the party, Father Jan Albrecht advocated the segregation of Catholic and Jewish children in schools.[19] It is true that, in its 1925 programme, the PSChD drew attention to the need to respect the rights of national minorities, but at the same time that programme and all the others stressed how important it was to maintain the Polish national character of the state and to strengthen the preponderance of the Polish – that is to say, Catholic – component. It was held that the constitution should guarantee that the President would be a Polish national and a Catholic. The agreement known as the 'Lanckorona pact', which opened up the possibility of forming a government with the participation of the Christian Democrat representatives, and which was signed, in May 1923, by representatives of the PSChD, contains the following statement:

> Policy regarding the eastern boundaries should seek to heighten the sense of belonging to Poland and to support Polish colonization, the Polish character of large and small-scale industry, commerce, the Church, the education system and all cultural organizations.

The Christian Democrats made a distinction between 'acculturation to nationality', which they opposed, and 'assimilation into the nation', which they strongly recommended.[20] However, they were sometimes inconsistent and self-contradictory. In 1925 one of the party periodicals declared: 'It would be all to the good if people living in border areas [i.e. including those who were not Polish] were to be united within the Catholic Church.'[21] The 1931 programme demanded the loyalty of national minorities, promising in return that the state would respect all their political rights.

It is not at all difficult to detect signs of anti-Semitism in the programme of the Christian Democratic Party, and as time went on it became more and more a feature of the party's activities. The 1931 programme highlighted the need to curb, by legal and moral means, the 'excessive number' of Jews in the professions, in commerce, in industry and among the self-employed. Anti-Semitism was yet more marked in the constitutional clauses of 1933 referred to above. The 'Jewish question' was considered to be of prime national importance. On the one hand, all thought of racism, violence and brutality was eschewed: the Jews were free to exercise their rights just like any other citizens, but only, it was added, to the extent that they fulfilled their duty as citizens. On the other hand, however, it was widely asserted that the Jews wanted to dominate Polish society, that they presented a danger to Poland and that their influence must be quelled. A feature of Christian Democratic thinking had always been a very marked inclination to separate the Jews in Poland from the rest of the population. At the end of 1925, in a special resolution relating to national minorities, the supreme council declared itself in favour of this measure.[22] The cry often went up in the Christian Democrat press that Jews should be excluded from public and influential circles. The prospect of assimilating and acculturating the Jewish population met with scant enthusiasm, and it was felt that any assimilation would be acceptable only in so far as it was accompanied by a 'sincere' conversion to Catholicism. There was strong support, in the end, for the proposal that the Jews should emigrate from Polish soil. In the run-up to the Second World War the Christian Democrat press published further anti-Semitic attacks. Demands were made that the Jews should be excluded from any economic activity, and even that three million people of Jewish extraction should be deported.[23]

Finally, regarding the institutions of the state, the Christian Democrats strongly supported the republican system, the ideal of the legally constituted state, and parliamentary institutions in their conservative, and sometimes even authoritarian, form. Although coming out in favour of the secret vote, the *chadecja* rejected the principle of elections by direct suffrage. It demanded the right to the family vote, whereby parents were granted the right to vote on behalf of their under-age children. It also called for the guarantee of appropriate political influence for well-educated people, and the raising of the minimum age at which one could vote. The number of mandates should depend on the economic and cultural level of the constituencies. The demand was also made for separate representation for the Polish people in the eastern territories, where they were an ethnic minority. In the 1920s there were those who claimed that the right to vote should be granted only to those with a good command of the Polish language. Local autonomous powers were to be adapted to the economic, political and national situation obtaining in the locations concerned. The adoption of such measures was intended to strengthen the position of the Polish people in relation to the national minorities.

For the Christian Democrats, the 1921 constitution had been 'imposed' by the left. In December 1922 the Christian Democrat press contributed greatly to the upsurge in the atmosphere of nationalist hysteria, in which the first President of the Polish Republic was assassinated by a fanatic in the *endecja*. Until the end of the 1920s, the Christian Democrats called for the strengthening of executive power, especially that of the government, the President and the senate at the expense of that of the Diet. The experiences of the early years of the dictatorship of Piłsudski, characterized by the violation of the principles of the legally constituted state and the limiting of the role of parliament, prompted the Christian Democrats to make a partial modification to their programme. The 1931 programme stipulated that a strong and efficient state could not be an omnipotent state surpassing the limits of natural and divine law. After 1930 the need to increase the executive power was somewhat played down; the emphasis was now on opposing the introduction, in the system and the political life of the nation, of totalitarian measures and practices. One of the Christian Democrat deputies, Jan Szulik, protested against the draft constitution of 1935, pointing out that it 'formed the basis of a totalitarian State, which was contrary to Christian teaching and which could eventually foment revolutionary fever and reduce the strength and cohesion of the State'.[24] From 1935 onwards, the accusation, levelled at the *sanacja*, of having reinforced the totalitarian measures was a constant feature of the party propaganda. In October 1932, the supreme council of the PSChD adopted constitutional clauses. A guaranteed balance of executive and legislative power was demanded. Senior state leaders were to act as mediators. Parliament was to keep its two chambers, but the upper chamber was to undergo changes: it was to comprise administrative, economic and cultural representatives of local, autonomous authorities.

In the field of foreign policy, the concepts of Christian Democracy were in line with nationalist tradition of the kind associated with *endecja*. The party stressed the need for a political alliance with Great Britain and especially with France, but also with Czechoslovakia. Its 1925 programme broached the question of Poland's civilizing mission in the east. Poland was to become the guardian of the 'Mediterranean Christian culture', but it could not do so unless it had international influence. Although openly hostile to bolshevism and the USSR, the Christian Democrats stressed the importance of maintaining good relations with the Soviet Union.[25] As they saw it, what represented a grave and obvious danger for Poland's independence was the policy being pursued in Germany, to which the PSChD was strongly opposed. It systematically warned against the resurgence of German militarism and the warlike aims of the Third Reich, and was sharply critical of Poland's relatively pro-German foreign policy pursued throughout the 1930s by the Foreign Minister, Colonel Józef Beck. Christian Democrat politicians repeatedly called for a strengthening of the state's defence capabilities.

THE CHRISTIAN DEMOCRATIC PARTY IN POLISH POLITICS

From the outset, the members of the PSChD displayed considerable political ambitions. The party was noticeably active in parliament. The number of its deputies and senators reflected not so much the influence in society of the party, or the views of the electorate, as the result of electoral alliances with other parties and, in general, the balance of political forces. Six parliamentary elections were held in Poland during the inter-war period. Christian Democracy participated in them as an autonomous party just once – in 1928. On three occasions it formed part of an alliance: with the right – in 1919 and 1922 – and with the centre in 1930. In 1935 and 1938 it boycotted the elections. In the first Polish parliament (1919–22) the PSChD obtained 25 to 29 seats (some 6.5 per cent of the parliamentary total). In the second (1922–28), the number of Christian Democrat deputies came to 43–44 (10 per cent), which placed the party in fourth position. After 1926 its results were much more modest. In the 1928 election the Christian Democrats won 18 seats, and in 1930 only 15. It must be pointed out that the elections of 1928 and 1930 took place under pressure from the state administration and, in 1930, in an atmosphere of political terror, which skewed the results obtained by the parties. In 1934 the PSChD had eleven deputies in the diet, and in 1935 only eight. The party was represented by eight senators in the senate in 1923, and by six in 1928. After 1930 the party was no longer represented in the senate. During the 1920s the clergy, through the party, was relatively well represented in parliament: four clerics in each of the first two Diets.

In the early years of the Second Republic, the Christian Democrats, despite their programmatic differences, were close to the *endecja* and lived under its umbrella. In 1925 Ludomir Czerniewski, a senior member of the party, wrote:

> Between the nationalist movement and Christian Democracy there are not, and there could not be, any fundamental contradictions ... Nationalism, concerned as it increasingly is about moral rights and traditional historic values, consequently paves the way to an awareness of the preponderance of the religious ethic, and to nationalism based on the Christian ethic.[26]

The National Democratic Party studied and supported the views of the PSChD in the fields of education, culture and morals. On the matter of social policy, the Christian Democrats were less conservative and endeavoured to adopt a moderately reforming position. In the 1930s, as the National Democrats drew nearer to totalitarian ideologies, so the paths of the *endecja* and the Christian Democrats began to diverge. The PSChD found itself more and more isolated, both politically and ideologically. It lost the support of the Church, severed its links with the National Democratic Party, remained firmly opposed to the *sanacja* regime and, for ideological reasons, was in no position to forge lasting links with the Socialist Party. Its only potential allies were a few sections of the peasant movement. So it was that, in a Catholic country, a party that strove to mould society in ways stemming directly from the teaching of the Church found itself abandoned by the Catholic hierarchy and cut off from the other major political parties.

The PSChD was the cornerstone of the Christian social movement and of the Christian trade union movement. Among youth organizations, the party remained closest to Odrodzenie, a Catholic student association. During the 1930s, however, all these ties were considerably loosened, but the major role in this sphere was played by the Christian trade unions. The trade union movement was the second area, after parliamentary activity, in which the party was particularly involved. This movement – Chrześcijańskie Zjednoczenie Zawodowe (ChZZ), a Christian trade union alliance founded in 1921 – was for a long time distinctly fragmented.[27] It did not succeed in establishing a national confederation, which is why it was so eager to collaborate with the Christian Democrats who were represented in Warsaw. Its partial unification was not achieved until 1931. The alliance, along with two other much larger groups, one dominated by the socialists and the other by the NPR and the nationalists, constituted one of the most influential elements in the Polish trade union movement in the inter-war years. Its membership, though, was scarcely one-third of that of either of the other two groups. In the period 1921–24 the Christian trade unions had a membership of some 150,000, but subsequently that number dropped sharply, such that in 1928 they had 60,000 members out of a total of 800,000 unionized workers, and in 1935 about 53,000 out of a total of 670,000. The merger between the PSChD and the NPR brought with it the trade unions that were affiliated to them. Thus was created the most powerful trade union confederation, but the Labour Party did not profit more politically from the merger. Fairly soon – in early 1939 – the new trade union began to show signs of its sympathies for the government camp.

In Poland there was a deep split in what was called 'political Catholicism', accounting for its political weakness. From the outset, the nationalist element in it was much more powerful than the Christian Democrat element. The sympathies of the general public inclined more towards the *endecja* than towards the Christian Democratic Party, and the Church was of the opinion that it lost on both fronts: not only that of the *endecja* throughout the 1920s, but also that of the *sanacja* in the 1930s. The Christian Democrats' programme moved away from the principal tendencies of the time. Advocating the idea of social solidarity, it could find no evidence of it in the 1920s, particularly in the early years with their social tensions and relatively radical welfare programmes. The 1930s were more promising for the fostering of solidarity and corporatism, but the Christian Democratic Party, weakened by that time, let itself be overtaken by the *sanacja* and Catholic Action. The weakness of both the Christian democratic movement and the party was more to do with politics than with ideology.

On the matter of the social welfare programme, the dividing line separated the nationalist right from the socialist and peasant left. Given the extreme socio-economic backwardness of the country, aggravated both by the acute economic crisis, which was particularly severe in Poland, and the dictatorial manner of the leaders of the *sanacja*, the conflicts and contrasts grew more intense. The conciliatory, indecisive and hybrid nature of the Christian Democratic Party's programme, the conservatism of which was hidden by a veil of Christian and radical phraseology, met with scant public support. Moreover, the party, which was not very homogeneous, was also weak intellectually.[28] None of its representatives – not even Korfanty himself – can be said to have been of any great political note in the 1920s. The actions taken by the party reflect its intellectual weakness and also that of its programme.[29] They lacked coherence and determination; the PSChD was at a loss as to what position to adopt regarding key political issues. Its feebleness and lack of cohesion can be detected in the wording of documents published by the party. 'The party did not like to express itself clearly, and endeavoured to model its style on that of the Church.'³⁰

The policy of the *sanacja* camp, in seeking to undermine and even destroy the opposition parties, including the PSChD, was probably instrumental in weakening the party even more. At the beginning of 1934, as has already been mentioned, a group of eminent party members such as the former Prime Minister, Ponikowski, the former ministers Stefan Piechocki and Stefan Smólski, and Ludwik Gdyk, the former chairman of the Diet, left the party. What prompted this, apart from the ploys of the *sanacja*, was the bickering that plagued the party leadership. The four members concerned were at loggerheads with Korfanty. To some extent, the Christian Democrats were all aware of the weakness of the party, and in 1931 Father Jan Piwowarczyk, one of the most intelligent members, wrote:

> In the parliamentary reports and in the publications of recent years, Christian Democracy played a part which was less than prominent. There were occasions when one had the impression that it did not exist. It was no longer mentioned or even taken into consideration.³¹

RELATIONS BETWEEN THE CHURCH AND THE CHRISTIAN DEMOCRATIC PARTY

The primary cause of the weakness of the party was the poor support it received from the Church, and it must be said that this support became more half-hearted over the years. This gave rise to a vicious circle: the dwindling of support from the Church added to the weakness of the Christian Democratic Party, which in turn made the Catholic hierarchy more disinclined to offer its support. The PSChD never became a 'Catholic' party, in that it did not represent the official position of the Polish Catholic Church. It should be noted that throughout the inter-war years the Polish bishops recognized no party as being Catholic, and gave neither official nor even merely unofficial support to any of them. Nevertheless, the Christian Democratic Party was Catholic in the sense that its policies were grounded in the teaching of the Catholic Church. In 1936 Korfanty, who was fully aware of this, wrote:

> No political or social group can claim to be the representative of Catholicism and call itself Catholic. No party can declare itself to be Catholic; it can only declare that it wishes to observe the principles of Catholic morality in social and political life. Catholicism cannot be the platform of any political group.³²

The attitude of Church leaders to the PSChD was broadly benevolent until the late 1920s, but subsequently their stance changed rapidly. The Church maintained officially that opposition to the ruling regime could not be justified on religious grounds, which is what the party did occasionally. In talks with Archbishop Aleksander Kakowski in the spring of 1930, Józef Chaciński asked for the support of the Church for his party. His request was flatly refused, however. A year later, the archbishop stated quite simply that the opposition of the PSChD to the government – i.e., the *sanacja* régime – which was based on 'Christian principles', was meaningless and unjustified.[33] Despite this, the Christian Democrats remained fairly rigidly opposed to the regime. In September 1930 Korfanty was arrested and sent to the detention camp in Bereza Kartuska; in 1935 he was forced to leave the country. In the archbishop's social council founded at the end of 1933, there was just one PSChD militant, Father Piwowarczyk, mentioned above. The council did not ally itself to the programme of any political party. It would appear that, had it not been for the war, 'the bulk of the social and political forces which formed the Christian-social movement, would have been gathered in the government camp. The Labour Party would have been in a minority among the Christian-social forces.'[34]

Discussions about the launch of a 'Catholic' party in Poland went on throughout much of the twenty-year inter-war period. Opinions among the priests and Church leaders regarding the possibility of a 'Catholic' party on the political scene were deeply divided. When the matter was seriously debated in 1921, one of the churchmen who was deeply involved in political activity made the following cautionary observation:

> The founding of a Catholic party would run into difficulty in that the ablest Catholic people involved in politics have for some time already been active in those groups whose programmes accord with Catholic principles. It is to be feared, then, that such a party – at least for the time being – would be particularly hesitant and lacking in competence. To entrust, therefore, the administrative representation of Catholicism in the cut and thrust of politics to some lightweight party, boasting of being avowedly Catholic, would be a manifest loss, not a gain for the Church.[35]

This statement explains what was to be the lot of the Christian Democratic Party. For the Church, the party was useful, but by no means indispensable. No 'Catholic' party was ever launched. This was for almost the same reason that led to the decline – indeed, in the 1930s to the death-throes – of the PSChD. Even if a 'Catholic' party had been formed and even if it had been very strong and influential, it would still have been merely one of the handful of parties active in Poland. In the political situation obtaining there in the pre-war period, the Church profited from the domination of groups that sought its favour and were prepared to accept its point of view, since it could not be held responsible for their mistakes or failures.[36]

Under the Second Republic, all the political groups of the right and the centre declared their respect for religion and the Church, and claimed Catholicism as the basis of their ideology and their political activity. The left was unresponsive to the stratagems of the Church, but in general was conciliatory towards it; only the communists, a marginal political force, adopted a firm and unbending response. The left made very few direct attacks on Church institutions as such, and even fewer on religion. Lay members of various shades of opinion were weak, and since they all acknowledged and respected the authority of the Church, there was no reason for the Church openly to favour any particular political party or viewpoint. A Catholic intellectual stated in 1935: 'Catholic political parties need to be established only when Catholicism is under threat from either strong lay groups or another faith backed by parties governing in breach of the laws of the Church.'[37] From the late 1920s on, the Church started to support and pin its hopes on Catholic Action. The decision to establish it in Poland was taken in 1926, and its Polish head office was opened in Poznań in November 1930. Catholic Action was meant to be independent of political parties, and made a point of avoiding coming into conflict with the authorities. Years later, one of the Christian Democrat activists recalled:

> When the vice-president of the PSChD once more approached one of the Church dignitaries in 1928 in order to persuade him that the methods adopted by Catholic Action were undermining the work of Pope Leo XIII – i.e. Christian Democracy – the dignitary said that the Catholic authorities had stipulated the aims and methods of Catholic Action and so should respect them and not the views of Christian Democracy.[38]

Even Catholic Action did not succeed in occupying the place in Polish social life that the Church would have wished. The weakness of the Christian Democratic Party resulted ultimately from the conservatism of the Catholic hierarchy in Poland and the homespun nature of Polish Catholicism.

TOWARDS THE SECOND WORLD WAR: THE LABOUR PARTY

The Labour Party was formed in 1937 as a result of the merger between the NPR, launched as early as 1905, and the Christian Democratic Party.[39] The merger had been mooted back in the 1920s, and in the period

1929–31 it was on the brink of being brought about. Korfanty became the leader of the new party, but in practice it was run in his absence in exile by the chairman of the NPR, Karol Popiel. People having hardly anything to do with Christian Democracy, such as Haller and General Marian Kukiel, shared in the running of the party. Of the activists of the former PSChD, Father Zygmunt Kaczyński, the director of the Catholic Press Agency and former parliamentary deputy, played a major role. Behind the scenes an important part was also played by Sikorski, the head of the Morges Front. The NPR was further prompted to merge with the PSChD by the demands of the political situation and by shared roots in the National Democratic Party, with whose programme it had much in common – for instance, an ideology of solidarity and decidedly anti-socialist leanings. The NPR was nearer the political centre and the PSChD tended more to the right. Like the Christian Democratic Party, the Labour Party[40] was weak. From 1937 until the outbreak of the war it was still finding its feet. The Catholic hierarchy refused to give the party its direct support.[41] It adopted a stance of firm opposition to the government. In political life it carried very little weight except in Silesia, and had scant public support. As far as can be calculated, it probably had a membership of about 20,000.[42]

The other groups of a Christian democratic nature were of practically no political significance. Until August 1923 there was Narodowe Zjednoczenie Ludowe, or the National Peasants' Party (NZL), which was eventually absorbed by one of the major peasant parties. Its history was marked by a great many disagreements and splits. Until the end of the 1920s, in the once Austrian part of Poland, there was Polskie Stronnictwo Konserwatywno-Ludowe, or the Polish Conservative Peasants' Party (PSKL). This was an ultra-conservative party actively supported by the Church, to which it owed its political position, although it must be noted that this was insignificant on a national scale. Stronnictwo Radykalno-Chłopskie, the Radical Peasant Party of Father Eugeniusz Okoń, so called because it advocated radical agrarian reform and collaborated with the far left – including the communists – cannot really be seen as belonging to the Christian democratic tradition.

When the war broke out the Labour Party was still not fully operational. In the period 1939–45, however, it was as active in occupied Poland as it was in exile, first in France and later in Great Britain. At home the party leaders and activists were soon engaged in undercover activities, setting up the structures of the clandestine Polish state. However, they worked with renewed determination in the period after the fall of France in June 1940 – a bitter blow that lessened the prospect of eventual victory over Nazi Germany and forced leading public figures in Poland to draw up long-term political plans. Unlike many political parties, the Christian Democrats decided not to form their own armed resistance units. Even though there were a few of them at the start of the period of the occupation, they soon joined forces with the Polish undercover Home Army, the Armia Krajowa (AK), under the orders of the legal Polish government in exile in London. By contrast, in the realm of politics, the activity of the Christian Democrats was outstanding. Their political standing in the life of the occupied country received a considerable boost following the party's merger with Unia, a clandestine organization composed mainly of Catholic intellectuals, that had been formed in 1940 from five small groups of Catholic militants intent on taking action – including military action – to oppose the occupying Nazi forces. Operating in the big cities such as Warsaw and Cracow, Unia was more like a somewhat loosely knit social movement than a clearly defined political body.[43]

In exile during the war, the Christian Democrats played a more important role than they had ever taken in Poland before 1939, including the period prior to 1926. The main leaders of the party – Haller, Colonel Izydor Modelski, and especially Popiel, its chairman – were forced into exile following the defeat of Poland in September 1939. In October of that year the premiership was entrusted to General Sikorski, who, as a politician, was very close to the Labour Party and maintained numerous personal contacts with its leaders. Sikorski headed the government in exile for three and a half years, until his tragic death in July 1943. His successor, Stanisław Mikołajczyk of the Peasant Party (PSL), fulfilled the role of Prime Minister until October 1944. Like Sikorski, he was on good terms with the Labour Party. Along with the PSL, the Nationalist Party (SN) and the Socialist Party (PPS), the Christian Democrats were the mainstay of the two successive governments. This four-party alliance was firmly welded together by a hearty distrust, sometimes bordering on outright hostility, that they harboured towards many of the representatives of the *sanacja* regime who still occupied many responsible posts among the emigrants and within the organs of the state, especially the army. Undoubtedly, among the emigrants, the Labour Party soon became a major political force, stabilizing the state institutions and being instrumental in settling the many conflicts which plagued the leading exiled officials.

The programme adopted by the Labour Party on 15 July 1945[44] was, broadly speaking, a continuation of the main threads of the 1937 programme. Owing to the bitter experiences of the time, however, a few changes were introduced; they reflect the state of mind obtaining in Poland at that momentous time. Many points are striking by their social radicalism. Corporatist ideas were discreetly dropped. In the field of economics, the party pressed vigorously for a broadening of control by the state, which was granted the right to oversee 'income and profits obtained by private persons', and even the right to check whether 'private estates are disposed in accordance with the demands of morality and the needs of the nation'. The programme set out plans for the nationalization of the most important and sensitive sectors of the Polish economy: the major banks, heavy industry and mining. In its foreign policy, Poland displayed evident and pronounced anti-German sentiments, as in its demand for a considerable westward extension, at Germany's expense, of Polish territory, and there were frequent calls for the partitioning of Germany in political discussions. At the same time, the Christian Democrats strongly defended the pre-1939 frontier between Poland and the USSR. In the months just before Soviet troops entered Poland, however, some party activists discreetly adopted a subtly more flexible stance on the subject. The close political alliance with France, Great Britain and the United States was seen to be a determining factor in the foreign policy of the future democratic Poland, but on the other hand the Labour Party stressed the importance of good relations with the USSR. Finally, a new element in the party's programme was the proposal for the creation of a grand confederation of the Central European states in the region stretching from the Baltic to the Adriatic and the Black Sea. This idea, broadly welcomed by the Polish politicians in exile after 1939, met with widespread approval in political circles under occupation in Poland itself. The sovietization that Poland underwent in 1944 put an end to that extension of the programme of the inter-war Polish Christian Democratic Party. Very soon the party itself was no more.

NOTES

1 The only leader of the Christian Democrat Party to attract historians' attention. The monograph by Marian Orzechowski, *Wojciech Korfanty. Biografia polityczna* (Warsaw 1975), remains the definitive study, although the author's views are somewhat dated.
2 For a general and balanced account, see Jerzy Kłoczowski (ed.), *Histoire religieuse de la Pologne* (Paris 1987), pp. 429–61.
3 Such is the conclusion reached by Jerzy Wisłocki in his definitive study of the concordat: Jerzy Wisłocki, *Konkordat polski z 1925 roku. Zagadnienia prawno-polityczne* (Poznań 1977).
4 On the political interdependence and ideological interference between the nationalist right and the Catholic Church, see Bogumił Grott, *Nacjonalizm chrześcijański. Narodowo-katolicka formacja ideowa w II Rzeczypospolitej na tle porównawczym* (Cracow 1996).
5 Andrzej Micewski, *Z geografii politycznej II Rzeczypospolitej* (Warsaw 1964), p. 142.
6 On the links between the two groups, see Henryk Przybylski, *Chrześcijańska Demokracja i Narodowa Partia Robotnicza w latach 1926–1937* (Warsaw 1980) and Jacek M. Majchrowski, *Stronnictwo Pracy, działalność polityczna i koncepcje programowe 1937–1945* (Warsaw and Cracow 1979), pp. 20–7. The NPR was particularly influential in Pomerania. See Roman Wapiński, *Dzialalność Narodowej Partii Robotniczej na terenie województwa pomorskiego w latach 1920–1930* (Gdańsk 1962).
7 Jerzy Holzer, *Mozaika polityczna II Rzeczypospolitej* (Warsaw 1974), p. 409.

8 Micewski, *Z geografii*, p. 159. See also Majchrowski, *Stronnictwo Pracy*, pp. 11–20.
9 It is virtually impossible to establish the exact number, mainly because the party archives were destroyed in a fire during the war. Konstanty Turowski, *Historia ruchu chrześcijańsko-demokratycznego w Polsce* (Warsaw 1989), p. 276. See also Przybylski, *Chrześcijańska Demokracja*, pp. 55–7, and Andrzej Andrusiewicz, *Stronnictwo Pracy, 1937–1950. Ze studiów nad dziejami najnowszymi chadecji w Polsce* (Warsaw 1988), pp. 11–12.
10 Andrzej Paczkowski, *Prasa Drugiej Rzeczypospolitej, 1918–1939* (Warsaw 1972), p. 58.
11 'Intelligentsia' is a fairly broad term in Poland. It generally refers to white-collar workers.
12 *Program Polskiego Stronnictwa Chrześcijańskiej Demokracji (PSChD) uchwalony na II Ogólnopolskim Kongresie Stronnictwa z 31 maja – 1 czerwca 1925* (Łomża 1925), p. 9.
13 Quoted in Micewski, *Z geografii*, p. 151.
14 Especially in Ludwik Caro, *Zmierzch kapitalizmu* (Poznań 1935).
15 Micewski, *Z geografii*, p. 152.
16 *Program Polskiego Stronnictwa*, p. 13.
17 Ibid., p. 2.
18 Wacław Bitner, 'O prawdziwe oblicze "Partii Katolickiej" w dwudziestoleciu', *Więź*, no. 62 (1963), pp. 110–12, here p. 112.
19 Turowski, *Historia ruchu*, p. 242.
20 *Zarys programu Polskiego Stronnictwa Chrześcijańskiej Demokracji* (Cracow 1925), p. 21.
21 *Hasło*, 15 September 1925.
22 Turowski, *Historia ruchu*, p. 319.
23 Czesław Strzeszewski, 'Chrześcijańskie stronnictwa polityczne', in idem, Ryszard Bender and Konstanty Turowski (eds), *Historia katolicyzmu społecznego w Polsce, 1932–1939* (Warsaw 1981), pp. 453–480, here p. 461.
24 Quoted in Micewski, *Z geografii*, p. 175.
25 Waldemar Bujak, *Historia Stronnictwa Pracy, 1937–1946–1950* (Warsaw 1988), pp. 32–6.
26 *Hasło*, 3 August 1925.
27 Ryszard Hermanowicz, *Chrześcijański ruch zawodowy w Polsce, 1918–1939* (Rome 1973), p. 123.
28 A few decades later, a party activist expressed the view that the lack of intellectuals was the main reason for the weakness of Christian Democracy in inter-war Poland. See Stefan Kaczorowski, 'Kilka sprostowań o partii katolickiej', *Więź*, no. 62 (1963), pp. 104–9, here p. 109.
29 In its statement of 1931, the third conference demanded, among other things, that 'women whose husbands earn enough money to support their families should be made redundant'. See Turowski, *Historia ruchu*, p. 375.
30 Bożena Krzywobłocka, *Chadecja 1918–1937* (Warsaw 1974), p. 176. Krzywobłocka's study is very biased, and includes a number of errors. However it has the merit of being based on a great many original sources.
31 *Głos Narodu*, 17 November 1931.
32 *Polonia*, 14 June 1936.
33 Wiesław Mysłek, *Kosciół katolicki w Polsce latach 1918–1939 (Zarys historyczny)* (Warsaw 1966), p. 188.
34 Micewski, *Z geografii*, p. 188.
35 Kazimierz Lutosławski, quoted in Krzywobłocka, *Chadecja*, p. 55.

36 Majchrowski, *Stronnictwo Pracy*, p. 40.
37 Adam Vetulani, 'Dążenia powojennej polityki konkordatowej', *Przegląd Powszechny*, no. 207 (1935), pp. 294–310, here p. 306.
38 Bitner, *O prawdziwe*, p. 112.
39 On the Labour Party, see Andrusiewicz, *Stronnictwo*; Bujak, *Historia Stronnictwa*; Majchrowski, *Stronnictwo*.
40 After 1939, when in exile, it called itself the Christian Democratic Labour Party.
41 According to Edward Kosibowicz, 'Sprawozdanie z ruchu religijnego, naukowego i społecznego. Sprawy Kościoła', *Przegląd Powszechny*, no. 216 (1937), pp. 118–28, here pp. 126–7.
42 Turowski, *Historia ruchu*, p. 414.
43 Ibid., p. 447; Andrusiewicz, *Stronnictwo*, pp. 162–91; Bujak, *Historia Stronnictwa*, pp. 110–16.
44 *Program Stronnictwa Pracy* (Cracow 1945). See Konrad Sieniewicz, *Le parti chrétien du travail polonais* (Rome 1975), pp. 28–37.

9

Middle-class Governmental Party and Secular Arm of the Catholic Church: The Christian Socials in Austria

Helmut Wohnout

On the eve of the First World War, the Christlichsoziale Partei, or Christian Social Party, had already developed from its origins in the urban milieu of Vienna to a classic *Reichspartei* that identified with the continued existence of the monarchy and its institutions.[1] The established Catholic Conservative groupings had to cede the leading role to the more dynamic Christian Socials, with their radical social reform programme, in almost all German-speaking areas of the western Cisleithenian part of the empire. The Christian Socials also succeeded in achieving a majority outside Vienna, by way of the farmers' associations that they had founded. When in 1907 a union took place with the Catholic Conservatives in the Reichsrat, the parliament of the Austrian part of the monarchy, the Christian Socials formed the largest parliamentary party, subsequently participating in coalition governments, which at the outset included Albert Gessmann as Minister for Employment and Alfred Ebenhoch as Minister for Agriculture. In addition, some of their leading representatives were advisers to Franz Ferdinand, the successor to the throne.

The fact that the Christian Socials were, from this time on, part of the government, brought with it new responsibilities for the state. On the other hand, it lost the social reform impetus that it had originally had. In addition, the social structure of the Christian Social Party changed for good in the years before the First World War. In rural areas, where it was dominated by farmers' organizations, as well as in the towns, it became a party of proprietors. This first became clear in the government elections of 1911, when the Christian Socials lost the electoral bastion of Vienna only a year after the death of Karl Lueger.[2] At this time the party ideology became more unified. Lueger had begun by wanting to cover the entire middle class, with the exception of the extreme German nationalists. What followed was the reorientation of the party towards political Catholicism.

THE RULING PARTY OF THE FIRST REPUBLIC

After Lueger's death and as a result of the heavy losses the party suffered in Vienna in 1911, the Christian Socials shifted the focus of their attention away from the capital, where the party had originated, to the regions. In other words, the focus shifted away from the lower-middle class to the conservative farmers. The ensuing antagonism between the Viennese Christian Socials, who were strongly marked by the personality of Ignaz Seipel, and to which belonged Richard Schmitz, Carl Vaugoin, Viktor Kienböck or Friedrich Funder, the chief editor of the *Reichspost*, which acted as the party's official organ,[3] and the regional representatives such as Johann Nepomuk Hauser from Upper Austria, Rudolf Ramek from Salzburg or Jodok Fink and Otto Ender from Voralberg, was to permeate the party up until 1933.

The Christian Socials began by playing a leading role in the forming of the new state after the end of the First World War. In February 1919 they emerged from the first elections as the second strongest party, with 69 deputies (as opposed to 72 Social Democrats and 26 German Nationalists), and a coalition government was formed together with the Social Democrats, with Jodok Fink as Vice-chancellor. This coalition turned out to be simply a marriage of convenience, however, as the parties became increasingly alienated from each other. Mainly ideological and philosophical issues widened the gulf between them and formed the prelude to the *Kulturkampf* of the First Republic.[4] After the breakdown of the Renner–Fink government in the summer of 1920, it was still possible in a provisional cabinet under the Christian Social, Michael Mayr, to plan the republican constitution together,[5] before co-operation with the Social Democrats finally collapsed. The elections of October 1920 brought the Christian Socials a relative majority of votes and deputies, something that was to change only in 1930.[6]

The era that now began, with the centre-right coalitions between the Christian Socials and German Nationalists and their increasingly more aggressive confrontation with Social Democracy, is very much the era of Ignaz Seipel. Seipel, who was a cleric of very high intellect, became the Professor for Moral Theology at Vienna University in 1917, succeeding the leading Christian Social thinker, Franz Martin Schindler. He was, from this time on, a member of the party leadership's inner advisory circle.[7] A year earlier he had already attracted attention with his comprehensive study of the nationality problem.[8] In October 1918, when Heinrich Lammasch, whom Seipel knew from their days in Salzburg, called on him to take part in the last imperial government, the meteoric rise of the charismatic priest really began. He was quickly to become the dominant figure in a party that, since Lueger's death, had been weakened by a power vacuum and several leadership crises. Seipel had already pulled strings behind the scenes at the transition from the monarchy to the republic, which the Christian Socials supported without enthusiasm for political reasons. He also negotiated the constitutional compromise of 1920 with Otto Bauer, and in doing so achieved the last 'great consensus'[9] between the Christian Socials and the Social Democrats. In 1922 he finally emerged from the second league and formed the middle-class coalition with the German Nationalists that was to exist for the rest of the decade. Seipel had already taken over the leadership of the party in June 1921. While the Christian Social representatives from the regions wanted an understanding with the Social Democrats, the group around Seipel prevailed. As a result of the experiences with the Social Democratic city administration in 'red Vienna', this section could be maintained only by 'vigorous' national politics. The Social Democrats experienced parallel developments with the reduced moderate wing around Karl Renner, being increasingly edged out by the radical 'Austrian-Marxist' group around Otto Bauer, who was Seipel's great political as well as intellectual opponent.

SOCIAL BASIS AND RELATIONSHIP TO THE CHURCH

In the 1920s, the theorists of the Christian Socials and the Christian Workers' Movement drafted comprehensive plans for a broad settlement of their interests. These plans were based on the teachings of the papal encyclical, *Rerum novarum*. The party was, however, from the formation of the First Republic onwards, torn between divergent philosophical and social interests. It strove to meet conservative tendencies on a cultural-political level, but economically and politically tried to fulfil the demands of the farmers and the lower-middle class.[10] This often meant taking protectionist measures to favour the domestic economy. Just after the war, the Christian Socials supported the nationalization of heavy industry, limited land reform and a series of noteworthy socio-political laws for cottage industry workers, agricultural and forestry workers, domestic servants and public and private employees.[11] In December 1918, in their election manifesto for the constitution of a national assembly, they demanded comprehensive social reforms, including the introduction of an unemployment and health insurance and a pension scheme.[12]

These demands were soon pushed into the background. Those reforms, especially in social policy, that were not realized at the time of the 'great coalition' with the Social Democrats were not accomplished by Seipel's government either. Seipel and his Finance Minister, Viktor Kienböck, did not push for social reforms because of the rigid policy of fiscal consolidation of the 1920s. Due to the prevailing desperate economic situation and the determination of Seipel and Kienböck to make healthy state finances the highest priority, there was no room for social policy measures that would make for social equality and improve the miserable situation in which a large sector of the population found itself.

By the end of 1925, the principle of the absolute priority of fiscal consolidation led to rationalization, mainly in the form of early retirement for more than eighty-three thousand civil servants. There was a dramatic increase in unemployment, and a rise in prices that hit the workers and the less well-off middle class hardest.[13] On the other hand, this did not prevent the Christian Socials from taking protectionist measures when their own clientele was to benefit, as for example in the case of agricultural customs protectionism.[14] Seipel's biographer, Klemens von Klemperer, admits that Karl Renners' criticism that the 'old liberal economic system' was the basis for Seipel's economic and financial policies, largely corresponded to reality.[15] The party had, however, at that time drifted far away from the social reform tradition of Karl von Vogelsang and Franz Martin Schindler.

In the last years of the monarchy, the Christian Socials had taken a strict clerical line on all societal issues. They understood themselves to be the secular arm of the Catholic Church, which had previously been protected by the ruling dynasty in its supremacy. This development was superficially strengthened by the activities of numerous 'priest-politicians', with Seipel at the helm and the Upper Austrian governor, prelate Johann Hauser. In the 1920s, the Social Democrats twice organized a movement among their followers promoting the leaving of the Church. This led to additional polarization and to a *Kulturkampf* mood.

The close adherence to Catholic teaching had other consequences, too. The Catholic tradition of anti-Judaism, predating the Second Vatican Council, made it easy for a large section of the Christian Socials to adopt a secular anti-Semitic way of thinking.[16] Hostility against Jews based on political or social arguments, above all that of the common cliché of Jewish dominance in the economy and culture and the resulting subversive influence on society, was common among the Christian Socials. This had been so since the days of the mayor of Vienna and party founder, Karl Lueger. To quote the manifesto of 1926: '[. . .] the Christian Social Party is combating the disproportional power of the subversive Jewish influence in spiritual and economic spheres'.[17] Anti-Semitic prejudice fell on fertile ground, above all in those places where it went hand in hand with resistance to the modern age and the interrelated tendencies towards secularization. Anti-Semitism, often linked with anti-liberalism, was for many Christian Socials a personal form of expressing their criticism of modern society.[18] In addition, anti-socialism in the form of anti-Marxism was taking on increasingly dogmatic forms, partly obvious and partly beneath the surface with anti-Semitic undertones.[19] This was connected to the fact that a large group of leading politicians in the Social Democratic Party was of Jewish origin. Thus there were Christian Social functionaries who saw great merit in their party having been first to recognize the 'Jewish threat'.[20]

The Christian Socials wanted to protect the political power of the Catholic Church and to keep its wide-reaching sphere of influence within society as intact as possible. Its fight against Social Democracy took on ever more radical forms in the sphere of Church politics and the *Kulturkampf*. This was one of the reasons why the Christian Socials began to develop and move ever further away from the Social Democratic Party in its social policies, treading an uncompromising anti-Marxist, capitalist path. Christian Social philosophy in its original, anti-capitalistic sense was only realizable in the agrarian sector, first and foremost through the massive promotion of co-operative societies.[21]

The *Kulturkampf* of the 1920s meant, in political practice, primarily a battle of resistance against civil marriage and, most importantly, against secularized schools. The Social Democrats, as well as the Christian Socials, regarded the school question as the central point in the socio-political debate, and both sides believed that they could at least influence, if not direct, long-term societal and political development through it. The Christian Socials made the 'moral-religious education' of the country's youth their battle cry. What they actually meant by this was the retention of the school system, which was traditionally based on primary and secondary levels, and making use of the great possibilities of Church influence. Key points in the Social Democrats' school reform programme were a standardized system of lower-secondary schools and an uncompromising secularization of the school system. As school regulations were laid down in the constitution, and any change at the national level required both Christian Social and Social Democrat support, 'red Vienna' developed into the hotly contested experimentation field of the left. The Christian Socials accused Social Democracy of subordinating its school policy to the primacy of an ideology based on the 'class struggle', putting heavy pressure on Vienna's Catholic teachers. As Seipel raised the demand for confessional schools to being the explicit imperative of Christian Social policy, and in 1926 replaced the moderate Christian Social Minister for Education, Emil Schneider, with the 'hardliner' Richard Schmitz, the irreconcilable differences between the two great 'ideological parties' regarding school issues seemed to be immovably sanctioned up until the end of the First Republic.[22]

Much of the ideology of the Christian Socials was religiously motivated. Seipel himself coined the expression 'the rehabilitation of souls'.[23] As a result of the anti-modernistic scepticism of Church teaching, Christian Socials' clericism implied a pronounced ambivalence towards liberal and pluralistic democracy of the kind to be found in Western Europe. With the rise of anti-democratic and authoritarian currents in Europe at the end of the 1920s and beginning of the 1930s, currents that affected the Church, the problems that the Christian Socials had with democracy and a multi-party system became evident. This was to be seen, above all, in the case of Ignaz Seipel, whose sympathy for authoritarian currents was ever increasing. When the foundation of Catholic Action by the Church put an end to the diversity of Catholic associations, it was a hard blow for the Christian Socials, as these associations had served the party as a background and contributed a great deal to Christian Social socialization. In the autumn of 1933, the bishops' conference demanded from Catholic clerics that they lay down their political mandates across the nation. The Bishop of Linz, Gföllner, was the driving force behind this decision. He openly favoured authoritarian currents.[24] Many Christian Socials thought that this meant the end of the party, and instinctively they were right. The Christian Socials lost their most important support when the Catholic Church disassociated itself from them.

PARTY STRUCTURES AND VOTERS

The social composition of the followers and voters for both large parties changed very little during the entire First Republic. The Christian Social Party was predominantly supported by farmers and the middle class. The Social Democrats were the centrally organized workers' party. This 'two-fold tightening of the party structure, ideologically and according to class'[25] consolidated both large societal camps. A greater process of erosion, starting at the beginning of the 1930s, led to the National Socialists' landslide success in the provincial elections in 1932.[26]

The Christian Socials did not, moreover, arrive at a homogenous organizational profile before 1933. The party's structure, according to Ernst Bruckmüller, 'partly implemented a corporatist model'.[27] What was meant by this was that the party's weight lay in its organized professional groups. Most influential was the Reichsbauernbund, the Association of Farmers, which had been formed in 1919 as an independent association and was active within the party as well as outside it.[28] Alongside the farmers there was the Christian Workers' Movement, which had been founded by Leopold Kunschak and was equipped with an organizational basis. Concerning the self-employed, Julius Raab succeeded in 1932 only in achieving the transformation of the German–Austrian Trade Association into an 'independent organization of professions within the context of the Christian Social Party'.[29] In the autumn of 1933, as the party was nearing its end, the Reichsgewerbebund, the Trade Association, was created following the farmers' example.

The party's power lay, at this time, in its far-reaching, autonomous, individual regional organizations. The organizational structure of these was very diverse, and embedded in an elaborately developed associational culture of political Catholicism. This was similarly true of the press. Party functions were often combined with those in Catholic organizations, which in turn led to the recruiting of the majority of functionaries and employees from their ranks. A modern party apparatus based on a tightly structured organization could not develop in these conditions. The Christian Socials had only had a party manifesto since 1926. This was, however, rather general and its statements were almost entirely defensive. At the national level, the *Klub* or parliamentary party formed the centre of power. The *Klub* leadership became the real political decision-making body of the Christian Socials.[30] Friedrich Funder described this *Klub* as the 'high command of the party'[31] and not the party leadership, which was mainly limited to dealing with organizational issues and propaganda. The extent to which the Christian Social Party structure was merely built on sand was to become clear during the process of its break-up. The party organization showed practically no resistance.

THE REPUBLIC, *ANSCHLUSS* AND EUROPE

Numerous reservations were built into the Christian Social commitment to the democratic republic. If some Christian Social regional organizations stood clearly for the transition to a republic in 1918–19, then it was possible for Seipel and the Cardinal of Vienna, Gustav Piffl, to show a high degree of flexibility because of their accommodating attitude guided by Thomistic thinking. Seipel, as minister in the last imperial government, had already formulated the decisive passage in the manifesto of 11 November 1918, after recognizing the untenable position of the monarchy. Unlike the German Emperor Wilhelm II two days previously, Emperor Karl did not formally resign, but only gave up (as he called it) all interest in the business of the state. Seipel had not chosen this wording, as some later argued, in order to facilitate later restoration, but to make the transition from monarchy to republic easier for conservative groups and to win their support for the building up of a new state.[32] All the same, he saved his party from a difficult clash between republicans and legitimists by this clever approach, and consequently contributed to the almost completely smooth transition from monarchy to republic in Austria. Its neighbours, Bavaria and Hungary, did not experience such a peaceful transition. The reservations about the republic that were found within the party became stronger over time, however, rather than weaker. Ernst Hanisch reckons that in 1918–19 most Catholics would have supported the continued existence of the monarchy.[33] The republic was frequently seen as being a necessary evil that one did not wish to get too used to or identify with.[34] These currents were first articulated in the weekly journal, *Das Neue Reich*, which was edited by the Catholic publicist Josef Eberle and had a large circulation among the Catholic educated class. It severely criticized the constitution of 1920, and the republican sympathizers in the Christian Social Party came under attack.[35]

Concerning the question of a possible *Anschluss* or integration into the German Reich, in the first shock of the collapse of the Habsburg Monarchy the Christian Socials let themselves be carried away by the pro-German feeling of the moment and the support for it among the Social Democrats and German Nationalists. A more discriminating attitude soon began to prevail, however. Seipel did not allow himself to be pinned down conclusively, but the immediacy of the wish for the *Anschluss* with Germany was replaced by a rather diffuse, Catholic-inspired *Reichsromantik*, or emotional attachment to the old German Reich prior to 1806. *Reichsromantik* in the final analysis left open the question of whether integration with Germany, or the return to a union of nations in the Danube region consisting of the successors of the dual monarchy, was being striven for. The Christian Socials never came to terms with Austria's forced existence as a small state. In the provisional national assembly of 1918–19, the possibility of a Danube federation was discussed and the Christian Social speaker, Josef Schraffl, aired the plan for a possible federation with the successor states of the monarchy.[36] Such plans were not grounded in real politics because these states were not interested in them. This did not, however, prevent their occasional resurrection in Christian Social foreign policy. Sections of the party first of all searched for a solution in conflicting ways. In the spring of 1921, individual Christian Social-led provincial governments began to prepare for a referendum about integration into Germany. They threw the party into a deep crisis, leading among other things to the resignation of the Christian Social-led government of Michael Mayr. Only at the party conference in June 1921, at which he formally took over leadership of the party, did Seipel manage to convince the regions to accept the reality of the situation created by the Peace Treaty of Saint Germain.[37]

Foreign policy, and above all the idea of Austria taking on a major role in Europe again, was Seipel's real strength. Although he began to concern himself intensively with foreign policy only when he became Chancellor, Seipel gained his reputation as a statesman of European proportions through this area and left his party, which had hardly any profile regarding foreign policy, far behind. Unlike almost all other leading politicians in the country, he recognized early on that under the international law of the Treaty of Saint-Germain, the conditions for new forms of international collaboration existed for the small Austrian nation.[38] When in 1922 Austria seemed about to collapse financially, he achieved a first success for the new republic with the Geneva Protocol and associated assistance from the League of Nations, amounting to 650 million gold crowns. This averted state bankruptcy. The foreign capital necessary for the revitalizing of the state's finances was, however, subject to a rigid domestic policy and the renewed prohibition of any *Anschluss* before 1942. In the course of the Geneva revitalization, Seipel won the high international reputation that led, among other things, to his being elected Vice-president of the League of Nations at its ninth assembly in 1928.

Thinking along the lines of the supranational categories of the monarchy, Seipel and Austria could not and did not want to come to terms with the role of small nation that the country had been allotted in the Treaty of Saint-Germain. If Seipel was one of the few in a position to combine small state politics with European responsibility, then it could be said that he was nevertheless impregnated by the memories of the old supranational empire. His position can be aptly illustrated by a letter in 1928, in which he wrote that Austrians were by their very nature 'Empire people' and did not wish to cultivate an Austrian consciousness based on a small-sized nation. It was not a task for 'those inhabiting the Karolingian Ostmark and the descendants of the victors against the Turks', as he loftily called the Austrians, 'to just cultivate their own little patch, showing it to strangers for an entrance fee'.[39]

At the beginning of the 1930s, the National Socialist *Anschluss* propaganda emanating from Germany became all the more vehement as the Christian Socials felt themselves prompted to present Austrian independence as a 'buffer' against the East, and to persist in emphasizing the German character of the country. Therefore, Central European collaboration came automatically into play. Kurt Schuschnigg, who since 1927 had been a Christian Social member of the Nationalrat, the parliament, and Minister for Justice since the beginning of 1932, declared in the early summer of that year in a speech to the monarchistic Reichsbund of Austrians, that the small nations that had come into existence after the First World War would not be capable of surviving unless they decided quickly

> to create a new form of large economic structure of some kind in Europe. Our Austria would thus be ensured its honourable role as a leading protagonist and cultural mediator in Central Europe. This is the way which would really lead to a third *Reich*.[40]

The Christian Socials began to promote Austria as the actual Catholic nucleus of German cultural and spiritual life. This was suppressed by an aggressive Prussian imperialism emanating from Germany, and history had shown just what a disadvantage this was. Thus the thoughts took shape that were to lead in the authoritarian period to the doctrine of Austria being the second, the better German state – a doctrine that had very little mass appeal. All in all, it can be said that within the three large political camps of the inter-war period the Christian Socials were those who had the least desire to opt for the *Anschluss*. The party, one of the leading pillars of the old monarchy and supranational system, was not prepared to see national unity as its goal. The Catholic idea of an Austrian-led Reich rather than one under German leadership, had clearly influenced their conception of unification with Germany.[41]

THE ROLE OF CORPORATISM WITHIN THE PARTY

The increasing disappointment and aversion of the middle-class camp to the republic went hand in hand in the late 1920s with an increasing sympathy for corporate and authoritarian patterns of thought. Rejection was concentrated above all on two elements in the Austrian constitution: first, proportional representation, and second, the dominant position of legislative power. It was hoped that with the constitutional amendment of 1929, which followed the trend of the time in shifting the weight of power from parliament to the head of state, wind would be taken out of the sails of anti-democratic currents. For many Christian Socials the amendment showed too many marks of compromise with the Social Democrats to be satisfactory, however.[42]

In the early 1930s, the disassociation of large sections of political Catholicism from the democratic principles of the state was to a large extent a result of Seipel's change of stance. The more the conflicts between Social Democrats and Christian Socials increased in intensity in the second half of the 1920s, the more Seipel's stance regarding his political rivals changed from being pragmatic to highly dogmatic and uncompromising. He began to set his 'true democracy' against the 'dictatorship of the proletariat', which had been hinted at in the 1926 Linz programme of the Social Democrats. Seipel's readiness to include non-parliamentary factors in his political calculations increased steadily, especially after the fire at the Palace of Justice on 15 July 1927, and the new campaign initiated by the Social Democrats that promoted leaving the Church. He gave more and more support to the Heimwehr, the paramilitary movement for the defence of the country, and showed his solidarity publicly in his speech in Tübingen in July 1929.[43] Furthermore, he repeatedly suggested the setting up of a corporatist assembly as a second chamber. Not being able to push this through in the reform of the constitution in 1929 after retiring from the chancellorship, he remained in a minority with this plan within his own party, even in 1930. This, together with his deteriorating health, led to his retirement from the party leadership. The regional party organizations who were still in favour of democracy had outvoted him, while the Viennese group around his successor, Carl Vaugoin, and Richard Schmitz increasingly aligned itself to a corporate stance.[44]

Neo-corporatist ideas had a certain tradition in the Christian Social programme because of their previous introduction by Karl von Vogelsang and his circle.[45] They remained non-binding, however. It was never completely clear if the ideas would, in practice, develop in the direction of Vogelsang, based on professional bodies, or the more social-corporatist direction of Franz Martin Schindler. A fresh impetus was given to the efforts to create a new corporate system in the country by the social encyclical *Quadragesimo anno*, published by Pope Pius XI in May 1931. This illuminated, in a few passages, the basis of a professional corporatist society and economy, and instigated the formation of professional corporatist bodies with the intention that members of the same profession should be able to form free associations connected with those professions. Although the encyclical avoided giving concrete instructions for the implementation of its programmatic aims, Seipel knew how to interpret the circular letter for his own purposes. For Seipel, a rebuilding of society and organizing of the professions went hand in hand with the undoing of the democratic state that had been in existence up until that time. His interpretation of the encyclical, which represented a narrowing down of the papal circular letter, was almost unquestioningly recognized by political Catholicism in Austria. That leading theorists in Germany such as Oswald Nell-Breuning and Gustav Gundlach did not see the corporatist system as being contradictory to parliamentary democracy was scarcely registered in Austria.[46] With Seipel's very individual idea of what was corporatist, the ideological basis was formed in the Christian Social programme on which the authoritarian experiments of 1933–34 to 1938 could be launched.[47]

THE DECLINE OF THE CHRISTIAN SOCIALS AS A PARTY

After the November elections of 1930 had ended in a fiasco for the Christian Socials – the party lost its relative majority in parliament – and the long-term German Nationalist coalition partner had gone astray, the Christian Social Party skidded from one crisis to another. It was in this situation that the agrarian expert and Christian Social Agriculture Minister, Engelbert Dollfuss, formed his first government in which he only had a very small majority, together with his coalition partners, the Agrarian Landbund and the Heimwehr. He managed to get the Lausanne loan through parliament after great efforts, and also a further loan of 300 million schillings, in return for another extension of the prohibition of the *Anschluss* before 1952. This was in the summer of 1932, and was met with strong resistance from the Social Democratic opposition. From this point on, the confrontation with Social Democracy became more and more intense. The events of 4

March 1933 surrounding the paralysing of parliament after the unexpected resignation of three presidents of the Nationalrat caught the leaders of the Christian Social Party and Dollfuss quite unprepared. Independently of each other, the party and the Chancellor were prompted to the same resolution, namely to carry on governing, first of all without parliament.[48] Dollfuss was not actually committed to an anti-democratic course from the very start of his time in government. On the contrary, as documented in Franz Schausberger's study, he had never belonged to Seipel's inner circle, and speculated about the possibility of a great coalition.[49] It was only in the throes of the government struggle over the Lausanne loan that he broke with Social Democracy and democratic parliamentarism.

While Dollfuss was returning from a party event in Carynthia on 5 March 1933, the party leaders, Carl Vaugoin, Leopold Kunschak and Karl Buresch, met near Vienna. All three agreed that the situation demanded authoritarian government. It was thought that in this way the Social Democrats could be forced into constitutional reform. When Dollfuss returned from Carynthia, he also suggested the same procedure. Influenced by the Reichstag elections in Germany in March 1933 in which the National Socialists once again achieved a relative majority, the leadership of the Christian Socials wanted to push through a far-reaching emergency decree and other Christian Social demands that had remained unfulfilled in the constitutional reform of 1929.[50] In the following weeks, the most influential figures in the Christian Social leadership, together with Dollfuss, successively changed their original idea for an organizational reform of the Nationalrat and the establishment of a regional and corporatist chamber to replace the Bundesrat as a second chamber, as had been laid down in the 1929 constitution. They now spoke about comprehensive constitutional reform as a basic prerequisite for the reconstitution of parliamentary structures.

Not all of the Christian Social Party leadership was prepared to go along with this unconditionally. This showed itself most clearly within the party in the resignation of the highly respected Minister for Social Affairs, Josef Resch, on 11 March 1933. Resch did not want to take joint responsibility for an anti-parliamentary course as a member of government, and in taking this step he drew personal consequences from what was, in his opinion, misguided policy. Not only individuals, but also entire groups within the disparate Christian Social Party were committed to a democratic course. The Christian Workers' Movement was one of these groups; others were the Lower Austrian farmers led by Josef Reither, and the Upper Austrian and Voralberg party sections that had already in 1930 considered leaving the parliamentary group of the Christian Socials in protest against the pro-Heimwehr policies of Seipel and Vaugoin.[51]

In the course of the spring of 1933, Dollfuss began to gradually move away from the idea of a return to parliamentary democracy of a West European nature. Crucial events connected with this were the Christian Social conference in Salzburg and the Heimwehr's celebration of the defeat of the Turks at the battle of Kahlenberg 250 years previously. Tens of thousands of Heimwehr members from all over Austria gathered in the garden of Schönbrunn castle. Added to this came increased pressure from fascist Italy not to return to a democratic multiparty system. The first personal meeting between Dollfuss and Benito Mussolini had already taken place in Rome at Easter, on 13 April 1933, and since that encounter the Italian dictator had put pressure on the Chancellor not to 'turn back'. The party conference that took place on 5–7 May 1933 in Salzburg did not take the course that Engelbert Dollfuss had expected. He had come to Salzburg in the hope that he would be asked to become party leader, but Vaugoin was re-elected. Dollfuss did not allow his disappointment to show. Yet the estrangement of the Chancellor from his own party and from the idea of the multiparty state was probably accelerated by this experience. The Christian Social leaders did not recognize this for quite some time, however.[52] In addition, important members of the party were in favour of an authoritarian government as a consequence of the anti-parliamentary rhetoric of the 1930s. It was not clear to them that with the end of parliamentary democracy, the political parties carrying this system would also be challenged.

The appointment of the highly respected governor of Vorarlberg, Otto Ender, to the position of minister in the chancellory responsible for constitutional questions, was tactically a clever move by Dollfuss. Ender had the reputation of being a pronounced democrat. In autumn 1933, however, the transition to authoritarian government took place step by step. In the frequently quoted *Trabrennplatz* speech that Dollfuss made on 11 September 1933 at the Vaterländische Front event on the periphery of the Catholic Congress, he said very little that was concrete about the future state structure. He reiterated his rejection of parliamentarism in the form it had taken up to that time, however: 'Parliament has inactivated itself. It has died of its own demagogy and formalism. This Parliament . . . will never and must never return again.'[53] He implemented his announcement that the 'time for party government' was now over with such determination, however, that he surprised even his own party friends. The events that took place around 12 February 1934, the 'revolt' of the Social Democratic paramilitary Schutzbund in Linz, which was followed by the Social Democratic workers' uprising and the ensuing short but intensive civil war, meant a further shifting of the internal balance of power in favour of the authoritarian wing and the Heimwehr. With the end of Social Democracy, the fate of the Christian Social Party was also sealed. Symptomatic of the beginning of the end of an era was the replacement of the pronouncedly democratic Upper Austrian leader Josef Schlegel by the regional leader of the Vaterländische Front and confidant of Dollfuss, Heinrich Gleissner. This was after the president of the Catholic Volksverein, Josef Aigner, had been forced to resign by Bishop Gföllner and the backbone of the Christian Socials in Upper Austria, one of its main centres, had been broken.[54]

During a visit to Vienna from 18–20 January 1934, the Italian Under-Secretary of State for Foreign Affairs, Fulvio Suvich, advised the Chancellor of Mussolini's unmistakable expectations: the battle against Marxism as well as the setting into motion of a clearly anti-parliamentary-corporatist constitutional reform, and the further pushing through of the Vaterländische Front as the sole 'unity party' instead of the democratic party organizations. Suvich demanded from the Chancellor not only a banning of Social Democracy, but also Dollfuss's separation from the democratic forces within the Christian Social Party.[55] In the weeks and months after 12 February 1934, the party was completely disconnected from all essential political decision making. Meetings of the party leadership no longer took place. The drafting of the new constitution lay in the hands of a small committee of ministers that included the Christian Socials Ender, Schuschnigg and Schmitz. Schmitz and Schuschnigg had, by this time, already separated themselves ideologically from the Christian Socials. The only one of the three to retain links with his party was Ender. Although it is often thought that he was in fact the creator of the authoritarian constitution of 1934, in reality he had to content himself with the function of editor of the constitution. Its contents carried more marks of the Heimwehr ideologist and State Secretary in the Dollfuss government, Odo Neustädter-Stürmer,[56] who in April 1934 – appropriately – could claim: 'Our ideas have now become those of the state.'[57] The stance of the Christian Socials in these months was quite diverse. One section was limited to the paramilitary forces or the Vaterländische Front. They fully identified with the new authoritarian state. Other sections, partly in the context of the political structures that were still in existence, such as the Christian Workers' Movement, withdrew into inner exile. A third group was resigned to the state of affairs and consoled itself with the hope that the old ideology of their party, such as the corporatist idea that was supposedly founded on Catholic social teaching, would reawaken under the new conditions.

All that was left was for the Christian Social Party to liquidate itself. The parliamentary party met on 14 May 1934 and dissolved. The party leadership discontinued its activities after a final meeting on 27 September 1934.[58] The party's news service was transformed into the Christliche Pressezentrale. This was led by the last party leader, Emmerich Czermak, who had been called in by Dollfuss to be its 'liquidator',[59] and Theodor Innitzer, who put Catholic Action in charge of the Pressezentrale.

If one wonders why the Christian Socials more or less just resigned themselves to their fate, and were partly actively involved in their own decline and demise, then the following can be said to sum it up. First, increased scepticism in middle-class circles regarding parliamentary democracy had been apparent since the late 1920s and was in keeping with the European trend of the time. An intuitive rejection of the republic, which had arisen out of the revolutionary overthrow of the monarchy in 1918–19 played a role, as did the phenomenon of belated parliamentarism and the corporatist-authoritarian ideas of Othmar Spann, who instigated near euphoric enthusiasm in the circles of young academics in the inter-war period with his book, *Der wahre Staat*. Reading this book and attending Spann's lectures was a compulsory part of the syllabus for the young Catholic intelligentsia at the University of Vienna.[60] The late anti-democratic tendencies of Seipel, who remained the Christian Socials' mentor long after his death in the summer of 1932, were also important. In addition, anti-democratic tendencies dominated most Catholic publications in the early 1930s. Newspapers such as Josef Eberle's *Schönere Zukunft*, and in part also Friedrich Funder's *Reichspost*, paved the way for the transformation of multiparty democracy into an authoritarian state. Moreover, developments in Germany also had an impact on Austria. The Christian Socials misjudged the *Präsidialkabinette* under the leadership – or at least with the participation – of Zentrum politicians, first and foremost Heinrich Brüning and Franz von Papen. Paradoxically, the German example of 1932–33, which led the country from being a party state into the National Socialist dictatorship, did not serve the Christian Socials as a warning but rather as an example to be emulated. Men like Reich President Paul von Hindenburg, and Franz von Papen, enjoyed uncritical praise in Christian Social publications and propaganda.[61] As the political reality of the new dictatorship in Germany became clear, it was already too late for the Christian Socials in Austria.

CHRISTIAN SOCIALS IN THE GOVERNMENT CAMP 1934–38 AND CONTINUITIES IN THE SECOND REPUBLIC

Although the Christian Socials had stopped existing as a party, Christian Social currents within the heterogeneous government camp in authoritarian Austria continued to play a role. In 1934, those Christian Socials who did not – like Kurt Schuschnigg or Richard Schmitz – fall into line with the authoritarian state, had their backs to the wall. When in the autumn of that year it came to the allotting of positions in new corporatist authoritarian law-making bodies, which had been set up in 1934, the Heimwehr, which was at the peak of its power, won through convincingly against the Christian Socials. Its members occupied a third of the seats in the state council alone.[62] When one thinks about how small the former parliamentary party of the Heimwehr had been in the Austrian parliament in comparison with the Christian Socials, and that countless state council members like, for example, those representing the religious communities, were not politically active, then one can really appreciate how far the Heimwehr had got. The comparatively modest representation of the Christian Socials was partly because, after the dissolving of the party, they found themselves in a phase where they were weak and seemed to have lost their way. The ones who were able to assert themselves were those who had a paramilitary organization to back them up, such as the Ostmärkische Sturmscharen or the Freiheitsbund of the Christian Workers' Movement.

After a relatively short period the old elites returned into state functions, however. The Heimwehr had passed its zenith, and as a result of its declining influence within the government camp former Christian Social politicians began to take up key positions again. This was in part because Schuschnigg could no longer do without their expertise. The new Chancellor, having succeeded Dollfuss after his assassination, aligned himself with those who had indispensable expertise. Thus Kienböck became president of the central bank and a close economic adviser. Resch returned to the government as Minister for Social Affairs in May 1936. Ender, who had been rather elbowed out in 1934 when he was president of the auditing office, returned in 1937, replacing Neustädter Sturmer, and took up the task of 'the continued construction of corporatist structures' as Schuschnigg's influential adviser.[63] Schuschnigg naturally availed himself of the services of former Christian Social politicians when they could help to integrate interest groups into the government camp. This was the case with Julius Raab, who was the uncontested leader of the influential Gewerbebund. It cannot be said, however, that Schuschnigg, who had himself come from the right wing of the Christian Social Party, organizing his own militia, the Ostmärkische Sturmscharen, relied exclusively on former Christian Social politicians.[64] He surrounded himself with a group of men who either came from the civil service, like Guido Schmidt and Hans Pernter, or who were members of different militias and had managed to a certain extent to detach themselves from them. In choosing such men, Schuschnigg showed a certain aversion to party politicians of the old school. A significant example of his choice for the inner circle was the popular poet and Heimwehr functionary, Guido Zernatto, who was from Carynthia. He was appointed general secretary of the Vaterländische Front by Schuschnigg. It was partly because of him that only a very small number of the strategic positions in the Vaterländische Front were held by former Christian Social politicians. Schuschnigg moved towards a reconciliation with the Christian Social camp in the last phase of his time in government. He learned once again to appreciate his former party friends as reliable partners in Austrian independence, because of the ever increasing German pressure and the presence of marked nationalists like Arthur Seyss-Inquart and Edmund Glaise-Horstenau within the government camp who were forced on him. Four ministers who had been Christian Social deputies before 1933 were part of the government formed in February 1938. As a result of this, Christian Social politicians were persecuted by the National Socialists directly after the *Anschluss* for being opponents of the new regime. Many were arrested and sent to the concentration camp at Dachau.[65]

In conclusion, it is necessary to briefly discuss the question of continuity in Austria from the inter-war period to 1945. It is remarkable that almost all the leadership of the newly formed Austrian People's Party were former Christian Socials who had not been linked to the authoritarian course to too great a degree.[66] There were two distinct groups. Older Democrats like Kunschak or Reither, who between 1934 and 1938 had had the reputation of having supported the authoritarian course only reluctantly and dragging their feet, formed one group. The second group consisted of men of the up-and-coming generation, such as the first Chancellor of the Second Republic, Leopold Figl, or the first secretary general of the party and Education Minister from 1945–52, Felix Hurdes. They came from the Christian Social camp, but had played only a minor role from 1934–38 and were arrested by the National Socialists between 1938 and 1945. After the end of the war they were in no way compromised, and went on to establish the People's Party in a consciously chosen organizational discontinuity, but with many connections in terms of personnel and ideology in the years up to 1938. Important differences to the previous party were already evident in the clear backing away from the resolute clerical course of the inter-war period (albeit with a continuing close ideological connection to the Catholic Church), in favour of a people's party open to all confessions.

Lines of continuity to the First Republic, which reflected certain basic characteristics of the emergence of Christian democracy in Europe after 1945, can be traced in two directions.[67] On the one hand there was, as a basic premise, the supposition of a society made up of social classes reflected in the structure of the party. On the other hand, some were pleased to be able to continue a certain tradition of organization from the First Republic. The Christian Social Party had been dissolved in 1934, but the Farmers' Association, the Christian Workers' Movement and the Gewerbebund continued to exist within the newly formed corporatist structures up until 1938. The Farmers' Association retained its supremacy in all political questions by way of the corporatist Agriculture and Forestry Association, which was established in June 1935.[68] The Gewerbebund was, to quote Julius Raab, 'a strongly centralized' association and one with a 'strong and authoritarian leadership'[69] and a monopoly of interest representation, just as the Christian Workers' Movement had in the context of the unions.[70]

This fact has received too little attention from historians in connection with the history of the founding of the Austrian People's Party. One exception is Michael Gehler, who has demonstrated, in a case study of the Tirol, how the tradition of internal corporate-professional representation was relaunched during the founding phase of the People's Party.[71] In fact, this party established itself in the spring of 1945 in the provinces and through professional organizations. Those exponents who emerged to become the leading government elite were those who had had political experience in the inter-war period, and for whom the post-war thesis of Austrians having been the first victims of National Socialist Germany corresponded to their own personal experiences.[72]

One exception was the heavyweight, Julius Raab. As Trade Minister in Schuschnigg's last government, he had been in too exposed a position in the final phase of authoritarian Austria. On top of this came his Heimwehr past, as well as the fact – obviously because of the intervention of the Lower Austrian National Socialist *Gauleiter* Hugo Jury – that he had never been arrested during the National Socialist period. In December 1945, because of pressure from the allies, these facts led to his not being eligible to become Trade Minister in Figl's cabinet.[73] He had to wait until 1953 before entering government, but when he did so it was to be as Chancellor.

NOTES

1 For the development of the Christian Social Party prior to 1918, see John W. Boyer, *Culture and Political Crisis in Vienna. Christian Socialism in Power, 1897–1918* (Chicago, IL 1995); idem, 'The End of an Old Regime. Visions of Political Reform in Late Imperial Austria', *Journal of Modern History*, vol. 58, no. 1 (1986), pp. 159–93; idem, *Political Radicalism in Late Imperial Vienna. The Origins of the Christian Social Movement, 1848–1897* (Chicago, IL 1981); Ernst Bruckmüller, 'Die Entwicklung der Christlichsozialen Partei bis zum Ersten Weltkrieg', *Christliche Demokratie, Vierteljahresschrift für Zeitgeschichte, Sozial-, Kultur- und Wirtschaftsgeschichte*, vol. 9, no. 4 (1991/92), pp. 343–68; Anton Staudinger, 'Christlichsoziale Partei', in Erika Weinzierl and Kurt Skalnik (eds), *Österreich 1918–1938. Geschichte der Ersten Republik*, vol. 1 (Vienna, Graz and Cologne 1983), pp. 249–76, here pp. 249–53.

2 Regarding Lueger, see Richard S. Geehr, *Karl Lueger. Mayor of Fin de Siècle Vienna* (Detroit 1990); Ludwig Reichhold, *Karl Lueger. Die soziale Wende in der Kommunalpolitik* (Vienna 1989); Kurt Skalnik, *Dr. Karl Lueger. Der Mann zwischen den Zeiten* (Vienna 1954); Brigitte Hamann, *Hitlers Wien. Lehrjahre eines Diktators* (Munich 2001 [1996]), pp. 393–435.

3 The *Reichspost*, which was founded in 1894, actually belonged to the Catholic Church. The paper's line was almost exclusively determined by Friedrich Funder, who had been chief editor since 1902, had acted as publisher since 1904 and led the paper until its demise in 1938. For Funder's biography, see his two autobiographical works: *Von Gestern ins Heute. Aus dem Kaiserreich in die Republik*, 3rd edition (Vienna 1971), and *Als Österreich den Sturm bestand* (Vienna

1957). See also Hedwig Pfarrhofer, *Friedrich Funder. Ein Mann zwischen Gestern und Morgen* (Vienna, Graz and Cologne 1978).
4 Erika Weinzierl, *Prüfstand. Österreichs Katholiken und der Nationalsozialismus* (Mödling 1988), pp. 16–17.
5 For Michael Mayr, see Hermann J. W. Kuprian, *Zwischen Wissenschaft und Politik. Die politische Entwicklung Michael Mayrs von 1907 bis 1922*, Ph.D. (University of Innsbruck 1986); idem, 'Michael Mayr', *Neue Deutsche Biographie*, vol. 16 (Berlin 1990), p. 10.
6 In the Nationalrat elections of 17 October 1920, the Christian Socials won 85 seats, the Social Democrats 69 and the German Nationalists 28. In the elections of 9 November 1930, the last in the First Republic, the Social Democrats had the relative majority with 72 seats. The Christian Socials won 66, the so-called Schoberblock (a merger of the German Nationalists and the Landbund) 19 and the Heimwehr, 8. The National Socialists, who were standing for the first time, gained 111,000 votes, but no parliamentary deputy.
7 See Klemens von Klemperer, *Ignaz Seipel. Staatsmann einer Krisenzeit* (Graz, Vienna and Cologne 1976 – Shorter English original 1972); Friedrich Rennhofer, *Ignaz Seipel. Mensch und Staatsmann* (Vienna, Cologne and Graz 1978).
8 Ignaz Seipel, *Nation und Staat* (Vienna and Leipzig 1916).
9 Ernst Hanisch, *Der lange Schatten des Staates. Österreichische Gesellschaftsgeschichte im 20. Jahrhundert* (Vienna 1994), p. 269.
10 For the frequent mystification of the term middle class (*Mittelstand*) among the Christian Socials and later the People's Party, see Ernst Bruckmüller, 'Die ständische Tradition – ÖVP und Neokorporatismus', in Robert Kriechbaumer and Franz Schausberger (eds), *Volkspartei – Anspruch und Realität. Zur Geschichte der ÖVP seit 1945* (Vienna, Cologne and Weimar 1993), pp. 281–316, here 306–7.
11 Staudinger, *Christlichsoziale Partei*, pp. 254–6.
12 'Das Wahlprogramm der Christlichsozialen Partei 1918', in Klaus Berchtold (ed.), *Österreichische Parteiprogramme 1868–1966* (Vienna 1967), pp. 356–9, here p. 358.
13 Unemployment levels peaked in 1926 at 11 per cent, but subsequently fell. They were to rise dramatically after 1930 as a result of the world economic crisis, and reached a record level of 26 per cent in 1933. For statistics in the public sector, see also Ernst Bruckmüller, 'Sozialstruktur und Sozialpolitik', in Weinzierl and Skalnik, *Österreich 1918–1938*, vol. 1, pp. 381–436, here pp. 406–8.
14 See Peter Meihsl, 'Die Landwirtschaft im Wandel der politischen und ökonomischen Faktoren', in Wilhelm Weber (ed.), *Österreichs Wirtschaftsstruktur gestern – heute – morgen. Strukturwandlungen der österreichischen Volkswirtschaft in der Vergangenheit und ihre Bedeutung für Strukturprobleme der Gegenwart und der Zukunft*, vol. 2 (Berlin 1961), pp. 551–837, here pp. 785–91.
15 Klemperer, *Seipel*, p. 174.
16 For Christian Social anti-Semitism in the inter-war period, see Anton Staudinger, 'Katholischer Antisemitismus in der Zwischenkriegszeit', in Gerhard Botz, Ivar Oxaal, Michael Pollak and Nina Scholz (eds), *Eine zerstörte Kultur. Jüdisches Leben und Antisemitismus in Wien seit dem 19. Jahrhundert* (Vienna 2002), pp. 261–80. More impartial, Bruce F. Pauley, *From Prejudice to Persecution: A History of Austrian Antisemitism* (Chapel Hill 1992) (Vienna 1993), pp. 199–222.
17 In his 1932 commentary about the party programme, Richard Schmitz wrote proudly that anti-Semitism had, 'since the origins of the movement, been a part of the Christian Social character': *Das christlichsoziale Programm. With explan-*

atory notes by Richard Schmitz (Vienna 1932), p. 67. For an assessment of the programme as a whole, as well as Seipel's stance on anti-Semitism, see Klemperer, *Seipel*, pp. 210–12; for an estimation of Lueger's anti-Semitism, see along with John Boyer's essential work, the pointed evaluation of Wolfgang Maderthaner and Lutz Musner, who arrive at the conclusion that Lueger's anti-Semitism was not racist but more 'casuistic and populistic'. See Wolfgang Maderthaner and Lutz Musner, *Die Anarchie der Vorstadt. Das andere Wien um 1900*, 2nd edition (Frankfurt/Main and New York 2000), pp. 203–8, here p. 203. For a comprehensive overview of Lueger's anti-Semitism, see also Hamann, *Hitlers Wien*, pp. 410–18.

18 Those representatives of the Christian Socials who most identified with the democratic system of the First Republic were, remarkably, those who were often most open to anti-Semitic propaganda. This was true of the founder and decade-long leader of the Christliche Arbeiterbewegung, the Christian Workers' Movement, Leopold Kunschak and the last leader of the Christian Social Party, Emmerich Czermak. Helmut Wohnout, 'Die Janusköpfigkeit des autoritären Österreich. Katholischer Antisemitismus in den Jahren vor 1938', *Geschichte und Gegenwart. Vierteljahreshefte für Zeitgeschichte, Gesellschaftsanalyse und politische Bildung* vol. 13, no. 1 (1994), pp. 3–16, here pp. 7–9.

19 'Anti-socialism in the guise of anti-Marxism was always mixed with anti-Semitic motives in the Christian Workers' Movement.' Anton Pelinka's comment about the Christian Workers' Movement can be almost completely transferred to the party as a whole, even though it was the Christian Workers' Movement that actually propagated anti-Semitic propaganda in the form of racism as a part of their policy. Anton Pelinka, 'Christliche Arbeiterbewegung und Austrofaschismus', in Emmerich Tálos and Wolfgang Neugebauer (eds), '*Austrofaschismus*'. *Beiträge über Politik, Ökonomie und Kultur 1934–1938*, 4th edition (Vienna 1988), pp. 121–32, here p. 130; idem, *Stand oder Klasse? Die christliche Arbeiterbewegung Österreichs 1933–1938* (Vienna, Munich and Zurich 1972), pp. 213–33.

20 National Archives, Washington, DC, Record Group 59: General Records of the Department of State 1930–39, 863. 416/104. The *Reichspost* reported in 1933: 'that is why it is a distortion of the facts to say that anti-Semitism is an invention of National Socialism . . .' *Reichspost. Unabhängiges Tagblatt für das christliche Volk*, 1 November 1933.

21 Around fifty dairy co-operatives were founded or extended between 1926 and 1929, for example, with help from the remainder of the 1922 loan from the League of Nations. See Martina Deutsch, '*Der Völkerbund-Molkereikredit: Erstellung und Verlauf der Kreditaktion für den Ausbau des österreichischen Molkereiwesens (1926–1938)*', Thesis (University of Vienna 1998).

22 Regarding Schmitz, see Fritz Braun, *Der politische Lebensweg des Bürgermeisters Richard Schmitz. Beiträge zur Innenpolitik der ersten Republik Österreich und zur Geschichte der Christlichsozialen Partei*, Ph.D. (University of Vienna 1968). Regarding Emil Schneider and his replacement by Anton Rintelen and then Richard Schmitz, see Gertrude Brinek and Helmut Wohnout, 'Emil Schneider – Zwischen pädagogischer Profession und politischem Augenmass', in Klaus Plitzner and Wolfgang Scheffknecht (eds), *Minister Dr. Emil Schneider. Ein Unterrichtsminister aus dem 'schwärzesten Österreich' 1883–1961* (Schwarzach 2001), pp. 197–230.

23 Klemperer, *Seipel*, p. 203.

24 See Harry Slapnicka, 'Vor 50 Jahren: Abzug des Klerus aus der Politik', in *Theologisch-praktische Quartalschrift*, vol. 131, no. 3 (1983), pp. 242–50.

25 Klemperer, *Seipel*, p. 123.
26 Regarding the 1932 elections, see Franz Schausberger, *Ins Parlament, um es zu zerstören. Das 'parlamentarische' Agi(ti)eren des Nationalsozialisten in den Landtagen von Wien, Niederösterreich, Salzburg und Vorarlberg nach den Landtagswahlen 1932* (Vienna, Cologne and Weimar 1995), pp. 91–193.
27 Ernst Bruckmüller, *Die ständische Tradition*, p. 288.
28 Ernst Bruckmüller, 'Interessenvertretung der Bauern', in Emmerich Tálos, Herbert Dachs, Ernst Hanisch and Anton Staudinger (eds), *Handbuch des politischen Systems Österreichs. Erste Republik. 1918–1933* (Vienna 1995), pp. 352–70, here pp. 357–67.
29 Michael Dippelreiter, 'Julius Raab und der Gewerbebund', in Alois Brusatti and Gottfried Heindl (eds), *Julius Raab. Eine Biographie in Einzeldarstellungen* (Linz 1986), pp. 97–105, here p. 100.
30 Walter Goldinger, 'Einleitung', in idem (ed.), *Protokolle des Klubvorstandes der Christlich sozialen Partei 1932–1934* (Vienna 1980), pp. 7–18, here p. 11.
31 Funder, *Als Österreich den Sturm bestand*, p. 107.
32 Klemperer, *Seipel*, pp. 79–80.
33 Ernst Hanisch, *Die Ideologie des Politischen Katholizismus in Österreich 1918–1938* (Salzburg 1977), p. 6.
34 Klemens von Klemperer has described Germany and Austria as 'improvised democracies', whose democratization was not the result of political development over a long period, but mainly a by-product of military defeat and the collapse of autocratic and monarchical rule. Klemens von Klemperer, 'Das nachimperiale Österreich, 1918–38: Politik und Geist', in Heinrich Lutz and Helmut Rumpler (eds), *Österreich und die deutsche Frage im 19. und 20. Jahrhundert. Probleme der politisch-staatlichen und soziokulturellen Differenzierung im deutschen Mitteleuropa* (Vienna 1982), pp. 300–17, here p. 302.
35 Regarding Josef Eberle, see Peter Eppel, *Zwischen Kreuz und Hakenkreuz. Die Haltung der Zeitschrift 'Schönere Zukunft' zum Nationalsozialismus in Deutschland 1934–1938* (Vienna, Graz and Cologne 1980), pp. 34–44; Alfred Diamant, *Die österreichischen Katholiken und die Erste Republik. Demokratie, Kapitalismus und soziale Ordnung 1918–1934* (Vienna n.d.), pp. 129–31.
36 Klemperer, *Das nachimperiale Österreich*, p. 311.
37 Friedrich Funder, *Vom Gestern ins Heute*, pp. 509–10; see also Hermann J. W. Kuprian, 'Tirol und die Anschlussfrage 1918 bis 1921', in Thomas Albrich, Klaus Eisterer and Rolf Steininger (eds), *Tirol und der Anschluss. Voraussetzungen – Entwicklungen – Rahmenbedingungen 1918–1938* (Innsbruck 1988), pp. 43–74.
38 Klemperer, *Das nachimperiale Österreich*, p. 309.
39 Klemperer, *Seipel*, p. 247.
40 Zentrum zur Aufbewahrung historisch-dokumentarischer Sammlungen (CChIDK), Moscow, Ostmärkische Sturmscharen, 506 – 1 – 7, 'Der österreichische Gedanke. Aus einer Rede des Bundesministers Dr. Kurt Schuschnigg im Reichsbund der Österreicher' (typed manuscript, n.d.).
41 Klemperer, *Das nachimperiale Österreich*, p. 311.
42 For the constitutional reform of 1929, see Klaus Berchtold (ed.), *Die Verfassungsreform von 1929. Dokumente und Materialien zur Bundes-Verfassungsgesetz-Novelle von 1929* (Vienna 1979); Gernot D. Hasiba, *Die Zweite Bundes-Verfassungsnovelle von 1929. Ihr Werdegang und wesentliche verfassungspolitische Ereignisse seit 1918* (Vienna, Cologne and Graz 1976).

43 For the transcript of the Tübingen speech, see Ignaz Seipel, *Der Kampf um die österreichische Verfassung* (Vienna and Leipzig 1930), pp. 177–88.
44 Helmut Wohnout, *Regierungsdiktatur oder Ständeparlament? Gesetzgebung im autoritären Österreich* (Vienna, Cologne and Graz 1993), pp. 45–8.
45 For the corporatist ideological legacy that lasted up until the beginnings of the Christian Social movement, see in summary Bruckmüller, 'Ständische Tradition', pp. 282–92.
46 Oswald von Nell-Breuning, *Die soziale Enzyklika. Erläuterungen zum Weltrundschreiben Papst Pius' XI. über die gesellschaftliche Ordnung* (Cologne 1932), p. 155; for Gundlach, see Benno Karpeles, *Klassenkampf, Faschismus und Ständeparlament. Ein Beitrag zur Diskussion über die berufsständische Neuordnung* (Vienna 1933), p. 28.
47 Wohnout, *Regierungsdiktatur*, pp. 52–3.
48 For the Christian Social role after 5 March 1933, see Anton Staudinger, 'Die Mitwirkung der christlich-sozialen Partei an der Errichtung des autoritären Standesstaates', in *Österreich 1927 bis 1938. Protokoll des Symposiums in Wien, 23–28. Oktober 1972* (Vienna 1973), pp. 68–75; idem, 'Christlich soziale Partei und Errichtung des "Autoritären Ständesstaates"', in Österreich', in Ludwig Jedlicka and Rudolf Neck (eds), *Vom Justizpalast zum Heldenplatz. Studien und Dokumentationen 1927 bis 1938* (Vienna 1975), pp. 65–81.
49 Franz Schausberger, *Letzte Chance für die Demokratie. Die Bildung der Regierung Dollfuss im Mai 1932. Bruch der österreichischen Proporzdemokratie* (Vienna, Cologne and Weimar 1993).
50 For the influence of the elections in Germany on the decision made by the Christian Socials to take the authoritarian path, see Gerald Stourzh, 'Die Aussenpolitik der österreichischen Bundesregierung gegenüber der nationalsozialistischen Bedrohung', in idem and Birgitta Zaar (eds), *Österreich, Deutschland und die Mächte. Internationale und österreichische Aspekte des 'Anschlusses' vom März 1938* (Vienna 1990), pp. 319–46, here pp. 320–2.
51 Anton Staudinger, Wolfgang C. Müller and Barbara Steininger, 'Die Christlichsoziale Partei', in Tálos, Dachs, Hamisch and Staudinger (eds), *Handbuch des politischen Systems Österreichs. Erste Republik 1918–1933*, p. 174.
52 Wohnout, *Regierungsdiktatur*, p. 80.
53 Dollfuss's *Trabrennplatz* speech in Edmund Weber (ed.), *Dollfuss und Österreich. Eines Mannes Wort und Ziel* (Vienna and Leipzig 1935), pp. 19–45, here p. 26.
54 Harry Slapnicka, *Christlichsoziale in Oberösterreich. Vom Katholikenverein 1848 bis zum Ende der Christlichsozialen 1934* (Linz 1984), pp. 298–303.
55 Suvich was in agreement about this demand with the leader of the Heimwehr, Ernst Rüdiger Starhemberg, who issued an ultimatum to Dollfuss on 5 February 1934. See Fulvio Suvich, *Memoire 1932–1936. A cura di Gianfranco Bianchi* (Milan 1984), pp. 269–71.
56 See in summary Helmut Wohnout, 'Politisch-juristische Kontroversen um die Verfassung 1934 im autoritären Österreich', in Erika Weinzierl, Oliver Rathkolb, Rudolf G. Ardelt and Siegfried Mattl (eds), *Justiz und Zeitgeschichte. Symposionbeiträge 1976–1993*, vol. 2 (Vienna 1995), pp. 833–48, here pp. 837–40.
57 Quotation from *Der Heimatschützer. Offizielles Organ des Österreichischen Heimatschutzes*, 28 April 1934.
58 Peter Huemer, *Sektionschef Robert Hecht und die Zerstörung der Demokratie in Österreich. Eine historisch-politische Studie* (Vienna 1975), p. 277.

59 Funder, *Als Österreich den Sturm bestand*, p. 79.
60 Othmar Spann, *Der wahre Staat. Vorlesungen über Abbruch und Neubau der Gesellschaft*, 5th edition (Graz 1972).
61 Barbara Haider, 'Die Diktatur der Vernunft. Die Präsidialkabinette Brüning und das christlichsoziale Lager in Österreich', in Wohnout, *Demokratie und Geschichte*, vol. 2 (1998), pp. 194–227, here p. 220.
62 Wohnout, *Regierungsdiktatur*, pp. 193–228.
63 Ibid., pp. 356–9.
64 For a biography of Schuschnigg, see Anton Hopfgartner, *Kurt Schuschnigg, Ein Mann gegen Hitler* (Graz, Vienna and Cologne 1989).
65 See *Gelitten für Österreich. Christen und Patrioten in Verfolgung und Widerstand* (Vienna n.d. [1988]).
66 There was only one exception: the Foreign Minister, Karl Gruber, who had his roots in the resistance movement. Michael Gehler, 'Vom Telegraphenamt zum Ballhausplatz. Karl Gruber und Österreichs Aussenpolitik bis zum Scheitern der Staatsvertragsverhandlungen 1927–1949', Thesis (University of Innsbruck 1999), pp. 300–462.
67 Bruckmüller, 'Die ständische Tradition', p. 294.
68 Wohnout, *Regierungsdiktatur*, p. 266.
69 Referat des Präsidenten Ing. Julius Raab bei der 1. Innungsmusterkonferenz (konstituierende Sitzung des Hauptausschusses des Bundes der österreichischen Gewerbetreibenden) am Freitag den 6. September 1935 im Haus der Kaufmannschaft in Wien, Karl von Vogelsang-Institut, Vienna, Julius Raab-Archiv, Korrespondenzen 1945–54.
70 Pelinka, *Stand oder Klasse?*, p. 108.
71 Michael Gehler, 'Die Volkspartei in Tirol 1945–1994', in Kriechbaumer and Schausberger, *Volkspartei*, pp. 645–700, here pp. 645–7.
72 Gerald Stourzh, 'Erschütterung und Konsolidierung des Österreichbewusstseins – Vom Zusammenbruch der Monarchie zur Zweiten Republik', in Richard G. Plaschka, Gerald Stourzh and Jan Paul Niederkorn (eds), *Was heisst Österreich? Inhalt und Umfang des Österreichbegriffs vom 10. Jahrhundert bis heute* (Vienna 1995), p. 308; idem, *Um Einheit und Freiheit. Staatsvertrag. Neutralität und das Ende der Ost-West-Besetzung Österreichs 1945–1955* (Vienna, Cologne and Graz 1998), p. 26.
73 Manfried Rauchensteiner, *Die Zwei. Die Grosse Koalition in Österreich 1945–1966* (Vienna 1987), p. 67.

10

Collaborating with Horthy: Political Catholicism and Christian Political Organizations in Hungary

Csaba Fazekas

Hungarian historians usually place the birth of political Catholicism during the last decade of the nineteenth century.[1] The first independent Catholic organization within the Hungarian political party system, the People's Party (Néppárt), which was closely tied to the activities of Nándor Zichy, was founded in 1895. The party came into being as a result of the new laws of 1894–95, which had been inspired by the spirit of liberalism. The legislation reorganized Church–State relations in Hungary and instigated an extraordinarily spirited resistance on the part of Catholic prelates. The first of these new laws made civil marriage mandatory, while the second required the registration of births by the state. These were followed by laws that granted legal equality to the Jewish faith and guaranteed the free practice of religion.[2] Similar conflicts with the Catholic Church had already accompanied urbanization and the growth of a middle-class culture during the so-called reform era, immediately before 1848. At that time, political Catholicism first developed in Hungary under the leadership of Canon Mihály Fogarassy, who was its first representative. He aimed at defending the Catholic Church in the public sphere by organizing politically and establishing a mass movement for winning over laymen.[3]

Although the revolution of 1848 was accompanied by the elimination of some elements of the Catholic Church as a State Church and the loss of some of its feudal privileges, the comprehensive rearrangement of Church–State relations did not come about during the period of absolute rule that followed the failure of the revolution. Thus, modifications essential from the perspective of the development of a civic society were considerably delayed. Both the achievements of 1848, and the interests of the Habsburg dynasty, were taken into account in the Compromise of 1867 between Hungary and Austria. The character of the Compromise impressed itself on the entire era from 1867 to the First World War. With the exception of a brief period, the Liberal Party of Free Thinkers, or Szabadelvü Párt, ruled Hungary from

1867 to 1918. Central to its programme was the maintenance of domestic order and the establishment of the legal framework for a civic society. Naturally, these priorities also made their influence felt in Church–State relations. Political Catholicism developed as a defensive reflex,[4] partly in response to the challenges posed by a developing civic society and partly in response to the need for maintaining a social role for the Church. During the 1890s the People's Party, led by Zichy, attempted to limit the ecclesiastical laws and to retain the position of the Catholic Church in the social and political spheres.

During the age of dualism, the main issue in party politics in Hungary revolved around the acceptance or rejection of the Compromise of 1867. The People's Party, however, was organized in order to serve different ecclesiastical and ideological interests. From 1906 to 1910 it served briefly as part of a governing coalition and adopted the name Parliamentary People's Party, or Országgyülési Néppárt. During this time it lost its connection to the currents of early-twentieth-century Catholic renewal. The Catholic Church, incapable of adjusting to the many aspects of legal reform, assumed a stance of hostile opposition to the liberal State, and its role in public life was not by accident labelled 'militant Catholicism'. These developments help to explain why the effects of the Catholic renewal, which began in the wake of the 1891 encyclical, *Rerum novarum*, remained limited in Hungary. The number of clergy who were willing to defend the interests of Catholicism with a mixture of democratic and social teachings remained small, and their long-term significance only showed considerably later.

One of these clergy, a prelate from Győr named Sándor Giesswein, who had participated in a meeting on Christianity and society in Vienna in 1899, four years later founded and led the first organization in Hungary dedicated to the problems of social Christianity. This organization was viewed with distrust, however, by the majority of the ecclesiastical elite. It was all too typical of Catholicism in Hungary at the beginning of the twentieth century that the social or reform Catholicism of the Bishop of Székesfehérvár, Ottokár Prohászka, was received with similar scepticism by the ecclesiastical hierarchy, whose leaders were composed primarily of the landowning sons of nobles and aristocrats. At one point Prohászka was even placed on the Church Index of unacceptable authors. His influential work of 1907 was revealingly entitled *Modern Catholicism*. Giesswein believed that under the influence of the 'spirit of the age', the People's Party would eventually lose its 'militant' stance and become infused with democratic reforms – above all, the right to vote – that were being demanded by social Catholicism. Consequently, he initially opposed the formation of a Christian Social Party, which was organized by his own followers in 1907. Three years later a disappointed Giesswein left the People's Party and became the most influential leader of the

National Christian Socialist Party, or Országos Kereszténiyszocialista Párt.[5]

In a speech in 1910 Giesswein outlined his programme, which was was a significant initial interpretation of modern Christian democracy. He understood Christian democracy not in terms of 'militant' conservative Catholicism, but in the spirit of a social policy desirous of developing a civic society. His toleration of the non-Hungarian nationalities and his pacifism during the First World War, which was exceptional in Hungary, sprang from his deeply religious sensibilities and his democratic convictions. All this aroused the indignation of the representatives of 'militant' Catholicism and of a significant portion of the prelates. Nevertheless, the Archbishop of Esztergom and Primate of Hungary, János Csernoch, often supported Giesswein.[6] At the same time, it is also true that until 1918 the main field of the Christian Socialists' not very effective activities remained the various social organizations and not party politics. They were able to play a greater role only after their unification with the People's Party as the Christian Social People's Party, the Keresztényszociális Néppárt, in 1918, but were unable to take full advantage of this development. On 31 October 1918, the democratic revolution led by Mihály Károlyi engulfed Budapest. It placed great value on democratic reforms and enjoyed the popular support of the masses, who had become disillusioned by the war. These supporters included many clerics. Giesswein and Prohászka, as well as the Christian Socialists, hailed the collapse of the 'old regime' and believed that the Hungary of the great estate owners would at last be replaced by a social order based on the social teaching of the Church. At the end of 1918 and the beginning of 1919 the prelates also acknowledged the changes, and at this time the most serious preparations were under way for the establishment of an autonomous national Catholic Church.

Giesswein and Prohászka accepted not only the democratic revolution with cautious patience, but also hoped for acceptable solutions from the Hungarian Soviet Republic, which came to power through a *coup d'état* on 21 March 1919. But in its ecclesiastical policies the Communist government of Béla Kun did not distinguish between aristocratic prelates and the Christian socialist parish priests. Indeed, it made no difference between the various religious groups and ecclesiastical organizations either. Through the hastily established Office for the Liquidation of Religious Affairs, the Vallásügyi Likvidáló Hivatal, the Kun government attempted either to entirely expropriate the churches, or to eliminate them, or to at least make their situation untenable. The complete aping of Russian Soviet policy degenerated into a hostile anticlericalism. By the fall of the dictatorship on 1 August 1919, the Kun government's ecclesiastical policy had managed to arouse the disgust of even the non-religious segments of the population.[7]

THE IDEOLOGY OF 'CHRISTIAN NATIONALISM'

Before analysing the development of Catholic parties in inter-war Hungary, it seems necessary to briefly review the ideology of the age, or what has been called 'Christian nationalism'. Not only in the realm of Church–State relations, but also in the political system and public life, this ideology became completely fused with the developments in Hungary during the period between the two wars. The ideology of Christian nationalism was nothing less than the complete identification of the interests of the Hungarian state, or rather its leading institutions and organizations, and those of the historical churches. The main causes for the birth of Christian nationalism can be found in the general conditions existing in Hungary between 1918 and 1920. Over and beyond the problems arising from the lost war, the revolutions, the communist dictatorship, the loss of two-thirds of Hungary's territory resulting from the Treaty of Trianon of 1919–20, the political isolation arising from the later Little Entente between Rumania, Czechoslovakia and Yugoslavia, many thought that the nation needed not only to re-establish its economic system and political structure but also to restore a Hungarian national spirit. According to this concept, 'foreign ideologies' had disturbed the Hungarian people's spiritual world and were directly responsible for its tragedy. Consequently, traditional religion had to be aggressively supported in all areas of public life. The ideologists of the government that came to power after 1919 claimed that turn-of-the-century liberalism had prepared the way for the democratic revolution and the communism that followed. Therefore they rejected not only the democratic revolution and communism, but the entire liberal age. They established a single front against everything from moderate liberalism to communism, and juxtaposed against it Christian nationalism.

As a result, the regime that came to power after 1919 sought from the very beginning to establish close working relationships with the historical churches, above all with the Roman Catholic Church. Interestingly, Miklós Horthy, who was a member of the Reformed Church and often promoted Protestants into high government positions, encouraged this policy more than anyone else. Shared interests motivated the accommodation. For its part, the Catholic Church hoped to restore its authority, which had been shaken by the earlier reform of Church–State relations during the liberal era. Horthy and his allies, for their part, needed the moral authority as well as the social organization and activities of the Church.

Indeed, the symbiosis was so extensive that the Catholic Church, through its role in public life and its economic position, came essentially to be identified with the political authorities. Gyula Szekfü, a leading historian and intellectual in Hungary between the two wars, appropriately referred to the Catholic Church as 'neo-baroque [and] triumphalist'. In a letter of 18 August 1919 – at the very beginning of the Horthy era – addressed to the ecclesiastical leadership, the new Minister of Culture and Education, Károly Huszár, made clear the state's need for an active role of the churches in public life.[8] On the ecclesiastical side, Csernoch described State–Church relations in the renewal of Hungary as similar to the relationship between body and soul. Many clerics, both Catholic and Protestant, subscribed to this view. Kunó Klebelsberg, the politician who was most intimately involved in cultural affairs during the 1920s, declared at a Catholic conference that for the nation's economic and political problems, 'the most effective treatment is Catholicism. The resources of the state are not sufficient for the reconstruction of the soul. Therefore, I am opposed to the idea of the separation of Church and State.'[9] The state assigned a number of public functions to leading clerics. For example, the government regularly submitted its important social and educational proposals to the bishops and sought their approval. The Catholic Church retained its huge estates. Furthermore, it received large subsidies from the treasury and enjoyed a virtual dominance in education.[10] In 1938 the World Eucharistic Congress was held in Budapest. The conference became a showpiece for Catholicism, and an expression of the intertwining of the Church and the State.[11]

Christian nationalism thoroughly penetrated Hungarian society in the inter-war period. Despite Hungary's significant territorial losses at the end of the First World War, the relative proportion of the population belonging to each denomination remained unchanged. Approximately two-thirds of the population were Roman Catholic, which thus remained the dominant faith in the country. Nevertheless, the influence of the traditional Protestant churches, which organized some 27 per cent of the population, remained significant. Among the Lutherans, and especially among the Reformed Church, considerable debate ensued on the proper relationship of their churches to the state. Should they preserve their traditional Protestant autonomy, or should they develop close working relationships with, and increasing dependence on, the state? In the end the latter view prevailed, and the Protestants, by narrowing their differences with the Catholics to the sphere of theology, joined the Christian nationalist system. Nevertheless, they could not alter its fundamentally Catholic character. But it should be noted that they did not have any desire to enter into the party politics of the age. They acknowledged Christian politicking as an exclusively Catholic domain. As a result, the Protestants generally voted for the governing, and not for a Christian party.

The Horthy system provided opportunities for social and political activism, but firmly rejected any democratic reforms. Anyone who called any core elements of the existing system into question, or rejected any of the teachings of Catholicism, ended up in the group of 'enemies of the nation'.

Communists, social democrats, principled Jews, or neo-Protestant members of movements outside the historical churches were all considered part of this unsavoury category.[12] Christian nationalism not only rejected all leftist social movements, both that of the illegal communists and that of the tolerated Social Democrats, but also embraced a doctrinaire opposition to the West, especially the United States. In general, Christian nationalism favoured agrarian over urban interests and was coloured by an anti-Semitism that derived primarily from its religious and moral views. Its tendency to exclude was manifested by the common use of the adjective 'Christian'. This ideology did not seek so much to determine who was a Christian, as to determine who was not.

The most important foreign policy goal of the Horthy system was the revision of the territorial arrangements of the peace treaties, in other words the restoration of Hungary as it had existed before the First World War. The Horthy system simultaneously blamed both the Western victors and the neighbouring states for these changes. Nationalism was all-pervasive, and the Horthy system often emphasized not the equality of the various European nations but the special role and 'mission' of Hungary. It considered internationalism as a kind of leftist phenomenon, which must be firmly resisted. In matters relating to Christianity, not its universalism but the uniqueness of Hungarian Catholicism played the central part.[13]

POLITICAL CATHOLICISM DURING THE FORMATION OF THE HORTHY SYSTEM[14]

Within the Horthy system, the directions and possibilities for action by political Catholicism were determined largely by the multilevelled intertwining of the Church and the State. Characteristically, during the entire era the promotion of Church interests in political life was understood to be an immediate task not for various Christian groups, but for the ecclesiastical elite. Furthermore, the powerful and centralized state considered the clergy, and not any interested larger social or political groups, as its partner in formulating and executing religious policy. Almost overnight after 1919, Christian nationalism became the organizing principle in public life. Whatever lay outside of it could at best define itself as something beyond the confines of the established order. Political alternatives could only be adumbrated within the camp of those who accepted the ruling Christian nationalist ideology. This led to two important consequences. First, in Christian politicking the room to manoeuvre became quite limited; and second, political Catholicism was not represented by one large and powerful party. Indeed, quite the opposite happened. During the inter-war years a remarkably rapid polarization led to a political Catholicism divided into numerous parties, organizations and alternatives, that were separated by shifting boundaries. Its supporters sometimes united and sometimes split into opposing factions. The actions of individual personalities were often central to the political conflicts, rather than well-developed political parties.

Before the First World War, political Catholicism had constituted an alternative formulated by those opposed to the civil state, while under the Horthy system political Catholicism became part of a political order that considered itself Christian. From the first moment the basic question was: could an independent Christian power, with its own identity and profile, emerge in the given political situation? Horthy and his associates from the very beginning emphasized that the limits of Christian politicking would be determined, by the state and the ecclesiastical elite allied with it. For Catholic political movements, only two alternatives remained. On the one hand they could embrace political opposition, which had always been a particularly difficult task for them. On the other, they could accept the harsh reality of joining the party that happened to be in power. The representatives of political Catholicism strove during the entire era to escape the status of supporting the government without being formally a part of it, by developing Christian democratic or Christian socialist alternatives.

The two faces of Christian politicking could be discerned in the organization of public life, even during the Rumanian occupation immediately after the collapse of the Hungarian Soviet Republic. On 8 August 1919 Pál Teleki and István Friedrich founded the Christian National Party, the Keresztény Nemzeti Párt, which declared: 'We can only save our homeland of one thousand years from its final destruction if every Hungarian Christian joins together into one political party.' The need for a unified and universal party proved to be a fiction even at that moment. Nevertheless, this party above all emphasized that 'the Christian world view and the national goals' must prevail at all costs. A few days later, on 14 August, Sándor Giesswein and the journalist István Haller reformulated the programme of the Christian Social Party, with the similar goal of rescuing the country from the destruction wrought by the war and the revolutions. But in the spirit of *Rerum novarum*, their effort concentrated primarily on the humane handling of social problems.[15] The Christian Socialists soon fused with the party led by Károly Huszár and the prelate Sándor Ernszt, and established the short-lived Christian Social and Economic Party, or Keresztény Szociális és Gazdasági Párt. During the autumn of 1919, as the coalition partner of István Friedrich's government, it played an important role in the formation of the new political system. Earlier Hungarian Christian socialism had concentrated on working through the organized labour movement. Now it had the opportunity to shape the political face of the country. In Hungary the definition of Christian socialism derived from Ottokár Prohászka, who, similarly to the

Austrian-German Christian social tradition, sought to define the movement not as a Christian version of socialism but as a social version of Christianity.[16] Giesswein acted in the same spirit. At that time, however, others embraced the term 'Christian' to advance different political agendas, such as one Budapest-centred party that considered itself to be a radical Christian socialist group, and attempted to organize and motivate the suburban proletariat by appeals to anti-Semitism.

A power vacuum allowed Giesswein's Christian Socialists briefly to become part of the government. The previous governing parties fragmented, as the Social Democrat or liberal forces found themselves completely on the defensive. Under the shadow of the Rumanian occupation and the difficult circumstances, Friedrich's Christian government vegetated without being able to implement its social programme. This was so because the only significant political force, Miklós Horthy, who was recognized by the entente powers, and his army, were not yet in Budapest. They would enter the capital only in the middle of November. In order to bring about a Christian policy of the right, the Christian Nationalist Party of Friedrich and Teleki joined together with the Christian National Unity Party, or Keresztény Nemzeti Egyesülés Pártja (KNEP), in October 1919. This fusion brought with it the subordination of the latter to the former. For this reason Giesswein did not join the newly formed party alliance, and together with others continued to work on the organization of Christian socialist groups. In the interest of Christian political unity the fusion was supported by the bishops; and only under these circumstances did the representative of the entente, George Clerk, consider the government an acceptable negotiating partner.

The parliamentary elections of 1920 were intensely fought and often corrupted by tactics of violent intimidation, but in the end the National Smallholders and Agricultural Party, the Országos Kisgazda- és Földmívespárt, organized by a smallholder, István Nagyatádi Szabó, captured the most seats. The Smallholders barely edged out the Christian National Unity Party and the other parties, including the independent Christian Socialists who were not able to play a significant role. The corrupt electoral tactics, the use of the police against the opposition and the open employment of tactics of intimidation remained typical of Hungarian elections during the entire period. Szabó's party also defined itself in accordance with Christian ethics. Instead of depending on the large estates, however, the Smallholders relied primarily on the support of the small farmer and won the election by promising land reform. Another Christian political organization, the Christian Smallholders and Agricultural Party, or Keresztény Kisgazda- és Földmívespárt, led by Gyula Andrássy, was opposed to such large-scale land reform.

With the signing of the peace treaty in 1920 the country regained its independence. It became obvious that in a truncated Hungary a new power structure would emerge, and in close connection with it a new political structure, which would modify the possibilities of Christian politicking. The political structure included a unicameral legislature with limited legal authority, and a central apparatus with considerable legal powers. It was a monarchy 'without a king', where the person of the Regent occupied the very centre of power. Horthy not only determined who would be the Prime Minister and removed him from office, but he also firmly retained the entire institutional structure of the political system in his own hands.

After a period of rapidly changing prime ministers between 1919 and 1921, István Bethlen was entrusted with the task of forming a government. His name would become associated with the consolidation of the Horthy system and the stabilization of the new Hungarian economy, as well as the foreign and domestic policies of the 1920s. Bethlen did not particularly approve of independent Christian politicking. He was convinced that the internal stabilization of the country demanded a dominant governing party that enjoyed overwhelming majorities in parliament, and he did everything he could in order to bring such a party into existence. This is how the system worked from 1922 until the end of the Horthy era, and Christian politicking thus remained confined within very narrow boundaries. In the interest of consolidation Bethlen relied on the Smallholders Party and not on the Christian KNEP, which embodied several different political strands and had entered an internal crisis by the end of 1921. The KNEP then collapsed, and its disappointed leaders such as Prohászka turned away from politics, convinced that their Christian social programme could not be realized. Bethlen believed that Christian nationalist ideology would best be directed by the bishops as a direct part of their role in public life. In order to alleviate social conflicts he came to an agreement with the Social Democratic Party. In this way he deprived the Christian Socialists of the possibility to organize successfully among the workers. Bethlen decided that he would entrust Christian nationalist politicking not to an independent Christian Party, but to a governing party that was thoroughly subservient to the state and obedient to the government. Bethlen's policy was to some extent motivated by the decision of most Christian Party politicians – with the exception of the Christian Socialists – to support the restoration of Charles IV, a policy that the entente powers strictly opposed, thus undermining Bethlen's strategy of reconciliation. Nevertheless, the elections of 1922 brought success for Bethlen's tactics. The so-called Unity Party, or Egységes Párt, organized around the Smallholders Party, won approximately 60 per cent of the seats in parliament. The independent Christian political representatives barely won any mandates at all. Thus, beginning in 1923, political Catholicism was forced to look for different solutions.

FROM THE YEARS OF CONSOLIDATION TO THE GREAT DEPRESSION[17]

During 1923–24 political Catholicism attempted to concentrate its strength in two large political parties. Under the leadership of Haller, the National Christian Socialist Party, the Országos Kereszténycszocialista Párt, was formed in February 1923. The party enjoyed the support of the lower clergy. Haller and Miklós Griger, a parish priest who played a decisive role in the leadership of the party, above all objected to the absence of democratic reforms. The party was founded in opposition to Bethlen's government, because universal suffrage and social reforms had not been achieved. Eight deputies joined it. Yet after 1923 Bethlen's policy of consolidation to improve the economy helped to alleviate social conflicts. Under the leadership of the Archbishop of Esztergom, János Csernoch, the clergy now determinedly distanced itself from the possibility of an oppositional Christian politicking and supported the government's policy unambiguously. Haller abandoned his opposition in 1925 and fused his Christian Socialist Party with the Christian Party that supported the government. From then onwards Christian socialism became a marginal – albeit discernible – phenomenon in Hungarian political life until 1944. Its followers tried several times to establish new political parties, but without success. Within the unified Christian Party the social conscience and democratic programme of the Christian Socialists disappeared. At the same time anti-Semitism and conservative opposition to capitalism and liberalism gained ground. Primarily due to their links with the Workers' Movement, the Christian Socialists enjoyed some success in organizing labour unions, however.

The other main current of political Catholicism supported Bethlen's policy of consolidation. The members of this group called themselves Christian Democrats. It is important to keep in mind, however, that this did not constitute Christian democracy in the modern sense of the word. Rather, it served as non-governmental support for Bethlen's policy.[18] The Hungarian Christian Democrats clearly distanced themselves from liberal Catholicism and democracy. They relied on an extremely conservative aristocracy. János Láng, a parliamentary representative of the Christian Party, attempted to clarify the concept of Christian democracy in 1924. He rejected in their entirety the values of civic society and the nineteenth-century liberal state. He demanded 'the democratic right to vote, but only for those who are able to exercise it responsibly. I also demand basic freedoms, but only for those who can exercise them legally and justly.'[19]

In 1923 János Zichy, who shared Bethlen's basic ideas, began to play a prominent role in national politics. He represented Bethlen's policy in the garb of political Catholicism. In that year Zichy organized the fragments of the Christian Party into a new conservative political group, which consistently followed a policy of supporting the government. Aside from its marked Christian religiosity, the party's autonomy was indicated by two significant characteristics of its ideology: legitimacy and agrarianism. During this era it was more agreeable both for the Horthy system and the Catholic Church to have a Christian Party that supported and preserved legal, as well as historical, continuity and relied on the wealthy aristocracy, rather than a Christian socialist movement based on the democratic desires of the petit bourgeoisie and the workers. Zichy quickly obtained the backing of the bishops and established the Christian National Economic Party, the Keresztény Nemzeti Gazdasági Párt. The prelate, Sándor Ernszt, joined it, and so did Károly Wolff, another major figure in this movement. But the most important leader became the prelate József Vass, who until his death in 1930 served as the Minister for Welfare and was one of Bethlen's most important and reliable supporters.

In 1925 Haller's Christian Socialist Party combined with Zichy's party under the name Christian Economic and Social Party, or Keresztény Gazdasági és Szociális Párt (KGSZP), which remained the hub of Christian Party politics until 1937. When Vass joined the government, the new Christian party in effect became a part of the governing coalition, which severely limited its ability to manoeuvre and constantly forced its leaders to define their positions. The party supported without reservation not only Bethlen's government, but also the entire Horthy system. Its leaders were constantly called on to clarify their positions in regard to the party's autonomy. For many, it seemed that they had become a part of Bethlen's well-organized Unity Party. One might say that over time any emphasis of the one main difference between the Christian Party and the government party – the question of the monarchy – became purely a matter of tactics. The unenunciated policy was that Horthy and Bethlen had consigned the Christian Party to the status of a reserve. They hoped that in the case of the government failing, or having to confront a crisis in parliament, it would not be forced to share power with the liberals or with leftist forces. Nevertheless, the internal political stability of the Horthy system remained intact. During twenty-five years, only one government proposal failed to gain the necessary backing in parliament. For its part, the KGSZP adapted to its assigned role. The party seldom made its voice heard on specific proposals and remained content to echo the position of the government; when it chose to disagree with the government, the KGSZP did so mainly to maintain the appearance of autonomy. Through these lukewarm political displays the party lost most of its credibility by the 1930s. This was also reflected in its shrinking voter base. Zichy himself designated the position of his party within the existing political system: 'Our party took on a thankless task when it wedged itself between the government and the opposition because Hungarians love two things: either a share of power, or to mouth off to their hearts' content. We avoid both.'[20]

The party described itself as 'Christian democratic' because this profile was required by both the Horthy system and the Church. Csernoch, and after 1927 his successor Jusztinián Serédi, rapidly adopted the policy enunciated by Pius XI in his 1922 encyclical, *Ubi arcano Dei*. The Pope desired an end to a separate Christian political party and urged the integration of Catholics into different political organizations. Csernoch understood this to mean that the interests of the Church could be realized through different parties, above all through the representatives in parliament of the government party. Bishop Gyula Czapik expressed the guiding idea quite clearly at a Church conference in 1924: 'Under today's conditions the notion of a single Catholic political party would only do harm.'[21] Bethlen was grateful to the Church for its unquestioning support of the Horthy system. He provided the ecclesiastical leadership with considerable opportunity to influence policy, especially in educational and social matters; and in 1926, with the active participation of the ecclesiastical elite, Bethlen restored the upper house.

Due to the enthusiastic backing of the prelates and the network of parishes, the KGSZP enjoyed a nationwide organization. Only in Budapest did it fail to establish any significant local organization. This was due to the fact that the Christian politicians in the capital who supported Bethlen without reservation had their own political party. Under the leadership of Károly Wolff and András Csilléry, a dentist, the Christian Community Party, or Keresztény Községi Párt (KKP), constituted one of the most unusual political organizations not just in the history of political Catholicism, but in the whole Horthy era. It was unique largely because, as Wolff and his followers observed, after the First World War roughly one-fourth of Hungary's population came to be concentrated in Budapest, and the cosmopolitan capital that had suddenly swelled so enormously had entirely different political and social problems to those in the countryside. The KKP belonged to the KGSZP's right wing. In parliament, its representatives formed an alliance with the KGSZP, but in local Budapest politics they did not. Instead, in local matters the KKP pursued a considerably more radical Christian nationalist policy. Contrary to the KGSZP's ineffectiveness, the KKP could mobilize the capital's non-Jewish population. Between 1920 and 1939 the KKP proved to be an effective rival of the Social Democrats and the Liberals. With the help of the national government it steadily maintained control of Budapest's municipal government.

Among the unique characteristics of Wolff's party were the following. Of the various forms of political Catholicism, co-operation between Catholics and Protestants came about in Budapest alone. Furthermore, the KKP's ties to the bishops were far looser, while its connections with the parish clergy and ordinary laymen, as well as with the urban masses, were much stronger than those of the KGSZP. Largely due to the activities of the KKP, Budapest – where the largest number of workers were concentrated – was a citadel of Social Democracy like contemporary Vienna, but, unlike the Austrian capital, it also became 'Christian Budapest'. This development can best be explained by reference to the capital's unique social mix. Wolff and his allies had nothing to do with the wealthy aristocracy that formed the backbone of the KGSZP, and their social goals. They also opposed the city's significant number of liberal democrats and Social Democrats, as well as the petit bourgeois Jews and the Jewish intellectuals. While the prelates considered the wealthy Jews as potential allies, the Christian petit bourgeoisie leaned towards extreme anti-Semitism. Practically without any support from the prelates, the KKP significantly expanded the membership of the capital's parishes. Within the ranks of the KKP, the moderate anti-Semitism of the KGSZP was combined with racism, anti-capitalist demagogy and populism. Thus the KKP served as an incubator for the far right of the 1930s.

The moral standing of the KGSZP was further eroded by the fact that the bishops and the government assigned no significant tasks to the party, save to support the government and the Church. On the surface, the party represented a unified Christian political organization. It constantly strove to unify the various manifestations of political Catholicism. Naturally, the diversity inherent within Christian politicking led to a series of internal disputes and disagreements, which could not be masked by the unity displayed during elections. At least four important currents could be discerned within the party: the so-called 'counts', a legitimist, aristocratic, agrarian group, which included men such as János Zichy; the remnants of the pre-1918 People's Party, which included Huszár, Ernszt and Vass; the radical right, including Wolff, Csilléry and the KKP in general; and finally the Christian Socialists, such as Haller, Griger, János Tobler and József Szabó.

Largely due to its alliance with the Unity Party, the KGSZP proved to be quite successful during the parliamentary elections of 1926. Next to the governing party with its huge representation of 170, the KGSZP with 35 parliamentarians formed the second largest bloc. The internal make-up of the party, however, changed significantly, as the Christian Socialists largely dropped out. In large part the Christian Socialists lost their seats in parliament because their urban, especially Budapest, following abandoned them for the Social Democrats. Until the end of the 1920s, the KGSZP as a non-governmental party that nevertheless supported the government continued to function more or less well. It was the Great Depression and the resulting political change that forced Christian politicking into a renewed transformation.

THE TRANSFORMATION OF POLITICAL CATHOLICISM[22]

In the elections of 1931 the KGSZP appeared to have maintained the same level of parliamentary representation it had enjoyed since 1926. But soon after the new parliament met, the tensions that had earlier been kept on the back burner erupted into open conflict. After the death of Vass, Ernszt became the Minister for Welfare, and in 1931 after the fall of Bethlen he became Minister of Religion and Education. Thus, Ernszt became the decisive personality in the Christian Party. He recognized that the social consequences of the Great Depression strengthened the social movement and the extreme right. The social tensions had already polarized the Christian Party in 1929, when the industrialist Friedrich broke with the programme of consolidation and formed a new party, the Christian Opposition, or Keresztény Ellenzék. In 1931 József Szabó founded a short-lived organization, which was based on elements of the KGSZP, the Christian Socialist Party, or Kereszténysocialista Párt; and in 1932 Griger created the Legitimist People's Party, or Legitimista Néppárt.

The most important development, however, proved to be that in the autumn of 1931 Ernszt and the KGSZP were not willing to back the government of Gyula Károlyi, which had succeeded Bethlen and desired to ease the crisis by drastically reducing social expenditures. Ernszt left the government, and the coalition of the KGSZP and the governing party came to an end. After a short while, the KGSZP adopted a curious type of opposition that backed the government. The ineffectiveness of the Christian Party at the beginning of the 1930s resulted from several factors that had come to bear simultaneously. Ernszt was mistaken in believing, at the end of 1931, that his party could play a decisive role in the government that would come about after the crisis. Gyula Gömbös was entrusted with the task of forming a government in 1932, and his four years in office would be marked by a radical move to the right. Gömbös had no need for a Christian coalition partner. Indeed, he was captivated by the idea of establishing a one-party state. With the reorganized government party now known as the Party of National Unity, the Nemzeti Egység Pártja, Gömbös won a comfortable victory in 1935. At the same time the Christian Party lost over half of its seats in parliament. Its poor showing resulted in part from the fact that the reorganized Independent Smallholders Party, the Független Kisgazdapárt (FKGP), which inspired the peasantry with its social programme, robbed the Christian Party of a portion of its support. Increasingly ineffective, the Christian Party found itself caught between two unsavoury alternatives. On the one hand, it disliked Gömbös's dictatorial methods, which aped those of Italian fascism. On the other hand, it felt uncomfortable in the role of opposition, as it had a fundamental interest in the stability of the Horthy system. Only one possibility remained for the party's politicians: to represent the alternatives that still remained within the system. Potentially the best of these were the social reforms championed by the Christian Socialists, but only as long as they did not threaten the interests of the great landowners.

Thus, the elections of 1935 resulted in a serious defeat for the Christian Party. Only one solution offered a way out of the cul-de-sac: the unification of all its forces into one party. Only János Zichy and Ernszt were able to accomplish the new integration of Christian politicians. In 1937 they brought together KGSZP, the Christian Opposition, and the Legitimist People's Party and formed the Unified Christian Party, or Egyesült Keresztény Párt (EKP). For the first time they took up a position of opposition in parliament, and for a while this party solved the problem of bringing together the different Christian politicians into a unified political party. But since the EKP's leaders were the same as those of the formerly separate parties, the new unified party faced the same internal divisions as its predecessor. Indeed, with Csilléry as Vice-president, it was obvious that fascist elements were included in the organization. During the 1930s the most important issue in Hungarian domestic politics had become the relationship to fascism. Stemming largely from its Catholicism, the EKP condemned right-wing radicalism, but by the end of the 1930s, along with the entire Horthy system, it had drifted to the right. The EKP desired to continue the role of 'reserve' that it had inherited from the Bethlen era, but by that time there was neither need nor opportunity for that. Its support for the new government of Béla Imrédy, which proposed a Catholic social programme in 1938, proved to be the EKP's biggest mistake. Imrédy's government quickly became merely a continuation of Gömbös's previous rule. Under Imrédy, the Hungarian parliament also passed the first discriminatory laws against Jews. In the end the Christian Party fell, together with Imrédy's government.

The increasing ineffectiveness of the Christian Party led to numerous Catholic movements that did not enjoy the backing of the clergy. Among the most important of these was the movement in western Hungary led by the priests József Mindszenty (Pehm) and Zoltán Nyisztor, which desired to renew Catholic politicking on the basis of a conservative right-wing legitimist ideology.[23] In the elections of 1939, the Unified Christian Party received only four parliamentary seats. This development accurately reflected the situation of political Catholicism at the end of the 1930s. Most of the former backers of the EKP voted for the government party, which by this time had been reorganized by Pál Teleki, the Prime Minister, into the Hungarian Life Party, or Magyar Élet Pártja. Those former supporters of the EKP who opposed the rightist trend went over to the opposition parties, especially to the Smallholders; while the radicals joined the right-wing parties. Among the latter the members of the Christian Community Party, which had dissolved in 1939, formed a significant camp. Openly sympathizing with the Nazis, this group came to lead the radical right in Hungary and from its symbol acquired the designation Arrow-Cross Party, or Nyilas Keresztes Párt. The elections of 1939 brought the party considerable advances with 28 seats. But other fascist groups benefited as well. For example, the Christian Nationalist Socialist Front, or Keresztény Nemzeti Szocialista Front, which had broken off from the EKP, openly attempted to reconcile National Socialism and Christian politicking.[24] As the most undiluted followers of the Nazis, the Arrow-Cross Party would take power in Hungary after Horthy's departure in 1944.

In 1943, the EKP under Zichy's leadership transformed itself into the Christian People's Party, the Keresztény Néppárt, and declared that it wished to return to its original programme of 1895. This step spoke for itself. By the last years of the Second World War Christian politicking no longer had any meaningful content. The new direction became manifest at a conference held at Győr in 1943, which emphasized that Christian political activity ought to be characterized by democracy and neo-liberalism, and not by social activism. In 1944, under the leadership of József Pálffy and István Barankovics, the participants of the Győr gathering founded the Christian Democratic People's Party, or Keresztény Demokrata Néppárt. This organization openly espoused a form of Western-style Christian democracy that would operate within the bounds of a system clearly based on civic democracy.[25]

Political Catholicism as a whole contained three main currents. First, a conservative Catholicism that was primarily represented by such leaders of the Christian Party as Ernszt and Zichy. This strain kept its distance from fascism. Opposed to the conservative political philosophy were the Catholic followers of fascism. One of these, a young priest from Győr named József Közi-Horváth, argued that the growth of the far right ought to be harmonized with Catholicism. The Catholic Church in Hungary felt unable to move against the domestic fascists, because these right-wingers considered themselves good Christians and often attended mass in their fascist uniforms. In short, they did not proclaim a neo-pagan ideology as the National Socialists did in Germany. Third, there existed a form of democratic Catholicism, which found its chief elaboration in various social organizations and exercised almost no influence on party politics. In the 1930s, for example, many Catholics who were prominent in public life joined the Ottokár Prohászka Society.[26] Its followers were active primarily in literary societies and in the press. Later they became conduits for anti-fascist reform Catholicism. Due largely to the opposition of the prelates, this form of political Catholicism came to consider forming a political party only during the last days of the Horthy system. Their ideal was French neo-Catholicism, and its chief adherents included Gyula Szekfő, György Széchényi and Jenő Katona.

We should be aware that during the 1930s, Hungarian political Catholicism became less and less coloured by party politics, and the role of Catholic social organizations and movements became more pronounced. These were often directly inspired by *Quadragesimo anno*, the

1931 encyclical of Pope Pius XI. The Horthy era in Hungary brought with it a flowering of public Catholicism. Various groups of the faithful, youth organizations and women's associations arose quickly one after another. On the one hand, these bodies mobilized large masses of people; on the other, they also demonstrated the social influence of the Catholic Church. At first these were organized throughout the country by the National Catholic Alliance, and after 1934 by Actio Catholica. It is, however, important to note that during the 1930s these organizations did not remain purely social groups, but sought to fill the void created by the hopeless situation of the Christian Party. One of the immediate consequences of *Quadragesimo anno* was the appearance in Hungary of corporatism, which reflected the obvious inadequacies of the Christian Labour Union Movement. Actio Catholica organized the representatives of the various professional bodies. Despite the fact that these groups operated in accordance with the rules of an authoritarian order, they later sheltered autonomous movements that rejected fascism. Three Catholic social organizations of the second half of the 1930s deserve special attention: the National Alliance of Catholic Youth and Agricultural Organizations, the Katolikus Agrárifjúsági Legényegyletek Országos Szövetsége (KALOT), which appropriated the social teaching of the Church most thoroughly, the Professional Organization, Hivatásszervezet, and the Parish Workers' Division or Egyházközségi Munkásszakosztályok (EMSZO). The first two were led by Jesuits, the third group arose from the bottom up. Although many of the EMSZO's leaders opposed democracy and thus aided totalitarianism, a number of them later turned against fascism and were sent to concentration camps during the German occupation of Hungary.[27]

THE SOCIAL HISTORY OF POLITICAL CATHOLICISM

Having adumbrated the history of political Catholicism between the two wars, it is necessary to make a few general observations on the social basis of the movement. In somewhat simplified form, voting in Hungary reflected three separate patterns: Budapest, the other larger cities, and the villages. Generally the biggest difference between the cities and the villages was that in the urban areas the presence of the organized industrial workers and Jews increased opposition against the Horthy system. At the same time the urban intellectuals and officials generally supported it. The rural peasants strongly backed the government and the Christian parties. This support was reduced only during the 1930s, with the rise of the reorganized Smallholders and the rural organization of the Social Democrats.

Miskolc in north-eastern Hungary can serve as a typical example of a larger provincial town. Unlike Budapest, Miskolc lacked a liberal bourgeois opposition, and in practice the inhabitants of the town divided into two camps. The worker colonies of the large government-owned companies and industrial plants, and the Jewish petit bourgeoisie, turned Miskolc into a stronghold of Social Democracy. They fought constant battles with the supporters of the governing party, who included Christian 'intellectuals' such as teachers, officials and employees, as well as refugees from the northeastern territories lost under the terms of the Treaty of Trianon, the non-Jewish petit bourgeoisie, and the anti-Semitically inclined proletariat. The Christian Nationalist forces attracted attention through constant demonstrations and increased activism. The sharp political and social cleavages were revealed in 1925, when some desired to separate the professional organizations into 'national' and 'non-national', or Jewish sections.[28] In local politics the voters actually voted according to local concerns and not national parties' interests. Among the villagers, on the other hand, the governing party and the Christian Party held overwhelming sway. In Szabolcs county in the north-east, many did not vote because in a number of districts only the government party ran candidates. In the rural areas the limited suffrage was further curtailed by the practice of public voting and the forceful backing of the governing party by the police. The basic operation of the Horthy system made any thought of organizing an opposition based on the support of the peasantry entirely illusory.[29] Protestants actually voted for the government party and disliked the Christian parties. For Protestants in the 1930s, only the Independent Smallholders Party was a conservative alternative in opposition. In counties with a Protestant majority the FKGP received many votes, but was quite unsuccessful in Catholic territories.

Within the ideology of Christian nationalism, the Christian political parties usually revealed a clearly defined social composition. It is indicative that beginning in the second half of the 1920s most of the divisions within the party resulted from disagreements between the Christian Socialists and the Christian Democrats. The latter were organized around agrarian interests, which included not only wealthy aristocrats but also peasants. The Christian Socialists, on the other hand, were stronger in urban areas.

Due to a lack of appropriate sources, there are no detailed studies of the social structures of the different Christian parties. Based on a number of contemporary reports, it has been possible to analyse the information given by those who joined the Christian Nationalist Party, the first such party to be formed. The active party members – not the voters – were most often officials, teachers, members of the lower middle class and the so-called Christian 'intellectuals'. Most were between thirty and forty years of age and a relatively large number were women. The majority were Catholics, although the party's officially declared goal remained 'the unification of all Christians into one party'. The later Christian parties were openly organized for the defence of Catholicism, and thus were rejected by the Protestants. With the exception of the KKP and several Christian socialist groups, the membership of the later parties came from voters who supported the government. The anti-Semitism of the Christian parties excluded not only the petit-bourgeois Jews but also the wealthier Jewish citizens, who enjoyed certain social connections to various groups of aristocrats. In a typical example, when the Budapest lawyer Ferenc Rósa asked to be admitted into the Christian Nationalist Party, he was rejected as 'formerly Jewish'. The rejection came despite Rósa's fervent Catholicism; and only after a long debate would the party accept his baptism of twenty years earlier.[30]

The analysis of their social composition indicates that nearly every Christian party of the era began as an effort to integrate, and of necessity proclaimed a programme for the entire country and for the whole society. This was so even in the case of the KGSZP and the EKP, both of which unambiguously supported the government and represented the aristocracy, the ecclesiastical elite and the middle class. Only a few Christian groups attempted to devote themselves primarily to specific social classes. The Christian Socialists, for example, consciously relied on the workers and employees of the Christian Labour Unions. The Christian parties to the right of those that supported the government, such as Friedrich's Christian Opposition, declared themselves to be entirely middle-class parties, and the KKP in Budapest also strove to appeal to the middle class.

CONCLUSION

The diverse structures of these parties make useful generalizations rather difficult. It is, however, a fact that the Christian parties of the era made only half-hearted efforts at the establishment of a multiparty system. Only those who were dissatisfied with the official Christian parties engaged in such efforts. The official Christian parties could not create mass parties and political Catholicism did not become the stabilizing factor of the Horthy system. In this respect, nationalist political Catholicism was unsuccessful. This failure is striking, since in neighbouring Austria, where political developments followed a pattern similar to that of Hungary, political Catholicism enjoyed considerably more success. Two main factors can account for this difference. First, the absolute majority established and enjoyed by the governing party did not allow the independent Christian parties a great deal of room to manoeuvre; and second, the leadership of the Catholic Church not only co-operated with the government but became a part of it. The ecclesiastical leadership developed a unique division of labour with the political authorities. The maintenance of the political power of the Church demanded opposition to all changes, especially radical ones. As a result, the parties of political Catholicism participated in public life more as ideological organizations than as political parties. Thus, when a historian of modern Hungary looks for examples of Christian democracy in the past, he or she will not normally concentrate on the inter-war period. Instead, he or she will look to Prohászka and Giesswein before the First World War, or to the party of István Barankovics, which emerged only towards the end of the Second World War, in 1944.

NOTES

1 For the history of the Hungarian Roman Catholic Church, see Gabriel Adriányi, *Fünfzig Jahre ungarischer Kirchengeschichte 1895–1945* (Mainz 1974); Jenő Gergely, *Katolikus egyház, magyar társadalom 1890–1986. Prohászkától Lékaiig* (Budapest 1989); idem, *A katolikus egyház története Magyarországon, 1919–1945* (Budapest 1997). The most useful edition of documents is Margit Beke (ed.), *A magyar katolikus püspökkari tanácskozások története és jegyzőkönyvei 1919–1944 között*, 2 vols (Munich and Budapest 1992). For Hungarian political Catholicism in general, the best work to date is Jenő Gergely, *A politikai katolicizmus Magyarországon (1890–1950)* (Budapest 1977). For a general overview see also idem, 'Keresztény pártok, 1919–1944, hatalom és egyház között', *Társadalmi Szemle*, no. 8–9 (1991), pp. 132–41.
2 See for example Csaba Csapodi, *Gróf Zichy Nándor* (Budapest 1993); Moritz Csáky, *Der Kulturkampf in Ungarn. Die kirchenpolitische Gesetzgebung der Jahre 1894/95* (Graz, Vienna and Cologne 1967); Gábor Salacz, *A magyar kultúrharc története, 1890–1895* (Pécs 1938); Gábor Salacz, *Egyház és állam Magyarországon a dualizmus korában, 1867–1918* (Munich 1974); Dániel Szabó, 'A Néppárt megalakulása', *Történelmi Szemle*, no. 2 (1977), pp. 169–208; Miklós Szabó, 'Új vonások a századfordulói magyar konzervatív politikai gondolkodásban', *Századok*, no. 1 (1974), pp. 3–65.
3 Pongrácz Sörös, A kath. klérus törekvései az 1843/44. országgyűlés egyházi ügyeinek tárgyalása alatt, *Katholikus Szemle*, no. 10 (1901), pp. 865–90; Csaba Fazekas, 'The Dawn of Political Catholicism in Hungary, 1844–1848', *Hungarian Studies*, no. 1 (1998–99), pp. 13–26; idem, '"Az idő ránk is terhesedett". Adalék a politikai katolicizmus reformkori történetéhez', in László Veres and Gyula Viga (eds), *A Herman Ottó Múzeum Évkönyve, XXXV–XXXVI* (Miskolc 1997), pp. 255–72; idem, 'Katolikus egyháziak "platformja" a Konzervatív Pártban', in András Molnár (ed.), *Az Ellenzéki Nyilatkozat és a kortársak* (Zalaegerszeg 1998), pp. 73–112.
4 Jenő Gergely, 'Szabad egyház a szabad államban? A politikai katolicizmusról', *Népszabadság*, 14 August 1993, p. 19.
5 For Christian socialism during the first two decades of the twentieth century, see Jenő Gergely, *A kereszténysszocializmus Magyarországon 1903–1923* (Budapest 1977).
6 On Giesswein, see for example Jenő Gergely, 'Giesswein Sándor, a politikus', in *Demokrácia – kereszténység – humanizmus. Giesswein Sándor, a modern kereszténydemokrácia előfutára* (Budapest 1994), pp. 29–41; Zoltán Kovács, 'Giesswein Sándor és a kereszténysszocialista mozgalom', in ibid., pp. 42–7.
7 See for example Andrew C. Janos and William B. Slottman, *Revolution in Perspective. Essays on the Hungarian Soviet Republic of 1919* (Los Angeles, CA and London 1971); György Balanyi, 'Egyház és vallás', in Gusztáv Gratz (ed.),

A bolsevizmus története Magyarországon (Budapest 1921), pp. 585–618; Tibor Hajdú, *A Magyarországi Tanácsköztársaság* (Budapest 1969); Csaba Fazekas, '"Vallásügyi Likvidáló Hivatal" 1919–ben', in Ferenc Pölöskei and Gyula Stemler (eds), *Múltból a jövöbe. Tanulmányok* (Budapest 1997), pp. 63–101.
8 Föegyházmegyei Levéltár, Eger, Archivum Novum, Nos. 2637–2972 (1919).
9 *Nemzeti Újság*, 14 October 1924, p. 7.
10 For the close connections between the Catholic Church and the State in inter-war Hungary, see Péter László, 'Church–State Relations and Civil Society in Hungary: a Historical Perspective', *Hungarian Studies*, no. 10 (1994), pp. 1–31; Jenő Gergely, 'Adatok a magyarországi katolicizmus helyzetéröl a két világháború között', *Levéltári Szemle*, no. 3 (1996), pp. 615–38. For the ecclesiastical policy of the inter-war Hungarian state, see for example Andor Csizmadia, *A magyar állam és az egyházak jogi kapcsolatainak alakulása és gyakorlata a Horthy-korszakban* (Budapest 1966).
11 Jenő Gergely, *Eucharisztikus világkongresszus Budapesten – 1938* (Budapest 1988).
12 Csaba Fazekas, *Kisegyházak és szektakérdés a Horthy-korszakban* (Budapest 1996).
13 On Christian democracy in inter-war Europe, see generally Niels Arbøl, *A kereszténydemokrácia Európában* (Budapest 1994 [Italian 1990]).
14 See in particular Jenő Gergely, 'A politikai katolicizmus átrendezödése a bethleni konszolidáció elsö felében (1920–1926)', *Századok*, no. 5–6 (1990), pp. 670–707; Ferenc Glatz, 'Konszolidáció és keresztény politika. Megjegyzések Giesswein Sándor muködése kapcsán', in *Demokrácia – kereszténység*, pp. 73–89.
15 For the party programmes of the period, see Jenő Gergely, Ferenc Glatz and Ferenc Pölöskei (eds), *Magyarországi pártprogramok, 1919–1944* (Budapest 1991).
16 Compare the chapter by Helmut Wohnout.
17 For this period, see also Jenő Gergely, *A kereszténysocializmus Magyarországon, 1924–1944* (Budapest 1994).
18 For a comparison with the rather different traditions of the German Centre Party and the Italian People's Party, see the chapters by Jürgen Elvert and Tiziana di Maio in this book.
19 Gergely, 'A politikai katolicizmus', p. 682.
20 Ibid., p. 698.
21 Ibid., p. 687.
22 For this period, see in more detail Jenő Gergely, 'A keresztény párt és a katolikus egyház politikai útkeresése az 1930-as évek második felében', *Levéltári Szemle*, no. 2 (1990), pp. 47–63.
23 Jenő Gergely, 'Mindszenty (Pehm) József apátplébános és katolikus pártalapítási kísérletek az 1930-as években', *Múltunk*, no. 1 (1993), pp. 37–58.
24 Jenő Gergely, 'A magyarországi katolikus egyház és a fasizmus', *Századok*, no. 1 (1987), pp. 3–48.
25 Jenő Gergely, 'A Keresztény Demokrata Néppárt elötörténete, 1936–1944', *Mühely*, no. 1 (1984), pp. 3–22.
26 See also Sándor Sebestény, *A Bartha Miklós Társaság, 1925–1933* (Budapest 1981).
27 On the Christian social movements and corporations in the second half of the 1930s, such as, for example, EMSZO, KALOT, etc., see Zoltán Kovács K. and István Vida (eds), *Félbemaradt reformkor. Miért akadt el az ország keresztény humanista megújítása* (Rome 1990).

28 Katalin Bozsikné Mengyel, 'Miskolc polgárságának gazdasági és politikai viszonyai 1920–1930 között', in Ferenc Lendvai L. and Balázs Mezei (eds), *A Miskolci Egyetem Közleményei* (Miskolc 1994), pp. 17–32.
29 Gyözö Vinnai, 'Választások és önkormányzatok Szabolcsban 1919–1939 között', in Péter Hársfalvi (ed.), *Tanulmányok választásokról és önkormányzatokról Szabolcsban (1848–1948)* (Nyíregyháza 1994), pp. 61–98.
30 Magyar Országos Levéltár, R 316 (= Kornai János-hagyaték) 2, cs. 13. tétel. A Keresztény Nemzeti Párt iratai.

11

Catholic People's Parties in East Central Europe: The Bohemian Lands and Slovakia

Arnold Suppan

The First World War and its consequences not only radically changed the economic, social and spiritual life of the peoples in East Central Europe, but their political forms of organization as well. Prior to 1914 they were essentially determined by the Vienna Reichsrat, the Budapest parliament, the Berlin Reichstag and the Petersburg duma. The thesis propagated by Lenin advocating the independence of nations, and the principles advocated by US President Woodrow Wilson for the post-war period, came out of the breaking up of multinational great empires and the laying down of arms dictated by the Western entente. A whole new group of larger, so-called nation states came into being in East Central Europe, in which of course the new dominant nation mostly comprised less than 90 per cent of the entire population. Liberal democracy in the form of representative parliamentary government was introduced, modelled on those in France, Great Britain and the USA. A catalogue of individual freedoms and basic rights was codified and universal suffrage was accomplished, mostly with the inclusion of women. In 1919–20 elected constituent national assemblies created liberal parliamentary constitutions with various presidential and plebiscite elements. Even when the new electoral laws foresaw at least a right to vote by ticket, the role of parties was not constitutionally well regulated.[1]

The following parties put up candidates in the first elections after the First World War: first, the Catholic people's parties, which represented programmatically a synthesis between Catholic social thought and conservative tradition. They brought together and organized political Catholicism in Bohemia, Moravia, Slovakia and Slovenia. Support for political Catholicism in this part of East Central Europe came mainly from smallholders, the lower classes of civil servants and employees, and to a small degree from the conservative big landowners and the old property-owning bourgeoisie. The most important parties were Československá strana lidová, the Czechoslovak People's Party, for decades under the leadership of Jan Šrámek; Slovenská l'udova strana, the Slovak People's Party, under the likewise long-serving chairman Andrej Hlinka, after whom the party was named in the inter-war period; and the Slovene People's Party, Slovenska ljudska stranka, led for over two decades by its dominant chairman Anton Korošec, who, like the other two leaders, was a priest.[2]

Second, farmers' parties, which were specific to the party spectrum in East Central Europe, as they were closest to the societal structure, which was strongly permeated by the smallholders. In their programme they represented, on the one side, Catholic Conservative interests, and on the other, partly also social revolutionary demands, which were geared above all against the great landowners, especially the 'foreign nationals' in Poland, Czechoslovakia, Romania and Yugoslavia. The most successful of these parties in the 1920s were undoubtedly Wincenty Witos with his Peasants' Party, Polskie Stronnictwo Ludowe – Wyzwolenie; the Czech Antonín Švehla with his Republikánská strana československého venkova; István Nagytádi Szabó with the Országos Kisgazda- és Földmívespárt; and the Croatian Stjepan Radić with his Hrvatska pučka seljačka stranka. The three other Polish peasants' parties and the Slovak Slovenská strana národní a rolnická should also be taken into consideration.[3]

Third, national liberal parties in which the partly new and lay political class of higher civil servants, senior military officers, professors, teachers, diplomats, freelancers and journalists was concentrated, and which determined 'national' politics throughout many changes of government. Most important among these parties was the National Democratic Party in Poland and Czechoslovakia, as well as the Hungarian Magyar Elet Pártja under the authoritarian ruling Prime Minister, Gyula Gömbös.[4]

Fourth, social democratic parties that were supported primarily by the industrial workers were successful only in those countries where industry was correspondingly developed. This was the case in East Central Europe in the Bohemian regions, and that is why the Czech and German Social Democrats in Czechoslovakia were strongly represented. In the other regions, the Social Democrats were concentrated mainly in the big towns and cities and in industrial and mining areas.[5] Fifth, in most East Central European states the radical wings of the social democratic parties split off directly after the First World War and formed their own communist parties. These were, at the beginning, successful in Hungary and Yugoslavia, but after the outlawing of the parties they were subsequently able to retain ground only in Czechoslovakia.[6]

In the majority of the states in East Central Europe, after the elections of constituent assemblies there was a balance of power between middle-class and socialist parties resulting in the formation of Christian Democratic–Peasant–Social Democratic coalition governments, above all in Poland and Czechoslovakia. As early as after the second elections, however, with the exception of Czechoslovakia, the Christian Democrat and peasant parties and the national liberal parties increased their share of the vote and determined the formation of the government. This happened first in Hungary, then also in Poland and Yugoslavia. Thus the Slovene Korošec became the last Yugoslavian Prime Minister in July 1928 before the introduction of the dictatorship of the King.[7]

Liberal parliamentary democracy had already gained an increasingly bad reputation in the second half of the 1920s in most East Central European states. The parties reacted to the enormous number of problems, such as demobilization, conflicts about the drawing of borders, liberation payments, war debts, hyperinflation, supply and distribution crises and land reforms, with fundamentally conflicting ideas and programmes. They had to take into consideration, amid all this, their functionaries' ambitions not only in the public sector but also in the partly state-owned banks and insurance companies, chambers and health insurance companies, monopoly concerns and export businesses. Thus the Pětka in Czechoslovakia, a coalition of five parties – the Social Democrats, National Democrats, Agrarian Party, Christian Democrats and National Socialists – shared out the attractive state and semi-state positions among themselves. Not only the German, Hungarian, Ukrainian and Polish minorities went short here, but also the second national group in the state, the Slovaks. The minorities in Poland, Rumania, Hungary and Yugoslavia were in the same situation, as was the second recognized national group in Yugoslavia, the Croats. Highly educated Jews were given extra consideration in the sharing out of jobs in all the states; their assimilation into the nation state was, of course, expected of them.[8]

In Italy, despite the existence of an influential parliament with a young Catholic People's Party, Partito Popolare Italiano, a strong liberal centre and an active socialist left, it was left to the victorious state to give way to the *fasci di combattimento* – mostly militant action groups made up of uprooted soldiers from the Front – in rural areas and in the factories. The Italian example of the setting up of a fascist dictatorship was soon also seen in East Central Europe as a modifiable model for problem solving, especially when the effects of the agrarian price crisis were felt after 1927, and under pressure from mass unemployment with the world economic crisis after 1929. On 12 May 1926 Marshal Józef Piłsudski took over with the help of the army of a centre-right cabinet; on 6 January 1929 King Alexander I of Yugoslavia dissolved the Belgrade parliament and took over all executive power; on 21 September 1932 the Hungarian Vice-regent, Admiral Miklós Horthy, named his old friend Gyula Gömbös – an exponent of the nationalistic middle class – as Prime Minister of Hungary.[9]

These semi-dictatorial regimes strengthened the state executive at the cost of the parliamentary legislative and tried – not always successfully – to form state parties to secure the majority for themselves in often manipulated elections, taking the ideological *raison d'être* of their movements partly from nationalism, partly from corporatist and partly from Catholic social thought. Thus personal and political freedoms became greatly restricted; this was true not only with regard to socialist and communist parties, but also fascist and National Socialist groupings such as the Arrow-Cross Party in Hungary or the Ljotić group in Serbia. The public attitudes of many 'little dictators' were, of course, copied from Mussolini or Hitler, so that in the population at large the local differences, compared with fascism and National Socialism, became ever more blurred. Added to this was the general fear of bolshevism, without clearly recognizing how much the totalitarianism of National Socialism and bolshevism, with its leadership principle, monopoly of power, system of terror, and central governing of society and economy still differed from the authoritarian dictatorial regimes in East Central Europe.[10] How did the leading Catholic parties in Czechoslovakia act in this societal, ideological and political environment?

THE CZECH PEOPLE'S PARTY

The Czech People's Party (Československá strana lidová) came into being in January 1919, and was made up of Moravian and Bohemian groups. The starting point was the first 'Czech' Catholic assembly in Brno in 1894, at which Robert Neuschl, the main speaker, compared the social encyclical *Rerum novarum* with *Das Kapital* by Karl Marx. In September of that year 152 Bohemian and Moravian educational, journeyman and Christian societies founded the Křest'ansko-sociální strana pro Čechy a Moravu in Leitomischl, or Litomyšl. It saw its main programmatic task as being the 'solving of social issues on the basis of Catholicism'. Specialist societies were formed for putting Christian social reforms into action, and a common committee was established to co-ordinate the independent regional groupings. This function of the Christian Socials prompted other Catholic groupings in Moravia and Bohemia in 1896–97 to found Catholic national parties, which were supported above all by Czech farmers and tradesmen. The Catholic National Party and the Christian Socials were in 1906 already the strongest parliamentary parties in the Moravian regional diet, while they achieved only a single mandate in the 1908 Bohemian diet. But in the Reichsrat election in 1907 they won 17 mandates in the Bohemian regions combined.[11]

The Bohemian Society for Agrarian Youth (with 12,000 members), the Farmers (with 50,000 members), the Workers (with 20,000 members), 300 co-operative banks and Orel sports societies (with 2,600 members) were effective as societal organizations linked to and supporting the party. In Moravia, Silesia and Lower Austria the Katolický spolek českého rolnictva na Moravě, ve Slezsku a v Dolních Rakousích, the Catholic Association of Czech Farmers, had 21,000 members, the Agrarian Youth 23,140, the Christian-Social Workers 32,000, the 500 co-operative banks 60,000 and the Consumer and Housing co-operatives 13,925 members. This mobilization of the Moravian farmers and working class was a solid basis for the future.[12]

The lawyer Mořic Hruban from Olmütz (Olomouc), and the chaplain Jan Šrámek from Neutitschein (Nový Jičín), were the leading Christian Social political personalities. While the Moravian 'Clericals' were just behind the Social Democrats in the Reichsrat elections in 1907, gaining ten mandates, in 1911 they became clearly the strongest party with 128,000 votes (36.6 per cent of the Czech votes). They did lose three seats, however. What was remarkable in these elections was that Šrámek and Hruban's parties gained more than 90 per cent of their votes in the rural parts of east, south and west Moravia. The Catholic camp in Moravia distinguished itself from that in Bohemia in several aspects. The unanimity in Moravia was in contrast to Bohemia's inner strife. Apart from the traditionally more intensive religiosity in Moravia, what was of great importance was the antagonism between town and country, as the German element dominated in many Moravian towns. In Moravia, a confrontation between the Catholic and the non-Catholic parties developed. In Bohemia, however, the Social Democrats were on one side and the other parties on the other.[13]

During the First World War, Šrámek, Hruban and their party members represented the national political line of autonomy for the Bohemian regions within a federal Austria. Nevertheless, they took part in the Český svaz, the national council in Vienna in 1916, and later in the Národní výbor, an organization of Czech parliamentarians, in Prague. In September 1918 the leaders of both Moravian Catholic parties united their groups. Šrámek took over as leader and the elder Hruban had to be satisfied with the deputy leadership, although he was parliamentary party leader in the Reichsrat. Thus he was invited on 12 October 1918 with 30 deputies to Baden to see Emperor Charles I, from whom they demanded the immediate appointment of a Czech national government, Czech participation in the peace conference and the shifting of the Czech government into Bohemian territory. The Kaiser's manifesto tried to meet these demands in part, but was unable to hold back complete national political collapse in Prague on 28 October 1918.[14]

Parallel to the political currents that began the attempt to loosen and release the country from Vienna, especially during the First World War, but also in the period just prior to the war, was an anticlerical movement. In 1910, 96.5 per cent of Czechs described themselves as Roman Catholic, but in the industrial area around Pilsen (Plzeň), Kladno and Brüx-Dux (Most-Duchcov), as well as in the working-class suburbs of Prague, anticlerical socialistic agitation began to take effect and put down deep roots during the war. In the Czech part of Charles University the proportion of Catholics in the last semester during the war sank to under 90 per cent. The newspapers of the Free Thinkers and supporters of Thomas Garrigue Masaryk, who began to demand withdrawal from the Catholic Church directly after the end of the war, were partly responsible for this. Thus the new Czechoslovak People's Party, from the time of the beginning of the new state, experienced a strong anti-Catholic current. The otherwise mostly level-headed Masaryk, who had already left the Church long before 1914, returned now from emigration as new state President and declared, 'We have broken away from Vienna, we will also break away from Rome.' On 3 November 1918, the baroque pillar in the Old Town Square in Prague with the Virgin Mary on it was destroyed. In May 1919 the police even had to protect the statue of St Jan Nepomuk on the Charles Bridge.[15]

The strong anti-Catholic currents in Prague were, on the one hand, upheld by many politicians who had emigrated in the course of the First World War or had withdrawn into inner resistance against the Catholic Habsburg dominance, and on the other, they were upheld by many republican secondary school teachers and by a number of Catholic priests who lived in concubinage and contributed decisively to the founding of a 'Czech Church', often described as the 'Hus Church'. 'Legionaries' coming home from Italy, France, and the Soviet Union gave decisive support to the anti-Catholic mass movement. By 1921 1.5 million Czechs had already left the Roman Catholic Church. In the early years of the Czech Republic, 150,000 Catholics converted to Protestantism and the 'Hus Church' grew by 500,000 members. The 700,000 who remained had no confession at all, rising to 833,000 by 1930. The membership of the 'Czech Church' increased to 780,000. The proportion of Bohemian Czechs who were Catholic sank to 71 per cent within a decade, whereas it was still up at 89 per cent of the Moravian Czechs. Archbishop Count Huyn and Cardinal Skrbenský resigned, followed by the theology professor František Kordáč in Prague and the popular Cyril Stojan in Olomouc.[16] Thus the percentage of the Roman Catholic population in some Prague working-class areas sank by 40–50 per cent. In the Old Town, New Town and in the 'Lesser Town', it sank by only about 20 per cent, however. The number of Catholics in the Czech part of Charles University dropped dramatically: from 89.6 per cent in the winter semester of 1918–19 to 51.4 per cent in the same semester of 1921–22 and 46.7 per cent in 1925–26. Only in the second half of the 1920s was the proportion of Catholics able to stabilize at around 53 per cent.[17]

Although they were bound together in the revolutionary national assembly, the Social Democrats, National Socialists and National Democrats attacked the Catholic deputies strongly and repeatedly. They pushed through a series of laws, especially in 1919: the introduction of optional civil marriage; a loosening of divorce regulations; the allowing of exemption from classes in religion in the schools; the removal of crucifixes from schoolrooms; the forbidding of clergy from commenting on state and political life, the so-called pulpit paragraph; the exemption from setting up theological faculties at the new universities of Brno and Bratislava. Even more characteristic of the anti-Catholic stance was, of course, openly expressed hate. The Social Democratic deputy, Rudolf Bechyně, insulted his colleague Šrámek at the national assembly with: 'You will be thrown out, you black priest.' Bechyně, the free thinker, also slandered his comrades. A police report registered a speech he made in the Old Town Square on 15 May 1919: 'As the evening bells of the Týn Church began ringing . . . the crowd surged into the church . . . insulted the priest celebrating the mass . . . ; the police had to clear the church.'[18]

The overwhelming demand of the majority of members of parliament for radical reform of the property laws was felt by the Roman Catholic Church as a great threat, above all to the dioceses and the convents, monasteries and seminaries. In 1913, the archdiocese of Prague possessed 23,000 hectares, the metropolitan chapter St Vít 11,000 hectares, the premonstrate Tepl and Strahov between 9,000 and 10,000 hectares, and the Cisterian Hohenfurt (Vyšší Brod), the Kreuzherren Order, the Maltese Order and the Benedictine monastery of St Margaret each had between 5,000 and 6,000 hectares. The archbishopric in Olomouc held over 36,000 hectares, the German Order of the Knights over 10,000 hectares, the metropolitan chapter Olomouc between 8,000 and 10,000 hectares; in Austrian Silesia the bishopric Breslau (today Wrocław) had 33,800 hectares and the German Order of the Knights over 13,900 hectares. The reform of the property laws that was soon introduced expropriated 28 per cent of the entire property and redistributed it among 750,000 owners and leaseholders – predominantly Czech (and Slovak) smallholders. The powerful leader of the Agrarians, Antonín Švehla, had co-operated quite well with Šrámek on this issue. A coalition of these two party leaders hindered the complete split of Church and State in the constitutional commission.[19]

Not least because of the introduction of the vote for women, the Czech People's Party met with success in the first parliamentary elections in April 1920; with 7.5 per cent of all Czechoslovak votes they won 21 seats, and their coalition partner, the Slovak People's Party, won 12 seats with 3.8 per cent of the vote. In comparison, the Agrarians won 40 seats, the Social Democrats 74, the National Socialists 24 and the National Democrats 19. The German Social Democrats won 31 seats, the Farmers' Union 13 and the German National Party 12. As a member of the Czech five-party coalition (Pětka), Šrámek enhanced the position of his party (1925: 31 seats) and represented one of the main pillars of the political system in the 1930s in Czechoslovakia, although the People's Party fell back to 22 seats in the 1935 elections.[20]

The Czechoslovak People's Party's programme of 1919 contained enough social demands to make it attractive to the widest possible base in the population. The Catholic Church, in addition, gave its village priests organizational back-up. The sports society Orel was an especially active Catholic group and even proved to be competition for the extremely powerful Sokol organization. The *Čech* newspaper, led by the priest Horský and the main organ of political Catholicism, did not contribute much to Šrámek's modern course and continued to publish anti-republican and anti-Semitic articles. *Lidové listy* became the official organ of the party, which represented the moderate conservative-Christian-social majority of the People's Party. There were also weaknesses in the entire national structure of the party, as not only Slovakia and the Carpathian Ukrainians remained independent, but also the Bohemian and Moravian groups, which each retained their own leaders, secretaries-general and executive committees.[21]

Šrámek managed, however, to reconcile political Catholicism with the Czechoslovak republic. He achieved this, above all, by demonstrating that the Czech Catholics were just as loyal as the non-Catholic Czechs. There were problems, of course, with the widespread Hus cult, as the anniversary of the reformer's execution in 1415 was raised to the status of a national public holiday in 1925, an act that led to the papal nuncio leaving Prague. Šrámek was not afraid of presenting Hus as a revolutionary and a threat to the state in his day and of comparing him with the present-day communists. All of this was historically rather far from the truth. It was therefore not in the interest of the new republic to propagate Hussite revolutionary ideas, as they were trying at the same time to push through their authority over the German and Magyar minorities. Šrámek's Czech national leanings went so far that in 1925 he resisted the inclusion of the German Catholic activists in the coalition government, arguing that the Germans had their states in Germany, Austria and Switzerland, whereas the Czechs had only this one state in the whole world: 'The more intensively our Czech People's Party works with us to secure this state, all the more Christian it will be in appearance and therefore the State will be more national and Slavonic . . .'[22]

The German Christian Socials eventually joined the new coalition government in 1926, and Hlinka's People's Party did so once again in 1927. In February 1928 Šrámek took over as Prime Minister from Švehla, who was in bad health. Despite this leading position and the thousand-year jubilee of Saint Wenceslas in 1929, Šrámek did not increase the votes for his party. What is more, he increasingly got into conflicts with his Slovakian colleague, the priest Hlinka, and also with the leader of the Bohemian wing of the party, Stašek, who were both sympathetic to corporatist ideas. All the same the organization managed a first Catholic assembly that included all states and the participation of all nationalities, and in the presidential election in December 1935 all the Catholic parties in Czechoslovakia voted for the foreign minister, Edvard Beneš.[23]

Although the People's Party did not gain more seats than Hlinka's 'autonomic block' in the 1935 elections, namely 22, it played an important role in state politics until the end of the first Czechoslovak republic, although distancing itself increasingly from the Slovak, German and Magyar Catholics. The emphasis on Czech national ideology occurred at a time when the German Christian Socials increasingly embraced the nationalist Sudetendeutsche Partei and the Hlinka party moved towards Slovakian autonomy. If it had ever existed, the option of creating a multiethnic Catholic People's Party was certainly no longer possible after 1935. Thus the Communist Party remained the only multiethnic party.[24]

In the September crisis of 1938 it was Šrámek who stood most strongly with the National Democratic minister František Ježek against submitting to Hitler's demands. In their opinion the government had no right, according to the constitution, to give up any Czechoslovak territory; only the national assembly had this power. But President Beneš and the majority of the cabinet were under pressure from the British-French diplomatic note of 19 September demanding compliance, and reluctantly agreed to give up those territories mainly inhabited by German speakers. After the Munich Agreement the People's Party joined the National Front, and Šrámek went into exile after the German march into Prague. Beneš made him Prime Minister and he remained in exile until April 1945, when he returned to Prague. Šrámek's People's Party, integrated in the new Czech and Slovak National Front, stood in the elections of 26 May 1946 as the sole 'middle-class' party in the Bohemian regions. The Agrarians and National Democrats were no longer allowed to stand. While the Communists gained 40.17 per cent of the votes, the National Socialists 23.66 per cent and the Social Democrats 15.59 per cent, the People's Party achieved 20.23 per cent. Compared with the parliamentary elections of 1935, this meant a complete collapse of the political balance of power in the direction of socialism. This trend ended in the elections of May 1948 in the communist-dominated single-party system.

THE SLOVAK PEOPLE'S PARTY

On 19 December 1918 the priest Andrej Hlinka re-established the Slovak People's Party (Slovenská Ľudova Strana, SLS) in Žilina in the presence of over 300 people – among them the theologian Jozef Tiso. Hlinka had clearly opposed his metropolitan, the Archbishop of Esztergom, who was by birth the Slovak Ján Černoch, at the beginning of November 1918 and had spoken out very decisively for the Czecho-Slovak state. On 27–28 November Hlinka had called together around one hundred Slovak priest colleagues in Ružomberok and put together a first programme of action: the sending of 29 Slovak Catholic priests to the revolutionary national assembly in Prague; the creation of a Slovakian Church province with its seat in Nitra; the setting up of Catholic secondary schools; and the rejection of civil marriage.[25]

Hlinka was born in Černová in 1864, and went to the secondary school in Ružomberok and Leutschau (Levoča). He joined the newly founded Hungarian People's Party of Count Nándor Zichy as early as 1895, but changed his allegiance to the Slovak National Party in 1901. Although he had been ordained in 1889 and had been a priest and town councillor in Ružomberok, he was convicted of denigrating the Hungarian nation in December 1906, sent to prison for two years and made to pay a fine of 1,500 crowns. In March of the same year he founded the Slovak People's Party, as he no longer agreed with the nationalities programme of the Hungarian People's Party. In May 1906 he was suspended from the priesthood at the request of the Hungarian government. The Moravian Catholics intervened on his behalf, however, appealing directly to Pope Pius X at a mass demonstration in Velehrad. After a massacre of Hungarian gendarmes in Hlinka's home parish on the occasion of the inauguration of a church on 27 October 1907, 15 Slovakian demonstrators were shot. A petition followed from 30,000 Slovakian Catholics and he was finally reordained in April 1909. Despite nominal leadership of the party, Hlinka now devoted himself more to pastoral and social work.[26]

Prior to 1914, the Slovakian national movement faced insurmountable hurdles – in great contrast to the Czechs who had already built up a fully developed national society. Slovakian Upper Hungary was ruled socio-economically by the Hungarian aristocracy; the land was divided up into 19 counties, and administered by Hungarians or by Magyarized civil servants who were for the most part Hungarian gentry. Hungarian was the main language not only in the lower-secondary schools, but since 1907 in the primary schools. It was the teaching language in the teacher training institutions and in the seminaries. In the largest towns such as Pressburg, (Bratislava), and Kaschau (Košice), but also in a series of regional towns, the German, Magyar and Jewish middle class was dominant. The great majority of Slovakian smallholders, land workers and craftsmen respected this social, economic and political hierarchy. After the collapse of political power in November 1918, only 35 of 12,447 former Hungarian state civil servants remained in the service of the Czechoslovak republic, 18 of 948 county civil servants, 11 of 823 town civil servants, 33 of 1,133 regional civil servants, 10 of 660 secondary school teachers and one of 464 judges. Young Slovakian academics thus had the chance of rapid promotion; due to a lack of adequately qualified people, however, many Czechs took over the new posts, right the way through to the Carpathian Ukraine.[27]

It was only in the spring of 1918 that the new movement took its place in Slovakian political life. On 1 May 1918 the Slovakian National Party organized a meeting in Liptovský Svätý Mikuláš, and the main speaker, Vavro Šrobár, initiated a resolution demanding self-determination and a Czech–Slovak union. On 24 May at the meeting in Turčiansky Svätý Martin, the aim of creating an independent Czecho-Slovak state consisting of Bohemia, Moravia, Silesia and Slovakia was clearly defined. Hlinka, who also participated, stated: 'The thousand-year marriage with the Magyars has foundered. We must separate.' On 30 May 1918 Czech and Slovak organizations in the USA signed the Resolution of Pittsburgh: 'We approve of the political program which aims at the union of the Czechs and Slovaks in an independent state composed of the Czech Lands and Slovakia. Slovakia shall have her own administrative system, her own Diet and her own courts.' Shortly after 1918, however, many young Slovakian lawyers were given positions as high sheriffs and deputy sheriffs, as leading functionaries in regional administration and as judges and state solicitors; but there was no mention of Slovakia having its own administrative system until 6 October 1938.[28]

The coming into being of Czechoslovakia was the dominant issue: the recognition of the Czechoslovak national council as an independent government by the Western powers; the political collapse in Prague on 28 October 1918; and the declaration of the Slovakian national council, on 30 October 1918 in Turčiansky Svätý Martin, of the union of the Slovaks with the Czechs to form the Czechoslovak nation. The majority of those delegates present were Protestant, but Andrej Hlinka signed the call to the people of Slovakia. However, in November 1918 Hungarian troops occupied the town and arrested the president of the national council.[29] In the same month dividing lines began to emerge among the political elite in Slovakia. Šrobár, who had studied in Prague, took over the Slovakian 'government' and led it with other, mostly Lutheran 'Hlasists' – pronounced followers of Masaryk – along the lines of Prague centralism. Milan Hodža, a lawyer, who had studied at the universities of Budapest and Vienna and had represented his nation in the Hungarian parliament since 1905, had joined the so-called Belvedere Circle in 1908, and started setting up a Czechoslovak agrarian party. Hlinka renewed the Slovakian People's Party.[30]

Hlinka's People's Party programme demanded autonomy for Slovakia and spoke clearly against Prague centralism. In September 1919 Hlinka secretly tried to get support in Paris, but without success. Thus in February 1920 the party delegates voted for the central Czechoslovak constitution, although reserving their demand for autonomy until later. The election results of 1920 showed clearly, however, that the majority of Slovakian Catholics had not voted for the People's Party. After all, the Prague government parties concerned themselves with improving the standard of living in the entire Slovakian population: the citizens had all democratic freedoms; the state created 84 secondary schools, as well as Komenský University in Bratislava, a national theatre and a philharmonic orchestra. Reform of the property laws freed only 247,000 hectares for redistribution and many factories were still inferior compared to their new Czech competitors. On 1 January the Matica Slovenská, or Slovak Heritage Foundation, was established and at once began its wide-ranging educational work among the rural population.[31] The organization had first been set up in 1863 by the Catholic bishop, Štefan Moyses, and the Lutheran superintendent, Karol Kuzmány, as the central cultural institution to advance the Slovak language and culture in the Hungarian half (from 1867) of the Habsburg monarchy. In the inter-war period, however, as well as after its refounding in the 1990, it became more and more aggressively nationalistic.

The constitution had laid down 'Czecho-slovak' as the official state language and minority languages were recognized by authorities and law courts only in regions with at least a 20 per cent minority population. The Slovaks in 1921 made up only about 16 per cent, however, whereas the Germans in the state as a whole constituted over 23 per cent and the Hungarians 5.5 per cent. In figures, this meant that in Slovakia in 1921, 745,000 Hungarians, 461,000 Russians and Ukrainians and 150,000 Germans, as well as a larger number of Jews and Gypsies, lived alongside 1.9 million Slovaks. Slovaks thus made up a majority of only 60 per cent of the population. According to the 1930 census, 71.6 per cent of the Slovak population were Catholics, 16.5 per cent Lutherans, 6.4 per cent Unitarians (Ukrainians) and 4.1 per cent Jews.[32]

Already during the founding of the party Hlinka had unequivocally made it clear that his party would uphold Christian Catholic principles in all walks of public life, the economy and social welfare and would do its utmost for the culture of the Czechoslovak state. The SLS demanded, as an immediate measure, a change of course in Kramář's government's church and school policy. From 1920 it also called for a reversal of the 'Czechifying' of the Slovak administrative system, a demobilization of the Czech troops stationed in Slovakia and measures to improve the competitive position of the Slovakian economy. Hlinka decisively rejected the idea of a unified 'Czechoslovak' nation, a cornerstone of the Czechoslovak constitution, and demanded that Slovakia have its own independent administration with its own federal state parliament and law courts, as had been forshadowed in the Pittsburgh Resolution.[33]

The SLS's leadership committee was in the early years almost without exception composed of Catholic clerics, such as the priests František Jehlička, Ferdiš Juriga and Jozef Buday. Jozef Tiso, who between January 1927 and October 1929 took part in a Prague coalition government as Health Minister, came somewhat later. Among these clerics in the early years were, however, quite a few 'Magyarons' of Slovak origin who had been educated at Hungarian seminaries before 1918. Only after 1925, the year that the party's name was changed to Hlinkova Slovenská Ľudová Strana (HSĽS) did laymen enter the party presidium and the executive committee in the person of professor Vojtěch Tuka, who had been removed from his Bratislava chair of international law, and Karol Sidor. If Jehlička was Hlinka's most important adviser from 1918 on, then Tuka took over this role from 1921. Tuka was chief editor of the party paper *Slovák*, and as secretary general of the HSĽS (from 1926) was very influential. He created the Rodobrana organization from veterans and students, based on the fascist model. It was, however, banned by the Prague government in 1927 as a threat to the state. Tuka's propaganda machine against communism, socialism, freemasonry and Czech free thinking ensured him the sympathy of the clerics. Also his political-economic rather than race-based anti-Semitism found wide resonance. In October 1929 Tuka was convicted of treason. Yet many of his followers continued on his radical nationalistic course and demanded full independence for a Slovakian national state.[34]

After 1918, especially, party members with conservative leanings, who under Hungarian dominance had carried the process of the emergence of the Slovakian nation in their roles as teachers, notaries, small landowners and tradesmen, gathered round the Catholic clerics. This 'prelate wing' accepted the Czechoslovak state, but demanded greater consideration of the Slovaks in central and regional administration, an intensifying of economic development and the upholding of cultural autonomy. The party was supported in particular by two groups of voters: on the one side, the not so highly educated smallholders (under five hectares) of northern and central Slovakia, and on the other, the Catholic population of the small and medium-sized towns, to whom the HSĽS appealed through the Christian Union movement to a considerable number of workers and above all to many railway workers. Lastly, the HSĽS had access to sections of the young intelligentsia, such as the Bratislava university students who expected of the People's Party that they would get more and better administrative posts in the law courts and schools, in the railways and at the post office and even in the police and army. The smallholders and farmers with larger farms in the southern and western part of Slovakia voted for the Agrarian Party under the leadership of Milan Hodža, whereas the larger part of the growing group of industrial workers voted for the Social Democrats or Communists.[35]

Hlinka, who as the long-standing leader (1913–38) determined the aims of the party and the course of its parliamentary wing practically single-handed, expanded the party from a Catholic society of notables to a real People's Party with 36,501 members by 1935. His slogans, such as 'The Slovak language in Slovakia', 'Slovakia for the Slovaks', or 'The Pittsburgh

Agreement must become part of the constitution', helped him to become popular and gave him a feeling of personal power. In the parliamentary elections of 1920 the HSL'S gained only 21 per cent of the Slovak votes, but by the 1925 elections this had already risen to 32 per cent. After entry into government, and the Tuka trial, the party fell back to 28 per cent in 1929, rising again to 30 per cent by 1935 and reaching over 35 per cent of the votes in the local elections in May and June 1938. The HSL'S was from 1925 the strongest single Slovakian party, but stood in opposition to a majority of Czechoslovak parties – Agrarians, Social Democrats and Communists. We can therefore presume that with Hlinka's death in August 1938, a majority of ethnic Slovaks found the main points of the HSL'S programme – self-administration of Slovakia and the upholding of cultural and economic autonomy – justified and were in agreement with them.[36]

The collaboration between the Slovakian Party and the Czech People's Party worked above all in the early years and mostly in religious matters. With the introduction of the Hus commemoration day as a public holiday in 1925, some Czech Catholics defended Hus as a national personality, while the Slovakian Catholics rejected him as a heretic. Regarding the issue of the upholding of confessional schools in Slovakia, Šrámek supported his fellow priest Hlinka, although this problem hardly existed in the Bohemian Lands at the elementary school level because state elementary schools had dominated in Cisleithania. However, in this case the Slovak People's Party defended the old Hungarian legacy with a network of confessional schools: in the 1931–32 school year, alongside 1,511 public Slovakian schools in Slovakia there were still 1,117 Roman Catholic, 398 Lutheran, 162 Uniate, 23 Calvinist and 36 Jewish schools with Slovakian as the teaching language. With regard to the new ordering of the relationship between the Czechoslovakian state and the Roman Catholic Church, the Hlinka Party demanded a concordat, but was finally content with the *modus vivendi* of January 1928 between Prague and the Vatican: no Czechoslovakian diocese should in future go beyond the state borders and no part of the Czechoslovak republic should be under church authority coming from outside the country. This meant a separation of the Slovakian diocese from what, until that time, had been the jurisdictional areas of the Hungarian archbishoprics of Esztergom and Eger. What is more, the Pope had in future the power to appoint the archbishops, bishops and other important positions, so that the Czechoslovakian government had only a political veto.[37]

A trusting political collaboration between Hlinka and his leadership group on the one side and Masaryk, Beneš and other representatives of Prague 'Castle' on the other had never really existed between 1918 and 1938. Hlinka saw in Masaryk the embodiment of anti-religious and liberal-socialist tendencies. Masaryk saw in Hlinka a symbol of clericalism and provinciality. The HSL'S even denied President Masaryk its vote in the re-election of 1927 and 1934, but yielded to Vatican influences in voting for Beneš in December 1935. The background to the tensions between the 'Castle' group and the Hlinka party was, of course, also the non-recognition of Slovakia as an independent state and Prague's unbudging support for the idea of a Czechoslovak nation. This is why the political influence of the Hlinka party in Prague was limited; it did not even permeate the cultural work of the Matica Slovenská, nor the celebration in honour of the 'Slovakian' Prince Pribina, a figure from the early Middle Ages, in Nitra in August 1933. Quite the opposite was the case, so that not even leading Slovakian members of the Prague government like Milan Hodža and Ivan Dérer gave enough attention to the exceptional position of their homeland.[38]

During the world economic crisis the level of unemployment in the Bohemian Lands was higher than in Slovakia (in February 1933 in Bohemia it was 31.0 per cent, in Moravia 33.3 per cent and in Slovakia 21.7 per cent), as there was much more temporary employment available in the latter. This is why Hlinka's autonomists argued against Prague's employment policies. They had far less to be concerned about than the ethnic Germans, who were hit far more seriously by unemployment (up to 40 per cent). The election successes of the Sudetendeutsche Partei in 1935 and 1938, as well as the progressively more and more aggressive eastern European policies of Hitler, strengthened the radical Tuka wing within the HSĽS. After Hlinka's death, it was no longer satisfied with 'national autonomy' but demanded more and more clearly full sovereignty in an independent state. Karol Sidor, the chief editor of *Slovák*, followed a polonophile course, while Tuka, who was rehabilitated in October 1938, increasingly shifted his allegiance to the Germans. In the summer of 1938, the so-called Hlinka Guard was founded as a military organization belonging to the Slovak People's Party, and after the Munich Agreement the long striven-for autonomy was finally achieved in the Second Czechoslovak Republic.[39]

The Slovak People's Party had put forward three suggestions for autonomy between 1922 and 1938. The first of these was presented to the Prague parliament in January 1922 and only foresaw as 'common interests' the army, foreign policy, the constitution, the presidency, currency and public transport. The second proposal of May 1930 tried to extend the theoretical autonomy that Slovakia had achieved to the Carpathian Ukrainians. This autonomy was anchored in the constitution, but had never been realized. The third proposal for autonomy was finally presented to the Prague parliament in June 1938 and was signed by Hlinka. In the Žilina Agreement of 6 October 1938, the Agrarians, the National Socialists, the Slovakian National Party, the Small Tradesmen's Party and the Fascists all came together, but not the Social Democrats. On 7 October 1938 a Slovakian government was formed for the first time, with Jozef Tiso as Prime Minister.

The constitution, foreign policy, national defence, citizenship, currency, taxes, customs duties and monopolies, railways and the postal service remained common with the Czech part of the state. Autonomous Slovakia lost a large part of southern Slovakia to Hungary through the First Vienna Arbitration on 2 November 1938. In this part of the country the majority of the population was Hungarian. The state that was proclaimed on 14 March 1939 at the parliament of Bratislava, under pressure from Hitler, was from the beginning a satellite of the so-called Third Reich.[40]

Tiso, Hlinka's successor and between 1939 and 1945 President of the independent Slovakia, described the object of the political efforts of his party in his defence speech at the National Court in March 1947 as '. . . none other than the Slovakian people – to allow them to be an independent, confident and contented people . . . This people should be helped to become morally and economically independent . . . The People's Party programme aimed not only at material interests but also the spiritual, the cultural and higher ideals . . .'[41]

The participation of Tiso and Tuka's government in the deporting of Jews from Slovakia can surely not be said to belong to these 'higher aims'. Neither could the entry into war against the Soviet Union and the Western Allies. That is why it came as no surprise that Hlinka's People's Party was banned after the war, and even at the elections in May 1946 was no longer tolerated. The contribution that the Slovakian People's Party made to the formation of the Slovakian nation in the first half of the twentieth century has to be recognized, however, as decisive for Slovakian confidence in its nationhood.

NOTES

1 Joseph Rothschild, *East Central Europe between the Two World Wars* (Seattle, WA and London 1990), pp. 3–25.
2 Arnold Suppan, Valeria Heuberger and Klaus Koch, 'Parties and Elections 1917–1947', in Österreichisches Ost- und Südosteuropa-Institut (ed.), *The 1990 Elections in Central, East and South-East Europe. Atlas East and South-East Europe 6.1 – G3* (Vienna 1991), pp. 17–21.
3 See Heinz Gollwitzer (ed.), *Europäische Bauernparteien im 20. Jahrhundert* (Stuttgart and New York 1977). The long-standing Hungarian Prime Minister, István Count Bethlen, began as early as 1922 to infiltrate the Smallholders' Party and thus secured himself a parliamentary seat.
4 Karl Bosl (ed.), *Die Erste Tschechoslowakische Republik als multinationaler Parteienstaat* (Munich and Vienna 1979); Helmut Slapnicka, 'Die böhmischen Länder und die Slowakei 1919–1945', in *Handbuch der Geschichte der böhmischen Länder*, vol. 4 (Munich and Vienna 1974), pp. 2–150; Andrzej Albert, *Najnowsza historia Polski 1914–1993* (London 1994); Iván T. Berend and György Ránki, *East Central Europe in the 19th and 20th centuries* (Budapest 1977).

5 Alice Teichova (ed.), *Central Europe in the Twentieth Century. An Economic History Perspective* (Aldershot and Brookfield 1997); Michael Kaser and E. A. Radice (eds), *Economic History of Eastern Europe 1919–1975*, 3 vols (Oxford 1985–86).
6 Julius Braunthal, *Geschichte der Internationale*, vol. 2, 3rd edition (Berlin and Bonn 1978); see also Norbert Leser, *Zwischen Reformismus und Bolschewismus. Der Austromarxismus zwischen Theorie und Praxis* (Vienna 1968).
7 Richard J. Crampton, *Eastern Europe in the Twentieth Century* (London and New York 1994), pp. 31–176.
8 Antonín Klimek, *Boj o hrad*, 2 vols (Prague 1996–98); Arnold Suppan, *Jugoslawien und Österreich 1918–1938. Bilaterale Aussenpolitik im europäischen Umfeld* (Vienna and Munich 1996), pp. 52–75.
9 Renzo de Felice, *Le interpretazioni del Fascismo* (Rome and Bari 1991); Peter F. Sugar (ed.), *Native Fascism in the Successor States, 1918–1945* (Santa Barbara, CA 1971).
10 Antony Polonsky, *The Little Dictators. The History of Eastern Europe since 1918* (London 1975); Magda Adám, *Richtung Selbstvernichtung. Die Kleine Entente 1920–1938* (Budapest and Vienna 1988).
11 Jan Heidler, *České politické strany v Čechách, na Moravě a ve Slezsku* (V Praze 1914), pp. 47–51; Karel Hruby, 'Kirche und Arbeiter', in Ferdinand Seibt (ed.), *Bohemia Sacra. Das Christentum in Böhmen 973–1973* (Düsseldorf 1974), pp. 258–68.
12 Heidler, *České politické strany*, pp. 58–9; Jiří Malíř, *Od spolků k moderním politickým stranám. Vývoj politických stran na Moravě v letech 1848–1914* (Brno 1996), pp. 254–9.
13 Malíř, *Od spolků*, pp. 347–48 and 352ff.
14 Arnold Suppan, 'Christlich-demokratische Parteien bei den Tschechen', *Christliche Demokratie*, vol. 4, no. 3 (1986), pp. 137–48.
15 Jaroslav Pecháček, 'Die Rolle des politischen Katholizismus in der ČSR', in Bosl, *Die Erste Tschechoslowakische Republik*, pp. 259–69, here pp. 261–2; Jan Havránek (ed.), *Dějiny University Karlovy*, vol. 3 (Prague 1997), pp. 365–6.
16 Ferdinand Peroutka, *Budování státu. Československá politika v letech popřevratových*, 4 vols, 2nd edition (Prague 1936); *Statistická příručka Republiky Československé*, vol. 2 (Prague 1925) and vol. 4 (Prague 1932).
17 Antonín Boháč, *Hlavní město Praha* (Prague 1923), p. 81; Slapnicka, 'Die Böhmischen Länder', pp. 41ff.
18 Peroutka, *Budování státu*, vol. 2, pp. 635–56 and vol. 3, pp. 1457–80.
19 Roman Sandgruber, *Österreichische Agrarstatistik 1750–1918* (Vienna 1978); Harry Klepetař, *Seit 1918. Eine Geschichte der Tschechoslowakischen Republik* (Ostrava 1937).
20 Jiří Sláma and Karel Kaplan, *Die Parlamentswahlen in der Tschechoslowakei 1935–1946–1948* (Munich 1986); Gregory Campbell, 'Die Tschechische Volkspartei und die Deutschen Christlichsozialen', in Bosl, *Die Erste Tschechoslowakische Republik*, pp. 291–303, here pp. 295ff.
21 Campbell, 'Die Tschechische Volkspartei', pp. 296ff; Miloš Trapl, *Politika českého katolicismu na Moravě 1918–1938* (Prague 1968), p. 35.
22 Pecháček, 'Politischer Katholizismus', p. 266; Trapl, *Politika českého katolicismu*, pp. 71–2; see also idem, *Political Catholicism and the Czechoslovak People's Party in Czechoslovakia* (New York 1995).
23 Campbell, 'Die Tschechische Volkspartei', pp. 302–3.
24 Victor S. Mamatey and Radomír Luža (eds), *A History of the Czechoslovak Republic 1918–1948* (Princeton, NJ 1973), pp. 161–2; Milan Otáhal,

'Czechoslovakia behind the Iron Curtain (1945–1989)', in Mikuláš Teich (ed.), *Bohemia in History* (Cambridge 1998), pp. 306–23.
25 Milan D. Ďurica, *Dejiny Slovenska a Slovákov v chronologickom prehl'ade* (Košice 1995), p. 120; Jozef Lettrich, *History of Modern Slovakia* (Mississauga, Ontario 1955), pp. 68–9.
26 Stanislav J. Kirschbaum, *A History of Slovakia. The Struggle for Survival* (New York 1995), pp. 145–57.
27 Kirschbaum, *Slovakia*, pp. 156–7; Lettrich, *Slovakia*, pp. 39–40. See also Ludwig von Gogolák, *Beiträge zur Geschichte des slowakischen Volkes*, vol. 3 (Munich 1967).
28 Dušan Kováč, *Dějiny Slovenska* (Prague 1998), pp. 174–5.
29 Lettrich, *Slovakia*, pp. 288–9.
30 Kirschbaum, *Slovakia*, pp. 147–8.
31 Ibid., pp. 172ff.
32 Kováč, *Dějiny Slovenska*, p. 186; State Office for Statistics Prague (ed.), *Statistische Übersicht der Tschechoslowakischen Republik* (Brno 1930), pp. 10–11.
33 Jörg K. Hoensch, 'Die Slowakische Volkspartei Hlinkas', in Bosl, *Die Erste Tschechoslowakische Republik*, pp. 305–22, here pp. 310–11.
34 Hoensch, 'Die Slowakische Volkspartei', pp. 312–14. See also Joseph M. Kirschbaum, *Slovakia: Nation at the Crossroads of Europe* (New York 1960), pp. 61–2.
35 L'ubomir Lipták, *Slovensko v. 20. storočí* (Bratislava 1968), pp. 103ff; Elizabeth Bakke, *Doomed to Failure? The Czechoslovak Nation Project and the Slovak Autonomist Reaction, 1918–38* (Oslo 1999), pp. 406–27.
36 Hoensch, 'Slowakische Volkspartei', pp. 315, 319. See also C.A. Macartney, *Hungary and Her Successors* (London 1937), p. 144.
37 Bakke, *Doomed to Failure?*, pp. 327–34. See also, Emilia Hrabovec, *Der Heilige Stuhl und die Slowakei 1918–1922 im Kontext internationaler Beziehungen* (Frankfurt/Main 2002).
38 Hoensch, 'Slowakische Volkspartei', pp. 314–15.
39 Bakke, *Doomed to Failure?*, pp. 398–406; Jörg K. Hoensch, *Die Slowakei und Hitlers Ostpolitik, Hlinkas Slowakische Volkspartei zwischen Autonomie und Separation 1938/39* (Cologne and Graz 1965), pp. 132ff.
40 Bakke, *Doomed to Failure?*, pp. 465–73.
41 Jozef Tiso, *Die Wahrheit über die Slowakei. Verteidigungsrede, gehalten am 17. und 18. März 1947 vor dem 'National'-Gericht in Bratislava*, edited by Jan Sekera (Munich 1948), pp. 113–14.

12

Catholic Politics or Christian Democracy? The Evolution of Inter-war Political Catholicism

Martin Conway

The purpose of this chapter is to serve as a conclusion to the series of national case studies presented above and to reflect on some of the more general conclusions that it is possible to derive from the wealth of analysis they contain.[1] Such an exercise must, given the very real diversity of Catholic political traditions and of the national political contexts in which they operated, be somewhat arbitrary. Catholic politics was too amorphous a phenomenon in the Europe of the 1920s and 1930s to be capable of reduction to a single satisfactory definition. Nevertheless, there is, I believe, a real virtue in engaging in a comparative analysis of this kind. During recent decades, there have been an impressive number of studies of Catholic political movements of the inter-war years that have enriched historical understanding of the complex mixture of spiritual, political and social impulses that underpinned their development. If there has, however, been a weakness in these excellent studies, it is that they have often been reluctant to reflect on the broader significance of their subject matter. Written within national historiographical traditions, they have understandably tended to emphasize national specificities at the expense of the broader trends shaping European Catholicism.[2] Moreover, the affiliation of many of their authors to a consciously Catholic tradition of historical research has led them to accept the nature of their subject as self-evident. Seen from this perspective, the existence of a distinctive Catholic political culture has been assumed rather than questioned; unifying factors have taken precedence over internal divisions; and continuities have appeared more important than ruptures. There is much that is valid in what one might term this 'organic' interpretation of Catholic political development.[3] Nevertheless, in attempting a comparative analysis of Catholic political movements, there is some value in seeking to transcend these implicit or explicit frontiers. Political Catholicism of the inter-war years needs to be viewed not merely from national and confessional perspectives, but also as a complex, rapidly shifting and European phenomenon.

THE FORTRESS MENTALITY

The essential starting point of any such comparative analysis must be that the phrase 'Catholic politics' is a meaningful and self-sufficient designation of what we are seeking to describe. It is meaningful, in the sense that Catholicism did constitute one of the major currents of inter-war European politics, in which the religious element was more than an accidental legacy of history. It is also self-sufficient, in that to dismantle the phenomenon into subsidiary currents with labels such as 'Christian democracy', 'clerico-fascism' or 'Catholic conservatism' seems neither natural nor conceptually useful. That such trends did exist is, of course, self-evident but, as the contributors to this book demonstrate, Catholic politics is best regarded as a unity rather than a sum of its constituent parts.[4]

The overriding purpose of Catholic political action in inter-war Europe was to rally the faithful in as large numbers as possible in the public sphere. There was, of course, nothing new in this goal. The mentalities and structures of inter-war Catholic politics owed much to the remarkably rapid emergence of Catholic political movements that had taken place in late-nineteenth-century Europe. The Catholic 'path into modernity', as Urs Altermatt has argued for the case of Switzerland,[5] was one that sought to create an enclosed world of distinctively and homogeneously Catholic spiritual, economic, social and ultimately political organizations. This defensive reflex, forged in the clerical–anticlerical conflicts of the pre-1914 years, continued to define much of the character of Catholic politics of the inter-war period. Its primary purpose was to use political power at the national and, perhaps more especially, the local level to protect the interests of the Church and of its affiliated archipelago of educational, social and economic institutions against the inimical actions of their opponents.

Defence was not, however, the only goal. What was distinctive about Catholic politics after the First World War was the increasing confidence with which Catholic parties proposed programmes and policies of relevance to the needs of society as a whole. In part, this change reflected the pressure of external events. The dictates of electoral and interest-group politics, as well as the exercise of governmental power, obliged Catholic movements to define their attitudes towards an increasing range of problems. But it was also the consequence of the emergence of a more activist mentality within Catholic ranks, which had its origins in the spiritual and social changes taking place within the religion. The new mood of spiritual militancy encouraged by the papacy during the 1920s, as well as the emergence of a generation of younger Catholics less constrained by the predominantly conservative preoccupations of their elders, served to inject a new energy into Catholic politics of the inter-war years. Although the extent of this change can easily be exaggerated,[6] it helps to explain the new tone of self-confidence – and on occasions of intransigence – that characterized much Catholic campaigning during the 1920s and 1930s. Catholicism, it seemed, was concerned not merely to defend its rights, but also to advance its political, social and economic ideas.

This distinctive combination of defensive and offensive concerns found its expression in the dominant metaphorical vision of Catholicism as a *fortress*.[7] No other image was as characteristic of Catholic self-representation during the 1920s and the 1930s as that of the Church and the faithful as a bastion of order and truth in a disordered and corrupt world. Represented repeatedly in papal encyclicals, election posters and the speeches of priests and politicians, the metaphor of the fortress was one that simultaneously reflected and reinforced the prevailing *Weltanschauung* of many European Catholics. If its origins lay in the discrimination experienced by many European Catholics before 1914, this fortress image also derived its strength from more urgent contemporary concerns. The understandable sense of dislocation felt by many amid the disruptions of war, changes of political regime and economic crisis, as well as renewed attacks by state authorities and radical movements on the autonomy of the Church, served to reinforce the self-image of the Catholics as a distinct community, united by their values and alone possessed of a solution to the manifold ills of the current age.

What, then, were the consequences of this fortress definition of Catholicism? Three, it seems to me, emerge strongly from the chapters in this book and other recent research. The first is that political Catholicism operated within *frontiers*. These frontiers were both real and imagined, reflecting the political realities within which Catholic parties functioned and, more importantly, their perception of those realities. One ineluctable reality was the existence of national frontiers throughout Europe that were in many respects more defined and less permeable than in either the pre-1914 or post-1945 eras. Thus, although common trends were evident in Catholic politics throughout Europe, the parties operated within strictly national contexts. As the contributions to this volume illustrate, Catholic parties made some gestures in the direction of international co-operation. Moreover, both within Catholic youth movements and some intellectual groups there was an interest in pan-Europeanism, which expressed Catholic distrust of the liberal and fascist cult of the secular nation state.[8] But it is clearly all too easy to exaggerate the significance of these straws in the wind in the light of the role played by Christian democrat parties in the processes of European integration after 1945. Catholic politics of the inter-war years operated overwhelmingly within a national mould, seeking to achieve its goals within, rather than across, national frontiers.

In addition to these external frontiers, there were also the internal and less visible frontiers of confession. Catholic parties derived from their fortress mentality a strong sense of their differentness, and consequently of the existence of a frontier between Catholics and non-Catholics that could not and should not be transgressed. In fact, this frontier was already an anachronism. Social and economic modernization had long since destroyed any possibility of maintaining a self-contained Catholic community. Importantly, however, most Catholic political movements in inter-war Europe behaved as if a frontier between Catholics and non-Catholics remained both natural and desirable. Just as the Catholic Church displayed little interest in the tentative ecumenical initiatives of the era, so Catholic parties sought to ensure that electoral and confessional frontiers mirrored each other as closely as possible. Their objective during election campaigns was not to reach out to new audiences, but to mobilize as effectively as possible those who by dint of religious observance or other forms of social definition were perceived as forming part of the Catholic community.[9]

The logic of this electoral goal led Catholic parties to emphasize both their exclusively Catholic character and the uniqueness of the spiritual and political principles that defined their policies. Although the various dictates of coalition politics, bourgeois (or rural) self-defence and patriotic unity on many occasions led the parties to collaborate with other political forces, there was no slackening in this affirmation of a distinct Catholic identity. Indeed, the inter-war years probably constituted the modern high-water mark of such self-imposed Catholic distinctiveness. In retrospect, this can seem difficult to understand. Viewed with the benefit of hindsight, the clerical–anticlerical struggles of the nineteenth century appear to have become a spent force in the politics of the 1920s and 1930s. The future for Catholic parties, it seems, lay in forging a new centrist politics capable of appealing to social constituencies wider than those of the Catholic faithful.

Little of this was, however, visible to the Catholic politicians of the inter-war years. Fears of a revived Liberal–Socialist alliance based on the shared bond of anticlericalism remained vivid, and appeared to find confirmation in the anti-Catholic tone of the new Czechoslovak state or in the confrontational politics of the Spanish Second Republic.[10] With the relative decline of liberal parties in many areas of Europe, it was now socialism that provided the enemy against which Catholic parties defined themselves. It is easy to lose sight of the extent to which Catholic political energies in inter-war Europe were devoted to the goal of countering the materialist and, above all, atheistic doctrines of Marxist socialism. Such fears were of course heightened, especially in Central Europe, by the emergence of Soviet communism. The spectre of revolution, manipulated by the agents of Moscow, constituted the ultimate evil of Catholic propaganda. It was, however, the more immediate and omnipresent challenge of non-communist socialism that constituted the principal challenge for most Catholic parties. In Italy, for example, in the volatile years following the First World War, it was Socialist electoral success that provided much of the stimulus to the wildfire growth of the *popolari* as the guarantors of Catholic interests. As Tiziana di Maio shows in her chapter, even as the Fascists became the greater threat, an alliance of Catholics and Socialists proved impossible. It is perhaps above all in studies of local politics that the primacy of the Catholic–Socialist rivalry becomes evident. Not merely in prominent cities such as Vienna but, more characteristically, in the small and medium-sized communities that constituted the norm in inter-war Europe, struggles between Catholics and Socialists for control of the levers of municipal power provided much of the mobilizing energy behind Catholic political action.[11]

Attempts to reach out across the political divide between Catholics and non-Catholics generally amounted to little more than 'a dialogue of the deaf'.[12] In Germany, as Jürgen Elvert shows, the replacement of Wilhelm Marx by Ludwig Kaas as chairman of the Centre Party in 1928 marked a retreat from a centrist definition of the party to one of the defence of particularist Catholic and regional interests. In France, the Popular Democratic Party (PDP) constituted perhaps the most striking example in inter-war Europe of an attempt to construct a Catholic-inspired identity that subordinated confessionalism to a broader social and political agenda. But, as Jean-Claude Delbreil demonstrates, it was one that by the 1930s had effectively fallen between two stools: the PDP had failed to rally non-Catholics to its reformist programme, or to convince sufficient numbers of Catholics that it was the representative of their interests. Confessionalism, it seemed, was a more reliable mobilizer of political loyalties in much of Catholic Europe in the inter-war years than many of its more secular alternatives. Nowhere perhaps was this truth more evident than in Austria, where, as Helmut Wohnout's chapter importantly illustrates, the Christian Social Party adopted a more narrowly confessional identity than had been the case prior to the death of Karl Lueger in 1910. The only (partial) exceptions to this trend were those new states that emerged after the First World War. In the Irish Free State, both major political traditions, Fine Gael and Fianna Fáil, courted Catholic support, rendering superfluous the creation of an explicitly Catholic party.[13] Similarly, in Poland, the link between confessional identity and political behaviour remained relatively weak. As Leszek Kuk demonstrates, in a situation in which almost all of the ethnically Polish parties expressed support for the values of Catholicism, the Church saw little reason to create an official Catholic Party and the Christian Democrats of the Polskie Stronnictwo Chrześcijańskiej Demokracji (PSChD) received little clerical support.[14]

The second dominant characteristic of Catholic parties as presented in this book is that, to borrow from the language of political science, they were *milieu* parties. Because they operated within the rich network of

Catholic associations that had expanded across Europe from the mid-nineteenth century onwards, they possessed few of the formal organizational structures supposedly characteristic of modern political movements. Indeed, as several contributions to this volume make clear, they were in many respects scarcely parties at all. In Belgium, Switzerland or Austria, for example, the Catholic 'parties' of the 1920s had few members, scant financial resources of their own and highly informal decision-making structures. This was not a sign of their weakness; on the contrary, it demonstrated the degree to which they were integrated within the supportive environment afforded by Catholic associations. In some respects, this once again appears anachronistic. The informality of much Catholic politics was often the legacy of the notable politics of the nineteenth century, and it is not surprising that many Catholic political leaders of the 1920s and 1930s strove to create efficient and hierarchical party structures better suited to the needs of modern politics. It would be misleading, however, to present the milieu character of many inter-war Catholic parties as merely a legacy of the past. It also reflected the manner in which the transition to mass politics had occurred in many Catholic areas of Europe from *circa* 1880 onwards. This had taken the form of the creation of 'pillarized' parallel societies of socialists, Catholics, liberals and, in some regions, Protestants, each possessed of their own social, economic and cultural organizations. Catholic parties were an expression of this reality: rather than autonomous 'stand alone' movements, they were the extension into the political sphere of their pillar.[15]

The Church – and, more especially, its personnel, financial resources and press – formed one element of the milieu that enveloped these Catholic parties, but not the dominant one. Perhaps one of the most striking features of the analyses presented in the preceding chapters is the relatively limited prominence that the authors accord to the role of the Church. Catholic parties might have been, as their opponents never tired of declaring, the disguised agents of the Church, but the accusation tended to be true in a more general than in a specific sense. Catholic parties defended with an uncomplicated determination the interests of the Church, while the informal influence of Catholic prelates and priests within the national, and particularly the local counsels of Catholic parties was substantial. But the parties had outgrown their origins as agents of clergy-directed mobilization. If clerical figures such as Luigi Sturzo, Ludwig Kaas, Jozef Tiso and Ignaz Seipel played prominent roles, they nevertheless remained exceptions to the rule that Catholic politics had essentially become a politics of the laity, and more especially of a laity that had acquired its training and experience within Catholic spiritual, economic and cultural associations.

This evolution was one element of a wider change gradually taking place in the nature of the Catholic community. That the Church lay at the heart of the Catholic fortress remained clear; but that the Church hierarchy consequently had a natural right to leadership of the Catholic community was much less certain. There was now more than one class of officer within the Catholic army, and the fortress metaphor itself encouraged a functional specialization of responsibilities. Political, economic and spiritual organizations each had their own role to play, and bishops and clergy recognized (albeit often reluctantly) that they had to accord a certain autonomy to these movements. This renegotiation of the power relations within the Catholic community was as yet more implicit than explicit, and was to some extent contradicted by the determined efforts of the papacy under Pius XI and, more especially, Pius XII to construct a more hierarchical definition of Catholic power.[16] Nevertheless, within the political sphere, there was a mutual recognition on the part of the party leaders and the Church hierarchy of the distance that should exist between Church and party. The parties were therefore neither dependent on the Church nor independent from it; rather, they co-existed alongside it within the interlocking and still expanding networks of spiritual movements, trade unions, insurance leagues and women's and youth groups which constituted what John Boyer in his chapter aptly terms the Catholic 'social civilization'.

The third attribute of this fortress Catholicism was in large part the consequence of the factors already outlined. These were parties based upon the *primacy of unity*. Whether in the Low Countries, Italy or Central Europe, the parties strove to be the single political voice of the Catholic population. A somewhat authoritarian cult of unity suffused much Catholic politics of the inter-war years. The unity of the faithful was assumed to be both natural and necessary, while to establish a dissident Catholic grouping or, worse still, to support a non-Catholic party was regarded not merely as a different political choice but as a betrayal. Only in France was this pursuit of unity largely absent. Although a movement such as General de Castelnau's Fédération Nationale Catholique (FNC) posed in the 1920s as the representative of all French Catholics, the differences of tradition, region and of ideology within French Catholicism were in practice always too forceful to make unity anything other than a very distant dream. Almost uniquely in Catholic Europe, a culture of political pluralism (but certainly not of democracy) existed within inter-war French Catholicism, and was only temporarily disrupted by the enthusiasm with which the overwhelming majority of French Catholics welcomed the establishment of the Vichy regime in 1940.[17]

THE DIFFICULTIES OF UNITY

The principal challenge that faced Catholic politics was that, while the aspiration for unity was widespread in Catholic ranks, it proved to be difficult to achieve and to maintain in the circumstances of the inter-war years. Catholics felt themselves to be united, but often found themselves to be divided. Why was this the case? In part, the answer lies in ideological disputes within Catholic ranks, as well as in the divergent choices made by Catholics in response to events such as the rise of Italian fascism and the establishment of the Weimar Republic. However, the most important and in many respects novel explanation to emerge from the chapters in this book is that of socio-economic conflict. The economic difficulties of the inter-war years, combined with the increasingly assertive presence within Catholic ranks of groupings committed to the defence of the sectional interests of the working class, farmers and the bourgeoisie, drained Catholic parties of much of the sense of common purpose that they had managed to retain, albeit often with some difficulty, during the pre-1914 era.

Two social fault-lines had a particular impact on Catholic politics: first, that between the middle and working classes; and second that between a newly militant rural population and the defenders of urban interests. Both posed a more direct challenge to Catholic unity than to any other political tradition. If socialism or liberalism had acquired by the inter-war years what one might term a social 'centre of gravity', Catholic movements were composed more than ever of diverse social constituencies. This cross-class, pillarized character constituted their greatest strength: by appealing to confessional identity over and above sectional interest, Catholic parties could reach out to a mass audience in a much more direct manner than their rivals. But this same social diversity presented them with their most serious challenge. As movements that sought to win simultaneously the support of the middle classes, rural populations and the working class, Catholic parties were engaged in an attempt to defy the gravity of material interest. Not surprisingly, this was a feat that they often found difficult to achieve.

The most durable of these fault-lines was that between the middle and working classes. As Wilfried Loth has argued, the unity of the Centre Party of the pre-1914 years was already being undermined by the divergent material interests of its social components.[18] After 1918, this problem became both more intense and more general. A series of often traumatic economic upheavals appeared to threaten middle-class savings, businesses and career structures as well as the more general fabric of bourgeois life in much of Europe. In response, there was an upsurge in middle-class defence organizations, which insistently demanded effective protection and redress from the state. Catholic parties, with their predominantly bourgeois leaderships and substantial middle-class electorates, could scarcely remain immune from these campaigns. Indeed, throughout the 1920s and early 1930s, many Catholic parties tended to degenerate into little more than vehicles for bourgeois and lower-middle-class demands on issues such as taxation, economic policy and welfare reform. Moreover, the more general ideological reorientation evident in much Catholic politics during the inter-war years, away from a passive acceptance of liberal parliamentarism towards models of authoritarianism and corporatism, was strongly influenced by middle-class dissatisfaction with a political and economic system that no longer seemed protective of their interests.[19]

This middle-class ascendancy within Catholic ranks was challenged by an expanding and newly confident network of Catholic working-class organizations. If the 1890s and 1900s were the formative period in the development of Catholic trade unions, insurance leagues and pressure groups, it was undoubtedly in the inter-war years that they came of age. Several factors underlay this process. The general expansion in levels of trade unionism, and its expansion into new regions and industrial sectors, offered Catholic unions opportunities for recruitment. The tentative structures of industrial corporatism emerging in some areas of Europe also increased the incentive for women and white-collar workers to organize in trade unions. The most important driving force, however, was the gradual emergence of a distinct Catholic working-class consciousness that took its religious faith as its basis, but which dispensed with its *fin-de-siècle* legacies of paternalism and social deference. This was a Europe-wide phenomenon that flourished in areas as diverse as north-eastern Italy and Polish Silesia, but had as its heartland a band of territories stretching from areas of western Germany such as the Saarland, through the southern Netherlands and Belgian Flanders into northern France. Throughout this region, class consciousness and Catholic identity were parallel processes, each reinforcing the other and invested with an additional momentum by long-standing and more recent forms of social and political discrimination. The consequence was the development of a Catholic trade unionism and associational culture, that, through its reliance on a combination of confessional solidarity, effective organization and a pragmatic approach to industrial conflicts, proved to be a formidable rival for the socialist movement.[20]

Perhaps not surprisingly, Catholic political movements were slow to adapt to this change from below. Bourgeois leaderships resisted the demands of Catholic working-class groups for a greater role in policy making, as well as for places on electoral lists and within government. The consequent tensions severely strained Catholic political unity during the 1920s. Dissident 'Christian democratic' electoral organizations and networks were established in a number of areas, that, although reluctant to reject explicitly the dogma of confessional solidarity, nevertheless challenged the pretensions of established Catholic parties to be the sole representatives of Catholic opinion. In Hungary, as Csaba Fazekas shows, the populist demagogy of the Keresztény Községi Part (KKP) in Budapest split from the more conservative (and middle-class) Keresztény Gazdasági és Szociális Párt (KGSZP). In Germany, Adam Stegerwald and Catholic trade unionists in the Deutscher Gewerkschaftsbund (DGB), established in 1919, considered and then drew back from breaking with the Centre Party to create a deconfessionalized political movement; while in Belgium, as Emmanuel Gerard's chapter demonstrates, the Catholic Party became all but polarized during the 1920s and early 1930s between competing working-class and middle-class sub-organizations.[21] In Poland, by contrast, the working-class and petit-bourgeois electorate of Silesia provided – as Leszek Kuk shows – the most reliable basis of support for the PSChD, prompting a significant defection of middle-class votes to the authoritarian politics of the governmental camp during the 1930s.

While struggles for influence between bourgeois and working-class groups have remained a persistent theme of Catholic politics during the twentieth century, the second source of socio-economic tension, that of urban–rural conflict, was more acute and specific to the particular circumstances of the inter-war years. One of the significant themes to have emerged from the wealth of local studies of politics in the 1920s and 1930s published in recent years has been the importance of urban–rural tensions, and more especially the almost insurrectionary mood fostered in many rural areas by the price controls of the First World War and its aftermath, as well as by the wider structural crisis faced by many sections of European agriculture during the 1920s and the Depression years. Threatened by sudden falls in market prices for their produce, indebted by investments in new machinery and subjected to increased levels of taxation and social security contributions, many small farmers in Western and Central Europe experienced a significant and lasting decline in their living standards.[22]

These rural grievances, and the fierce resentments that they provoked against urban populations and governments seemingly more concerned about the need for cheap food than for the interests of agricultural producers, placed Catholic parties in an especially painful position. While most Catholic parties had long relied on rural areas of high religious practice for much of their electoral support, both their middle-class leaders and working-class trade unionists were responsive to more urban concerns. The tensions provoked by the consequent balancing act affected almost all Catholic parties. In Italy after the First World War, the Fascists were the beneficiaries of the inability of the *popolari* to reconcile the interests of their urban supporters with those of a rural population radicalized by economic difficulties and by the socialist unionization of agricultural labourers.[23] In Germany, farmers' movements formed a disruptive and highly vocal interest group within the local politics of the Centre Party, while the Christian Social governments of the 1920s in Austria endeavoured to retain the support of their predominantly rural electors tempted by the authoritarian populism of movements such as the Heimwehr.[24] As Lukas Rölli-Alkemper demonstrates, the Schweizerische Konservative Volkspartei (SKVP) faced much the same difficulty in seeking to respond to the grievances of its supporters in the rural cantons of the so-called *Stammlande*, while also reaching out to the expanding numbers of Catholic migrants in the major cities. In Poland, the predominantly urban leadership of the PSChD failed to rally significant rural Catholic support, while in Hungary the KGSZP lost much of its rural electorate to the more consistently agrarian Independent Smallholders Party. Finally, in Belgium, both of the major dissident movements to emerge within Catholic ranks during the inter-war years, Rex and the Flemish Nationalists of the Vlaamsch Nationaal Verbond (VNV), derived much of their support from rural populations alienated by the apparent failure of the Catholic Party to perform its accustomed role as the guarantor of agrarian interests.[25]

Given the prevalence of socio-economic tensions between their middle-class, working-class and rural supporters, it is scarcely surprising that the Catholic parties of the inter-war years found it difficult to articulate programmes that went beyond the rehearsal of specifically Catholic concerns. When they did try to do so, as in the economic and social programme of the SKVP in 1929, or the manifestos issued by the Centre Party in the latter Weimar elections, they singularly failed to win unanimous endorsement even within their own ranks.[26] In Hungary, Catholic unity proved impossible, as the successive Catholic parties failed to reconcile their ideological and more especially social components. Should we therefore conclude, in the manner of Wilfried Loth, that the Catholic parties of the inter-war period were doomed to dissolve into their constituent socio-economic elements as outmoded relics of the Catholic transition to modernity?[27] Such an interpretation would in fact seem overly deterministic. As the example of the Belgian Catholic Party illustrates, the replacement of outmoded confederal structures by a more centralized structure could do much to limit damaging internal disputes. Moreover, to concentrate on the national political difficulties of Catholic parties risks neglecting the manner in which confessional difference remained a durable reality in the local and regional political cultures of much of modern Europe.

Nevertheless, the impact of socio-economic tensions did constitute a serious challenge to the unitary structure of national Catholic political parties. Especially when compared with the pre-1914 Catholic parties and to Christian Democracy after the Second World War, the parties of the inter-war years can be seen to have lacked the means both of mediating conflicts within their own ranks and of resolving the economic problems of society as a whole. Nowhere was this difficulty more acutely evident than in Germany. The Centre Party was in many respects the archetype of a modern Catholic party, yet its history during the Weimar Republic was, as Jürgen Elvert explains, one of gradual disintegration into its constituent social and regional elements. Viewed too often by historians through the distorting prism of 'the rise of Nazism', this unravelling of the Centre Party was in fact a much more complex and multifaceted process, but one which can be seen as encapsulating many of the problems encountered by Catholic parties in inter-war Europe.

CATHOLIC POLITICS OR CHRISTIAN DEMOCRACY?

The conclusion that therefore rightly emerges from the analyses presented in this book is that the history of Catholic politics in inter-war Europe cannot be reduced to a simple tale of success or failure. Certain criteria of success were emphatically present: Catholic parties were among the most electorally successful in Europe, and played a major role in national and local government. More generally, there was an indisputable energy and intellectual vitality in Catholic politics, which in turn reflected the remarkable resilience demonstrated by the Catholic religion in a time of rapid social and cultural change. At the same time there were also clear elements of failure. The framework of unitary Catholic parties inherited from the pre-1914 era no longer seemed capable of accommodating the social and ideological constituencies present within Catholicism. Sectional rivalries threatened spiritual unity, dissident political movements emerged and occasionally flourished, while some Catholics abandoned entirely the confessional framework of politics in favour of secular rivals of the left and right. If Catholic politics had therefore undoubtedly grown in scope and ambition during the inter-war years, it also became indisputably more divided.

The most striking manifestation of the fractures in the Catholic fortress was the support that millions of European Catholics gave to movements of the extreme right. No history of inter-war Catholicism is complete without recognition of the reality that a considerable proportion of European Catholics stepped outside of the parliamentary process to support by their votes, words or actions the movements of the authoritarian and fascist right. There were manifold examples of this process: if it was most dramatic in Austria, Spain and Italy, it also strongly influenced Catholic politics in states as diverse as France, Portugal, Belgium, Germany, Hungary, Croatia and Slovakia.[28] The scale of the phenomenon excludes its explanation as accidental. Although Catholic historians sometimes seem inclined to dismiss the 'authoritarian temptation' in Catholic politics of the inter-war years as no more than a product of particular national circumstances, it seems more plausible to assert a positive connection between Catholicism and the politics of the anti-democratic right. The legacy of nineteenth-century battles against the anticlericalism of the left, the social composition of the Catholic populations, the more militant character of Catholic spiritual and youth movements of the 1920s and the pervasive fear of communism, were all factors that rendered many European Catholics particularly susceptible to the rhetoric and prejudices of the anti-democratic right.

This was not, however, the entire story. In the case of those states, such as Fascist Italy and Nazi Germany, which experienced secular regimes of the extreme right, Catholic social organizations were rigorously repressed because they were perceived as threats to state power, and Catholic activists as well as some members of the clergy were often persecuted. Moreover, as a number of the contributors to this volume rightly stress, there also existed a current within Catholic politics that defined itself against the lure of the authoritarian right. Those *popolari* in Italy who refused to come to terms with the Fascist regime, the role played by Catholics in the Resistance in France, the Catholic workers' movement in Austria and Catholic dissidents within the Third Reich opposed the anti-democratic right, and in doing so often found themselves drawn, almost unconsciously, towards support for a Catholic form of democracy.[29] The question therefore arises as to whether we should regard these opponents of the extreme right, and indeed the wider currents of popular and working-class Catholic politics during the inter-war years, as manifestations of 'Christian democracy'? The term is a tempting one: it was used by many progressive Catholics themselves, especially when seeking to differentiate themselves from conservatives within Catholic ranks. In historiographical terms too, it provides a satisfying bridge between the Christian democratic experiments of the 1890s and 1900s and the Christian democrat parties of the 1940s and 1950s. Unsurprisingly, therefore, historians of Christian democracy have often seized upon democratic Catholic politicians of the inter-war years and presented them as precursors of the Christian democracy of the post-1945 era.[30]

The analyses presented in this volume seem to me to offer two correctives to this teleological, and in some respects sanitized, interpretation of twentieth-century Catholic politics. In the first place, to regard all those who used the term 'Christian democracy' as participants in a shared ideology creates a misleading impression of stability out of what was always a diverse and in some respects contradictory phenomenon. Christian democracy, as the case of Hungary well demonstrates, was a term capable of many meanings, some of which looked backwards rather than forwards. The ultramontane and anti-liberal origins of much of the social Catholicism and Christian democracy of the late nineteenth century are now widely accepted by historians.[31] The First World War in many respects marked a decisive watershed in the development of such ideas. Nostalgic visions of a world of medieval guilds and *ancien régime* monarchy largely disappeared, and the social Catholicism of the inter-war years had a much more pragmatic and realistic character. Nevertheless, an inertia of mentalities remained and, if some Catholic intellectuals and exiles of the 1930s seem very obviously to prefigure in their writings a post-1945 vision of Catholics as an active minority within a plural and secular society, they did not constitute the dominant current. Instead, most Catholic democrats of the inter-war years, as manifested for example in the workers' movements of the era, remained wedded to a more traditional definition of their actions as working within the Catholic pillar to create a distinctively Catholic form of social justice.

The second difficulty raised by use of the term 'Christian democracy' is that it strives too hard to build a continuity with the post-1945 era. Certainly, some of the contributors to this volume find trends within Catholic politics of the 1930s that pointed towards subsequent developments. Jean-Claude Delbreil, for example, describes the Popular Democratic Party as an essential step towards the establishment of the Mouvement Républicain Populaire (MRP) after the Second World War, while Emmanuel Gerard sees the formation of the Catholic Bloc in Belgium in 1936 as anticipating the creation of the Christelijke Volkspartij-Parti Social Chrétien (CVP-PSC) in 1945. These are valid points, but it would be misleading to extrapolate from them to present the Catholic politics of the inter-war years as a road that led to a logical terminus in Christian democrat politics after the Second World War. To do so would not merely impose a crude teleological perspective on the diverse trends evident within Catholic politics during the 1920s and 1930s, but also accord too great an importance to the years immediately after 1945 as the moment when a modern and pluralist Christian democracy was founded. As studies of Catholic politics in the later 1940s and the 1950s are now clarifying, there was in fact much in the Christian democrat politics of that era that recalled the rather undemocratic mentalities of the inter-war years. The real moment of transition perhaps occurred only in the 1960s, a decade which, it is fair to guess, will soon emerge as a major focus of work on Catholic politics.[32]

Catholic politics of the inter-war years therefore needs to be assessed on its own terms. Although often overshadowed in much writing on Catholic politics by prior and subsequent events, these years in fact constituted a decisive moment of experience, experiment and transition. This was evident in at least three respects. First, it was in the 1920s and 1930s that Catholicism established itself as one of the major electoral forces in modern European politics. Whatever the difficulties of unity experienced by many Catholic parties, they undoubtedly emerged as mass movements capable of competing effectively for the support of an increasingly sophisticated electorate. Second, the various ideological forms adopted by Catholic politics during the inter-war years, ranging from quasi-fascism to a putative Christian democracy, demonstrated the vitality of

THE EVOLUTION OF INTER-WAR POLITICAL CATHOLICISM

Catholicism as a political doctrine. Although there was no single definition of Catholic political values in inter-war Europe, the connection between religious faith and political ideology was decisively established. Finally, the rapid expansion in Catholic social and economic organizations, especially of farmers' leagues and trade unions, made Catholics powerful and indispensable participants in the politics of corporatist negotiation that was becoming the norm in much of Europe. In these various ways, Catholic politics had become not merely an integral element of modern European politics but also one of its most influential architects.

NOTES

1 I have largely dispensed with references to the other chapters in this book, and have limited the notes to a number of references to the other existing historiography.
2 On this point, I find myself in agreement with Stathis Kalyvas, *The Rise of Christian Democracy in Europe* (Ithaca, NY and London 1996), p. 12. In other respects, his political science interpretation of Catholic politics differs markedly from that presented here.
3 It is the German school of historical writing on Catholicism that has produced the most distinguished manifestations of such an approach, both in its virtues and occasionally its weaknesses. See for example the work of Rudolf Morsey and Winfried Becker (eds), *Christliche Demokratie in Europa. Grundlagen und Entwicklungen seit dem 19. Jahrhundert* (Cologne and Vienna 1988) and Winfried Becker (ed.), *Die Minderheit als Mitte. Die Deutsche Zentrumspartei in der Innenpolitik des Reiches 1871–1933* (Paderborn 1986).
4 I consider some of these methodological problems in greater detail in Martin Conway, 'Introduction', in Tom Buchanan and Martin Conway (eds), *Political Catholicism in Europe 1918–1965* (Oxford 1996), pp. 1–33.
5 Urs Altermatt, *Der Weg der Schweizer Katholiken ins Ghetto* (Zurich 1972).
6 For a perhaps rather maximalist account of this change, see Martin Conway, 'Building the Christian City: Catholics and Politics in inter-war francophone Belgium', *Past and Present*, 128 (1990), pp. 117–51.
7 See the chapter by Lukas Rölli-Alkemper in this book.
8 See for example Michael Gehler, 'Richard Coudenhove-Kalergi, Paneuropa und Österreich 1923–1972', in Helmut Wohnout (ed.), *Demokratie und Geschichte. Jahrbuch des Karl von Vogelsang-Instituts zur Erforschung der Geschichte der christlichen Demokratie in Österreich*, 2 (Vienna 1998), pp. 143–67. See also the chapters by Guido Müller and Wolfram Kaiser in this book.
9 The Netherlands provides perhaps the most emphatic manifestation of this phenomenon. See also Paul Luykx, 'The Netherlands', in Buchanan and Conway, *Political Catholicism*, pp. 219–47.
10 See the chapter by Arnold Suppan in this book as well as Mary Vincent, *Catholicism in the Second Spanish Republic* (Oxford 1996).
11 For a good example of the solidity of the Catholic–Socialist frontier in the context of a provincial city, see Charlie Jeffery, *Social Democracy in the Austrian Provinces, 1918–1934. Beyond Red Vienna* (London 1995), pp. 34–5, 148–50. See also the comments on the town of Miskolc in the chapter by Czaba Fazekas in this book.

12 Vincent, *Catholicism*, p. 257.
13 Dermot Keogh, *The Vatican, the Bishops and Irish Politics* (Cambridge 1986).
14 See also Antony Polonsky, *Politics in Independent Poland 1921–1939* (Oxford 1972), pp. 83–4, 241.
15 For a recent examination of this phenomenon, see Carl Strikwerda, *A House Divided. Catholics, Socialists and Flemish Nationalists in Nineteenth-Century Belgium* (Lanham 1997).
16 Marc Agostino, *Le Pape Pie XI et l'opinion publique (1922–1939)* (Rome 1991); Jean Chélini and Joël-Benoît d'Onorio (eds), *Pie XII et la cité: la pensée et l'action politiques de Pie XII* (Aix and Marseille 1988); Oliver Logan, 'Pius XII: *romanità*, prophesy and charisma', *Modern Italy*, 3/2 (1998), pp. 237–47.
17 James F. McMillan, 'France', in Buchanan and Conway, *Political Catholicism*, pp. 40–56.
18 Wilfried Loth, 'Integration und Erosion: Wandlungen des katholischen Milieus in Deutschland', in Wilfried Loth (ed.), *Deutscher Katholizismus im Umbruch zur Moderne* (Stuttgart 1991), pp. 266–81.
19 See also Dirk Luyten, 'Politiek corporatisme en de crisis van de liberale ideologie (1920–1944)', *Belgisch Tijdschrift voor Nieuwste Geschiedenis*, 24 (1993), pp. 107–84; Roland Ruffieux, *Le mouvement chrétien-social en Suisse romande 1891–1949* (Fribourg 1969), pp. 163–76.
20 See particularly Klaus-Michael Mallmann, 'Ultramontanismus und Arbeiterbewegung im Kaiserreich. Überlegungen am Beispiel des Saarreviers', in Loth, *Deutscher Katholizismus*, pp. 76–94; Strikwerda, *A House Divided*; Don Kalb, *Expanding Class. Power and Everyday Politics in Industrial Communities, The Netherlands, 1850–1950* (Durham and London 1997), pp. 44–50, 67–72. On Silesia, see the chapter by Leszek Kuk in this book as well as Anna Zarnowska, 'Religion and Politics: Polish Workers *c*. 1900', *Social History*, 16 (1991), pp. 299–316.
21 See also William Patch, *Christian Trade Unions in the Weimar Republic 1918–1933: The Failure of 'Corporate Pluralism'* (New Haven, CT and London 1985); Paul Wynants, 'La controverse Cardijn-Valschaerts (March–April 1931)', *Revue belge d'histoire contemporaine*, 15 (1984), pp. 103–36.
22 Robert O. Paxton, *French Peasant Fascism* (New York and Oxford 1997); Jonathan Osmond, *Rural Protest in the Weimar Republic: the Free Peasantry in the Rhineland and Bavaria* (New York and Basingstoke 1993); Kevin Passmore, *From Liberalism to Fascism: the Right in a French Province, 1928–1939* (Cambridge 1997); Shelley Baranowski, 'East Elbian Landed Elites and Germany's Turn to Fascism. The *Sonderweg* Revisited', *European History Quarterly*, 26 (1996), pp. 209–40.
23 See Paul Corner, *Fascism in Ferrara, 1915–1925* (London 1975).
24 See also Robert G. Moeller, *German Peasants and Agrarian Politics, 1914–1924: The Rhineland and Westphalia* (Chapel Hill, NC and London 1986); Alfred Diamant, *Austrian Catholics and the First Republic* (Princeton, NJ 1960).
25 See also Leen Van Molle, *Ieder voor allen. De belgische Boerenbond 1890–1990* (Leuven 1990), pp. 271–305.
26 See also Rudolf Morsey, *Der Untergang des politischen Katholizismus. Die Zentrumspartei zwischen christlichem Selbstverständnis und 'Nationaler Erhebung' 1932/33* (Stuttgart and Zurich 1977), pp. 20–33.
27 Loth, 'Integration und Erosion', pp. 277–8.
28 See Richard J. Wolff and Jörg K. Hoensch (eds), *Catholics, the State and the European Radical Right 1919–1945* (Boulder, CO 1987).

29 See also, for France, Renée Bédarida, *Les armes de l'esprit: Témoignage Chrétien (1941–1944)* (Paris 1977).
30 Recent examples of this interpretation include Noel D. Cary, *The Path to Christian Democracy. German Catholics and the Party System from Windthorst to Adenauer* (Cambridge, MA 1996); Jean-Dominique Durand, 'La mémoire de la démocratie chrétienne en 1945. Antécédents, expériences et combats', in Emiel Lamberts (ed.), *Christian Democracy in the European Union* (Leuven 1997), pp. 13–26. Other historians of Christian democracy prefer to pass over the inter-war years in silence, implying rather than proving some form of connection between the Christian democracy of the 1890s and that of the 1940s. For a striking example of such a silence, see Kalyvas, *The Rise of Christian Democracy in Europe*.
31 In relation to France, see Emile Poulat, 'Pour une nouvelle compréhension de la démocratie chrétienne', *Revue d'histoire ecclésiastique*, 70 (1975), pp. 5–38; Philip Nord, 'Three views of Christian Democracy in fin-de-siècle France', *Journal of Contemporary History*, 19 (1984), pp. 713–27.
32 See for example Maria Mitchell, 'Materialism and Secularism: CDU Politicians and National Socialism, 1945–1949', *Journal of Modern History*, 67 (1995), pp. 278–308. See also Conway, 'Introduction', pp. 28–33.

13

Anticipated Exile of Catholic Democrats: The Secrétariat International des Partis Démocratiques d'Inspiration Chrétienne

Guido Müller

Institutionalized co-operation between around fifty representatives of Catholic parties from eleven European countries[1] began at the end of 1925, and took place largely at eight congresses between 1925 and 1932. These were held in 1925 in Paris, 1926 in Brussels, 1927 in Cologne, 1928 in s'Hertogenbosch, 1929 in Paris, 1930 in Antwerp, 1931 in Luxemburg and 1932 in Cologne. One can see even in the choice of location just where the emphasis lay geographically, and also the strongly Western European orientation of co-operation between the Catholic parties. The preparation and work involved in the congresses was undertaken by an executive committee[2] that was active until 1939, and by an office in Paris. Collaboration followed in a very loose and increasingly non-committal form. This was even more the case from the late 1920s on, when the Vatican gave up on political Catholicism by first withdrawing its support for the Italian Partito Popolare. With the end of the German Centre Party in 1933 the European work largely broke down. The problem of discontinued co-operation was not solely a result of structural and political conditions in international relations in the inter-war period. What was decisive was, above all, the fact that Christian democratic ideas within the Catholic parties in the inter-war period were of very little importance. Such ideas were not representative of the confessional parties after the First World War. The attempts at transnational collaboration between individual Christian democratic politicians had therefore no direct effect on European politics.

The importance of co-operation was initially on the level of personal exchange between a small group of individual politicians, who repeatedly took part in international meetings. In addition, Christian democratic thinking played a role in the forming of a tradition of ideals for these politicians. They created an avant-garde in their time that was the basis for later developments after the Second World War, without causing any direct strains on continuity. This was true, on the one hand, for their attempts at building up a Christian democratic, Christian Social and interconfessional orientation. On the other, they count as being among the earliest ventures in co-operation of confessional parties in a transnational European context. Both were to achieve political relevance in Europe only after the end of the Second World War and during the Cold War. Until then, party politicians could only play a leading role in their own countries and on an international level in connection with experiences that were associated with the national collapse of states on the continent and with individual persecution and exile. The war and its ending by the great powers, the USA and USSR, was of special importance psychologically for the change of consciousness to a wider European and Christian democratic commitment. What was now often decisive for an outstanding political position in the West European states after 1945 was the relationship the confessional politicians had to the Western powers.

Possibly a further starting point for a European Christian democratic consciousness after 1945 were the early negative experiences in the Locarno era, alongside wartime experiences. Its continuity and importance should not, however, be overvalued. Only a very thin personal connection and continuity of ideals existed from the inter-war period to the period after the Second World War. This fine line was carried by the exile groups in Great Britain and later in the USA – by People and Freedom and the International Christian Democratic Union founded in 1940–41, and above all by their outstanding representatives, the Dutchman J. A. Veraart and the Italian Luigi Sturzo. The Anglo-American experiences carry at least as much weight for the later European and Christian democratic commitment as the older, rather unsuccessful experiences of the 1920s. More exact analysis is necessary here, however, that would take into consideration personal networking and the exchange of ideas among those in exile and the societies taking up those ideas.[3]

Thus we can conceive of the theme of this chapter, from the perspective of post-war history, as anticipated exile. In addition to this later development, important politicians who were participating in transnational collaboration in the 1920s were already at that time in exile. They had been driven out of their home countries and were indeed already exiled, such as the Italian Christian democrats. Luigi Sturzo was not only the initiator, but also a symbolic figurehead for the early Christian democratic collaborative ventures. Other representatives were increasingly isolated in their parties, for example the German Democrats and the internationally aligned politicians on the left wing of the Centre Party. Others were, with their party, marginalized in their own country. This happened to the French representatives. Finally, conservative Christian people's parties – such as those in Switzerland or in Austria – were hardly represented, or else only irregularly. They were stronger in international collaborations on other political and societal levels than within the Secrétariat International des Partis

Démocratique D'Inspiration Chrétienne (SIPDIC). A great diversity within European forms of co-operation in extremely different groupings and structures is especially characteristic of the inter-war period.

In the 1930s there was no more political space for the Christian democratic stance, and international activities suffered the same fate, apart from undertakings by those in exile. Dominating them were the concordat politics of the Vatican and the policies of authoritarian and fascist states, while the priorities of the Church hierarchy towards the laity were in the context of Catholic Action, with its mistrust of democratic parliamentarism. Right-wing Catholic anti-democratic currents became increasingly important in Europe in the 1930s, and marginalized Christian democratic tendencies even more strongly. They had, in any case, always been minority tendencies.

This is why an isolated examination of the theme that is concerned exclusively with the history of institutions and politics can only be seen to be fair from one side.[4] The dominant cultural and political-societal currents at that time were of decisive relevance for the success and significance of such an initiative. After 1919, however, the times were highly unfavourable for Christian democratic and transnational developments. These remained minority positions to which many were hostile. The period after the First World War was determined by a political, cultural and social crisis consciousness. Christian democratic co-operation also suffered in this scenario of a 'Christian civilization'. The governing economic and social insecurities led almost everywhere to the majority defending the traditional bastions of confessional convictions and positions. Thus the ideas of defence of the 'Occident', in connection to a Catholic movement of renewal, became increasingly attractive in the period from the 1920s to the 1950s.[5]

The political atmosphere was marked by sharp conflicts between two tendencies of the period. On the one hand, there was an ever-increasing and accelerated internationalization. This was demonstrated in the activities of the League of Nations and the beginnings of new international economic and security politics, a trend characterized by international economic cartels and security pacts. On the other hand, another movement – nationalistic regression – with its efforts towards self-sufficiency, isolationism and demarcation, set itself up in opposition.[6] Both currents crossed each other's paths in their attempts to bring about transnational parliamentary co-operation between Catholic parties. The individual representatives were initially concerned with gaining a large following for the new Christian democratic ideas and possibly finding understanding, alliance partners and support abroad. Opposition arose at the same time on different fronts: against social democracy and right-wing Catholicism, against retreating liberalism and against the rise of bolshevism and fascism. The transnational aspect and the idea of European solidarity was pushed by this ever more into the background.

ANTICIPATED EXILE OF CATHOLIC DEMOCRATS

INSTITUTIONAL AND POLICY DEVELOPMENTS

All the problems that were to occur later had their roots in the form taken by the founding of the SIPDIC in December 1925 in Paris. It took place on the initiative of the Italian, Christian democratic politician in exile, Luigi Sturzo, who had lived in London since 1924, in connection with the just-founded small French Parti Démocrate Populaire (PDP). This had orientated itself at its formation in autumn 1924, in both name and programme, towards Sturzo's Italian Partito Popolare (PPI) created in 1919.[7] In the French sister party, Georges Thibout, Marcel Prelot, Robert Cornilleau, Paul Simon, Henri Simondet, Raymond Laurent, Philippe de Las Casas and Louis-Alfred Pagès were especially interested in an international level. Thus the SIPDIC was initiated by two small political groups that were active on the periphery of the big confessional and political movements in their countries.[8] The important Catholic Party in Germany, the Centre Party, took part in the first Paris congress at which 34 delegates were present. France had 22 delegates, Belgium two, Italy two, Poland three and Germany five – although it was already represented by a travel group partially financed by the German foreign ministry.

The first Paris congress was an event that anticipated the internal exile of a minority. This minority was not only a small number of left-wing Christian democrats who were close to the unions. It was also a minority with a European disposition in a continent torn by increasing nationalism. The strong French presence, with a majority of chamber delegates and members of the executive commission of the party present, reflected the dominance of the host and guaranteed this role for future activities. The SIPDIC was, from 1925 on, always led by a Frenchman. After Laurent and Las Casas in the early years, Simondet took over in 1928. He was Professor of German at the École des Sciences Politiques in Paris. The strong French leadership from the very start had the effect of provoking German mistrust. Two representatives of the workers' wing of the Union catholique belge / Katholiek Verbond van België were present from Belgium – Hendrik Heyman and Father Georges Rutten. The Italians were represented by Sturzo and by the journalist Domenico Russo, who was resident in Paris at that time. Representing Germany from the very start were Joseph Joos and Helene Weber, both members of the Reichstag, the general secretary of the Centre Party, Heinrich Vockel and the director of the party newspaper *Germania*, Richard Kuenzer. Some sources also list the Paris correspondent for the *Germania* and *Kölnische Volkszeitung* newspapers, Henning Pfafferott, as being among the participants.[9] These Centre Party politicians made great efforts towards a German–French rapprochement.[10] The Italian, Sturzo, was looked on highly in Catholic democratic and pacifist circles both in France and on the left of the German Centre Party. That is why he seemed to be a suitable go-between for a Franco–German rapprochement. This rapprochement was recognized very quickly after the First World War as being the central problem for European co-operation.[11] Sturzo had already, at the start of the 1920s, striven towards an accommodation between victors and vanquished through the international parliamentary collaboration of democratically minded Christian politicians. With this aim in mind, he met representatives of the union wing of the Centre Party on his travels in Germany: people like Carl Sonnenschein, Joseph Wirth, Heinrich Brauns, Johannes Giesberts, Adam Stegerwald, August Pieper and Karl Muth. At the founding meeting of the SIPDIC in Paris on 12 and 13 December 1925, and at the second meeting in Brussels on 22 and 23 March 1926, only representatives of the Centre Party's left wing were present: Joos, Weber, Vockel and Kuenzer. They also participated in SIPDIC co-operation after 1925–26.

However, after the Locarno Treaty was signed in 1925 between seven European countries, including France and Germany, guaranteeing (among other provisions) the Franco-German border, the majority in the Centre Party saw an initiative stemming from French politicians – despite the PPI's support of Briand's policy of reconciliation – as still being suspect and part of French power politics. This was even more true after the political move to the right that the Centre Party undertook from 1928 onwards. Right-wing politicians critical of democracy in the Centre Party increasingly set the tone and were looking for partners in France other than the parliamentary PDP. Thus the French complained in 1932, at the SIPDIC Conference in Cologne, about the absence of representative Centre Party politicians – and this on German ground. The previous year, in Luxembourg, the Germans had even withdrawn completely and at short notice. With the clearing of the Rhineland by French troops in 1930, one of the last great successes of Stresemann's foreign policy – the aim of the rapprochement policy with France – had been in a certain sense accomplished for the especially strong Rheinland Centre Party.[12]

The founders of the SIPDIC were not interested in a Church-bound 'Catholic International'. The focus of their thinking was, rather, a political and inter-confessional 'international people's party'. Thus they explicitly kept their distance from the Church hierarchy. Already at this time the image of the 'white international' in opposition to 'red'-socialist and 'black'-Catholic internationals emerged.[13] While the Italians strove towards a permanent inter-parliamentary union, the French pushed through their idea of a central information office with a bulletin appearing regularly, thus strengthening their hold on a French headquarters. The Italians, for their part, were additionally weakened by their exile status.

Emphasis was placed on a non-political stance right at the start, in order to bridge national differences and domestic party peculiarities and priorities. According to the draft SIPDIC constitution:

the main aim of the association is to better realize the social and ethical aims of the different individual groups or parties in each state through the promotion of contacts among like-minded people, exchanging programmatic ideas and morally aligning the different groups and parties.[14]

An anti-fascist resolution suggested by Sturzo therefore attracted little support at the first Paris congress at the end of 1925. His suggestion at the next meeting, 'investigating fascism, bolshevism and defining the relationship of the Christian parties to socialism',[15] likewise had no resonance. The French, as well as the Germans, opposed the discussion of foreign policy – surely because of the attitude of their governments to Fascist Italy. The only outcome of the weakly attended second congress in Brussels in 1926 was a resolution about the relationship to democracy and the 'organization of peace' in Europe in accordance with the rules of the League of Nations.[16] In Brussels, there were only four delegations with a total of 14 participants present; three each from Belgium and Germany, six from France and two from Italy. The small number of delegates from so few countries facilitated the formulation of a substantial resolution. Polish representatives as well as invited parties from Lithuania, Austria, Switzerland and Czechoslovakia sent their apologies.

The participants in the resolution declared their allegiance to democracy because it was in accordance with the needs of the time. The resolution stated that the results of post-war difficulties were seen in fascism and bolshevism, both of which destroyed the lively relationship between state and people through the aggression of state institutions. Democracy had to battle against these dangerous political currents, avoiding both the rule of the masses and excessive individualism. True democracy was based on the appeal to moral forces, freedom, full respect for the human being and the upholding of Christian morality. The SIPDIC was never again to find such clear words. In this, it is clear just how far currents critical of democracy, or even anti-democratic currents themselves, had gained hold in the Catholic parties in Europe as early as the end of the 1920s. It is also worth noting that the founders of the SIPDIC, to avoid domestic political problems for the PDP, could also not agree on the term 'Christian democratic' and chose instead the rather long-winded Partis démocratiques d'inspiration chrétienne. Nor was there any talk of republicanism. It is surely not by chance that only a small number of representatives of the Locarno states took part. These states tried carefully to come to an agreement about more far-reaching political aims. Dutch and Central and Eastern European party representatives were characteristically missing.

In 1931 the executive committee, on French initiative, passed a declaration for securing peace by economic and political collaboration.[17] Apart from this, the representatives abstained from common political demonstrations and activities. Representatives from France, Belgium, Italy, the Netherlands and Germany could not agree either on their concept of democracy or on co-operative or organic state constitutions. There was more confusion over ideas and concepts than attempts at explanation and striving for agreement.[18] Getting to know one another and exchange of information were the focus. The European concept had transnational collaboration as its starting point. It was looking for a 'third way' between international pacifism and enforced regulation of conflicts. With the self-dissolution of the Centre Party in 1933, a substantial German partner was lacking. Although the work carried on up until 1939, its scope was now limited. Especially controversial among the remaining members was the Concordat between the German Reich and the Vatican of 1933 and Dollfuss's policies in Austria.

STRUCTURAL DEFICIENCIES IN EARLY CHRISTIAN DEMOCRATIC CO-OPERATION

There were many structural and institutional reasons greatly hindering collaboration between the – at most – some dozens of democratically orientated representatives of Catholic parties. Agreement was at first made more difficult by the weight of national traditions and characteristics, by the different national party structures and national loyalties, and above all by the arguments about the revision of the Versailles Treaty or the preserving of the status quo. This was especially clear in the refusal to enter into discussions and the expressions of mistrust between the Poles, the Germans and the French after Locarno in 1925, which made common concrete statements almost impossible. Second, the Catholic parties also had greatly different vote-catching potential, as well as very different positions in their respective systems of government.[19] Very large and strong parties, small parties from the margins and exiled individuals co-operated with one another. The form taken ranged from exile party to opposition party to small or large party in government. Thus their actual political weight varied, and they were bound to different degrees by their governments' foreign policies. Further, the emphasis placed on foreign policy in their home countries was very different. The Italians in exile could develop clearer democratic and international positions than could the representatives of the Centre Party, who had not only to take into consideration majority opinion within their party, but also German foreign policy.

Third, two irreconcilable and incompatible directions stood in opposition in the European Catholic parties. There was a progressive, democratic parliamentary direction and a conservative, traditional wing critical of parliamentarism and marked by the battle against the ideas of 1789 and by anti-modernism. Criticism of parliamentarism was widespread on the continent and an especially great obstacle for the SIPDIC.[20] In addition, the critical distance between the official Church and the initiators inevitably led to grave acceptance problems for party co-operation on the part of the Catholic Church hierarchy. The Vatican clearly claimed sole right to formulate policies on international issues. The Catholic Church feared unwelcome competition to its international disciplinary and supervisory authorities. The protection of national Church interests was, in its own view, of more importance than the protection of democracy and internationalism. The Lateran Treaties and Concordats with Italy in 1929 and Germany in 1933 reflect this preference. The SIPDIC initiative thus lacked the decisive backing of the Church hierarchy, without which outsider status within the Rome-orientated confessional parties was unavoidable.

A fifth reason that militated against the initiative from the point of view of contemporaries was that internationalism was despised as being politically 'red', that is to say, communist or socialist in the sense of the 'left internationals'. The work was thus limited to small groups, to the almost complete exclusion of the public. This stood in the way of greater participation from wider sections of the parties. As a result of the very different levels of power of the representatives in their national party and government structures, there was no effective co-ordination of substantial political initiatives. The German Reich Chancellors Marx and Brüning were looking to use the strong French-dominated SIPDIC only for their own ends. In relation to the national parties, governments and the Vatican co-operation took on an almost 'conspiratory character'.

Christian democratic party co-operation was like a pupil who is rather behind. It was suspected of imitating other international groups, above all the left-wing Socialist International and International Trades Union Congress. Compared with other Catholic international groups, it also appeared to arrive rather late. In the context of these confessional associations and organizations, a much more important role was played after the First World War by the Catholic union movement, the peace movement and other Catholic organizations.[21] Essential among these were the Confédération Internationale des Syndicats Chrétiens formed in Utrecht in 1920, the Union Catholique d'études internationales launched in the same year, and the Union Internationale des Etudes Sociales, also formed in 1920. This was also the year that Marc Sangnier created his European movement for peace and mutual understanding. His mass movement, which attracted above all the youth, and his party *Jeune République*, which stood further left than the PDP, played a much more important role in Franco–German rapprochement and the development of a Christian European consciousness than the limited SIPDIC with its few party representatives. Its character as a movement comprising many groups, circles and initiatives was, in addition in its societal and cultural form, much more characteristic of the period after the First World War than an organization built on party co-operation.[22] Lastly, the organization Pax Romana of 1921, the Lake Constance conferences for Christian politics from 1921 to 1926 and the Fédération des Unions intellectuels/Europäischer Kulturbund from 1922–24 to 1934 should be mentioned. All that remained for the SIPDIC was to be only in small parts an organization orientated to the future. It was a catchment organization for the anticipated exile of a minority working against the anti-democratic trend of the time, and active within the context of right-wing majorities in their own parties.

ALTERNATIVE SOCIETAL AND POLITICAL FORMS OF INTERNATIONAL CATHOLIC CO-OPERATION

In the period after 1918, there was only very limited and concealed international co-operation in the Catholic realm outside the direct sphere of influence of the Vatican. There were other, very much more representative and politically more important forms of transnational co-operation than the endeavours of some Catholic politicians in the SIPDIC in the 1920s. These initiatives, which were at the centre of transnational networks in the 1920s and 1930s, are described below.

To begin with, there were connections between young conservative philo-fascist and anti-parliamentary groups and associations.[23] The congress of the Europäischer Kulturbund of the Austrian Prince Karl Anton Rohan and his journal *Europäische Revue* give examples of this trend, as did the big international European congress of the Volta Academy in Rome in 1932 to mark the ten-year anniversary of the founding of the fascist system in Italy. Catholic representatives were prominently represented there. In the Franco–German rapprochement movement, conservative, anti-liberal and nationalist representatives began to play a more important role than the early pacifistic, internationalist and democratic initiatives stemming from the beginning of the 1920s.[24] Bilateral meetings between Germany and France, Germany and Austria and Germany and Italy often played a more important role after the First World War than the early multilateral European or international contacts.

Pacifistic internationalism like Marc Sangier's Sillon, the youth association that arose out of it and the international peace congresses, as well as the Catholic Peace Movement, were of more quantitative and qualitative relevance in the 1920s than the meetings of party representatives, although even they had no direct political effect.[25] The factor of individual personalities is much more important in international relationships in the inter-war period than that of institutions or organizations. Attention should be drawn to a range of personalities other than Sturzo: the Austrian, Catholic politician and publicist Ignaz Seipel, the Germans

Joseph Wirth, Wilhelm Marx and Franz von Papen and the Frenchmen Marc Sangier, Wladimir d'Ormesson and Jean de Pange.

Finally, political-cultural journals and intellectual discussion circles played a very decisive role, one that has only begun to be researched. This is true of *Abendland*, which was published in Cologne, Munich and Berlin. It arose from a project of the Romanist Hermann Platz and the philosopher Alois Dempf and first appeared during 1925–30. The journal, which was close in spirit to the Catholic reform movement, offered European discussions and Franco-German dialogue extensive space on its pages. Prince Rohan's *Europäische Revue*,[26] which had been in existence since 1925, enjoyed an even greater distribution, reaching out beyond the Catholic milieu into middle-class, liberal, young conservative and philo-fascist circles. Important European meeting centres up until 1933–34 were Pontigny, the Semaines Sociales and the annual congress of the Fédération des Unions Intellectuelles/Europäischer Kulturbund in Paris, Milan, Vienna, Frankfurt am Main, Heidelberg, Prague, Barcelona, Zurich, Krakow and Budapest.

As a result of the outsider status of SIPDIC politicians and the limits to institutionalized co-operation, attention should be drawn to societal and cultural cross-border contacts and exchange of ideas. In these contacts, the following themes were particularly controversial and were often consciously excluded in the congresses and work of the Christian democratic 'International': inter- and non-confessionalism and ecumenicity, criticism or acceptance of fascism and National Socialism, the relationship to the Catholic lay movement and to Catholic Action, the issue of collaboration with social democrats and the 'Abendland' discourse.[27] In these discourses, which cannot at this point be gone into further,[28] lay the potential for the development of a Christian democratic idea of international relationships, including those between people's parties, but not in the weak SIPDIC.

There is much work still to be done in examining even more closely in many areas just how far these ideals and discursive approaches from the 1920s and the early 1930s were strengthened and transformed by the experiences of the exiles after 1940 – above all in Britain and the USA – and the experiences of National Socialism and Stalinism. Serious reservations must, however, be registered against attempts by historians who wish to construct an unbroken line of continuity from the SIPDIC and the timid forays of the 1920s through to Christian democratic party co-operation in the so-called 'Geneva Circle' and the Nouvelles Équipes Internationales after 1945. Lines of tradition are not evident in the case of biographies. The participants in the meetings prior to 1933 and after 1945 belonged to different groups of people. Hardly any direct connections can be made concerning the content of transnational links and debates, due to a lack of discussion at the congresses in the 1920s and early 1930s. It is difficult to even speak about Christian democracy in the inter-war period in terms of parties. The anticipated exile of individual democratic representatives of Catholic parties in the 1920s was so strongly severed in the Second World War that a new beginning after 1945 appeared necessary, not only for the national confessional parties but also for international co-operation in Europe.

NOTES

1 Belgium: Ligue des Travailleurs Chrétiens de Belgique within the Catholic Party; Germany: Centre Party (Zentrum); France: Parti Démocrate Populaire; Italy: Partito Popolare Italiano (representatives in exile were Luigi Sturzo, Domenico Russo and Francesco L. Ferrari); Lithuania: Christian Democratic Party; Luxembourg: Rechtspartei/Parti de la Droit; Netherlands: Rooms-Katholieke Staatspartij; Austria: Christlich-Soziale Partei, Switzerland: Schweizerische Konservative Volkspartei; Czechoslovakia: Tschechoslovakische Volkspartei, and a Catholic Party from Hungary.
2 Seven extended meetings of the executive committee took place between 1933 and 1939.
3 See also Wolfram Kaiser's chapter in this book.
4 Roberto Papini, *The Christian-Democrat International* (London 1996); idem, *Il coraggio della democrazia. Sturzo et l'Internazionale popolare tra le due guerre* (Rome 1995).
5 Richard Faber, *Abendland. Ein politischer Kampfbegriff* (Berlin and Vienna 2002); Guido Müller and Vanessa Plichta, 'Zwischen Rhein und Donau. Abendländisches Denken zwischen deutsch-französischen Verständigungsinitiativen und konservativ-katholischen Integrationsmodellen 1923–1957', *Journal of European Integration History*, vol. 5, no. 2 (1999), pp. 17–47.
6 For the context of international relations, see Gottfried Niedhart, *Internationale Beziehungen 1917–1947* (Paderborn 1989); Rene Girault und Robert Frank, *Turbulente Europe et nouveaux mondes, 1914–1941* (Paris 1988).
7 Jean-Claude Debreil, *Centrisme et Démocratie Chrétienne en France. Le Parti Démocrate Populaire des origines au M.R.P. 1919–1944* (Paris 1990).
8 For more general information about the development of Catholic parties in Europe, see Jean-Marie Mayeur, *Des Partis catholiques à la Démocratie chrétienne XIX–XXe siècles* (Paris 1980).
9 Alwin Hanschmidt, 'Eine christliche-demokratische "Internationale" zwischen den Weltkriegen. Das "Secrétariat International des Partis Démocratiques d'Inspiration Chrétienne" in Paris', in Winfried Becker and Rudolf Morsey (eds), *Christliche Demokratie in Europa* (Cologne and Vienna 1988), pp. 153–88, here pp. 166–70.
10 See Jean-Claude Delbreil, *Les catholiques français et les tentatives de rapprochement franco-allemand 1920–1933* (Metz 1972).
11 See Guido Müller, *Deutsch-Französische Gesellschaftsbeziehungen nach dem Ersten Weltkrieg. Das Deutsch-Französische Studienkomitee und der Europäische Kulturbund im Rahmen deutsch-französischer Verständigungsbewegungen 1924–1933* (Munich 2004).
12 See the last issue of the Cologne journal *Abendland*, 1930; Franz Knipping, *Deutschland, Frankreich und das Ende der Locarno-Ära 1928–1931* (Munich

1987); Philipp Heyde, *Das Ende der Reparationen. Deutschland, Frankreich und der Youngplan 1929–1932* (Paderborn 1998).There has as yet been no analysis of the foreign policy and international relations of the Centre Party in the Weimar Republic. Considering its important role as a governmental party – not only because of its Reich Chancellors Wirth, Marx and Brüning – this is regrettable. See two interesting recent biographies with rather differing assessments of Chancellor Wirth: Heinrich Küppers, *Joseph Wirth. Parlamentarier, Minister und Kanzler der Weimarer Republik* (Stuttgart 1997); Ulrike Hörster-Philipps, *Joseph Wirth 1879–1956. Eine politische Biographie* (Paderborn 1998).

13 Luigi Sturzo, 'The White International', *People and Freedom*, 15 April 1941; Giuseppe Rossini, 'Primi tentative per una Internazionale bianca', in idem, *Il movimento cattolico nel periodo fascista* (Rome 1966), pp. 195–222; Roberto Papini, *Il coraggio della democrazia*, pp. 37–55.
14 Quotation taken from Alwin Hanschmidt, 'Eine christliche-demokratische Internationale'.
15 Heinrich Vockel, Bericht über eine Zusammenkunft Christliche Parteien Europas am 12. und 13.12.1925 in Paris. Historisches Archiv der Stadt Köln, Nachlass Wilhelm Marx, No. 225.
16 Hanschmidt, 'Eine christlich-demokratische Internationale', pp. 174–5.
17 See the resolutions in *Bulletin trimestriel du SIPDIC* in Hanschmidt, 'Eine christlich demokratische Internationale', pp. 174–5.
18 Ibid., pp. 177–81; Papini, *Il coraggio della democrazia*, pp. 171–215.
19 Stefano Bartolini und Peter Mair, *Identity, Competition and Electorate Availability. The Stabilisation of European Electorate 1885–1985* (Cambridge, MA 1990).
20 This was similarly true of the Interparliamentary Union and other party co-operation in the liberal-democratic or agrarian spectrum.
21 Dieter Riesenberger, *Die katholische Friedensbewegung in der Weimarer Republik* (Düsseldorf 1971); Michel Launay, *La CFTC, origines et développements 1919–1940* (Paris 1973); Jean-Dominique Durand, *L'Europe de la Démocratie chrétienne* (Brussels 1995).
22 Madeleine Barthelemy-Madaule, *Marc Sangier 1873–1950* (Paris 1973); Jean-Claude Delbreil, *Les catholiques français*; idem (ed.), *Marc Sangier, Témoignages* (Paris 1997).
23 Michael Arthur Ledeen, *Universal Fascism: The Theory and Practice of the Fascist International, 1928–1936* (New York 1972).
24 See the examples in Guido Müller, 'Gesellschaftsgeschichte und internationale Beziehungen: die deutsch-französische Verständigung nach dem Ersten Weltkrieg', in idem. (ed.), *Deutschland und der Westen: Internationale Beziehungen im 20. Jahrhundert* (Wiesbaden 1998), pp. 49–64.
25 Riesenberger, *Die katholische Friedensbewegung in der Weimarer Republik*.
26 Guido Müller, 'Von Hugo von Hofmannsthals "Traum des Reiches" zum Europa unter nationalsozialistischer Herrschaft: "Die Europäische Revue" 1925–1936/44', in Hans-Christof Kraus (ed.), *Konservative Zeitschriften zwischen Kaiserreich und Diktatur* (Berlin 2002), pp. 155–186.
27 See Müller and Plichta, 'Zwischen Rhein und Donau'.
28 See Emile Poulat, *Catholicisme, démocratie et socialisme: le mouvement catholique et Mgr Benigni de la naissance du socialisme a la victoire du fascism* (Tournai 1977); Jean-Marie Mayeur, *Catholicisme social et démocratie chrétienne* (Paris 1986); Doris von der Brelie-Lewien, 'Abendland und Sozialismus. Zur Kontinuität politisch-kultureller Denkhaltungen im Katholizismus von der

Weimarer Republik zur frühen Nachkriegszeit', in Detlev Lehnert und Klaus Megerle (eds), *Politische Teilkulturen zwischen Integration und Polarisierung. Zur politischen Kultur der Weimarer Republik* (Opladen 1990), pp. 188–219; Pierre Andreu, *Révoltes de l'esprit, les revues des années 30* (Paris 1991); Jutta Bohn, *Das Verhältnis zwischen katholischer Kirche und faschistischem Staat in Italien und die Rezeption in deutschen Zentrumskreisen (1922–1933)* (Frankfurt/Main 1992); Thomas Keller, 'Katholische Europakonzeptionen in den deutsch-französischen Beziehungen', in Hans Manfred Bock, Reinhard Meyer-Kalkus and Michel Trebitsch (eds), *Entre Locarno et Vichy. Les relations culturelles franco-allemandes dans les annees 1930* Vol. 1, (Paris 1993), pp. 222–33; Aram Mattioli (ed.), *Intellektuelle von Rechts. Ideologie und Politik in der Schweiz 1918–1939* (Zurich 1995); Thomas Keller, *Deutsch-Französische Dritte-Weg-Diskurse. Personalistische Intellektuellendebatten in der Zwischenkriegszeit* (Munich 2001).

14

Transnational Networks of Catholic Politicians in Exile

Wolfram Kaiser

Politically meaningful co-operation among Catholic parties in Europe had already become very difficult after Hitler's seizure of power in 1933.[1] After the outbreak of the Second World War and with the occupation of the Netherlands, Belgium, Luxembourg and France in 1940, such contacts could exist only in exile. The historical literature on political exile in Britain, the United States and other countries during the war is quite extensive. However, political exile is usually treated in a purely national context. Without doubt, questions of national collaboration and post-war reconstruction were of overriding importance to the majority of continental European politicians in exile. Transnational contacts and co-operation, however, also took place, and it is clearly crucial to know more precisely to what extent these contacts may have formed an organizational, or at least an intellectual, bridge to post-war European party collaboration and reconstruction.[2]

This chapter will analyse the contacts and co-operation among Catholic politicians in exile in Britain and the United States. After a brief survey of the Catholic experience of exile, it will discuss the degree of integration of these politicians in the Catholic communities in Britain and the United States and their contacts with the progressive democratic sections of these communities, especially with the People and Freedom Group founded in London in 1936. The chapter will then go on to assess the extent of transnational collaboration within the International Christian Democratic Union (ICDU), founded in London in February 1941, and the dominant ideas among the participating politicians for European reconstruction after the Second World War. It will thus be possible to assess the influence of the Catholic exile on the evolution of transnationalism in European Christian democracy from the inter-war to the post-war period and on the key issues of post-war reconstruction, especially economic and social reform, the future European or world organization and the German question.

EXILE OF CATHOLIC POLITICIANS 1925-45

Compared to the Social democrats, only relatively few Catholic politicians went into exile after 1922-25, 1933 or between the annexation of Austria in 1938 and the occupation of France in 1940. Initially, many conservative Catholics worked with the fascist and National Socialist regimes or with the German occupation forces, especially in Vichy France. Others, like the German and Italian post-war leaders Konrad Adenauer and Alcide De Gasperi, went into internal exile. Many, mostly younger, politically and socially more progressive Catholic democrats joined the national resistance. Georges Bidault succeeded Jean Moulin as leader of the French Resistance, collaborating closely with Pierre-Henri Teitgen, Paul and Alfred Coste-Floret and François de Menthon, all also leading figures in the Mouvement Républicain Populaire (MRP) after 1944.[3] Other Catholic politicians in the Resistance included Josef Müller, the first leader of the Bavarian Christian Social Union, and Felix Hurdes, the first secretary general of the Austrian People's Party. Moreover, while most communists fled to the Soviet Union and many social democrats to Britain, due to their links with the Labour Party, the numerically fewer Catholic politicians in exile were more dispersed, thus complicating any transnational contacts among them.[4]

The Catholic political refugees from Italy, Germany and Austria were initially very isolated politically, and their main problem was whether, and on what basis, to establish new links with the non-Catholic democratic political refugees, and especially with the socialists. When the Italian socialists and republicans had founded the Anti-Fascist Concentration in 1927, they had excluded the Partito Popolare Italiano (PPI) refugees because of the political support of the Vatican for Mussolini.[5] After a brief period of Popular Front collaboration between the socialists and communists after 1935, Sturzo established a close personal relationship with Count Sforza and other liberal and socialist refugees in the United States, but he refused to join the Mazzini Society of Italians in exile, which he regarded with some justification as a liberal anti-Catholic organization.[6] At the same time, many Austrian Christian Social politicians clung to the *Ständestaat* model for much longer than most Catholics within Austria and in the Austrian resistance, precluding closer contacts with the social democrats.

While the Catholic politicians from Italy, Germany and Austria concentrated on a rapprochement with other political groups from their own countries, the Catholic refugees from the Netherlands, Belgium, Luxembourg, France and East Central European countries, especially from Poland and Czechoslovakia, were naturally oriented primarily towards their national governments in exile in London and to official planning for post-war reconstruction.[7] Their transnational co-operation mainly took place at the governmental level, especially in the context of the negotiations between the Netherlands and Belgium about a customs union,[8] and of the bilateral talks leading up to the Polish–Czechoslovak Treaty of Confederation of January 1942.[9] Moreover, the establishment of other transnational contacts was further complicated by the fluctuation in the personnel of the governments in exile. The Belgian government, for example, started its work in London with only four ministers. August de Schryver, president of the Nouvelles Équipes Internationales (NEI) during the 1950s, arrived in Britain only at the beginning of August 1942. He was then on a mission in Washington and did not return to London until May 1943, when he became Interior Minister.[10] Shortly afterwards, in the early summer of 1943, Maurice Schumann, who was close to Charles de Gaulle and later played a prominent role in the MRP, had already left London when the Free French government moved to Algiers.

FACING BRITISH AND AMERICAN POLITICAL CATHOLICISM

At the political level, the Catholic politicians in exile had no natural partners in Britain and the United States, due to these countries' predominantly secular, non-confessional party traditions and the resulting absence of comparable Catholic parties. Unlike on the European continent – with the notable exception of Germany, Switzerland and the Netherlands – Catholicism formed minority cultures both in Britain and the United States that were politically entrenched, both for historical reasons and because they were at least partially identified with recent waves of immigration. The majority, especially of the Irish working-class immigrants, supported Labour, a preference that the Church leadership had publicly condoned in 1924–25.[11] In the United States, between 20 and 30 per cent of the population was Catholic in the 1930s. Many of the American Catholics, especially Italians and Poles, had come to the United States only from the 1880s onwards, and were still socially and politically dominated by the earlier waves of predominantly Protestant settlers of British and other North European descent. In the 1930s, they tended strongly to support Roosevelt's anti-capitalist rhetoric and New Deal economic policy.[12]

The profoundly disturbing experience of Catholic political refugees in the 1930s was the sheer extent of political support for Mussolini and Franco and the philo-fascism among the Catholic communities in Britain and the United States, which, as a result, were also generally the most ardent supporters of the policies of appeasement and of isolationism. When he arrived in Britain, Sturzo was struck by the extent to which the perception of fascist Italy seemed to be formed by the Rothermere press.

According to this view, Mussolini was the first Italian politician to have established an 'orderly' society. He was also staunchly anti-communist, a preference that united working-class Catholic Labour supporters and middle- and upper-class Protestant Conservatives. Even among the most staunchly anti-fascist, progressive Catholic democrats, many were attracted by the Portuguese corporatist constitution, *Estado Novo*, established by Salazar in March 1933.[13] These cleavages were highlighted by the political debate about the Spanish Civil War. Flint has shown that the Catholic press in Britain was initially sceptical about Franco's insurrection.[14] However, the atrocities committed by republican troops against the Church in the early phase of the war convinced not only the leading journal, *The Tablet*, that 'all those Spaniards who wish to see the Church survive in Spain will have had to side with the insurgents', who deserved at least moral support.[15] Catholic writers like Hilaire Belloc and Evelyn Waugh also supported Franco. Although the exact extent of support for Franco among working-class Catholics in Britain is disputed, it is clear that the religious cleavage largely overshadowed the class cleavage. Most Catholic Labour supporters, instead of siding with the Spanish socialists, were 'either neutral or thoroughly hostile towards the Spanish Republic'.[16]

Like Labour in Britain, it was the Democratic Party in the United States that was the almost natural political home of the socially disadvantaged Catholic immigrants, especially during the Roosevelt era. The 1930s, however, saw yet another attempt to establish a third party that would appeal to the idea of the traditional, rooted community and, being highly ambivalent about the process of modernization, would be more anti-capitalist and very hostile to internationalism. In many ways, this protest movement, like fascism in Europe, was the product 'of similar social and economic crises and drew from similar political traditions'.[17] However, it did not initially invoke racism or anti-Semitism. It strove for 'organic' social unity, but organized by small community institutions rather than by the state. Crucially, it lacked the charismatic leadership that Roosevelt exercised on the democratic left. The National Union for Social Justice was founded in December 1934, but its candidate in the 1936 presidential election, Congressman William Lemke, gained fewer than one million votes. The movement then became more radicalized and established contacts with American fascists.[18]

British appeasement policy during the 1930s was economically and politically motivated. Most Catholics staunchly defended it until the German aggression against Poland, and in some cases beyond the British declaration of war. It is indicative of the strength of the pro-appeasement feeling among Catholics in Britain that they often caused the greatest trouble for anti-appeasement politicians at the grassroots level.[19] Similarly, American policy towards Spain was influenced by well-organized Catholic opposition to arms sales to the republic. Roosevelt, who was personally inclined to support the republic, clearly refrained from doing so as a result of the aggressive lobbying by the Catholic Keep the Spanish Embargo Committee, which appealed to a very important Democratic constituency.[20]

In Britain and the United States, small groups of articulate, but hardly representative, liberal Catholics tried to provide an alternative intellectual and political focus and also to create a friendlier environment for Catholic politicians in exile. In Britain, the Catholic democratic tradition had been established and upheld mainly by the Christian Social Guild, founded in 1909, which had some 4,000 members in 1938.[21] A group of mostly middle-class Labour and Liberal supporters, many of them converts, eventually founded the People and Freedom Group in November 1936. According to one member, Anthony Moore, the group allowed progressive Catholic democrats for the first time 'to show an English Catholic contribution to political thought, to show too that Catholics did not necessarily support reaction'.[22] In the United States, liberal Catholics organized themselves against the so-called Christian Front and founded the Committee of Catholics for Human Rights with the support, among others, of John Ryan and Charles Miltner of the Catholic universities of Washington and Notre Dame.[23] Another American who was particularly concerned with aiding the Catholic politicians in exile was George N. Shuster. He had resigned from the *Commonweal* when it turned pro-Franco, and became president of the Catholic Hunter College in New York.[24] Later, partly on the initiative of Sturzo, the British People and Freedom Group also expanded across the Atlantic.

TRANSNATIONAL CONTACTS AND CO-OPERATION IN EXILE

The British People and Freedom Group consisted exclusively of Catholics, although some non-Catholics were linked to the group as 'friends'. Most members were middle-class and many were converts. Unlike the Catholic trade unionists, who had a tradition of close relations with the German Christian trade unions, many members of the People and Freedom Group had strong links with France, Belgium and Italy. According to the group's constitution, its general purpose was 'to promote a sound grasp of political and social problems, and to further the application of Christian principles to national and international life'.[25] The group regularly organized speeches, many of them by Catholic refugees, and it passed political resolutions. These were published in the newssheet *People & Freedom*, which appeared from 1938 and monthly during the war, and were also diffused through letters to the editor and other reports, mainly in Catholic publications, as well as in the *Manchester Guardian*, *The Times* and other daily newspapers. The group was relatively small, and its members often complained that their newssheet was not sold and read widely enough. On the other hand, it was not only read within Britain, but also by American Catholics, who later wanted to bring out a similar publication, and even by De Gasperi in the Vatican library.[26]

The People and Freedom Group's chairman during 1936–44 was Virginia Crawford. She was a co-founder of the Catholic Social Guild, a Labour borough councillor in London for 14 years, chairman during 1925–26 of the St Joan's Alliance, the Catholic women's suffrage society, and also editor of the anti-fascist journal, *Friends of Italian Freedom* from 1929 to 1931.[27] The group's honorary secretary responsible for the administrative work was Barbara Barclay Carter from 1936 to 1948, when she joined the United Nations in Geneva. Carter was born in the United States. Her father was American and her mother Irish. She grew up in England, and in 1921 converted to Catholicism and studied medieval history and literature at the Sorbonne in Paris, becoming a Dante specialist. She met Sturzo in 1924 and later lived with him and a female friend in a house in London. She translated many books by Sturzo and other Catholic politicians in exile into English and became involved in refugee politics.[28]

It is also important to note that some of the group's Protestant 'friends' were quite influential and assisted the Catholic democrats in establishing indirect links with Labour and Conservative opponents of appeasement, including Winston Churchill. Henry Wickham Steed, for example, was at that time a lecturer in Central European history at King's College, London. The Duchess of Atholl was another 'friend'. She was not initially interested in foreign policy, but had the unabridged German version of Hitler's *Mein Kampf* personally translated for her in 1935 and became a vociferous opponent of her own government's appeasement policy.[29] She advocated drastic increases in defence spending early on and even sided with the republic in the Spanish Civil War. She played a leading role in the All Party Committee for Spanish Relief and, after a personal visit to Spain, her book *Searchlight on Spain*[30] sold roughly 100,000 copies during the first week alone. Inside the Conservative parliamentary party she was considered an anti-fascist hawk and maverick, but she did have close relations with Churchill and Anthony Eden, who resigned as Foreign Secretary in February 1938, and with other critics of Chamberlain's policy.

The People and Freedom Group was clearly a key element in a transnational political network of Catholic democrats, which, however, was only a loose one. The group had close links, for example, with the French publication *L'Aube*, and Carter participated in a congress of *Les amis de l'Aube* in Paris in November 1937.[31] The guest speakers included, for example, Alfredo Mendizábal, a professor at the University of Oviedo, who was later in exile in the United States and had close contacts with Sturzo and the leading French Catholic philosopher Jacques Maritain; and Javier Landaburu, a former deputy of the Spanish Cortes who was later the Basque representative in the NEI. De Schryver often went to the lectures,[32] and many other Catholic politicians in exile in London would have done the same. The group's role in facilitating transnational contacts among Catholic refugees from different countries during the war is also underlined by the fact that Crawford, Carter and Sturzo conceived the idea of a successor organization to the inter-war secretariat in Paris, and that the foundation of the ICDU was prepared at a People and Freedom Group meeting on 21 November 1940.[33]

Although the group could not agree to come out in favour of the Spanish Republic, and instead argued for a negotiated settlement, it was generally ahead of public opinion in Britain, and most certainly of the government. In early 1939, for example, it passed strongly worded resolutions against anti-Semitism and the persecution of Jews in Germany, and for a joint Western effort to restrain Franco after the Nationalists' victory and to grant a wide amnesty for Republicans.[34] Just after the British declaration of war, the group demanded the inclusion of the leading Conservative dissidents Churchill, Eden, Duff Cooper and Lord Cranborne into a new and 'truly National Government'.[35] The British example inspired several American Catholics to found similar groups, also named People and Freedom, in American cities, often seeking the advice of Sturzo.[36] Groups were established in New York, where Shuster acted as chairman; in Boston, where some of its 25 members were associated with the Catholic Association for International Peace; in Notre Dame, where the university professor Willis D. Nutting was chairman; in Philadelphia, where the group was headed by a certain Godfrey Schmidt; in Los Angeles, and possibly in a few more American cities.

The American People and Freedom groups were not the only forum for fostering transnational contacts among Catholic politicians in exile. The Hunter College in New York organized many meetings and guest lectures, for example by the former Reich Chancellor and law professor at Harvard, Heinrich Brüning.[37] The small, but very active French École libre des Hautes Études, a small exile university within the New York School of Social Sciences, also organized many events and publications. At the same time, opportunities for transnational contacts were perhaps less important to the Catholic politicians in exile in the United States, especially in New York, as they also had contacts with the respective immigrant communities. This was true, for example, of the People and Liberty group under the chairmanship of Antony P. Ullo, which brought together Italian Americans and Italians in exile like Sturzo.[38]

Sturzo, Antonio de Onaindía, a Basque professor at the University of Madrid,[39] and others felt, however, that a separate organization, the ICDU, was needed to foster transnational contacts and to provide a platform for common thinking on post-war Europe. According to its constitution, the ICDU's main aim was to create 'permanent bonds of solidarity between the Christian Democratic movements in the various nations', and to organize them against 'the forces of materialism and totalitarian oppression, and for the triumph of organic and parliamentary democracy'.[40] The ICDU had the political backing of leading Catholic politicians like the Czechoslovak Prime Minister Jan Šrámek and General József Haller, chairman of the supreme council of the Polish Party of Labour and Minister of Education, who, together with Sturzo, formed the union's committee of honour. They did not, however, play an active role in it. Significantly, those union members, who were leading representatives of their parties and movements, tended to be from Central Europe and the Basque country, like František Hála, secretary general of the Czechoslovak Popular Party,[41] Michał Kwiatkowski, spokesman of the Party of Labour and a member of the Polish National Council,[42] and Manuel de Irujo, acting president of the Basques.[43]

It was certainly indicative of the relatively low importance attached to the union by leading West European politicians in exile that its chairmanship was given to J. A. Veraart, a professor at the University of Delft. Veraart had participated in congresses of the European Catholic parties in the inter-war period, but he was considered a political outsider within the Dutch party. In the early 1930s, he had been very critical of capitalism and parliamentary government, which at that time gave him a latently fascist and anti-democratic following.[44] He had left the Roman Catholic State Party in 1933 to found his own party, the Catholic Democratic League, but rejoined it in 1939. As a result, Veraart was not surprised to find the Dutch government in exile somewhat anxious when he arrived in London in May 1940.[45] He was first given a job in the Dutch justice ministry, and then became personal economic adviser to Prime Minister P. S. Gerbrandy in May 1942. Dutch support for his chairmanship of the ICDU, for which he was very enthusiastic, should therefore be seen as a promotion sideways to keep a politically controversial figure with a difficult personality as far as possible out of Dutch exile politics.[46]

During the war, Veraart organized regular meetings with guest speakers, who would lecture on the different national party traditions and on themes of common interest, such as economic and social reform and the German question. Veraart himself gave several such lectures, mostly on economic and social policy. These meetings seem to have been quite well attended. From 1943, however, and especially after the Allied invasion of 1944, when concrete post-war planning became urgent, they increasingly seemed 'too great a tax on their [the ICDU members'] time'[47] and no longer took place on a monthly basis. Thus, the ICDU did develop into a transnational forum for debate on post-war Europe, but it was a more modest affair than Veraart had planned in early 1941. At that time, he had hoped to make it the successor organization for more formalized party co-operation of the inter-war Paris secretariat. In particular, the individual members of the

ICDU failed to form larger national groups, with the notable exception of a Dutch group of some fifty members, organized by Veraart.[48] The ICDU, which had no secretariat and whose administrative work was done by Carter, its honorary secretary until 1944, also did not succeed in establishing an information service. According to initial plans, such a service would have provided the Catholic parties with economic and political facts and information on the other parties' policies.[49]

The analysis of the lectures and debates at the meetings of both the People and Freedom groups and the ICDU, as reported in *People & Freedom*, and of publications by Catholic politicians in exile in Britain and the United States, show three main themes: economic and social reform and the relationship between corporatism and liberal parliamentary democracy; plans for a world organization to succeed the League of Nations; and possible solutions to the German question. On the whole, the fundamental experience of exile in non-Catholic liberal democracies clearly led to a reconsideration and political downgrading of corporatist concepts for an 'organic' society. It is also true that, compared to the resistance, the Catholic exile put relatively more emphasis on creating a modern world organization. 'Europe' really only played a major role for a brief period around the time of the symbolic offer of Anglo-French Union by Churchill in June 1940. Finally, while the Catholic exile was largely agreed that a German economic recovery after the war was necessary for Europe as a whole, they still differed fundamentally by 1945 over Germany's political future and territorial questions.

'THIRD WAY' THINKING AND THE DECLINE OF POLITICAL CORPORATISM

When the Catholic political refugees arrived in Britain and the United States, their thinking on economic and social reform had been influenced for a long time by the discourse about the contribution corporatist institutions could make to better economic management and to greater social equality and cohesion. They often regarded such institutions as the key to a European 'third way' between, as they saw it somewhat simplistically, the laissez-faire capitalism of the United States and the centrally planned state economy of the Soviet Union. The reform rhetoric of the more left-wing Catholics was often quite violently anti-capitalist, and it remained so in exile. In his speech at the inaugural meeting of the ICDU in January 1941, for example, Veraart spoke of capitalism as a 'monster'.[50] Later in the same year he attacked the 'parasitic finance that [is] strangling the finest enterprises'.[51] In yet another speech he demanded forcefully that 'the empire of the money market over human life must be shattered'.[52] Sturzo, too, frequently attacked capitalism, and especially its American version with its 'secret monopolies' and massive 'capitalist speculation at the expense of the community'.[53]

Catholic politicians in exile were not agreed on the precise reasons for the patient's illness or, indeed, the best cure, but their common expectation was that as a result of the world economic crisis, the totalitarian challenge and the war, the old capitalist system would have to be replaced by a more efficient and socially just, non-socialist alternative. However, any enthusiasm for political corporatism had already declined during the 1930s, as a result of the experience with actual corporatist solutions that were imposed from above by fascist and authoritarian states and combined with the abolition of trade unions and political rights. This experience increasingly led to a greater emphasis on the need for the growth from below of *voluntary* corporatist institutions to act as intermediate authorities between private enterprises and the state with a much more limited scope. As the French Catholic democrat, Louis Terrenoire, put it in his essay for a joint European publication of the People and Freedom Group in 1939, the crucial question was clearly how to make corporatism 'reconcilable with the political regime founded on liberty'.[54] Sturzo wrote in his contribution to the same book that corporatist institutions absolutely had to conform with political democracy in 'the endeavour to realize the combination of Authority and Liberty in an order, in which . . . all adult citizens . . . participate'.[55] Thus the experience of fascism and National Socialism led to a marked shift in Catholic democratic thinking towards less authority and more liberty and a new emphasis on participation, also of workers, in economic decision making, independent of the exact form this would take.

In the case of the Catholic political refugees, especially in Britain, the relative shift from authority to liberty and – in the words of the ICDU's constitution – from 'organic' to 'parliamentary' democracy, was strengthened further by the experience of exile in a liberal parliamentary democracy that they came to respect and, sometimes, to admire. Sturzo's thinking, for example, became more individualistic in exile, and this was clearly the case for many other Catholic democrats. They were distressed by the extent of authoritarian and philo-fascist thinking in the Catholic minority communities in Britain and the United States. At the same time, they were impressed by the relative stability of these countries' political institutions and by the sheer tenacity with which especially the British defended their liberty. Sturzo valued what he saw as the pragmatism of the British, the non-ideological character of their social institutions and their tradition of international solidarity, reflected in their liberal refugee policy.[56] Sturzo did criticize what he saw as the lack of working-class integration into the British economic and political system. Nevertheless, he and most other Catholic political refugees came back from Britain and the United States with a changed normative hierarchy in which individual liberty was, relative to the sometimes conflicting aim of social cohesion, much more important than before, thus pointing the way intellectually towards the more liberal Christian democracy of post-war Western Europe.

FOR A WORLD ORGANIZATION, NOT A EUROPEAN FEDERATION

Their exile in Britain and the United States also seems to have contributed to a more Atlanticist view of post-war Europe among Catholic political refugees than may have prevailed in the resistance movements.[57] The application of federalist ideas to Europe only played a significant role in their debates and publications during 1939–40. At that time, Catholic politicians in exile did have loose contacts with the Federal Union, founded in Britain in 1938, and there was probably some degree of intellectual cross-fertilization. However, no prominent Catholic politicians with close links to the People and Freedom Group or the ICDU were represented on the European committee of the Federal Union.[58]

After the fall of France, Catholic politicians in exile on the whole supported regional projects for co-operation or integration, such as between Belgium and the Netherlands, Poland and Czechoslovakia, or for the Danube region, not least as an insurance against a resurgent Germany. In contrast, they mostly thought that a larger federal Europe was either unrealistic or even dangerous. Joseph Bech, the Christian Democrat foreign minister of Luxembourg, certainly believed that a wider 'European economic union' was 'for the time being, impossible'. In his speech at the Belgian Institute in London in February 1943 he suggested instead a regional customs union, such as the future Benelux, that could be extended to other states bordering on the Atlantic, principally France, but – he implied – not Germany or Italy.[59] The inclusion of Germany in any new organization, whether federal, intergovernmental or with a mixed institutional structure, was excluded more explicitly by Frans Van Cauwelaert, president of the Belgian chamber of deputies, in a speech he delivered in Washington in April 1942. Such a larger integrated Europe, Van Cauwelaert argued, would inevitably be dominated by Germany, and it was therefore crucial for the United States and Britain to play a leading role in the reconstruction of Europe and in any new organizations.[60]

When Catholic politicians in exile did advocate federalism after 1940, they applied the concept in a rather loose way to an imagined Atlantic community or even to the world. Not surprisingly, therefore, the Catholic refugees greeted the 1941 Atlantic Charter and its promise of a better world order with great enthusiasm. The Anglo-American initiative appeared to take up demands of the late 1930s, also made by the People and Freedom Group and Catholic refugees, for a more effective League of

Nations or, as the ICDU put it in a resolution in April 1943, a new 'Commonwealth of democratic nations'.[61] The members of the People and Freedom Group and of the ICDU spent much time after 1941 debating the best political and institutional formula for such a world organization. From mid-1943 onwards, however, they quickly became disillusioned with Allied great power politics, and the fact that the new organization would be neither democratic nor based on the principle of equality that alone would guarantee the continental European countries a real voice in future world affairs. The adherence of the Soviet Union, and the veto envisaged for the great powers, was incompatible with the lessons the Catholic refugees had drawn from the experience of the inter-war period, namely, that a world organization should consist only of democratic states that fully supported its principles, and should be principally concerned with protecting its smaller members against any hegemonic threat.[62] Their disillusionment was complete when Churchill publicly exempted enemy states and colonies from the Charter's guarantees. In March 1944, the People and Freedom Group protested vehemently that his redefinition of the Charter, as they saw it, 'knocks away the already frail foundations of a new international order'.[63] Sturzo wrote sarcastically one month later that if Turkey inconveniently remained neutral, 'sooner or later we shall have a declaration that "neutrals" without belligerent qualifications cannot enjoy the Atlantic Charter'. The Charter, he concluded, 'after so many torpedos, is well and truly sunk'.[64]

The idea of a new world organization had appeared so attractive not least because it could have acted as a true arbiter with respect to the post-war settlement. As such, it would not only have had a better claim to greater political legitimacy than the Allies at Versailles and Trianon in 1919–20; crucially, it might also have found solutions to the problems the Catholic refugees themselves could not agree upon, especially territorial questions. Instead, Churchill's public surrender of the universality of the Atlantic Charter made it absolutely clear that each nation would be able to secure its interests only through direct lobbying of the great powers. As a result, the Catholic refugees spent much of the last two war years exercising such influence as they had in Britain and the United States through their exile governments, or – especially in the case of Italy and Austria – through the media. It is indicative of this general trend that Sturzo became totally preoccupied towards the end of the war with defending what he regarded as Italian interests, especially its territorial integrity. Sturzo gave much space in his publications to analysing and condemning National Socialism, and he conceded that some German loss of territory in the East was clearly inevitable. In contrast, he mentioned fascism only in passing. It now almost seemed a historical accident. Sturzo argued that, especially in view of French collaboration in Vichy France, the Badoglio government deserved the same treatment as the Free French government. As if this did not apply to Germany, he also insisted that it was of central importance for Europe that the new Italian democracy should not be burdened with any loss of territory, be it the Trentino, South Tyrol or Istria.[65] South Tyrol and Istria had, of course, large non-Italian majorities. Thus, Sturzo's argument illustrates very well how much easier it was also for Catholic democrats to accept the Charter's principles – in this particular case the right to self-determination – than their actual application to concrete controversies.

NO SECOND VERSAILLES: THE GERMAN QUESTION

Directly or indirectly, the securing of national interests was in most cases linked to the German question. A minimum consensus existed among the Catholic refugees that, in the words of Paul Tschoffen, a Belgian councillor of state, 'there must be no economic war against a defeated Germany, first because it would not be Christian, and secondly because it would be fruitless';[66] and third, it should be added, because it would be disadvantageous for countries like Belgium, whose economies were traditionally closely tied up with the German economy. As Veraart summarized it, 'contrary to Versailles Germany must not be destroyed economically'.[67] Beyond such generalities, however, the Catholic politicians in exile were deeply divided as to the causes of National Socialism and their war aims.

The simplistic view of a German collective guilt was still widely held. For Tschoffen, for example, 'Germany as a whole was behind Hitler and guilty with him'.[68] Veraart, well known for his strongly anti-German views before the war, believed that National Socialism 'responded to something in the souls of the German people'.[69] Such views were often linked to the anti-Prussian sentiments that were also prevalent among other political groups at the time. In Sturzo's view, for example, the greatest danger was 'the Prussian mentality, as forged by the Teutonic Knights, the Brandenburgs, the Hohenzollerns and Bismarks [sic!], . . . of whom Nazism is the heir'.[70] The least that was required before the Germans might one day be reintegrated into the community of democratic states was, as Sturzo put it, 'a real moral and psychological purification'.[71] Others believed strongly in political securities that they did not yet see in some kind of European construction. Instead, many ICDU members wanted to go beyond the imposition, if necessary, of fully fledged federalism and saw the only real solution in the dismemberment of Germany. This country, Veraart argued in a speech on the future of Germany in March 1943, was an 'artificially big unit' and had to be divided into at least five different states. Veraart's statement was followed by an animated discussion. Carter insisted that 'lasting peace must rest on assent', but on the whole, many members were quite sympathetic to Veraart's propositions.[72]

Concerning changes in Germany's external borders, most Catholic politicians in exile were quite happy to go beyond the restoration of the pre-1938 situation. Among the more lenient suggestions for German cession of territory in the East were those Sturzo made, with the Italian situation in mind. He advocated some adjustments in Silesia and elsewhere, but categorically rejected the idea of giving the very predominantly German East Prussia to Poland. 'Mass deportation', he argued, 'would be a crime that the Allies cannot and must not commit.' Sturzo also insisted that 'those who think of the annexation of the Rhine valley are but unconscious warmongers', an assessment of a long-standing French ambition that was shared by practically all non-French Catholic politicians in exile.[73] On the other hand, the Polish ICDU representatives made the most far-reaching territorial demands even before the Soviet occupation and annexation of eastern Poland. Responding to a letter to the editor in *People & Freedom*, Kwiatkowski defended Polish demands for the annexation of East Prussia, 'the sword of Damocles' hanging over Poland. In his view, the 'expulsion of a few hundred thousand of Prussian Junkers who amply share the responsibility for all the crimes committed both in the first and the present world war' was perfectly justified.[74]

Whereas the Catholic politicians in exile still differed widely by 1945 over the future of Germany, the British People and Freedom Group took a very consistent view of this issue throughout the war. They were, of course, comparatively detached from the conflicts of the continent and, unlike many others, had no direct stake in the peace settlement. In a striking example of their detached analysis and in line with their previous policies, Crawford warned, in her first published comment after the British declaration of war, that 'we must resolutely cherish our sanity of judgement, our mental balance, our sense of moral values, our faith in all our Christian traditions of justice and charity even towards our enemies. Ultimately, we must work for a just and not a revengeful peace.'[75] Just as it had strongly protested after the destruction of Guernica in 1937, the People and Freedom Group also expressed its opposition to the indiscriminate aerial saturation bombing of German cities during the war.[76] Towards the end of the war, it strongly opposed the cession of territory predominantly inhabited by Germans, such as East Prussia. In reply to Kwiatkowski's demands, the Group's committee took the unprecedented step of publishing a formal resolution, together with his letter to the editor, to the effect that such large-scale annexations as he was envisaging,

> would be disastrous . . . Arguments founded on racial origin, the brutalities of mediaeval colonisation . . . or feudal suzerainty seem to us supremely irrelevant. Prussia is an integral part of Germany, and its forceable incorporation in Poland would weaken Poland herself and make the general pacification of Europe impossible.[77]

At a meeting of the People and Freedom Group in January 1945, Conrad Bonacina, Crawford's successor as chairman, insisted that 'a Carthaginian peace would be no peace', and that any large territorial changes would mean either 'huge transfers, with terrible human misery, or the incorporation of some millions of hostile people in the Polish State'.[78] In March 1945, the People and Freedom Group then protested against the Polish border changes which reflected 'a preoccupation with States rather than peoples – or, more basically, simply people – [which] implies an impenitent pursuance of the process that has made modern history a series of wars of ever more destructive range'.[79]

Their views on the future of Germany were consistent with their general belief system. They probably also thought that they were truly Christian, ethically right and morally superior. They were, of course, highly unpopular with the vast majority of the British, who had a mental image of the destruction of Coventry or real experience with German V1 or V2 rockets. They were also incompatible with the majority view among the Catholic politicians in exile. Thus, it must have taken even the financially and personally independent middle-class members of the People and Freedom Group some social courage to pronounce and publish them so consistently during the war. Of course, their pronouncements and resolutions had absolutely no effect on the wartime reality, as historians have come to know it. When the group protested against aerial saturation bombing, Churchill was about to consider the indiscriminate use of poison gas against German cities in the hope that this would shorten the war. When they opposed far-reaching territorial changes in East Central Europe, Stalin had already decided, with implicit British and American consent, to annex eastern Poland. When, finally, the group spoke out against large-scale resettlements, the expulsion of millions of Poles from eastern Poland and Germans from eastern Germany was already in full swing.

CONCLUSION

Without the British People and Freedom Group, the Catholic politicians in exile in Britain and – to a lesser extent – in the United States would have been even more isolated than they were, especially when they played no role in an internationally recognized government in exile. The members of the British and American branches of the People and Freedom Group formed a small minority within the Catholic minorities of those countries, both in terms of their social background and their political views. These views were highly consistent, and generally very advanced not only on the dominant thinking of the wider Catholic public, but also of British and American policy: from – in the British case – their opposition to Munich in 1938, to their vivid protest against the internment of 'enemy aliens' in 1940, through to their strong support for a constructive policy towards Germany in 1943–45. The Group also provided an important forum for transnational contacts among Catholic refugees, especially in Britain, and it contributed to the greater formalization of their co-operation in the ICDU. The American branches were much less significant, especially as transnational contacts among Catholic refugees were also facilitated by other institutions, such as the Hunter College and the École libre des Hautes Études in New York.

Transnational co-operation in exile was much less formalized than Veraart and others had hoped. The ICDU was effectively concerned with fostering contacts and debate among individual politicians in exile, and not with formal party co-operation. The majority of the ICDU members, including its chairman, did not play leading roles in their own parties, and this is especially true of the West Europeans. It is indicative of the comparatively low profile of these transnational contacts that most leading Catholic politicians, like Hubert Pierlot, the Belgian Prime Minister, and Šrámek and Haller, apparently never attended any meeting of the People and Freedom Group or the ICDU. De Schryver, who became the first leader of the post-war Belgian Parti Social Chrétien, sometimes did participate. Schumann was even the official French representative during 1942–43, but – as Carter recalled later – he took part only once to give a speech.[80] It is not surprising, therefore, that Onaindía concluded at the annual meeting in 1944 that the organization '[has] served a valuable purpose in enabling Christian Democrats of various nationalities to get to know one another . . . but it must be admitted that it [has] not attained the influence or development that might have been hoped'. One reason, Onaindía believed, was that so few prominent politicians participated, not least as a result of their high workload in their respective governments in exile.[81]

As a result, their transnational co-operation probably had a certain influence on the political thinking of individual ICDU members. However, it had little effect, if any, on the post-war planning in exile for national and European reconstruction. Moreover, there is no direct continuity, either institutionally or politically, from the rudimentary transnationalism in exile to Christian democrat party co-operation in the NEI and the Geneva circle after 1947.[82] Carter travelled in Europe during 1945–46, and she probably encouraged Christian democrat politicians like Jules Soyeur, Robert Bichet, Felix Hurdes and Martin Rosenberg, who anyway wanted to form transnational links, to proceed with their plans. It is also clear, however, that their motivations related to the joint experience of totalitarianism, the war, occupation and resistance and to the need for economic reconstruction and greater political cohesion of Western Europe in the early stages of the Cold War. It may well be the case that their limited ICDU experience made de Schryver, Schumann and a few other

Catholic refugees, who had a high political profile in Western Europe after 1945, value transnational party co-operation more highly. Compared to those Christian Democrats who had preferred the resistance or internal exile to exile abroad, however, these politicians were to play only a relatively marginal role in most parties and in the NEI.

Moreover, it is clear from the analysis of the speeches and debates at the meetings of both the People and Freedom Group and the ICDU that there is also no political continuity from the thinking of Catholic politicians in exile on such crucial issues as the future role of Britain in Europe or policy towards Germany, to post-war European reconstruction. The Catholic refugees were united in their much clearer rejection of political corporatism, but so were those Catholic politicians who had stayed on the continent during the war. They gave absolute preference to the creation of a new world organization of democratic states. They quickly became disillusioned with Allied policy long before the creation of the United Nations in 1945, but failed to advance alternative concepts. Finally, the experience of exile generally led the Catholic refugees to develop a strongly Atlanticist vision of post-war Europe that excluded the possibility of any continental European solution to the German question. With the notable exception of the German Catholics in exile, who almost universally regarded the 'European vocation', as the Centre Party politician Carl Spiecker called it,[83] as their salvation from National Socialism, the debates in exile clearly did not anticipate the later fundamental solution of the German question through integration, in the context of the European Coal and Steel Community and the European Economic Community. On the whole, therefore, transnational co-operation in exile had only a marginal effect on the development of both the new Christian Democrat parties and their transnational co-operation and of Western Europe after the war.[84]

NOTES

1 See the chapter by Guido Müller in this book.
2 Even Roberto Papini, *The Christian Democrat International* (Lanham, Boulder, CO, New York and London 1997 [Italian 1986, French 1988]) devotes only 1.5 pages to the Catholic exile.
3 On the French Christian democrat resistance and the formation of the MRP, see Pierre Letamendia, *Le Mouvement Républicain Populaire. Histoire d'un grand parti français* (Paris 1995). See also Maurice Vaussard, *Histoire de la Démocratie Chrétienne. I: France – Belgique – Italie* (Paris 1956), pp. 102–8; Ernest Pezet, *Chrétiens au service de la Cité. De Léon XIII au Sillon et au M.R.P. 1891–1965* (Paris 1965), p. 128.
4 On the Italian, German and Austrian exile, see for example Francesco Piva and Francesco Malgeri, *Vita di Luigi Sturz* (Rome 1972); Francesco Malgeri, *Luigi Sturzo* (Milan 1993); Charles F. Delzell, *Mussolini's Enemies. The Italian Anti-Fascist Resistance* (Princeton, NJ 1961); Joachim Radkau, *Die deutsche*

Emigration in den USA. Ihr Einfluss auf die amerikanische Europapolitik 1933–1945 (Düsseldorf 1971); Ulrike Hörster-Philipps, *Joseph Wirth 1879–1956. Eine politische Biographie* (Paderborn 1998); Helene Maimann, *Politik im Wartesaal. Österreichische Exilpolitik in Grossbritannien 1938–1945* (Vienna, Cologne and Graz 1975).

5 See Giuseppe Ignesti, 'Momenti del Popolarismo in Esilio', in Pietro Scoppolo and Francesco Traniello (eds), *I Cattolici tra Fascismo e Democrazia* (Bologna 1975), pp. 75–183, here p. 101.

6 Gabriele De Rosa, *Luigi Sturzo* (Turin 1977), p. 409.

7 On the exile governments in London, see in a European perspective, Martin Conway, 'Legacies of exile: the exile governments in London during World War II and the politics of post-war Europe', in Martin Conway and José Gotovitch (eds), *Europe in Exile. European Refugee Communities in Britain 1939–1945* (Oxford and New York 2001), pp. 255–74.

8 Pierre-Henri Laurent, 'Reality not rhetoric: Belgian-Dutch diplomacy in wartime London, 1940–1944', in M. L. Smith and Peter M. R. Stirk (eds), *Making the New Europe. European Unity and the World War II* (London 1990), pp. 133–41.

9 See also Feliks Gross, 'Views of East European Transnational Groups on the Postwar Order in Europe', in Walter Lipgens (ed.), *Documents on the History of European Integration. Vol. 2: Plans for European Union in Great Britain and in Exile 1939–1945* (Berlin and New York 1986), pp. 754–85; Detlef Brandes, 'Confederation Plans in Eastern Europe during World War II', in Michel Dumoulin (ed.), *Wartime Plans for Postwar Europe 1940–1947* (Brussels 1995), pp. 83–94.

10 Theo Luykx, 'De rol van August De Schryver in het politieke leven tot en met de Tweede Wereldoorlog', in *Veertig jaar Belgische politiek, Liber amicorum aangeboden aan Minister van Staat A.E. De Schryver ter gelegenheid van zijn 70ste verjaardag* (Antwerp and Utrecht 1968), pp. 121–211, here p. 199.

11 Tom Buchanan, 'Great Britain', in Tom Buchanan and Martin Conway (eds), *Political Catholicism in Europe, 1918–1965* (Oxford 1996), pp. 248–74, here p. 250. See also Joan Keating, 'The British Experience: Christian Democrats without a Party', in David Hanley (ed.), *Christian Democracy in Europe. A Comparative Perspective* (London 1994), pp. 168–81.

12 For a useful introduction to American Catholicism, see Jay P. Dolan, *The American Catholic Experience: A History from Colonial Times to the Present* (Garden City 1985).

13 See Joan Keating, 'Roman Catholics, Christian Democracy and the British Labour Mouvement 1910–1960', Ph.D. thesis (Manchester 1992), chapter 3.

14 James Flint, '"Must God go Fascist?" English Catholic Opinion and the Spanish Civil War', *Church History*, vol. 56, no. 3 (1987), pp. 364–74, here p. 367.

15 *The Tablet*, 1 August 1936.

16 Tom Buchanan, *The Spanish Civil War and the British Labour Movement* (Cambridge 1991), p. 107.

17 Alan Brinkley, *Voices of Protest. Huey Long, Father Coughlin, and the Great Depression* (New York 1982), p. 279.

18 Sheldon Marcus, *Father Coughlin. The Tumultuous Life of the Priest of the Little Flower* (Boston, MA and Toronto 1973), p. 127. On Coughlin, see also Ronald H. Carpenter, *Father Charles E. Coughlin. Surrogate Spokesman for the Disaffected* (Westport, CT 1998).

19 See, for example, Stuart Ball, 'The Politics of Appeasement: the Fall of the

Duchess of Atholl and the Kinross and West Perth By-election, December 1938', *Scottish Historical Review*, vol. LXIX, no. 1 (1990), pp. 49–83.
20 See Leo V. Kanawada, *Franklin D. Roosevelt's Diplomacy and American Catholics, Italians and Jews* (Epping 1982), pp. 49–70.
21 Joan Keating, 'Looking to Europe: Roman Catholicism and Christian Democracy in 1930s Britain', *European History Quarterly*, vol. 26, no. 1 (1996), pp. 57–79, here p. 64.
22 'General Meeting', *People & Freedom*, no. 4 (1939), p. 4.
23 Marcus, *Father Coughlin*, p. 158.
24 On Shuster who, after the war, temporarily became an American governor in Bavaria, see Thomas E. Blantz, *George N. Shuster: On the Side of Truth* (Notre Dame, IN 1993).
25 'People & Freedom', *People & Freedom*, no. 1 (1938), pp. 1–2.
26 'From the Christian Democrats of Italy [Alcide De Gasperi to Conrad Bonacina]', *People & Freedom*, no. 68 (1945), p. 2.
27 See the obituary by Barbara Barclay Carter, 'Virginia Crawford', *People & Freedom*, no. 108 (1948), p. 1.
28 See the obituary by Crawford's successor, Conrad Bonacina, 'Obituary – Barbara Barclay Carter', *People & Freedom*, no. 124 (1951), pp. 1–3.
29 Katherine Duchess of Atholl, Working Partnership. Being the Lives of John George, 8th Duke of Atholl and of his wife Katherine Marjory Ramsay (London 1958), p. 200.
30 Katherine Duchess of Atholl, *Searchlight on Spain* (London 1937).
31 'People & Freedom', *People & Freedom*, no. 1 (1938), pp. 1–2.
32 Philippe Chenaux, 'Bijdrage tot de internationale christen-democratie', in Wilfried Dewachter et al. (eds), *Tussen staat en maatschapsij 1945–1995. Christen-democratie in België* (Tielt 1995), p. 253.
33 'Reception for Leading Christian Democrats', *People & Freedom*, no. 18 (1940), p. 4.
34 'General Meeting', *People & Freedom*, no. 4 (1939), p. 4.
35 '"White War"', *People & Freedom*, no. 5 (1939), p. 1.
36 Luigi Sturzo to Miss Reilly, 14 January 1941, in *Luigi Sturzo, Scritti Inediti, vol. 3: 1940–1946* (Rome 1976), document 10.
37 George N. Shuster, *The Ground I Walked on. Reflections of a College President* (Notre Dame, IN and London 1961), p. 146.
38 Francesco Malgeri, *Chiesa, Cattolici e Democrazia. Da Sturzo a De Gasperi* (Brescia 1990), pp. 196–8.
39 'International Christian Democratic Union', *People & Freedom*, no. 20 (1941), p. 4, speaks of an 'initiative' of Onaindía.
40 'International Christian Democratic Union', *People & Freedom*, no. 22 (1941), p. 2.
41 On the Polish exile, see in greater detail John Coutouvidis and Jaime Reynolds, *Poland 1939–47* (Leicester 1986).
42 See Peter Henmos, *Die Emigration aus der Tschechoslowakei nach Westeuropa und dem Nahen Osten 1938–1945* (Munich 1989).
43 The Basque exile is treated in the context of Spanish opposition to Franco after 1939 in Sergio Vilar, *Historia del Anti-Franquismo 1939–1975* (Barcelona 1984).
44 Sjef Schmiermann, 'Prof. Dr. J. A. Veraart (1886–1955). Een recalcitrant katholiek democraat', *Jaarboek van het Katholiek Documentatie Centrum*, vol. 20 (1990), pp. 122–42, here p. 130. On Veraart, see also in more detail idem, 'Prof. Dr. J. A. Veraart (1886–1955). Aspecten van het politieke leven van een recalcitrant katholiek democraat', Ph.D. thesis (Nijmegen 1988).

45 Veraart's impression was that his Dutch colleagues, also from his own party, thought 'now we have this man here again'. Quoted in Schmiermann, 'Veraart', p. 134.
46 On Veraart's isolation among the Dutch politicians in exile in London, see also Louis De Jong, *Het Koninkrijk der Nederlanden in de Tweede Wereldoorlog*, vol. 9, part 2 ('s-Gravenhage 1979), pp. 1445–6.
47 'International Christian Democratic Union', *People & Freedom*, no. 48 (1943), p. 5.
48 Some additional information on this Dutch group can be gleaned from Veraart's own recollections in J. A. Veraart, 'Internationaal Werk in Londen. Fragmenten uit mijn Dagboek, 1940–1945', *Katholiek Cultureel Tijdschrift*, no. 3 (1946–47), pp. 56–63, here pp. 58–9.
49 In 1941–42, for example, the ICDU spent the minute sum of £10 on paper, stamps, etc., and until May 1943 it had dealt with only three requests for information from 'semi-official circles'. See 'Annual General Meeting [1942]', *People & Freedom*, no. 36 (1942), p. 4; 'International Christian Democratic Union', *People & Freedom*, no. 48 (1943), p. 5.
50 '"Some Principles of Democracy", by Prof. Veraart (Address given at the inaugural meeting of the International Christian Democratic Union, on January 28, 1941]', *People & Freedom*, no. 20 (1941), p. 2.
51 'Veraart, Christian Democracy: Economic and Social Programme', *People & Freedom*, no. 28 (1941), p. 3.
52 'International Christian Democratic Union', *People & Freedom*, no. 40 (1942), p. 4.
53 'Luigi Sturzo, "The Bolshevist Peril"', *People & Freedom*, no. 37 (1942), p. 1.
54 Louis Terrenoire, 'Corporatism and Democracy', in People and Freedom Group (ed.), *For Democracy* (London 1939), pp. 185–209, here p. 186.
55 Luigi Sturzo, 'Democracy, Authority, and Liberty', in People and Freedom Group, *For Democracy*, pp. 95–116, here p. 105.
56 David Forgacs, 'Sturzo e la Cultura Politica Inglese', in *Luigi Sturzo e la Democrazia Europea, a cura di Gabriele De Rosa* (Rome 1990), pp. 342–7, here p. 346.
57 G. M. V. Mans, 'Ideas of Netherlands Exiles on the Postwar International Order', in Lipgens, *Documents*, vol. 2, pp. 451–75, here p. 453, makes this point comparing the Dutch exile and resistance without, however, distinguishing according to party allegiance.
58 For a list of the committee members, see Walter Lipgens, 'Plans of Other Transnational Groups for European Union', in Lipgens, *Documents*, vol. 2, p. 802, footnote 3. On the Federal Union, see Richard Mayne and John Pinder, *Federal Union: The Pioneers* (London 1990).
59 Quoted in Walter Lipgens (ed.), *Europa-Föderationspläne der Widerstandsbewegungen 1940–1945* (Munich 1968), pp. 471–2.
60 Frans Van Cauwelaert, Dangers of a European Federation, 2 April 1942, reprinted in *Washington Post*, 10 May 1942.
61 'A New League of Nations Now. Proposal Endorsed by International Christian Democratic Union', *People & Freedom*, no. 46 (1943), p. 3.
62 This general view among Catholic refugees was expressed most coherently after the war by Luigi Sturzo, *Nationalism and Internationalism* (New York 1946).
63 'Downward Steps', *People & Freedom*, no. 57 (1944), p. 1.
64 'Sturzo, The Shade of Wilson and the Atlantic Charter', *People & Freedom*, no. 58 (1944), p. 1.

65 See especially Luigi Sturzo, 'Italy after Mussolini', *Foreign Affairs*, vol. 21, no. 3 (1943), pp. 412–26.
66 'International Christian Democratic Union. Annual General Meeting', *People & Freedom*, no. 61 (1944), p. 4.
67 'International Christian Democratic Union. "How to deal with Germany and the Germans"', *People & Freedom*, no. 58 (1944), p. 3.
68 'International Christian Democratic Union. Annual General Meeting', *People & Freedom*, no. 61 (1944), p. 4.
69 'International Christian Democratic Union. "How to deal with Germany and the Germans"'.
70 'Sturzo, A New Germany', *People & Freedom*, no. 9 (1940), p. 3.
71 Ibid.
72 'International Christian Democratic Union. "How to deal with Germany and the Germans"'.
73 'Sturzo, What to do with Germany', *People & Freedom*, no. 63 (1944), p. 1.
74 Michał Kwiatkowski, 'Poland and East Prussia', *People & Freedom*, no. 57 (1944), p. 3. The national Polish–German antagonism was of course strengthened by the religious divide between Catholic Poles and Protestant Germans in these parts of Germany.
75 'Crawford, Where We Stand', *People & Freedom*, no. 6 (1939), p. 1.
76 See, for example, 'Downward Steps', *People & Freedom*, no. 57 (1944), p. 1.
77 'Statement by the People and Freedom Group Committee', *People & Freedom*, no. 57 (1944), p. 3.
78 'Principles of Peace', *People & Freedom*, no. 68 (1945), p. 4.
79 'States or Peoples', *People & Freedom*, no. 69 (1945), p. 1.
80 Carter to Sturzo, 30 June 1945, Archivio Luigi Sturzo, f.201A, c.331, quoted in Roberto Papini, *Il Coraggio della Democrazia. Sturzo e l'internazionale popolare tra le due guerre* (Rome 1995), p. 246.
81 'International Christian Democratic Union, Annual General Meeting', *People & Freedom*, no. 61 (1944), p. 4.
82 See Michael Gehler and Wolfram Kaiser, 'Transnationalism and early European integration: the Nouvelles Équipes Internationales and the Geneva Circle', *Historical Journal*, vol. 44, no. 3 (2001), pp. 773–98.
83 Karl [sic!] Spiecker, *Germany – from Defeat to Defeat*, with a preface by Professor R.W. Seton-Watson (London 1945), p. 153.
84 Martin Conway, *Catholic Politics in Europe 1918–1945* (London 1997), p. 89, makes a similar point with regard to the Christian democrat resistance.

Index

Please note that references to endnotes are denoted by page number, followed by 'n' and note number.

Aalberse, P. J. M., 85, 88
Abendland (newspaper), 59, 261
Acerbos Law, 144
ACJB (Association Catholique de la Jeunesse Belge), 104, 110
ACJF (Association Catholique de la Jeunesse Française), 14, 116, 119
Actio Catholica, 71, 211
Action catholique spécialisée (France), 123
Action Française (AF): and Belgium, 102; condemnation by Pius XI, 122, 128; nineteenth century, 17, 27; and PDP, 121, 131; Switzerland, influence on, 75
Action Libérale Populaire (ALP), France, nineteenth century, 14, 17, 30, 31–2
ACW *see* Algemeen Christelijk Werkersverbond-Ligue Nationale des Travailleurs Chrétiens (National League of Christian Workers), Belgium
Adamski, Father Stanislaw, 154
Adenauer, Konrad, 51, 58, 60, 61, 266
Aengenent, J. D. J., 88
AF (Action Française) *see* Action Française (AF)
Agrarian Landbund (Austria), 182
Agrarian Party (Slovakia), 229, 231
Agriculture and Forestry Association (Austria), 188
Aigner, Josef, 185
Aktion Gewitter, 59
Albert, King, 97
Albrecht, Father Jan, 158
Alexander I (King of Yugoslavia), 219
Algemeen Christelijk Vakverbond-Confédération des Syndicats Chrétiens (Confederation of Christian Trade Unions), Belgium, 99
Algemeen Christelijk Werkersverbond-Ligue Nationale des Travailleurs Chrétiens (National League of Christian Workers), Belgium, 96, 98, 99, 100, 110
All Party Committee for Spanish Relief, 270
ALP (Action Libérale Populaire), France *see* Action Libérale Populaire (ALP), France
Altermatt, Urs, 236
Anderson, Margaret, 11, 15, 16, 21–2, 28
Andrássy, Gyula, 202
Anglo-American initiative, 275
Anglo-French Union (1940), 273
Anschluss (Austria), 57, 130, 179–81, 182, 266
Anti-Fascist Concentration (1927), 266
Anti-Revolutionary Party (Netherlands), 82
anti-Semitism: Austria, 32, 33, 175; Bohemia, 224; France, 14–15, 30, 32; Germany, 271; Hungary, 204, 207, 209, 313; Poland, 152, 159; Slovakia, 229; Switzerland, 69
Appello al paese (PPI), 142
Archambault, Paul, 125
Ariëns, Alphons, 87, 88
Armia Krajowa (AK), Polish undercover Home Army, 168
Arrow-Cross Party (Nyilas Keresztas Párt), Hungary, 209, 210, 220
Association Catholique de la Jeunesse Belge (ACJB), 104, 110

286

INDEX

Association Catholique de la Jeunesse Française (ACJF), 14, 116, 119
Association of Farmers (Reichsbauernbund), Austria, 177, 188
associationalism, 11, 26, 27
Associations Law (1901), France, 13
Assumptionists (French), 12–13
Atholl, Duchess of, 270
Atlantic Charter (1941), 275, 276
Austria: absolute priority of fiscal consolidation principle, 175; *Anschluss* (1938), 57, 130, 179–81, 182, 266; anti-Semitism, 32, 33, 175; Association of Farmers (Reichsbauernbund), 177, 188; Catholic Congress movement, 17; Christian Workers' Movement, 174, 177, 183, 185; Church/State relations, 18, 175–7; Compromise of 1867 (Austria and Hungary), 195, 196; German-Austrian Trade Association, 177; Habsburg Church, 17, 18, 31; isolation (1920s), 74; Lower, Crownland of, 19; in nineteenth century, 17–20; Palace of Justice fire (1927), 181; Reichsgewerbebund (Trade Association), 177, 188; *Ständestaat* system, 2, 73, 266; Tyrol, protests in, 18; Vienna, suppression of Social Democratic riots, 129, *see also* Christian Socials (Austrian) *and other Austrian parties*
Austro-Marxism, 28
Aventine Secession, 144

Bachem, Julius, 9, 29, 47
Barankovics, István, 210, 214
Bauer, Otto, 174
Bäuerliche Arbeitsgemeinschaft (Swiss agricultural committee), 70
Bavarian Christian Social Union, 266
Bayerische Volkspartei (BVP), 48, 49, 51, 52, 55–6, 59
Bechyně, Rudolf, 223
Beck, Josef, 68, 72
Beck, Józef, 161
bedrijfsorganisatie, 103, 109
Belgische Boerenbond (Belgian Farmers' League), 95, 96, 99, 100, 106, 108
Belgische Volksbond-Ligue démocratique beige (Belgian People's League), 95
Belgium, 94–114; nineteenth century, party formation in, 94–6; in 1920s, 96–103; in 1930s, 103–10; Church/State relations, 95, 109; Droite (Catholic parliamentary group), 98; European dimension, 110–11; federal formula, 100; Flemish provinces, 96; fragmented parties (1920s), 96–103; German invasion (1940), 111; Liberal Party, 95, 97, 98; Loppem cabinet, 98; nationalism, 96, 101, 102, 107, 109; Netherlands, separation from, 95; party formation (nineteenth century), 94–6; people's party, emergence (1930s), 103–10; proportional representation, 94–5; Rexist movement, 106–7, 108, 109, 111, 245; school war (1879), 95; Union Démocratique Belge, 112; Walloon area, 96, 107; war and occupation, 111–12
Belloc, Hilaire, 268
Belvedere Circle (1908), 227
Benedict XV (Pope), 121, 142, 145, 146
Beneš, Edvard, 225, 230, 231
Bereza Kartuska detention camp, 165
Berman, Marshall, 9
Bethlen, István, 203, 204, 205, 208
Bichet, Robert, 280
Bidault, Georges, 119, 133, 266
Bieler, Victor, 72
Bismarck, Otto von: Catholic Church, attacks on, 10; and German Centre Party, 10, 11, 48; *Kulturkampf* legislation, 16; resignation, 48
Blackbourn, David, 21, 23
Blaschke, Olaf, 21, 32
Błażejewicz, Tadeusz, 154
Blok der Katholieken van België-Bloc Catholique Belge (Catholic Bloc), Belgium, 103, 107, 109, 248
Blum, Léon, 132
Boerenbond (Belgian Farmers' League), 95, 96, 99, 100, 106, 108
Bohemia: Catholic groupings in, 220, 221; unemployment in, 231
Bohemian Society for Agrarian Youth, 220, 221, 223
Bologna PPI congress (1919), 138, 140
Bonacina, Conrad, 279
Bornewasser, J. A., 91
Boyer, John W., 3, 7–45
Brauns, Heinrich, 256
Breslau, property in, 223

287

Briand, Aristide, 121, 127, 128, 131, 256
Britain *see* United Kingdom
Brose, Eric, 29
Brüning, Heinrich, 54, 186, 259, 271
Brussels, 97, 99
Buchenwald concentration camp, 90
Buday, Jozef, 228
Buomberger, Ferdinand, 75
Bureau d'action civique (France), 117
Buresch, Karl, 183
bürgerlich leaders/colleagues, 12, 29
Bürgertum, 11
BVP (Bayerische Volkspartei), 48, 49, 51, 52, 55–6, 59

CAB (Christlichsozialer Arbeiterbund), Switzerland, 67
Cahiers de la nouvelle journée, 125, 128, 133
capitalism, 273–4
Cardijn, Joseph, 105
Caro, Ludwik, 158
Cartel des gauches, 97, 121, 131
Carter, Barbara Barclay, 270, 271, 280
Cary, Noel, 7, 29, 35
Catholic Action: and Austria, 177, 185; and Belgium, 94, 106, 110, 111, 112; democratic parliamentarianism, mistrust of, 254; and Poland, 163, 166
Catholic Association of Czech Farmers, 221
Catholic Association for International Peace, 271
Catholic Bloc (Belgium), 103, 107, 109, 248
Catholic Congress: movement, 17; and Austria, 184; and Germany, 51; and Switzerland, 70–1
Catholic Farmers' Organization (Switzerland), 71
Catholic Flemish Group (Katholieke Vlaamse Kamergroep), 97
Catholic Flemish League (Katholieke Vlaamse Landsbond), 97
Catholic Flemish People's Party (Katholieke Vlaamse Volkspartij), 107, 108, 109
Catholic Keep the Spanish Embargo Committee, 269
Catholic National Party, Moravia, 220
Catholic Party (Belgium), 94–115; nineteenth century, party formation in, 94–6; in 1920s, 96–103; in 1930s, 103–10; and Europe, 110–11; war/occupation, 111–12
Catholic Peace Movement, 260
Catholic People's Party (KVP), Netherlands, 91
Catholic Social Action (Netherlands), 88
Catholic Social Guild (UK), 270
Catholic Social Party (Parti Catholique Social), Belgium, 107, 108, 109
Catholic Union, Belgium, 99–100, 102, 103, 106
Catholic Workers' International, 111
Catholic Workers' Movement: and Netherlands, 86, 87, 89; and Switzerland, 67, 71
Catholicism, as 'pariah nation', 7
Cavazzoni, Stefano, 143
Čech (newspaper): 224
Centre Party (Germany) *see* Zentrum (German Centre Party)
Centrolew, 153
centrisme social, 123
Centro Nazionale Italiano, 144
Černoch, Ján (Slovak spelling; *see also* Csernoch, János), 225
Československá strana lidová (Czechoslovak People's Party), 217–18, 220–5, 230; farmers, support of, 220; founding of, 220; social programme, 224; women, vote for, 223; workers, support of, 220
Českýsvaz (Czech association), 221
CFP (Confédération française des professions), 118
CFTC (Confédération française des travailleurs chrétiens), 118, 124
Ch-NSP (Chrześcijańsko-Narodowe Stronnictwo Pracy), Poland, 151, 154
Ch-NSR (Chrześcijańsko-Narodowe Stronnictwo Robotnicze), Poland, 151
Chaciński, Józef, 153, 154
chadecja (Christian Democracy), Poland, 151, 160
Champetier Concordat, 123
Champetier de Ribes, Auguste, 122, 132
Charles I (Emperor), 221
Chaussée d'Antin, 17
Christelijke Landsbond van de Middenstand (National League of Christian Middle Class), Belgium, 96–7
Christelijke Volkspartij-Parti Social

288

INDEX

Chrétien (CVP-PSC), Belgium 103, 248
Christian Community Party (Keresztény Községi Párt), Hungary, 206, 207, 213, 243–4
Christian democracy, 75, 76, 236, 246–9
Christian Democratic People's Party (Keresztény Demokrata Néppárt), Hungary 210
Christian Democrats, Belgium, 100, 101
Christian Economic and Social Party (Keresztény Gazdasági és Szocialis Párt), Hungary *see* KGSZP (Keresztény Gazdasági és Szocialis Párt), Hungary
Christian Front (US), 269
Christian Labour Movement, Belgium, 97, 98, 110, 111, 112
Christian Labour Union Movement, Hungary, 211
Christian National Economic Party (Keresztény Nemzeti Gazdasági Párt), Hungary, 205
Christian National Party (Keresztény Nemzeti Párt), Hungary, 201
Christian National Unity Party (Keresztény Nemzeti Egyesüles Pártja), Hungary, 202
Christian Nationalist Socialist Front (Keresztény Nemzeti Szocialista), Hungary, 210
Christian Opposition (Keresztény Ellenzék), Hungary, 208, 209, 213
Christian Smallholders and Agricultural Party (Keresztény Kisgazda és Földmívespárt), Hungary, 202
Christian Social and Economic Party (Keresztény Szociális és Gazdasági Párt), Hungary, 201
Christian Social Guild (UK), 269
Christian Social People's Party (Keresztényszociális Néppárt), Hungary, 197, 210
Christian Social Workers' Movement (Switzerland), 73
Christian Social Workers' Union (Switzerland), 67, 73
Christian Socialist Party (Keresztényszocialista Párt), Hungary, 208
Christian Socials (Moravia), 220
Christian Socials (Austrian), 19–20, 172–94; First Republic, ruling party of, 173–4, 177, 188; Second Republic, 188–9; *Anschluss*, 57, 130, 179–81, 182;Church relations, 175–7; confessional identity, 239; corporatism, role within party, 181–2; decline, 182–6; election losses, 8; European co-operation, 129, 181–2; government camp, in (1934–38), 186–8; nationalism, 31; origins, 19; party structures, 177–8; social basis, 174–5; voters, 177–8, *see also* Austria
Christian Workers' Movement: Austria, 174, 177, 183, 185; Switzerland, 70, 71
Christlichsoziale Partei *see* Christian Socials (Austrian)
Christlichsozialer Arbeiterbund (CAB), Switzerland, 67
Chronique sociale, 119
Chrześcijanska Demokracja (Christian Democracy), Poland, 151
Chrześcijanskie Zjednoczenie Zawodowe (ChZZ), Poland, 162
Chrześcijansko-Narodowe Stronnictwo Pracy (Ch-NSP), Poland, 151, 154
Chrześcijansko-Narodowe Stronnictwo Robotnicze (National Christian Worker's Party), Poland, 151
Church Index of unacceptable authors, 196
Church/State relations: and Austria, 18, 175–7; and Belgium, 95, 109; and France, 15, 120–3; and Germany, 48–53; and Hungary, 195, 196, 198; and Italy, 138–9; and Netherlands, 84, 87; in nineteenth century, 9, 15, 18, 33; and Poland, 164–6; and Switzerland, 70–2
Churchill, Sir Winston, 270, 271
ChZZ (Chrześcijańskie Zjednoczenie Zawodowe), Poland, 162
CIL (Confederazione Italiana Lavoratori), Italy, 141
Circle of Mecheln, Cardinal Désiré Mercier, 73
Cité Chrétienne, la (periodical), 110
Civiltà Cattolica (Jesuit journal), 145
clericalism, in France, 15, 16
CNR (Conseil national de la résistance), 133
Cold War, 253, 280
collectivism, 9
Combat Group, 133

Comité National de Secours et d'Alimentation, 98
Committee of Catholics for Human Rights (US), 269
communism, as threat, 107
Communist Party (KPD), Germany, 48
concentration camps, 90
Concentrazione antifascista, 146
concordataires, 122
Confédération des Syndicats Chrétiens (CSC), Belgium, 99
Confédération française des professions (CFP), 118
Confédération française des travailleurs chrétiens (CFTC), 118, 124
Confédération Internationale des Syndicats Chrétiens, 259
Confederazione Italiana Lavoratori (CIL), Italy, 141
confessionalization, 71
Confino, Alon, 31, 32
Conseil national de la Résistance (CNR), 133
Conservative Party (Belgium), 95
Conservative People's Party (Switzerland) *see* SKVP (Schweizerische Konservative Volkspartei)
Conway, Martin, 8, 235–51
Cooper, Duff, 271
Corn-dealing Act 1926 (Switzerland), 69
Cornilleau, Robert, 120, 128, 131, 255
corporatism: Austria, 181–2; Belgium, 106, 109; decline, 273–5; France, 125–6; Germany, 54; Italy, 125, 126; Switzerland, 74
Coste-Floret, Alfred and Paul, 133, 266
Coudenhove-Kalergi, Richard, 128
Cranborne, Lord, 271
Crawford, Virginia, 270, 271
Crownlands (Austria), 19
Csernoch, János (Hungarian spelling; *see also* Černoch, Ján), 197, 199, 204
Csilléry, András, 206, 207, 209
cuius regio, eius religio principle, 81
CVP-PSC (Christelijke Volkspartij-Parti Social Chréteien), 103, 248
Czapik, Gyula, 206
Czechoslovakia: Catholic Association of Czech Farmers, 221; co-operative banks, 220, 221; Consumer and Housing co-operatives, 221; crisis (1938), 130; 'Hus Church', 222, 224;

People's Party (Československá strana lidová), 217–18, 220–5, 230; Polish alliance, 161; Polish–Czechoslovak Treaty of Confederation (1942), 267; Prague, political collapse (1918), 221, 222, 227
Czermak, Emmerich, 185
Czerniewski, Ludomir, 154

Dachau concentration camp, 188
Dahrendorf, Ralf, 1
Daladier, Édouard, 122, 123, 126, 130
Das Kapital (Karl Marx), 220
Das Neue Reich (journal), 178
de Bruyne, Edgar, 108
de Castelnau, General, 121
De Gasperi, Alcide, 144, 145, 146, 266, 270
de Gaulle, Charles, 267
de Irujo, Manuel, 272
de Jong, Jan (Archbishop of Utrecht), 85, 91
de Man, Hendrik, 108
de Menthon, François, 119, 133, 266
de Montenach, Georges, 74
de Mun, Albert, 14, 30
de Onaindía, Antonio, 271
de Pange, Jean, 261
de Reynold, Gonzague, 74, 75
De Rosa, Gabriele, 146
de Schryver, August, 267, 271, 280
Decurtins, Caspar, 72
Degrelle, Léon, 106, 109
del Val, Cardinal Merry, 12–13
Delacroix, Léon, 101
Delbreil, Jean-Claude, 116–35, 239, 248
democracy: authoritarian, 55; 'Christian', 75, 76, 236, 246–9; nineteenth century, 8, 21, 22, 28–30; 'popular' (PDP), 131; and ultramontanism, 21, 22
democratic personalism, 125
Dempf, Alois, 261
Der wahre Staat (Othmar Spann), 186
Deutscher Katholikentag (National Congress of Catholics), 51
Deutscher Gewerkschaftsbund (DGB), Germany, 244
Deutschnationale Volkspartei (DNVP), Germany, 48
DGB (Deutscher Gewerkschaftsbund), 244
Di Maio, Tiziana, 136–49, 239

Die Schildwache (fundamentalist paper), 67–8
DNVP (Deutschnationale Volkspartei), Germany, 48
Dollfuss, Engelbert, 55, 147, 182, 183, 185, 187, 258; *Trabrennplatz* speech (1933), 184
d'Ormesson, Vladimir, 261
Dransfeld, Hedwig, 50
Dreyfus affair, 14
Droite (Catholic parliamentary group), Belgium, 98
Durand, Jean-Dominique, 2

East Central Europe, 217–34; co-operative banks, 220, 221; Czech People's Party, 217–18, 220–5, 230; farmers' movements, 218; Slovak People's Party, 218, 223, 225–32, *see also* Hungary; Poland
Ebenhoch, Alfred, 172
Eberle, Josef, 178–9, 186
Ebertz, Michael, 23
École libre des Hautes Études (New York), 271, 280
economic and social policy: France, 123–6; Italy, 139–41; Switzerland, 72–4, 245
ECSC (European Coal and Steel Community), 2, 281
Eden, Anthony, 270, 271
EEC (European Economic Community), 2, 281
Egyesült Keresztény Párt (EKP), Hungary, 209, 210, 213
Egyházközségi Munkásszakosztályok (EMSZO), Hungary, 211
Egységes Párt (Unity Party), Hungary, 203, 205
EKP (Egyesült Keresztény Párt), Hungary, 209, 210, 213
Elvert, Jürgen, 46–64, 239, 246
encyclicals, papal *see Graves de communi re*; *Il Fermo Proposito*; *Quadragesimo anno*; *Rerum novarum*; *Ubi arcano Dei*
endecja (National Democratic Party), Poland, 150, 152; and Christian Democrats, 162; and National Liberal Parties, 218; nationalist tradition, 161; and NPR, 167; public support, 163
Ender, Otto, 173, 184
Enlightenment, 25, 34

equality, nineteenth century, 28–30
Ernszt, Sándor, 201, 205, 207, 208, 209, 210
Erzberger, Matthias, 49, 55
Esprit (French review), 108
Estado Novo, 2, 268
Etter, Philipp, 75
Europa (newspaper), 59
Europäische Revue, 260, 261
European Coal and Steel Community, 2, 281
European Economic Community (EEC), 2, 281
Evangelical League, 31
exile of Catholic politicians: 1925–45, 266–7; anticipated, 252–64; federalism, 275–6; German question, 277–9; at Le Havre (France), 97; political corporatism, decline, 273–5; *popolari* (Italy), 146; Jan Šrámek (Czechoslovakia), 225; Luigi Sturzo, 144, 147; 'third way' thinking, 273; transnational contacts/co-operation, 269–73; transnational networks, 265–85; Zentrum (German Centre Party), 59

family allowances: France, 125; Switzerland, 74
farmers' movements: Austria, 177, 188; Belgium, 95, 96, 99, 100, 106, 108; East Central Europe, 218, 221; Germany, 244; Moravia, 221; Switzerland, 69, 71, 72
fasci di combattimento (militant action groups), 219
fascism: Anti-Fascist Concentration (1927), 266; anti-fascist resolution (1925), 257; clerico-fascism, 236; Hungary, 210, 211; inter-war years, 244; philo-fascism, 267; and PPI, 143–4, 146, 147; as problem-solving model (East Central Europe), 219; proto-fascism, 32
Faulhaber, Michael von, 51
Fazekas, Csaba, 195–216, 243–4
Federal Union, 275
federalism, 56, 130, 275–6
Fédération des Associations Conservatrices et des Cercles Catholiques (Belgium), 95–6, 97, 99, 100, 101, 102, 106

Fédération des Unions intellectuelles/Europäischer Kulturbund, 260, 261
Fédération nationale catholique (FNC), 121, 122, 241
Fédération républicaine, 121, 131
Fédérations de républicains-démocrates, 117
Feigenwinter, Ernst, 72
Ferrari, Francesco Luigi, 129, 146
Ferry, Jules, 16
Festschriften, 25
Fianna Fáil, 239
Figl, Leopold, 188, 189
Fine Gael, 239
Fink, Jodok, 173
FKGP (Független Kisgazdapárt), Hungary, 208, 212, 245
Flanders, 99
Flamenpolitik (German), 96
Flemish language, 97
Flint, James, 268
Flory, Charles, 119
FNC (Fédération nationale catholique), 121, 122, 241
Fogarassy, Canon Mihály, 195
France: Action Française *see* Action Française (AF); Action Libérale Populaire (ALP) *see* Action Libérale Populaire (ALP), France; anti-Semitism, 14–15, 30, 32; Association Catholique de la Jeunesse Française, 14; Associations Law (1901), 13; Bureau d'action civique, 117; Church/State relations, 15, 120–3; clericalism in, 15, 16; corporatism, 125–6; Enlightenment, 25; Franco-German rapprochment, 127, 129, 142, 256, 259, 260; laic legislation (republican), 13; Ligue de la jeune République, 116–17, 126, 127, 132, 259; monarchism, 15; nationalism, 128; nineteenth century, 12–17; occupation (1940), 266; Oeuvre des Cercles, 14; and papacy, 20; Paris Peace Conference, 58; 'phoney war' (1939–40), 122–3, 130, 132; republicanism, 15, 16; Separation Law (1905), 8, 16, 17; Sillon movement *see* Sillon movement (France); socialism, 124, 126; Third Republic, 17; trade unionism, 118, 124; Union catholique d'études internationales (Paris), 74; Vichy regime, 132, 241, *see also* French Resistance; French Revolution; (Parti Démocrate Populaire) *and other French parties*
Franco, General Francisco, 130, 267, 268, 271
Franco-Soviet Pact (1935), 130
Franz Ferdinand (successor to the Austrian throne), 172
freedom of association/education, 95
Freemasonry, ban on (Switzerland), 71
Freiheitsbund, Christian Workers' Movement, 187
Freisinnig-demokratische Partei (Swiss Liberal Party), 65, 66, 68, 70
Frenay, Henri, 133
French Resistance, 266
French Revolution, 81, 116
Fribourg, 74
Friedrich, István, 201, 202, 213
Friends of Italian Freedom (anti-fascist journal), 270
Független Kisgazdapárt (FKGP), Hungary, 208, 212, 245
fundamentalism, Swiss Conservative People's Party, 69
Funder, Friedrich, 173, 178, 186
Fuzet, Édmond (Archbishop of Rouen), 16

Gambetta, Léon, 13–14
Gasparri, Pietro (Cardinal), 138
Gay, Francisque, 132
Gdyk, Ludwik, 164
Gehler, Michael, 189
Geistige Landesverteidigung, 75
Gemellis, Agostino, 139–40
General Research Committee (France), 133
Geneva Circle, 261
Geneva Protocol, 179
Gerard, Emmanuel, 94–116, 244, 248
Gerbrandy, P. S., 272
German Order of the Knights, 223
German–Austrian Trade Association, 177
Germania, 255
Germany: anti-Semitism, 271; Concordat with Vatican (1933), 258; Belgium, invasion of (1940), 111; Catholic Congress movement, 17; Catholic political traditions (1870–1914),

10–12; Church/State relations, 48–53;
exile, politicians in, 277–9; Franco-
German rapprochement, 127, 129,
142, 256, 259, 260;
Gewerkschaftsstreit, 16; history (after
1945), 7, 8; inter-war period (see-saw
policy), 60; isolation (1920s), 74;
Munich Agreement (1938), 225, 231;
nationalism, 32; Netherlands, invasion
of (1940), 90; Protestantism, 12, 15,
31; Saar region, reintegration of, 57,
see also National Socialists (NSDAP);
Zentrum (German Centre Party) *and
other German parties*
Gessmann, Albert, 172
Gewerkschaftsstreit (union struggle), 16,
29
Geyer, Michael, 7, 8, 35
Gföllner, Johannes Maria (Bishop of
Linz), 177
Gibson, Ralph, 21, 23
Gids op Maatschappelijk Gebied
(periodical), 110
Giesberts, Johannes, 256
Giesswein, Sándor, 196–7, 201, 202, 214
Glaise-Horstenau, Edmund, 188
Gleissner, Heinrich, 185
Gömbös, Gyula, 208, 218
Goseling, C. M. J. F., 90
gouvernement démocratique Poullet-
Vandervelde, 98
Grabski, Stanisław, 153–4
Graves de communi re (encyclical), 88,
104
Gravissimo officii, 16
Great Depression, 208
Great Tradition (Catholic cultural
experience), 20, 33
Grew, Raymond, 7–8, 27, 28
Griger, Miklós, 204, 207, 208
Gundlach, Gustav, 54, 56, 182

Hackhofer, Karl, 75
Hague, The, 83
Hainaut (Walloon province), 96
Hála, František, 272
Haller, General Józef, 154, 167, 168, 204,
205; and ICDU, 272, 280; Union of
Soldiers, 153
Haller, István (journalist), 201
Hanisch, Ernst, 178
Harris, Ruth, 21

Hastings, Adrian, 20, 31
Hauriou, Maurice, 125
Hauser, Johann Nepomuk, 173, 175
Hazareesingh, Sudhir, 20
Heimwehr (Austrian paramilitary
movement), 181, 182, 184, 186–7, 245
Heine, Heinrich, 81
Held, Heinrich, 55, 56
Heyman, Hendrik, 111, 255
Hindenburg, Paul von (Marshal), 186
Hitler, Adolf, 56, 111, 129, 225, 265;
Mein Kampf, 270, *see also* Mussolini,
Benito
Hivatásszervezet (Professional
Organization), 211
Hlinka, Andrej, 218, 224, 225–6, 227,
228, 229, 231; Hlinka Guard, 231
Hlinkova Slovenská L'udova Strana
(HSL'S), 229, 230–1
Hodža, Milan, 227, 229
Horthy, Miklós (Admiral), 198, 205, 219;
system, 200–3, 208, 209, 210
Horthy system, political Catholicism
during formation of (Hungary),
200–3
House of Savoy, 137
Houtart, Maurice, 102
Hruban, Mořic, 221
Hrvatska pučka seljačka stranka, 218
HSL'S (Hlinkova Slovenská L'udova
Strana), 229, 230–1
Hungarian Life Party (Magyar Élet
Pártja), 209, 218
Hungarian People's Party (Néppárt), 195,
196, 207, 226
Hungary, 195–216; anti-Semitism, 204,
207, 209, 213; Christian nationalism,
ideology, 198–200; Church/State
relations, 195, 196, 198; Compromise
of 1867 (Austria and Hungary), 195,
196; consolidation policy, 204; *coup
d'état* (1919), 197; Great Depression,
207; Horthy system, 200–3, 208, 209,
210; social history of political
catholicism, 211–13; transformation of
political catholicism, 207–11
Hunter College (New York), 271, 280
Hurdes, Felix, 188, 266, 280
'Hus Church' (Czechoslovakia), 222,
224
Huszár, Károly, 199, 201, 207
Huyn, Paul de (Archbishop), 222

ICDU (International Christian
  Democratic Union), 265, 271–2, 273,
  276, 280, 281
Il Fermo Proposito (encyclical), 137
Imrédy, Béla, 209
Independent Smallholders Party
  (Független Kisgazdapárt), Hungary,
  208, 212, 245
Independents (Switzerland), 69
Industrial Revolution, 26
Innitzer, Theodor, 185
Integrationspartei (integration party),
  29
integrists, 14
inter-war political Catholicism, 5,
  235–51; Christian democracy, 246–9;
  defence, 236, 237; fortress mentality,
  236–41; frontiers, 237, 238; *milieu*
  parties, 239–40; primacy of unity, 241;
  social programmes, 236–7; unique
  policies of, 238; unity difficulties,
  241–6; urban–rural conflict, 244
International Christian Democratic Union
  (ICDU), 265, 271–2, 273, 276, 280,
  281
International Confederation of Christian
  Trade Unions, 111
International Labour Organization
  (Geneva), 84
International Trades Union Congress,
  259
Internationale démocratique, 127
Irish Free State, 239
Italy: Church/State relations, 138–9;
  corporatism, 125, 126; Ethiopia
  invasion, 129; Mazzini Society of
  Italians in exile, 266, *see also* fascism;
  Mussolini, Benito; PPI (Partito
  Popolare Italiano) *and other political
  parties*

Jacini, Stefano, 141, 143
Jaspar cabinet (Belgium), 100
Jaspar, Henri, 101
Jehlička, František, 228, 229
Jesuits, 70
Jeune République, Ligue de la, 116–17,
  126, 127, 132, 259
Jewish people, antagonism towards *see*
  anti-Semitism
Ježek, František, 225
Joos, Joseph, 255

Juge, Alphonse, 132
Jungbauernbewegung (Young Farmers'
  Movement), 72
Jungbauernpartei (Young Farmers' Party),
  69
Juriga, Ferdiš, 228
Jury, Hugo, 189

Kaas, Ludwig, 52, 53, 239, 240
Kaczyński, Father Zygmunt, 167
Kahlenberg, battle of, 184
Kaiser, Jakob, 60, 61
Kaiser, Wolfram, 265–85
Kaiserreich, 46, 51
Kakowski, Archbishop Aleksander, 165
KALOT (Katolikus Agrárifjúsági
  Legényegyletek Országos Szövetsége),
  Hungary, 211
Kalyvas, Stathis N., 8
Karolingian Ostmark, 180
Károlyi, Gyula, 208
Károlyi, Mihály, 197
Katholiek Verbond van België-Union
  catholique belge, 96, 255
Katholieke Vlaamse Kamergroep
  (Catholic Flemish Group), 97
Katholieke Vlaamse Landsbond (Catholic
  Flemish League), 97
Katholieke Vlaamse Volkspartij (Catholic
  Flemish People's Party), Belgium, 107,
  108, 109
Katholikentage, *see* Catholic Congress
Katholischer Frauenbund (Catholic
  women's organization), 50
Katolický spolek českého rolnictva na
  Moravě, ve Slezsku a v Dolních
  Rakousích, 220–1
Katolikus Agrárifjúsági Legényegyletek
  Országos Szövetsége (KALOT),
  Hungary, 211
Kereszteny Demokrata Néppárt
  (Christian Democratic People's Party),
  Hungary, 210
Kereszteny Ellenzék (Christian
  Opposition), Hungary, 208, 209, 213
Kereszteny Gazdasági és Szocialis Párt
  (Christian Economic and Social Party)
  see KGSZP (Kereszteny Gazdasági és
  Szocialis Párt), Hungary
Kereszteny Kisgazda és Földmívespárt
  (Christian Smallholders and
  Agricultural Party), Hungary, 202

Keresztény Községi Párt (KKP), Hungary, 206, 207, 213, 243–4
Keresztény Nemzeti Egyesüles Pártja (KNEP), Hungary, 202, 203
Keresztény Nemzeti Gazdasági Párt (Christian National Economic Party), Hungary, 205
Keresztény Nemzeti Párt (Christian National Party), Hungary, 201
Keresztény Nemzeti Szocialista (Christian Nationalist Socialist Front), Hungary, 210
Keresztény Szociális és Gazdasági Párt (Christian Social and Economic Party), Hungary, 201
Kereszténysociális Néppárt (Christian Social People's Party), Hungary, 197, 210
Kereszténysocialista Párt (Christian Socialist Party), Hungary, 208
Ketteler, Wilhelm, 53
KGSZP (Keresztény Gazdasági és Szocialis Párt), Hungary, 205, 206, 207, 208, 209, 213; inter-war years, 244, 245
Kienböck, Viktor, 173, 174
KKP (Keresztény Községi Párt), Hungary, 206, 207, 213, 243–4
Klebelsberg, Kunó, 199
Kleindeutsches Reich, 46
Klemperer, Klemens von, 175
Klub (parliamentary party), Austria, 178
KNEP (Keresztény Nemzeti Egyesüles Pártja), Hungary, 202, 203
Kolfschoten, H. A. M. T., 90
Kölnische Volkszeitung (newspaper), 255
Königswinter circle, 54
Kordáč, František, 222
Korfanty, Wojciech, 150, 153, 154, 156, 164
Korošec, Anton, 218, 219
Közi-Horváth, József, 210
KPD (Communist Party), Germany, 48
Kubick, Paul, 67
Kuenzer, Richard, 255
Kuk, Leszek, 150–71, 244
Kukiel, General Marian, 167
Kulturkampf: and Austria, 18, 173, 175, 176; and German Centre Party, 47, 48, 49; and Netherlands, 82–3; in nineteenth century, 8, 10, 13, 16; and Swiss politics, 70, 71

Kun, Béla (government), Hungary, 197
Kunschak, Leopold, 177, 183, 188
Kuyper, Abraham, 82
Kuzmány, Karol, 228
Květ'ansko-sociální strana pro Cechy a Moravu, 220
KVP (Catholic People's Party), Netherlands, 91
Kwiatkowski, Michal, 272, 278

La voix du Nord, 133
Labour Party: Britain, 1, 266; Poland, 154, 156–7, 165, 166–9
Lake Constance conferences for Christian politics (1921–26), 260
Lammasch, Heinrich, 173
Lanckorona pact, 158
Landaburu, Javier, 270–1
Landesring der Unabhängigen (Switzerland), 69
Landtag (Prussian), 46
Láng, János, 204
Langlois, Claude, 15
Las Cases, Philippe de, 255
Lateran Treaties (1929), 145–6, 259
L'Aube (newspaper), 132, 270
Laurent, Raymond, 255
Le ralliement a-t-il échoué (Robert Cornilleau), 120
League of Nations, 254, 257; Austria, financial assistance for, 179; and German Centre Party, 57; PPI support, 142; Seipel Vice-president of (1928), 180; and Swiss membership, 74
Lebenshaltung aus Fürsorge und Erwerbstätigkeit (Helene Wessel), 57
Lega Italiana dei Diritti dell'Uomo (LIDU), 146
Legitimist People's Party (Legitimista Néppárt), Hungary, 208, 209
Leimgruber, Oskar, 73
Lemire, Abbé Jules, 15
Lemke, William, 268
Leo XIII (Pope), 14, 23, 24, 25, 53, 88, 166
Leopold III (King), 111
Liberal Party: Belgium, 95, 97, 98; Italy, 143–5; Netherlands, 82; Switzerland, 65, 66, 68, 70
Liberal Party of Free Thinkers, Hungary, 195–6

liberalism: and collectivism, 9; France, 124; inter-war years, 242; liberal-individualist myth, 34; nineteenth century heritage, 9, 27, 31; Poland, 155, 157; and PPI, 143–5; and socialism, 28, 86; and working-class plight, 53
Liberation (1944–45), 133
Liberté movement, 133
Lidové listy, 224
LIDU (toga Italiana dei Diritti dell'Uomo), 146
Lieber, Ernst, 12
Liège (Walloon province), 96
Ligue de la jeune République, 116–17, 126, 127, 132, 259
Ligue nationale de la démocratie (LND), 117, 127
Lijphart, Arend, 83
Linz programme, Austrian Social Democrats (1926), 181
Liptovský Svätý Mikulás, meeting in (1918), 227
Little Entente (Czechoslovakia, Romania and Yugoslavia), 198
Ljotić group, Serbia, 220
LND (Ligue nationale de la démocratie), 117, 127
Locarno Treaty (1925), 4, 256
Loppem cabinet, Belgium, 98
Loth, Wilfried, 11, 12, 28, 29, 242, 245
L'Ouest Éclair (newspaper), 119
Lueger, Karl, 19, 20, 172, 173, 239

McManners, John, 13
McMillan, James, 31
Magyar Élet Pártja (Hungarian Life Party), 209, 218
Malgeri, Francesco, 140
Malines, Catholic Congress (1936), 109
Mancel, Abbot, 119
Mann, Golo, 46
March on Rome (1922), 143
Maritain, Jacques, 108, 111, 270
Martin, Benjamin, 14
Marx, Karl, 220
Marx, Wilhelm, 52, 57, 239, 259, 261
Masaryk, Garrigue Thomas, 222, 227, 230–1
Mataja, Heinrich, 28
Matica Slovenská (Slovak Heritage Foundation), 228
Matt, Hans von, 68

Matteotti, Giacomo, 144
Maurras, Charles, 102, 128
Mayeur, Jean-Marie, 10, 14, 17
Mayr, Michael, 173, 179
Mazzini Society of Italians in exile, 266
Meier, Josef, 72
Mein Kampf (Adolf Hitler), 270
Méline, Jules, 16
Mendizábal, Alfredo, 270
Mercier, Cardinal Désiré-Joseph (Archbishop of Malines), 73, 98
mesonism (social philosophy), 73
Miglioli, Guido, 140
Mikołajczyk, Stanisław, 168
Miltner, Charles, 269
Mindszenty, József, 209
Miskolc (Hungary), 211–12
Mittelstand, 11
mittelständisch protest groups, 19
Mittelständische Arbeitsgemeinschaft (trade and commerce committee), 70
Modelski, Colonel Izydor, 168
Modern Catholicism (Ottokár Prohászka), 196
modernity, corporate, 9, 34
Moeller van den Bruck, Arthur, 58
Molony, John, 25
Momigliano, Arnaldo, 35
monarchism, France, 15
Mönchengladbacher Volksverein, 88
Moore, Anthony, 269
Mooser, Josef, 12, 26
Moravia: Catholic groupings in, 220, 221; farmers in, 221
Morges Front, 167
Moulin, Jean, 133, 266
Mounier, Emmanuel, 108, 111, 125
Mouvement Républicain de Libération (MRL), 133
Mouvement Républicain Populaire (MRP), 133, 248, 266
Moyses, Štefan, 228
MRL (Mouvement Républicain de Libération), 133
MRP (Mouvement Républicain Populaire), 133, 248, 266
Müller, Guido, 252–64
Müller, Josef, 266
Munich Agreement (1938), 225, 231
Musil, Robert, 18
Mussolini, Benito: attitudes, 268; British/American support, 267; meeting

with Engelbert Dollfuss, 184; and PPI (Italy), 125, 141, 143–4, 145; Vatican, support from, 266, *see also* fascism; Hitler, Adolf
Musy, Jean-Marie, 68, 75
Muth, Karl, 256

Naples (PPI) congress, 141
Národni výbor organization (National Council), Prague, 221
Narodowe Zjednoczenie Ludowe, 167
Narodowa Partia Robotnicza (NPR), Poland, 153, 162, 163, 166, 167
National Alliance of Catholic Youth and Agricultural Organizations (Katolikus Agrárifjúsági Legényegyletek Országos Szövetsége), Hungary, 211
National Catholic Alliance, Hungary, 211
National Christian Socialist Party (Országos Kereszténysocialista), Hungary, 197, 204
National Christian Worker's Party (Ch-NSR), Poland, 151
National Congress of Catholics (Deutscher Katholikentag), Germany, 51
National Democratic Party (ND), Poland *see endecja* (National Democratic Party), Poland
National Front, 225
National League of Christian Workers (Algemeen Christelijk Werkersverbond-Ligue Nationale des Travailleurs Chrétiens), Belgium, 96, 98, 99, 100, 108, 110
National League of Middle Class (Christelijke Landsbond van de Middenstand), Belgium, 96–7
National Liberals (Germany), 11
National Party (SN), Poland, 168
National Peasants' Party (NZL), Poland, 167
National Security Act 1922 (Switzerland), 69
National Smallholders and Agricultural Party (Országos Kisgazda- és Földmivespárt), Hungary, 202, 203, 218
National Socialism, 48, 58–9; Belgium, German invasion of (1940), 111; and French relations, 128; Netherlands, German invasion of (1940), 90; Reichstag elections (1933), 183; and SIPDIC, 147, *see also Anschluss* (Austria); Germany; Hitler, Adolf
National Union for Social Justice (US), 268
National Worker's Party, Poland, 154
nationalism: Belgium, 96, 101, 102, 107, 109; France, 128; Germany, 12, 32; Hungary, 198–200; nineteenth century, 12, 30, 31–2, 34
Nationalrat (Austria), 180, 183
Naumann, Friedrich, 49
Nazi regime *see* National Socialism
ND (National Democratic Party), Poland *see endecja* (National Democratic Party), Poland
NEI (Nouvelles Équipes Internationales), 261, 267, 271
Nell-Breuning, Oswald, 54, 56, 57, 182
Nemzeti Egység Pártja (Party of National Unity), Hungary, 208
neophytes, 129
Néppárt (Hungarian People's Party), 195, 196, 207, 226
Netherlands: Anti-Revolutionary Party (Protestant), 82; Belgium, separation from, 95; Catholic pillar, formation, 85; Church/State relations, 84, 87; founding, 80; German invasion (1940), 90; Liberal Party, 82; modernization, late, 81; neutrality policy, 83; nineteenth century, 80–2; pillarization, Dutch, 82; Polder tolerance model, 81; political changes (post-First World War), 88–9; Protestants in, 81, 82; as 'religious testing-ground', 81; s'Hertogenbosch conference (1928), 127; social differences, Catholic milieu, 85–6; socialism in, 82, 86, 88, 89–90; universal suffrage issue, 83, *see also* RKSP (Rooms Katholieke Staats Partij) *and other Dutch parties*
Neuschl, Robert, 220
Neustädter-Stürmer, Odo, 185
New Deal (US), 267
nineteenth-century heritage, 7–45; anti-Semitism, 14–15, 30, 32; Church, new order, 22–3; democracy, 28–30; equality, 28–30; nationalism, 12, 30, 31–2, 34; social theory/practice, 23–7; and twentieth-century challenges, for Catholics, 27–8, *see also* Belgium: nineteenth century, party formation in; Netherlands: nineteenth century

Nipperdey, Thomas, 21, 32, 34
Nolens, W. H., 83, 84, 87, 88, 89
Non expedit, 137
Nord, Philip, 22, 29, 30, 32
Nouvelles Équipes Internationales (NEI), 261, 267, 271
Novak, Michael, 25
NPR (Narodowa Partia Robotnicza), Poland, 153, 162, 163, 166, 167
NSDAP (National Socialism) *see* National Socialism
Nutting, Willis D., 271
Nyilas Keresztas Párt (Arrow-Cross Party), Hungary, 209, 210, 220
Nyisztor, Zoltán, 209
NZL (National Peasants' Party), Poland, 167

Oeuvre des Cercles (France), 14
Office for the Liquidation of Religious Affairs (Hungary), 197
Okoń, Father Eugeniusz, 167
Olomouc, property in, 223
'one man, one vote' principle, 95
Orel sports society, 220, 224
Országgyülési Néppárt (Parliamentary People's Party), Hungary, 196
Országos Kereszténysocialista (National Christian Socialist Party), Hungary, 197, 204
Országos Kisgazda-és Földmívespárt (National Smallholders and Agricultural Party), Hungary, 202, 203, 218
Ostmärkische Sturmscharen, 187
Ottokár Prohászka Society, 210
Notre programme de politique extérieure (manifesto), 128

Pagès, Louis-Alfred, 255
Pálffy, József, 210
Pan-European movement, 128, 237
papacy, 20, 23
Papen, Franz von, 54, 186, 261
'pariah nations' (socialism and Catholicism), 7, 35
Paris Peace Conference, 58
Parish Workers Division (Egyházközségi Munkásszakosztályok), Hungary, 211
Parliamentary People's Party (Országgyülési Néppárt), Hungary, 196

Parti Catholique Social (Catholic Social Party), Belgium, 107, 108, 109
Parti Démocrate Populaire *see* PDP (Parti Démocrate Populaire)
Partis démocratiques d' inspiration chrétienne, 257, *see also* SIPDIC (Secrétariat International des Partis Démocratiques d'Inspiration Chrétienne)
Partito Popolare Italiano *see* PPI (Partito Popolare Italiano)
Party of National Unity (Nemzeti Egység Pártja), Hungary, 208
Patto Gentiloni, 138
Paulskirche Parliament, 46
Pax Romana organization, 75, 260
PDP (Parti Démocrate Populaire), 116–35; and Action Française (AF), 121, 131; 'ascendant phase', 131; Catholic support, 119; Church relations, 120–3; *Conseil national*, 117; decline, 130–3; democratic personalism, 125; doctrinal issues, 123, 124–5; economic and social policy, 123–6; electoral losses, 3; European and international initiative, 126–30; founding of, 17, 116, 117, 131; handbook (1928), 124; inter-war years, 239; and Mouvement Républicain Populaire (MRP), 133, 248; party conference (1927), 124; philosophy, 124–5, 131; 'pre-Resistance' attitude, 132;*ralliement* policy, 122;religious problems, 122;and secularism, 121; sociological roots, 117–19; trade unionism, 118; welfare problems, 125, *see also* France
Peace Movement, 84
Peace Treaty, St Germain (1919), 179, 180
peasant parties, 167, 168, 218
Penal Law Act 1938 (Switzerland), 69
People and Freedom Groups (UK/US): Federal Union, lack of representation in, 275; founding of, 253, 269; German question, 278, 279; meetings, themes of, 273; political continuity among Catholic politicians, lack of, 281; transnational contacts, 270, 271; Virginia Crawford chairman of (1936–44), 270; world organization, 276

298

People and Liberty group, 271
People's Association (Switzerland), 72
People's League (Belgium), 95
People's Party: Austria, 188, 189, 266; Belgium, 107, 108, 109; Czechoslovakia, 217–18, 220–5; Hungary, 195, 196, 207, 226; Netherlands, 91; Slovak, 225–32; Slovakia, 218, 223, 225–32; Switzerland *see* SKVP (Schweizerische Konservative Volkspartei)
Perrier, Ernest, 73
Pesch, Heinrich, 54, 56, 73
Pétain, Philippe (Marshal), 132
Petersburg duma, 217
Pětka (Czechoslovakia), 219
Peukert, Detlev, 34
Pezet, Ernest, 129
Pfafferott, Henning, 255
'phoney war' (1939–40), France, 122–3, 130, 132
Picard, Louis, 104
Piechocki, Stefan, 164
Pieper, August, 9, 29, 256
Pierlot, Hubert, 104, 280
piety, 20–1
Piffl, Gustav, 178
Piller, Joseph, 75
Piłsudski, Marshal Józef, 151, 152, 153, 219
Piou, Jacques, 14, 30
Pius X (Pope), 16, 17, 23, 26, 30, 137, 226
Pius XI (Pope), 121–2, 128, 145, 182, 206, 211, 241
Pius XII (Pope), 91, 241
Piwowarczyk, Father Jan, 164
Platz, Hermann, 13, 261
Poels, H. A., 88
Poland: anti-Semitism, 152, 159; Church/State relations, 164–6; *coup d'état*, 151, 153; eastern, annexation of, 278; European co-operation, 129; as guardian of 'Mediterranean Christian culture', 161; Home Army (undercover), 168; Łódź conference, 157; Polish–Czechoslovak Treaty of Confederation (1942), 267; Union of Soldiers, 153, *see also endecja* (National Democratic Party), Poland; PSChD (Polish Christian Democratic Party)

Polish Conservative People's Party (Polskie Stronnictwo Konserwatywno-Ludowe), 167
Polish Party of Labour, 272
Politique (journal), 126, 128
Polskie Stronnictwo Chrześcijańskiej Demokracji *see* PSChD (Polish Christian Democratic Party)
Polskie Stronnictwo Konserwatywno-Ludowe (Polish Conservative People's Party), 167
Polskie Stronnictwo Ludowe, 218
Ponikowski, Antoni, 153
Popiel, Karol, 167, 168
Popular Christian Union, 151
Popular Democratic Party (France) *see* PDP (Parti Démocrate Populaire)
Popular Front: France, 122, 126, 132; Spain, 107
Popular Party (Italy) *see* PPI (Partito Popolare Italiano)
popularism, 120, 124, 138, 139, 143, 144; democratic, 131
Pourquoi pas? (Robert Cornilleau), 128, 131
PPI (Partito Popolare Italiano), 136–49, 219; agrarian policy, 139, 141; and Belgium, 104; Church connections, 138–9; democratic perspective, 145–7; economic and social programme, 139–41; electoral losses, 144; foreign and European policy, 141–2; founding of, 117, 138; and liberal state crisis, 143–5; non-confessionalism, 139; origins/general character, 137–8; and PDP, 129; Roman Question, 137, 138, 145; and SIPDIC, 255; societal basis, 138–9; Vatican, withdrawal of support from, 252, *see also* Italy
PPS (Socialist Party), Poland, 168
pragmatism, Swiss Conservative People's Party, 69
Prague: political collapse (1918), 221, 222, 227; property in, 223
Präsidialkabinette, 186
Prelot, Marcel, 124, 126, 255
Press and Information Bureau (France), 133
Pressezentrale (Austria), 185
Pribina, Prince, 231
Prohászka, Ottokár, 196, 197, 201–2, 203, 214

proportional representation (Belgium), 94–5
Protestantism: Germany, 12, 15, 31; Netherlands, 81, 82
Prussian-Austrian War (1866), 46
PSChD (Polish Christian Democratic Party), 150–71; Church relations, 164–6, 239; difficulties, 245; formation, 151, 152; organization, 154; party programme, 155–61; politics, 161–4; press organ, 154–5; social composition, 154–5; structure, 154, *see also* Poland
PSL (Peasant Party), Poland, 168

Quadragesimo anno (encyclical): and Austria, 182; and Belgium, 110; and France, 123; and Germany, 54, 55, 57; and Hungary, 210–11; and Netherlands, 90; and Poland, 155, 157, 158, *see also Rerum novarum* (encyclical)

R. K. Bedrijfsradenstelsel (works council), 89
Raab, Julius, 177, 188, 189
Räber, Joseph, 68
Rada Naczelna (supreme council), 154
Radić, Stjepan, 218
Radical Peasant Party (Stronnictwo Radykalno-Chlopskie), Poland, 167
Ramek, Rudolf, 173
rationalism, 34
Rechtsstaat (constitutional state), 34
Redfield, Robert, 20
Reeken, Dietmar von, 19
Reformation, 80
Reichsbauernbund (Association of Farmers), Austria, 177, 188
Reichsgewerbebund (Trade Association), Austria, 177, 188
Reichspartei, 172
Reichspost, 173, 186
Reichsrat, 172, 217; elections, 220, 221
Reichsromantik, 179
Reichstag, 57, 217
Reille-Soult, François, 125
Reither, Josef, 183, 188
Renard, Georges, 125
Renner, Karl, 174, 175
republicanism, France, 15, 16
Republikánská strana československého venkova, 218

Rerum novarum (encyclical): and Austria, 174; and Belgium, 95, 103; and Czechoslovakia, 220; and France, 116, 123; and Germany, 53, 54; and Hungary, 196; issue of, 24–5, 41n83; and Poland, 155, 158; and RKSP, 87–8; social question, 2–3, 24–5; and Union de Fribourg, 73, *see also Quadragesimo anno* (encyclical)
Resch, Josef, 183, 187
Résistance, 133
Rexist movement, Belgium, 106–7, 108, 109, 111, 245
Risorgimento, 146
RKSP (Rooms Katholieke Staats Partij), 80–93; bishops, stance of, 84–5; centre (socialism/liberalism), 85–7; formation, 82; founding, 87; inter-war period, 84; liquidation of, 90; quality parliamentary seats, 87; re-orientation (social-political), 88; *Rerum Novarum*, effect on conservatives in, 87; unity, 84–5, *see also* Netherlands
Robles, Gil, 147
Roes, Jan, 80–93
Rohan, Karl Anton (Prince), 260, 261
Rölli-Alkemper, Lukas, 65–79, 245
Roman Catholic State Party (Netherlands) *see* RKSP (Rooms Katholieke Staats Partij)
Roosevelt, Franklin D., 60, 267, 268–9
Rósa, Ferenc, 213
Rosenberg, Martin, 72, 280
Rothermere press, 267
Russo, Domenico, 129, 255
Rutten, Georges Ceslas, 111, 255
Ruys de Beerenbrouck, Charles, 83, 88
Ryan, John, 269

Sachsenhausen concentration camp, 90
Saint Germain Peace Treaty (1919), 179, 180
Saint Joan's Alliance (Catholic women's suffrage society), 270
Saint Wenceslas jubilee (1929), 224
Salazar, Antonio Oliviera, 147, 268
Salzburg Christian Social conference (1933), 184
Sammlung, 30
sanacja, 151–2, 153, 160
Sangnier, Marc: international co-operation, 259, 261; Internationale

démocratique, 127; Jeune République, 116–17, 126, 127, 259; Sillon *see* Sillon movement (France)
Savoy, Abbé André, 73
Schausberger, Franz, 183
Scheiwiler, Bishop Aloisius, 71, 72
Scherrer, Josef, 67, 71, 73
Schildwache movement, 68
Schindler, Franz Martin, 173, 175, 182
Schlegel, Josef, 185
Schmitz, Richard, 173, 181, 186
Schneider, Emil, 176
Schönere Zutunft (newspaper), 186
Schreiber, Georg, 57
Schumann, Maurice, 267, 280
Schuschnigg, Kurt, 180, 186, 187
Schutzbund (Social Democratic paramilitary), Austria, 184
Schweizerische Katholische Bauernvereinigung (Catholic Farmers' Organization), 71
Schweizerische Konservative Volkspartei (SKVP) *see* SKVP (Schweizerische Konservative Volkspartei)
Schweizerischer Katholischer Volksverein (SKVV), 68, 72
SDAP (Social Democratic Labour Party), Netherlands, 89, 91
Secrétariat International des Partis Démocratiques d'Inspiration Chrétienne *see* SIPDIC (Sécretariat International des Partis Démocratiques d' Inspiration Chrétienne)
Segers, P. W., 111
Seipel, Ignaz: and Austrian republic, transition from monarchy, 173–4, 178; on Austro-Marxism, 28; and authoritarianism, 177; and corporatism, 181; on education, 176; and foreign policy, 179, 180; and international co-operation, 260; pro-Heimwehr policies of, 183; role, 240
Selbstbildung (self-development), 26
Semaines sociales, 119, 126
Separation Law (1905), France, 8, 16, 17
Serbia, Ljotić group, 220
Serédi, Jusztinián, 206
Seyss-Inquart, Arthur, 99, 188
Schaepman, Herman, 82, 84, 87
s'Hertogenbosch conference (1928), 127
Schraffl, Josef, 179
Shuster, George N., 269

Sidor, Karol, 229, 231
Sikorski, General Władysław, 154, 168
Sillon movement (France): founding of, 116; nineteenth century, 15, 16, 17, 26, 30; in 1920s, 260
Simon, Paul, 132, 255
Simondet, Henri, 127, 255
Singer, Milton, 20
Singulari quadam, 29
SIPDIC (Secrétariat International des Partis Démocratiques d'Inspiration Chrétienne), 252–64; ACW participation in, 110–11; alternative societal/political forms, 260–2; Cologne Conference (1932), 256; draft constitution, 256–7; early co-operation, structural deficiencies, 258–60; establishment, 127, 255; institutional/policy developments, 255–8; Paris congress, 255; and PDP (France), 129; RKSP taking part in, 84; Sturzo, recommendations made by, 136, 147
Skrbenský, Lev (Cardinal), 222
SKVP (Schweizerische Konservative Volkspartei), 65–79; Church, relationship with, 70–2; diffIculties of, 245; economic and social programme, 72–4, 245; European conceptions (Swiss Catholic Conservatives), 74–5; founding, 72; fundamentalism, 69; history, 66; ideology, 66, 69; inter-war period, 66, 69; social basis, 66–70; Young Conservatives within, 67–8, 69, 71, 74, *see also* Switzerland
SKVV (Schweizerischer Katholischer Volksverein), 68, 72
Slovák (newspaper), 229, 231
Slovak Heritage Foundation (Matica Slovenská), 228
Slovak People's Party (Slovenska L'udova strana), 218, 223, 225–32; leadership committee, 228; Party programme, 227
Slovene People's Party (Slovenská ljudska stranka), 218
Slovenska ljudska stranka (Slovene People's Party), 218
Slovenská L'udova strana (Slovak People's Party), 218, 223, 225–32
Slovenská strana národní a rolnická, 218
SLS (Slovenská L'udova strana), Slovak People's Party, 218, 223, 225–32

Smith, Helmut Walser, 12, 22
Smólski, Stefan, 164
SN (Nationalist Party), Poland, 168
Social Democratic Party: Austria, 19, 20, 173, 174, 175, 182, 184; Netherlands, 89, 91; Poland, 150
Social Democrats (SPD), Germany, 1, 11, 29, 48, 49, 53, 144, 223
social question: *Rerum novarum* (encyclical), 2–3, 24–5; Zentrum (German Centre Party), 53–5
Social Security Act 1925 (Switzerland), 69
social theory/practice, nineteenth century, 23–7
Social Weeks, 88
socialism: Belgium, 95; France, 124, 126; inter-war years, 242; and liberalism, 28, 86; Netherlands, 82, 86, 88, 89–90; as 'pariah nation', 7, 35
Socialist International, 259
Socialist Parti ouvrier beige (Belgium), 95, 98
Socialist Party: Belgium, 97, 98; Poland, 150, 168
Socialist Unity Party, Germany, 61
solidarity principle, 56, 57, 89
Sonderweg, 7
Sonnenschein, Carl, 256
Soviet–German Pact (1939), 130
Soyeur, Jules, 280
Spahn, Peter, 12
Spanish Civil War, 107, 130, 268, 270
Spann, Othmar, 186
SPD (Social Democrats), Germany, 1, 11, 29, 48, 49, 53, 144, 223
Sperber, Jonathan, 11
Spiecker, Carl, 281
Šrámek, Jan, 218, 221, 223, 224, 225, 272, 280
Šrobár, Vavro, 227
Stammlande (Swiss heartland), 66, 67, 69, 245
Ständestaat system (Austria), 2, 73, 266
Steed, Henry Wickham, 270
Stegerwald, Adam, 244, 256
Stingl, Karl, 56
Stojan, Cyril, 222
Stresemann, Gustav, 57
Stronnictwo Pracy (Poland), 151, 154
Stronnictwo Radykalno-Chlopskie (Radical Peasant Party), Poland, 167

Stunde Null, 35
Sturzo, Luigi: on Atlantic Charter, 276; and Austrian Christian Social Party, role in riot suppression, 129; and capitalism, 274; economic and social programme (PPI), 140; and Europe, 127, 253; and fascism, rise of, 143; foreign policy, 127, 141; and Germany, 137–8, 146, 278; Pope, relations with, 128; popularism, 120, 124, 131, 138; PPI, 117, 136, 140; role, 240; SIPDIC, founding of, 255
subsidiarity principle, 89
Sudetendeutsche Partei, 225
Suppan, Arnold, 217–34
Suvich, Fulvio, 185
Švehla, Antonín, 218, 223
Switzerland: anti-Semitism, 69; Church/State relations, 70–2; corporatism, 74; Freemasonry ban, 71; Liberal Party, 65, 66, 68, 70; neutrality of, 74; People's Association, 72; protest movements, 69; *Stammlande* (heartland), 66, 67, 69, 245; Swiss Catholic People's Association (SKVV), 68, 72; Zurich, Catholic population, 67; *see also* SKVP (Schweizerische Konservative Volkspartei) *and other Swiss parties*
Syllabus errorum (1864), 146
Szabadelvü Párt (Liberal Party of Free Thinkers), Hungary, 195–6
Szabó, István Nagyatádi, 202, 218
Szabó, József, 207, 208
Szekfü, Gyula, 198
Szulik, Jan, 160

The Tablet, 268
Tardieu Plan, 129
Teitgen, Pierre-Henri, 133, 266
Teleki, Pál, 201, 202, 209
Témoignage chrétien, 133
Terrenoire, Louis, 274
Tessier, Gaston, 118
Teutonic Knights, 277
Theunis cabinet (Belgium), 98
Theunis, Georges, 101
Thibout, Georges, 255
Third Reich, 58, 59, 161, 247
Third Republic, France, 17
Tirpitz, Alfred von (Admiral), 49
Tiso, Jozef, 228, 231, 232, 240

Tobler, János, 207
Trade Association (Reichsgewerbebund), Austria, 177, 188
trade unionism (France), 118, 124
Treaty of Trianon (1920), 198, 276
Treaty of Versailles (1919), 57, 142, 258, 276
Trémintin, Pierre, 132
Trimborn, Carl, 29
Troeltsch, Ernst, 60
Tschoffen, Paul, 277
Tuka, Vojtěch, 229, 230, 231, 232
Turčiansky Svätý Martin, meeting in (1918), 227
Turin PPI congress (1923), 143–4

Ubi arcano Dei (encyclical), 206
Ulitzka, Karl, 52
Ullo, Antony P., 271
ultramontanism, 20, 21, 22, 113 nl
Unia organization, 168
Unified Christian Party (Egyesült Keresztény Párt), Hungary, 209
Union Catholique d'études internationales (Paris), 74, 259
Union de Fribourg, 72–3, 74
Union Démocratique Belge, 112
Union d'étude des catholiques sociaux, 116, 119
Union Internationale des Etudes Sociales, 259
Union of Soldiers (General Haller), Poland, 153
United Kingdom, 267–9; Anglo-American initiative, 275; Catholic Social Guild, 270; Christian Guild, 269; Federal Union founded in, 275; Labour Party, 1, 266; People and Freedom Group, 253, 270, 271, 273, 275, 276, 278, 279
United States of America, 267–9; Anglo-American initiative, 275; Democratic Party, 268; New Deal policy, 267; People and Freedom Group, 269, 271, 273
United States of Europe, 4, 129, 147
Unity Party (Egységes Párt), Hungary, 203, 205
universal suffrage (Netherlands), 83

Vallásügyi Likvidálo Hivatal (Office for the Liquidation of Religious Affairs), Hungary, 197

Van Cauwelaert, Frans, 97, 275
Van Roey, Cardinal Jozef-Ernest (Archbishop of Malines), 100, 109, 112
Van Zeeland, Paul, 104, 109; cabinet of, 107
Vass, József, 205, 207, 208
Vaterland (newspaper), 65
Vaterländische Front (Austria), 184, 185, 187
Vatican: and France, 121, 122, 123, 128; and Germany, 52; and Italy, 144, 146, 266; Mussolini, support for, 266; in nineteenth century, 25; and Poland, 156; PPI, withdrawal of support, 252; Second Vatican Council, 175, *see also* papacy
Vatican Council, 46
Vatican State, 137, 138
Vaugoin, Carl, 173, 181, 183
Veraart, J. A., 89, 253, 272, 273, 277
Versailles Treaty, 57, 142, 258, 276
Verschuur, T. J., 90
Vichy regime, France, 132, 241
VNV (Vlaamsch Nationaal Verbond), Belgium, 245
Vockel, Heinrich, 255
Vogelsang, Karl von, 26, 140, 175, 182
Volksgemeinschaft, 56
Volksverein für das Katholische Deutschland, 10, 29, 53–4
Volta Academy Congress (1932), 260
voting behaviour: Austria, 177–8; Germany, 11

Wallonia (Belgium), 97, 99, 107
Walter, Otto, 68, 71
Walther, Heinrich, 68
Waugh, Evelyn, 268
Weber, Christoph, 9, 21
Weber, Helene, 255
Weimar Republic, 34, 47, 49, 51, 55, 56, 60; establishment, 242; inter-war years, 245–6
Weltanschauungsgemeinschaft/weltanschauung, 28, 65, 66, 237
Wessel, Helene (*Reichstag* deputy), 57
Whig theory, 9
Wick, Karl, 75
Wilhelm II (German Emperor), 178
Wilson, Woodrow, 142, 217
Windthorst, Ludwig, 11, 48

Windthorstbunde (youth organization), 50
Wirth, Joseph, 51, 57, 256, 261
Witos, Wincenty, 218
Wittelsbach, House of, 51
Wohl, Robert, 32
Wohnout, Helmut, 172–94, 239
Wolff, Károly, 205, 206, 207
Workers' Democratic Party (Poland), 150
Workers' League, Belgium *see* Algemeen Christelijk Werkersverbond-Ligue Nationale des Travailleurs Chrétiens (National League of Christian Workers), Belgium
Workers' Movement, Hungary, 204
Working-Time Act 1924 (Switzerland), 69
World Eucharistic Congress, Budapest (1938), 199
Wyzwolenie, 218

Young Conservatives (SKVP), 67–8, 69, 71, 74
Young Farmers' Movement (Switzerland), 72
Young Farmers' Party (Switzerland), 69
youth groups: Association Catholique de la Jeunesse Française, 14; Bohemian Society for Agrarian Youth, 220, 221, 223; KALOT (Katolikus Agrárarifjúsági Legényegyletek Országos Szövetsége), 211; Windthorstbunde, 50; Young Conservatives (SKVP), 67–8, 69, 71, 74; Young Farmers' Movement, 72; Young Farmers' Party, 69

Zeitgeist, 46, 75
Zemp, Josef, 66
Zentrum (German Centre Party), 46–64; anchoring in society, 48–553; Bavarian path, 48, 51, 55–6; and Catholic Church, 47, 48–53; change, opposition to, 29; clerics in, 52–3; collapse (1933), 11, 48, 252, 258; diversity, 52; election losses, 8–9, 29, 48; Europe, 57–8; farmers' movements, 244; founding, 10, 46, 48; historical background, 46–7; influence, 3; intra-party orientation crisis, 52; and *Kulturkampf*, 47, 48, 49; membership, 50; Netherlands, influence on, 82; organization, weak level of, 50, 52; and PDP (France), 127; and SIPDIC, 255; Social Democrats, co-operation with, 144; social question, 53–5; solidarity, 56, 57; structure, 50–1; Sturzo, influence on, 137–8; Upper Silesian, 52; voters, Catholic, 11; Weimar Republic, history during, 245–6; Windthorst, leadership of, 11, *see also* Germany
Zentrumsstreit, 47
Zernatto, Guido, 187
Zichy, Nándor, 195, 196, 204, 205, 207, 209, 210, 226
Žilina Agreement (1938), 231